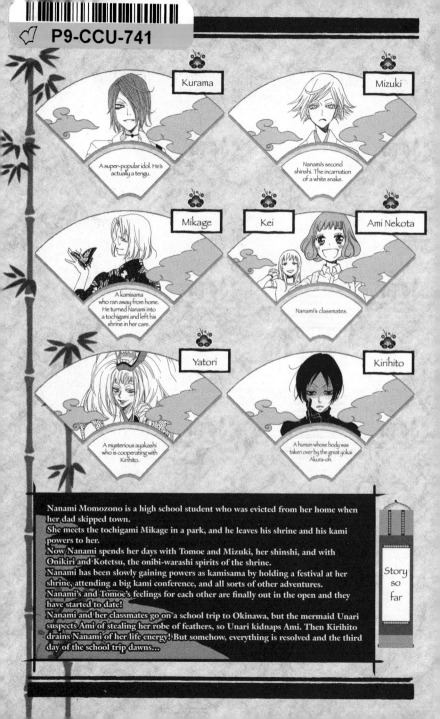

Kurama

A super-popular idol. He's actually a tengu.

Mizuki

Nanami's second shinshi. The incarnation of a white snake.

Mikage

A kamisama who ran away from home. He turned Nanami into a tochigami and left his shrine in her care.

Kei

Ami Nekota

Nanami's classmates.

Yatori

A mysterious ayakashi who is cooperating with Kirihito.

Kirihito

A human whose body was taken over by the great yokai Akura-oh.

Nanami Momozono is a high school student who was evicted from her home when her dad skipped town.

She meets the tochigami Mikage in a park, and he leaves his shrine and his kami powers to her.

Now Nanami spends her days with Tomoe and Mizuki, her shinshi, and with Onikiri and Kotetsu, the onibi-warashi spirits of the shrine.

Nanami has been slowly gaining powers as kamisama by holding a festival at her shrine, attending a big kami conference, and all sorts of other adventures.

Nanami's and Tomoe's feelings for each other are finally out in the open and they have started to date!

Nanami and her classmates go on a school trip to Okinawa, but the mermaid Unari suspects Ami of stealing her robe of feathers, so Unari kidnaps Ami. Then Kirihito drains Nanami of her life energy! But somehow, everything is resolved and the third day of the school trip dawns...

Story so far

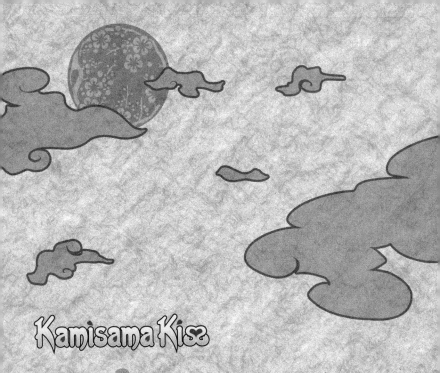

Kamisama Kiss

Volume 20
CONTENTS

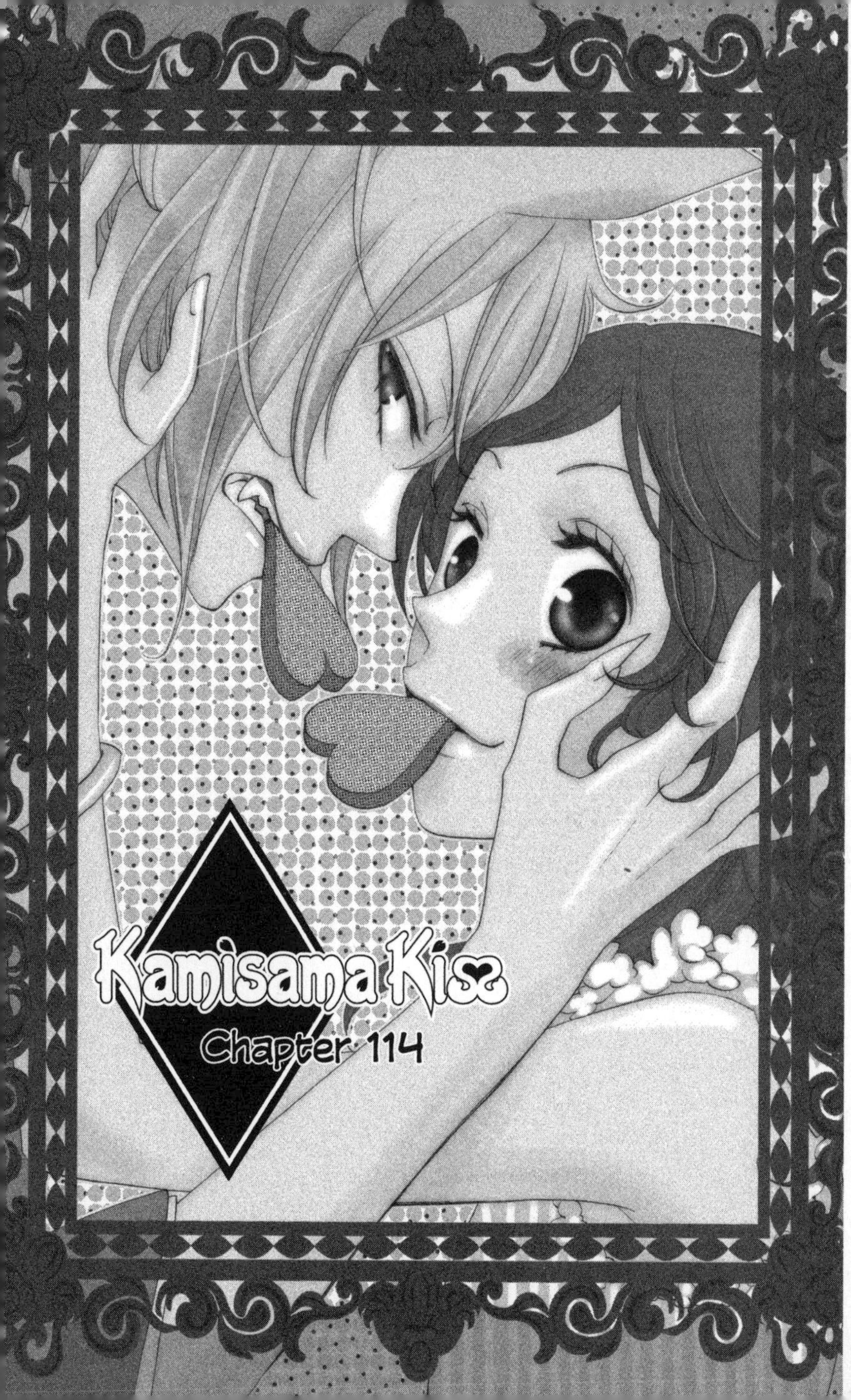
Kamisama Kiss
Chapter 114

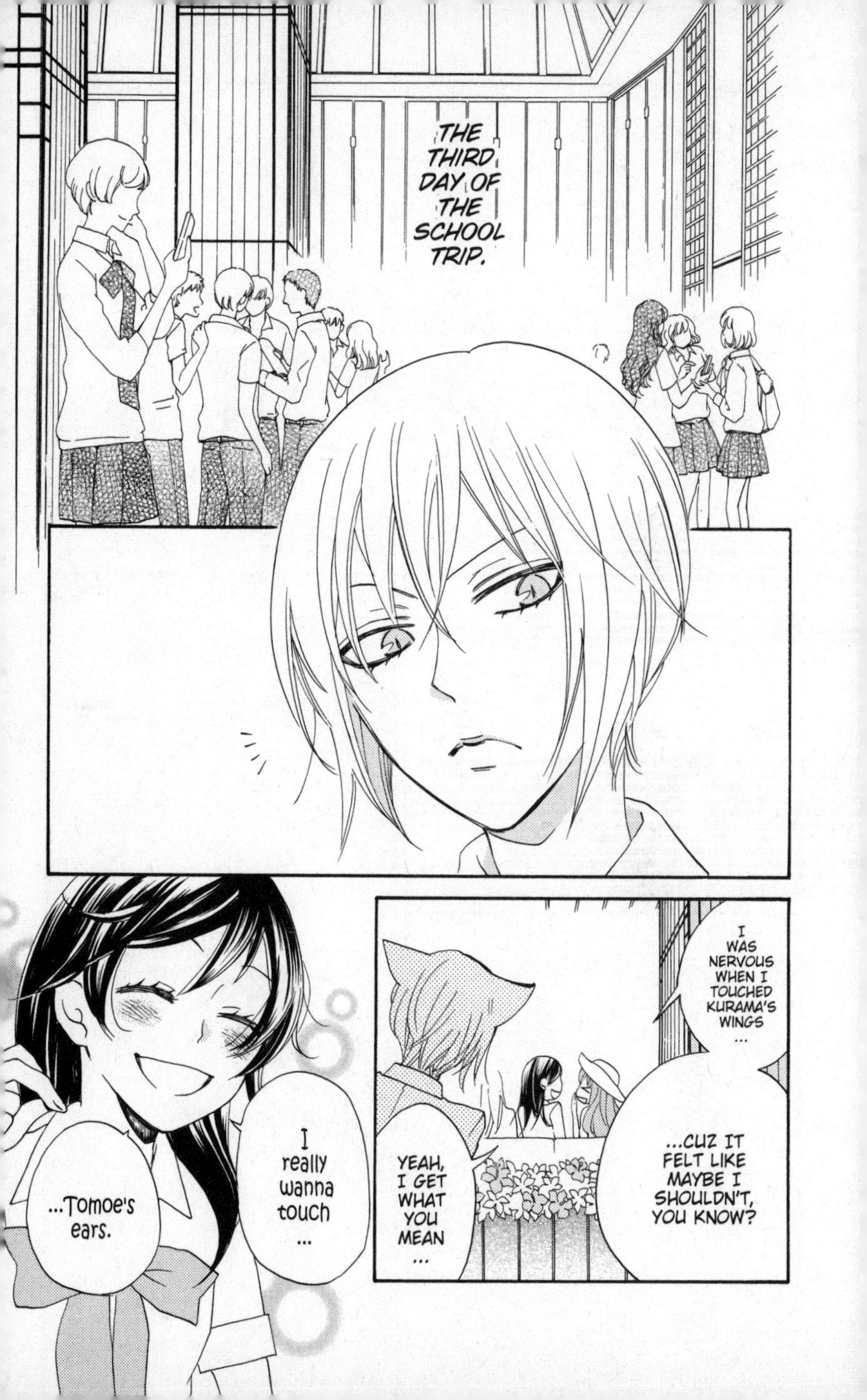
THE THIRD DAY OF THE SCHOOL TRIP.
I WAS NERVOUS WHEN I TOUCHED KURAMA'S WINGS ...
...CUZ IT FELT LIKE MAYBE I SHOULDN'T, YOU KNOW?
YEAH, I GET WHAT YOU MEAN ...
I really wanna touch ...
...Tomoe's ears.

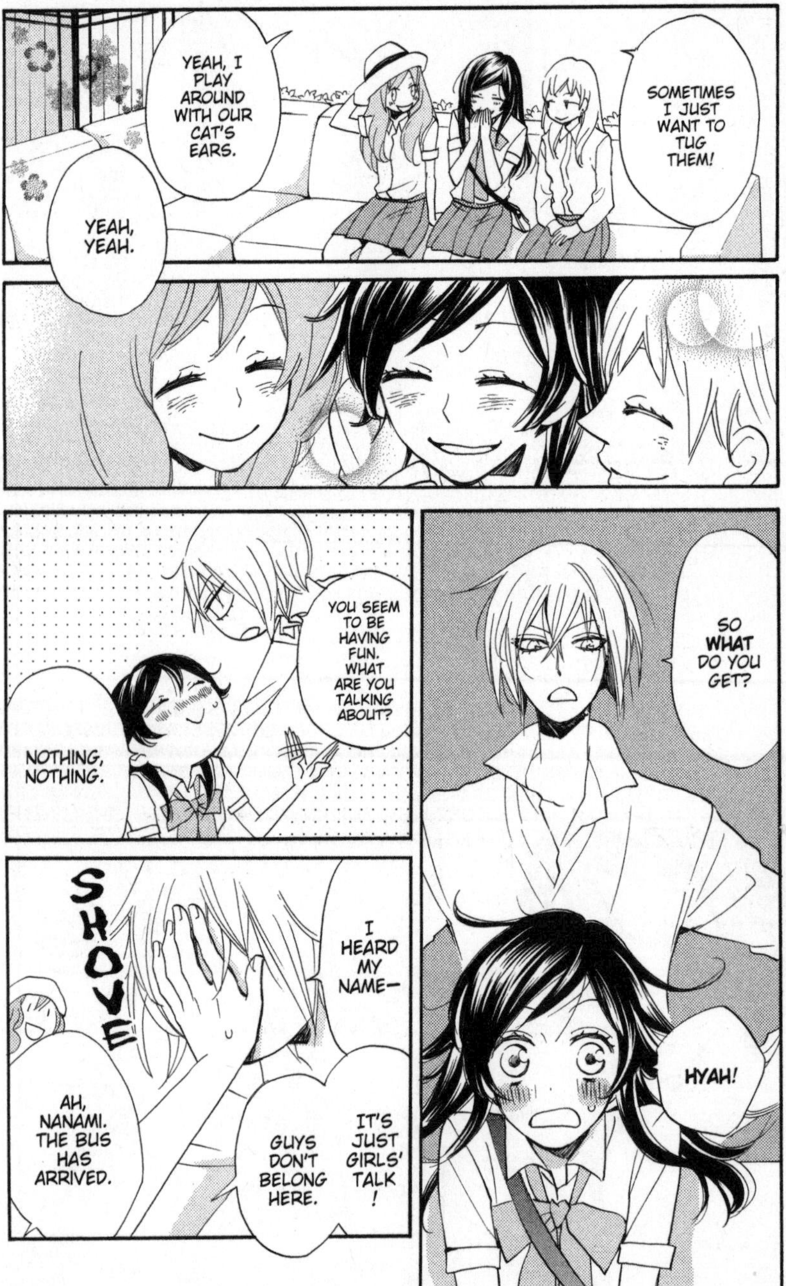
SOMETIMES I JUST WANT TO TUG THEM!
YEAH, I PLAY AROUND WITH OUR CAT'S EARS.
YEAH, YEAH.
SO WHAT DO YOU GET?
HYAH!
YOU SEEM TO BE HAVING FUN. WHAT ARE YOU TALKING ABOUT?
NOTHING, NOTHING.
I HEARD MY NAME—
SHOVE
IT'S JUST GIRLS' TALK!
GUYS DON'T BELONG HERE.
AH, NANAMI. THE BUS HAS ARRIVED.

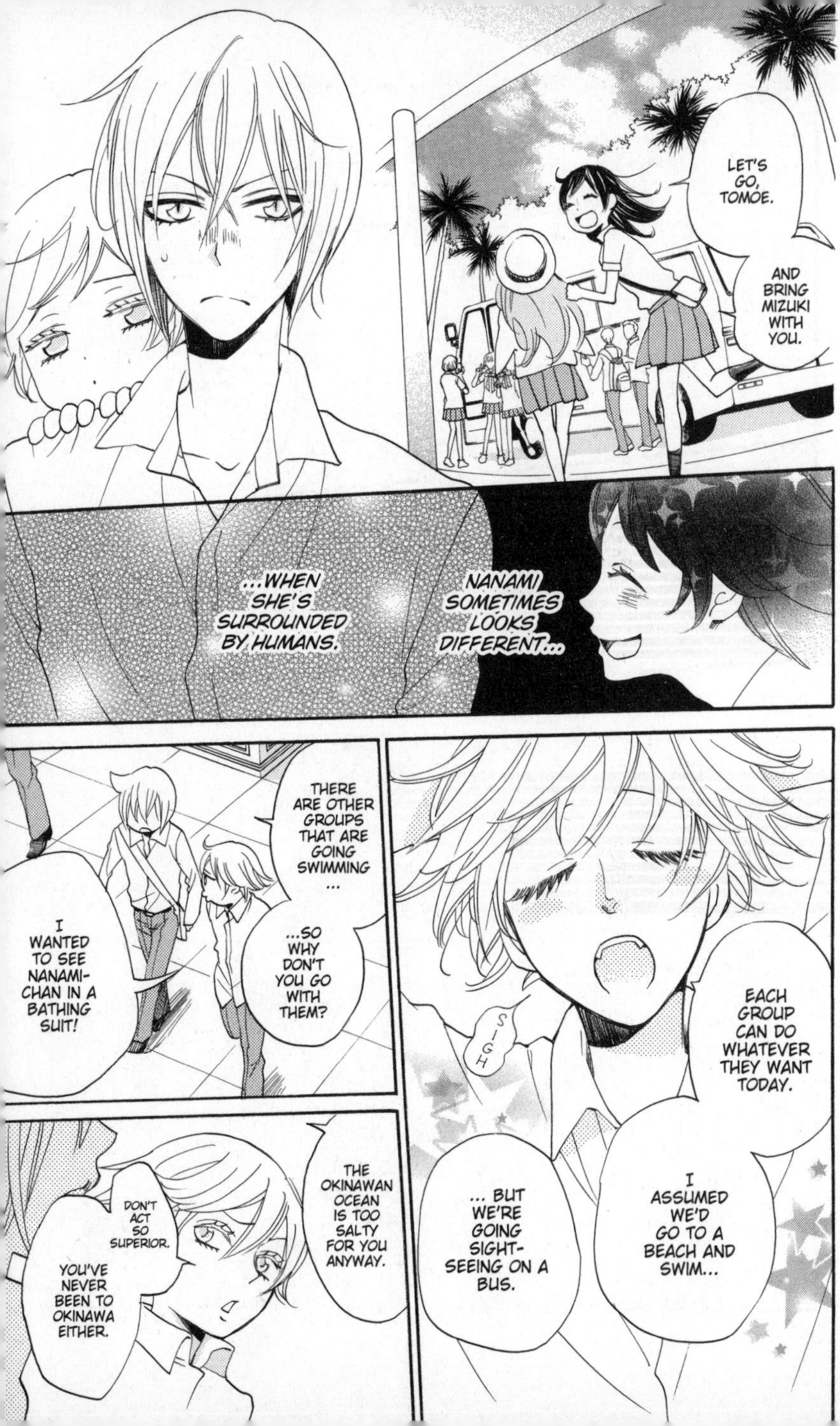
LET'S GO, TOMOE.
AND BRING MIZUKI WITH YOU.
NANAMI SOMETIMES LOOKS DIFFERENT...
...WHEN SHE'S SURROUNDED BY HUMANS.
EACH GROUP CAN DO WHATEVER THEY WANT TODAY.
SIGH
I ASSUMED WE'D GO TO A BEACH AND SWIM...
... BUT WE'RE GOING SIGHT-SEEING ON A BUS.
THERE ARE OTHER GROUPS THAT ARE GOING SWIMMING ...
...SO WHY DON'T YOU GO WITH THEM?
I WANTED TO SEE NANAMI-CHAN IN A BATHING SUIT!
THE OKINAWAN OCEAN IS TOO SALTY FOR YOU ANYWAY.
DON'T ACT SO SUPERIOR.
YOU'VE NEVER BEEN TO OKINAWA EITHER.

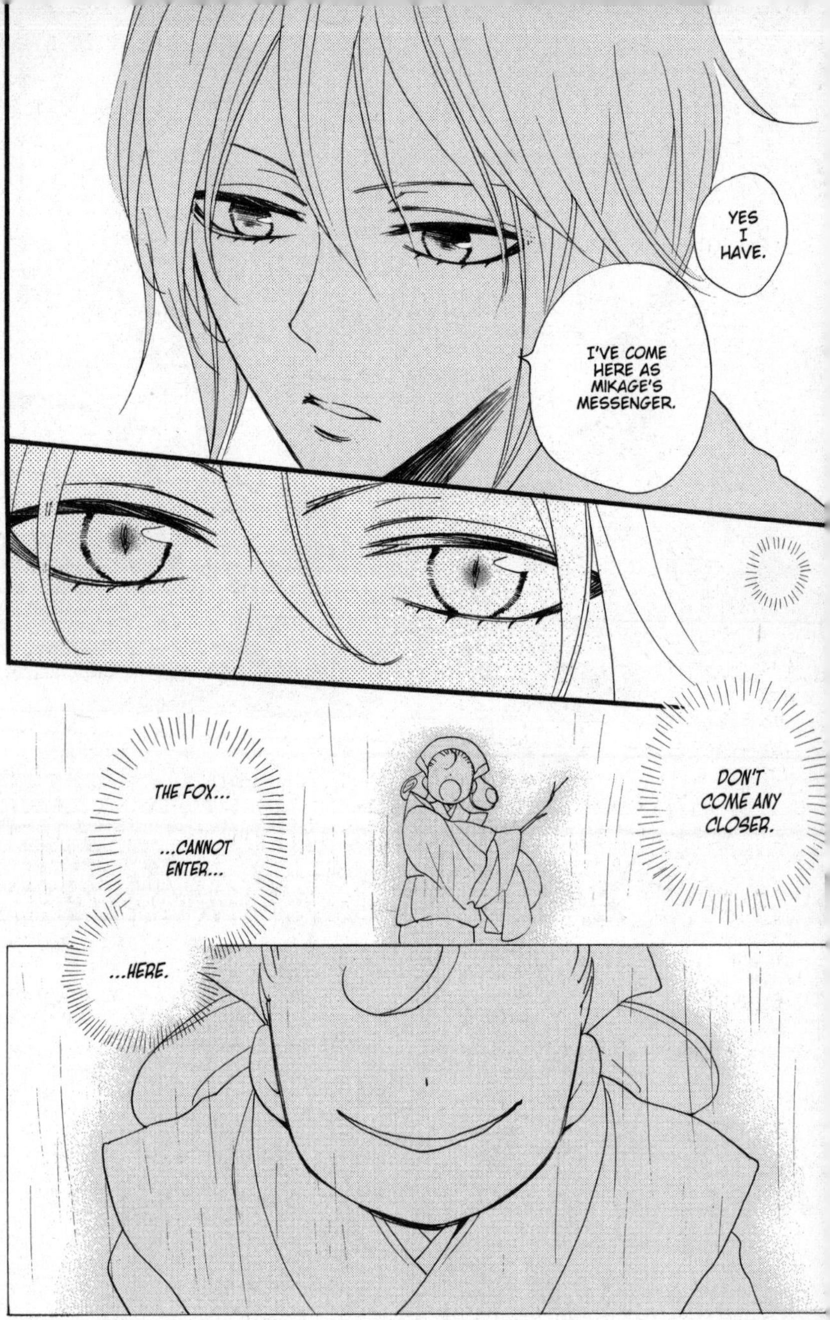
YES I HAVE.
I'VE COME HERE AS MIKAGE'S MESSENGER.
DON'T COME ANY CLOSER.
THE FOX...
...CANNOT ENTER...
...HERE.

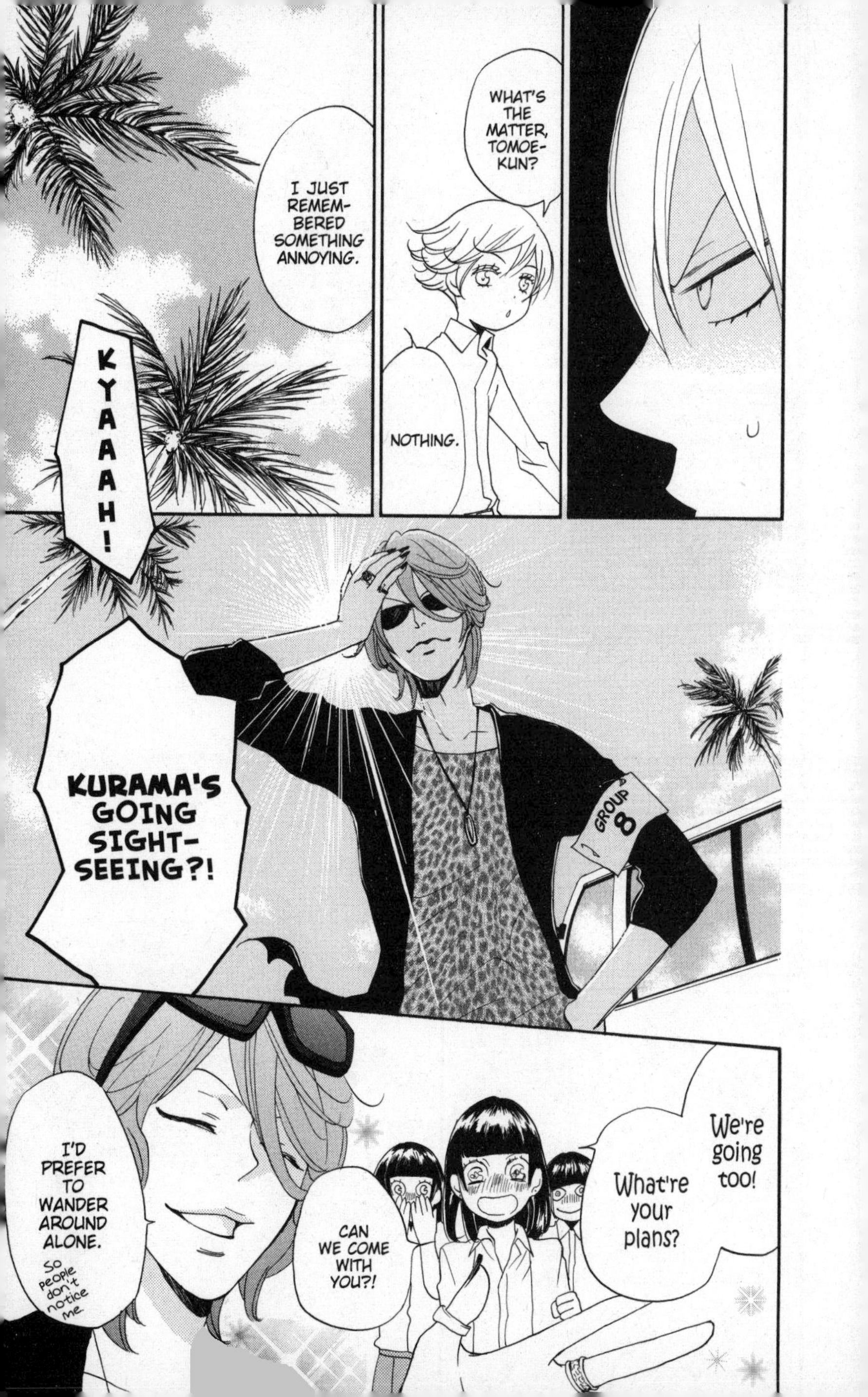
WHAT'S THE MATTER, TOMOE-KUN?
NOTHING.
I JUST REMEM-BERED SOMETHING ANNOYING.
KYAAAAH!
KURAMA'S GOING SIGHT-SEEING?!
GROUP 8
We're going too!
What're your plans?
CAN WE COME WITH YOU?!
I'D PREFER TO WANDER AROUND ALONE.
So people don't notice me.

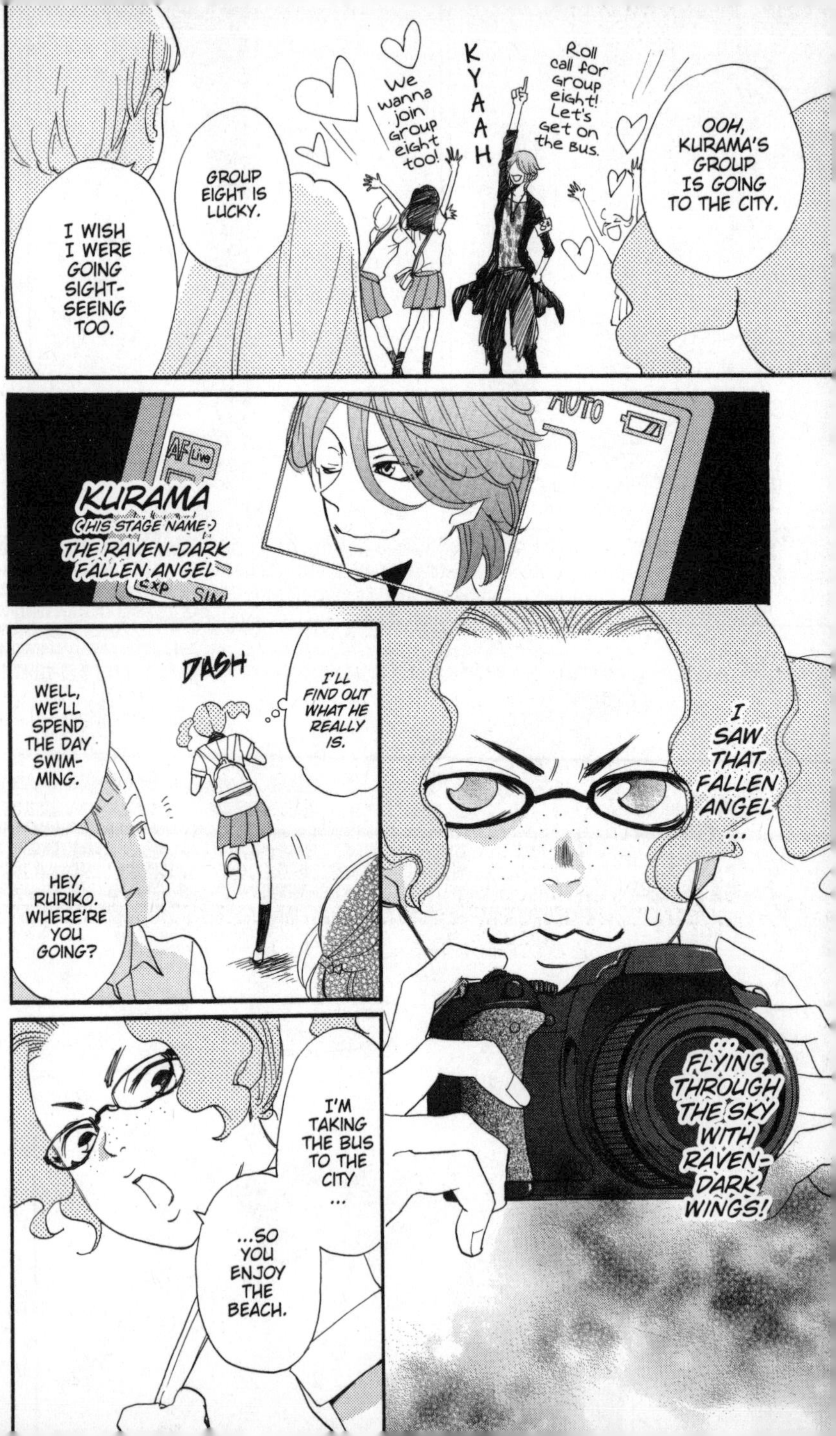
OOH, KURAMA'S GROUP IS GOING TO THE CITY.
Roll call for group eight! Let's get on the bus.
KYAAH
We wanna join group eight too!
GROUP EIGHT IS LUCKY.
I WISH I WERE GOING SIGHT-SEEING TOO.
AUTO
KURAMA (HIS STAGE NAME) THE RAVEN-DARK FALLEN ANGEL
I SAW THAT FALLEN ANGEL...
...FLYING THROUGH THE SKY WITH RAVEN-DARK WINGS!
I'LL FIND OUT WHAT HE REALLY IS.
DASH
WELL, WE'LL SPEND THE DAY SWIMMING.
HEY, RURIKO. WHERE'RE YOU GOING?
I'M TAKING THE BUS TO THE CITY...
...SO YOU ENJOY THE BEACH.

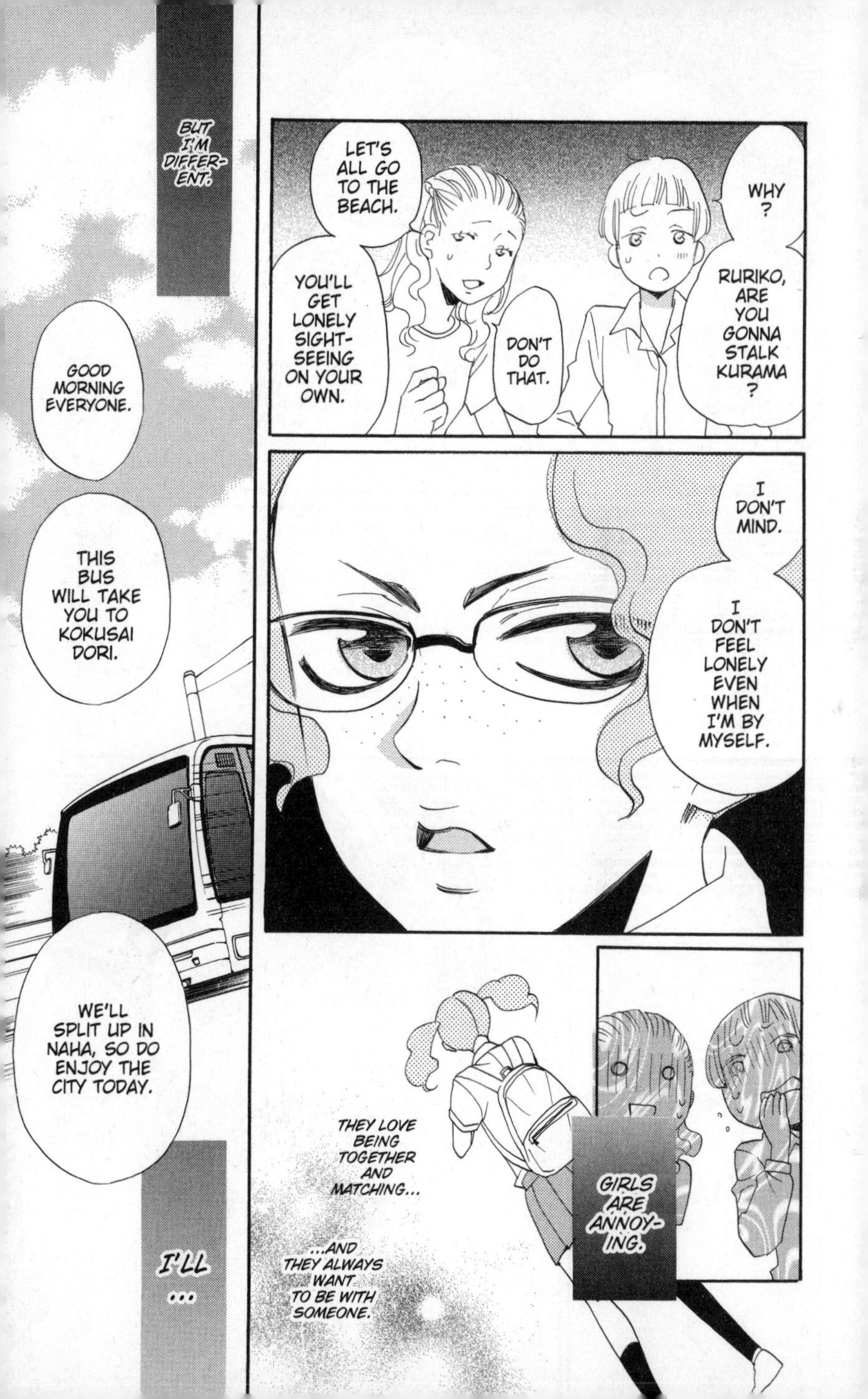
WHY?
RURIKO, ARE YOU GONNA STALK KURAMA?
LET'S ALL GO TO THE BEACH.
DON'T DO THAT.
YOU'LL GET LONELY SIGHT-SEEING ON YOUR OWN.
I DON'T MIND.
I DON'T FEEL LONELY EVEN WHEN I'M BY MYSELF.
GIRLS ARE ANNOY-ING.
THEY LOVE BEING TOGETHER AND MATCHING...
...AND THEY ALWAYS WANT TO BE WITH SOMEONE.
BUT I'M DIFFER-ENT.
GOOD MORNING EVERYONE.
THIS BUS WILL TAKE YOU TO KOKUSAI DORI.
WE'LL SPLIT UP IN NAHA, SO DO ENJOY THE CITY TODAY.
I'LL...

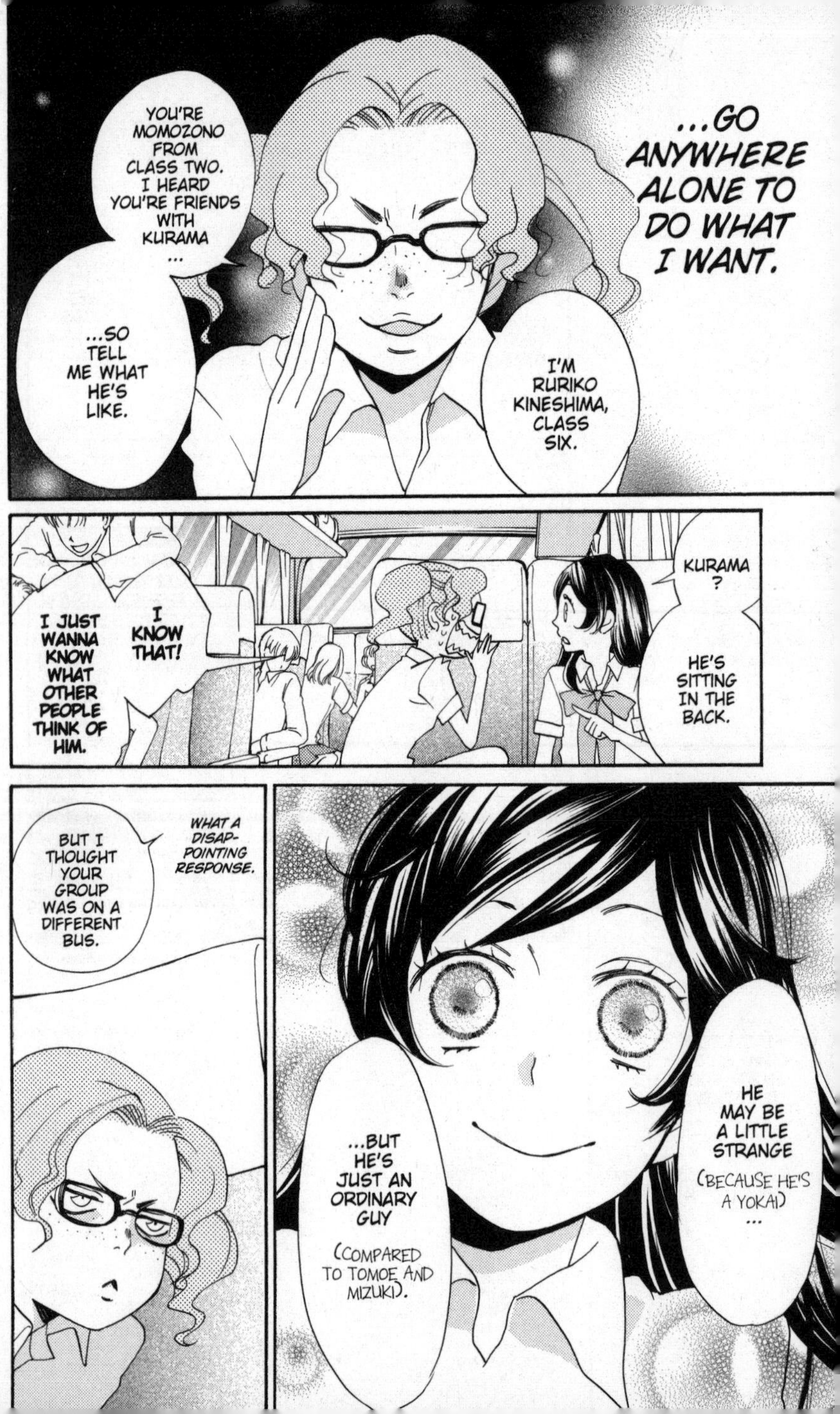
...GO ANYWHERE ALONE TO DO WHAT I WANT.
I'M RURIKO KINESHIMA, CLASS SIX.
YOU'RE MOMOZONO FROM CLASS TWO. I HEARD YOU'RE FRIENDS WITH KURAMA ...
...SO TELL ME WHAT HE'S LIKE.
KURAMA?
HE'S SITTING IN THE BACK.
I KNOW THAT!
I JUST WANNA KNOW WHAT OTHER PEOPLE THINK OF HIM.
HE MAY BE A LITTLE STRANGE
(BECAUSE HE'S A YOKAI) ...
...BUT HE'S JUST AN ORDINARY GUY
(COMPARED TO TOMOE AND MIZUKI).
WHAT A DISAP-POINTING RESPONSE.
BUT I THOUGHT YOUR GROUP WAS ON A DIFFERENT BUS.

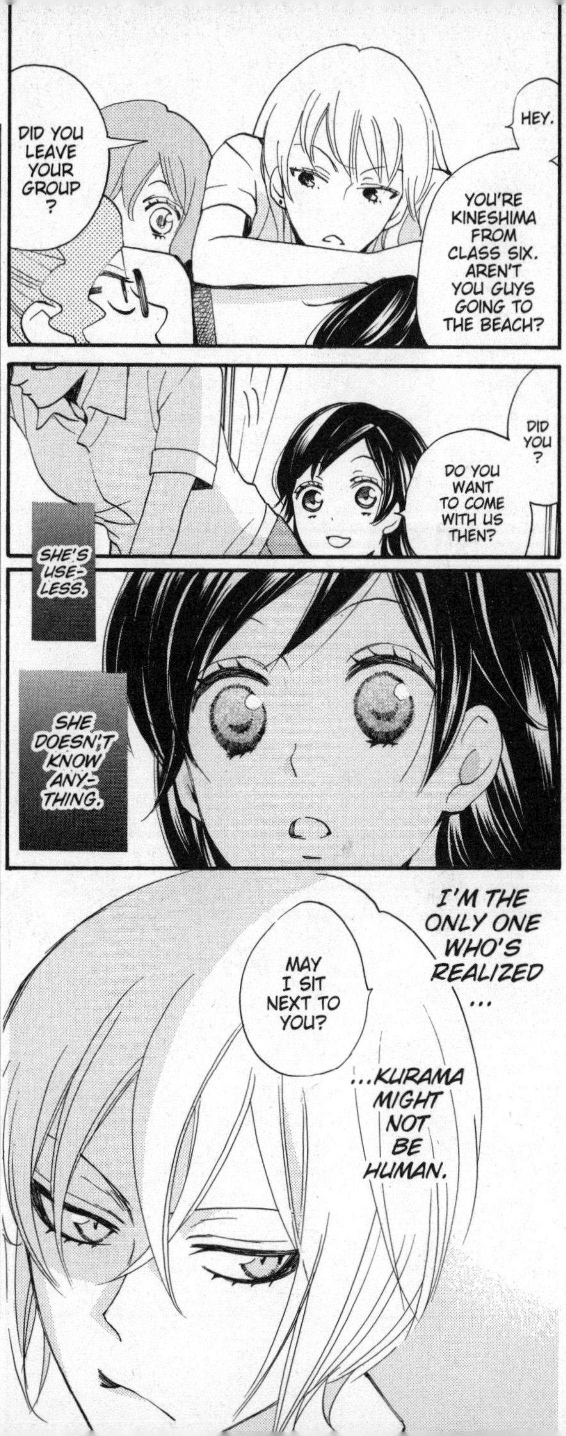
HEY.
YOU'RE KINESHIMA FROM CLASS SIX. AREN'T YOU GUYS GOING TO THE BEACH?
DID YOU LEAVE YOUR GROUP?
DID YOU?
DO YOU WANT TO COME WITH US THEN?
SHE'S USELESS.
SHE DOESN'T KNOW ANYTHING.
I'M THE ONLY ONE WHO'S REALIZED...
MAY I SIT NEXT TO YOU?
...KURAMA MIGHT NOT BE HUMAN.

Thank you for picking up volume 20 of Kamisama Kiss!

I'm flustered the series is now over 20 volumes long.

I am very grateful to my readers who've kept reading this series for a long time.

I hope you enjoy reading this volume as well.

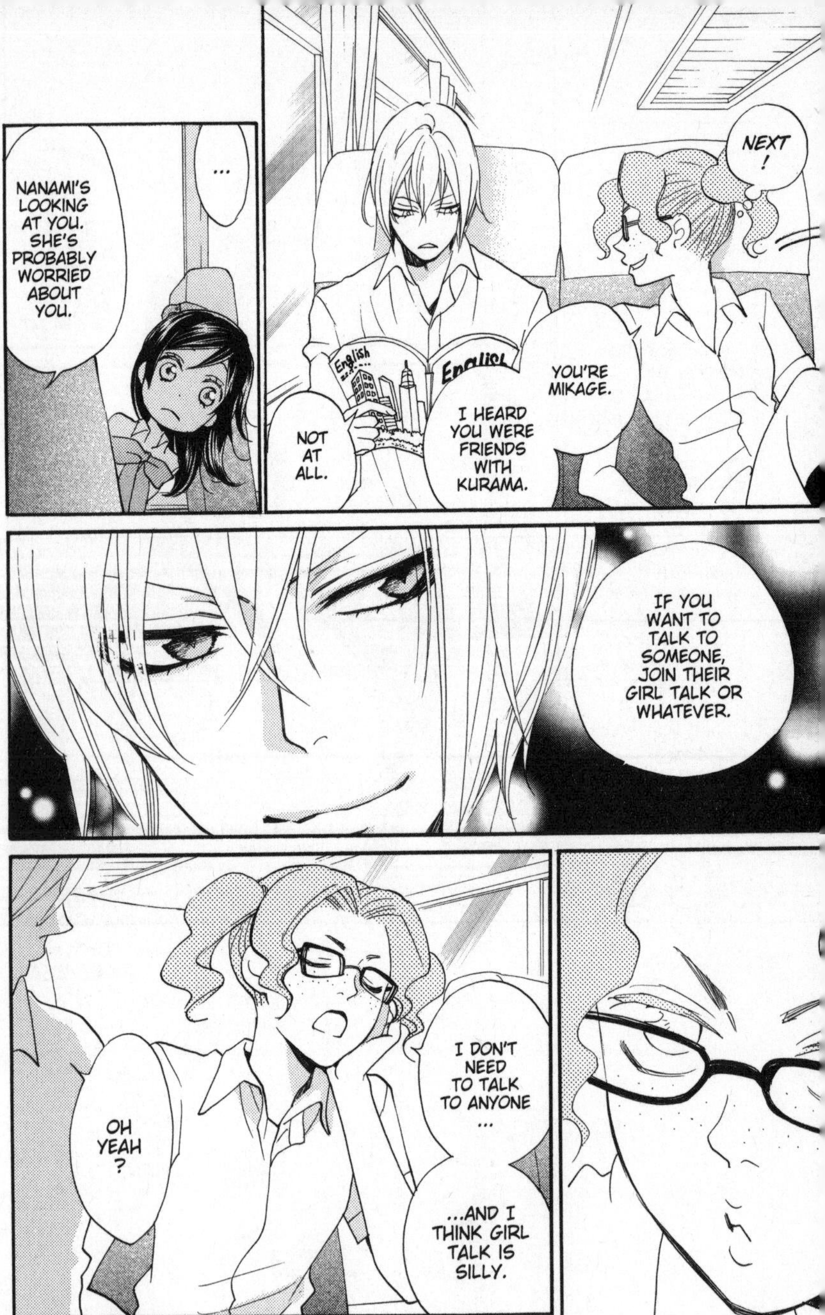
NEXT!
YOU'RE MIKAGE.
I HEARD YOU WERE FRIENDS WITH KURAMA.
NOT AT ALL.
...
NANAMI'S LOOKING AT YOU. SHE'S PROBABLY WORRIED ABOUT YOU.
IF YOU WANT TO TALK TO SOMEONE, JOIN THEIR GIRL TALK OR WHATEVER.
I DON'T NEED TO TALK TO ANYONE...
...AND I THINK GIRL TALK IS SILLY.
OH YEAH?

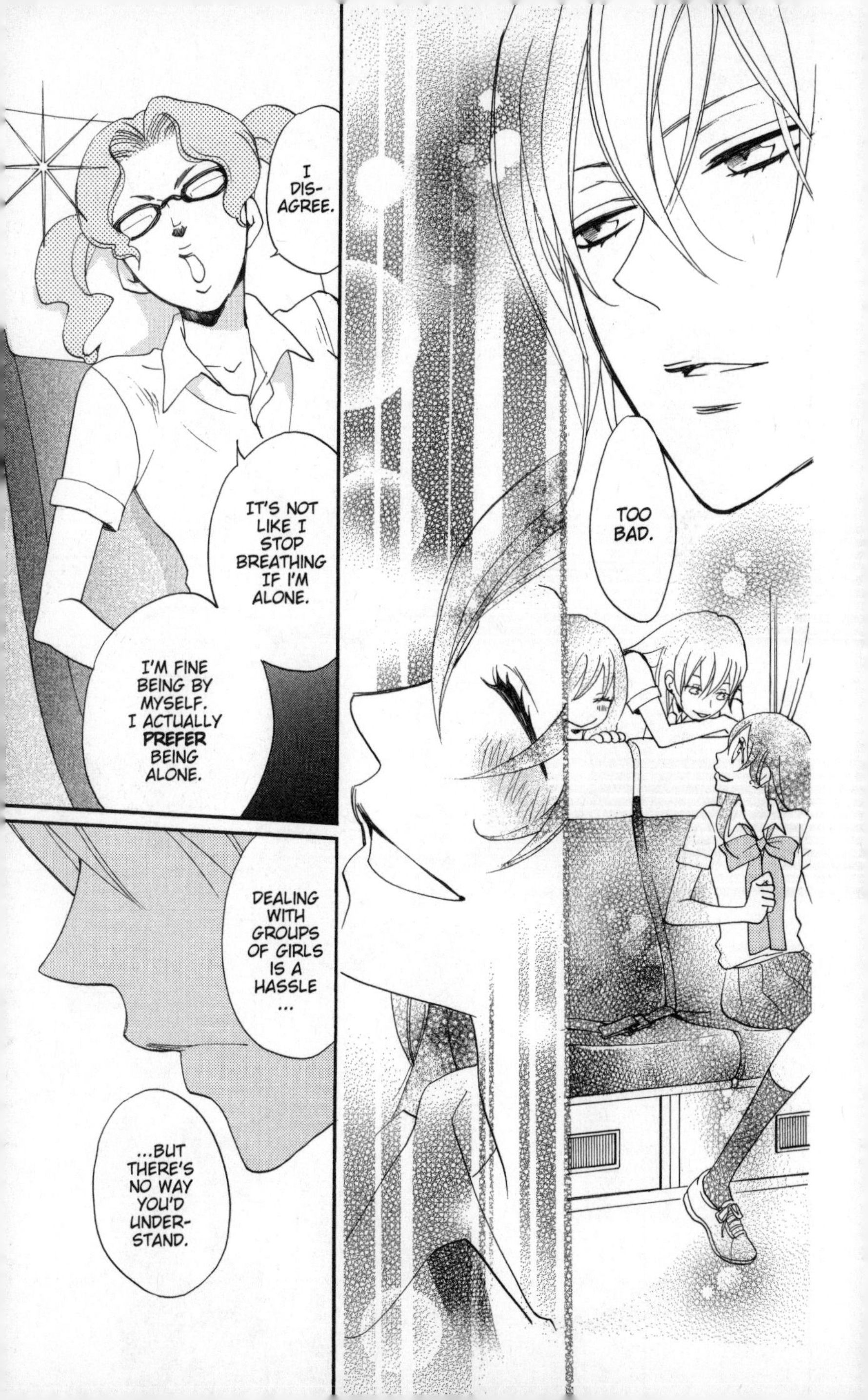
TOO BAD.
I DIS-AGREE.
IT'S NOT LIKE I STOP BREATHING IF I'M ALONE.
I'M FINE BEING BY MYSELF. I ACTUALLY **PREFER** BEING ALONE.
DEALING WITH GROUPS OF GIRLS IS A HASSLE...
...BUT THERE'S NO WAY YOU'D UNDER-STAND.

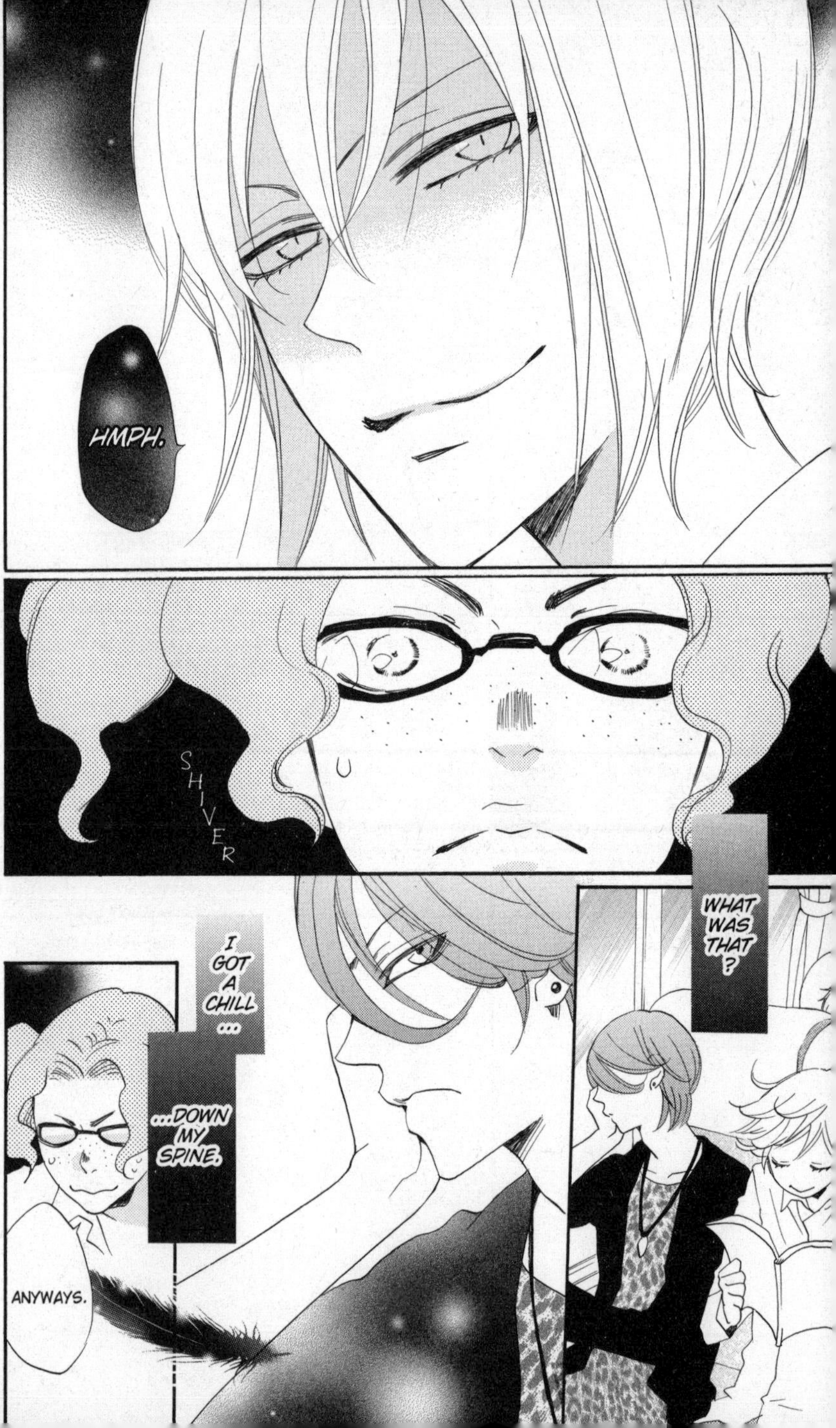
HMPH.
SHIVER
WHAT WAS THAT?
I GOT A CHILL...
...DOWN MY SPINE.
ANYWAYS.

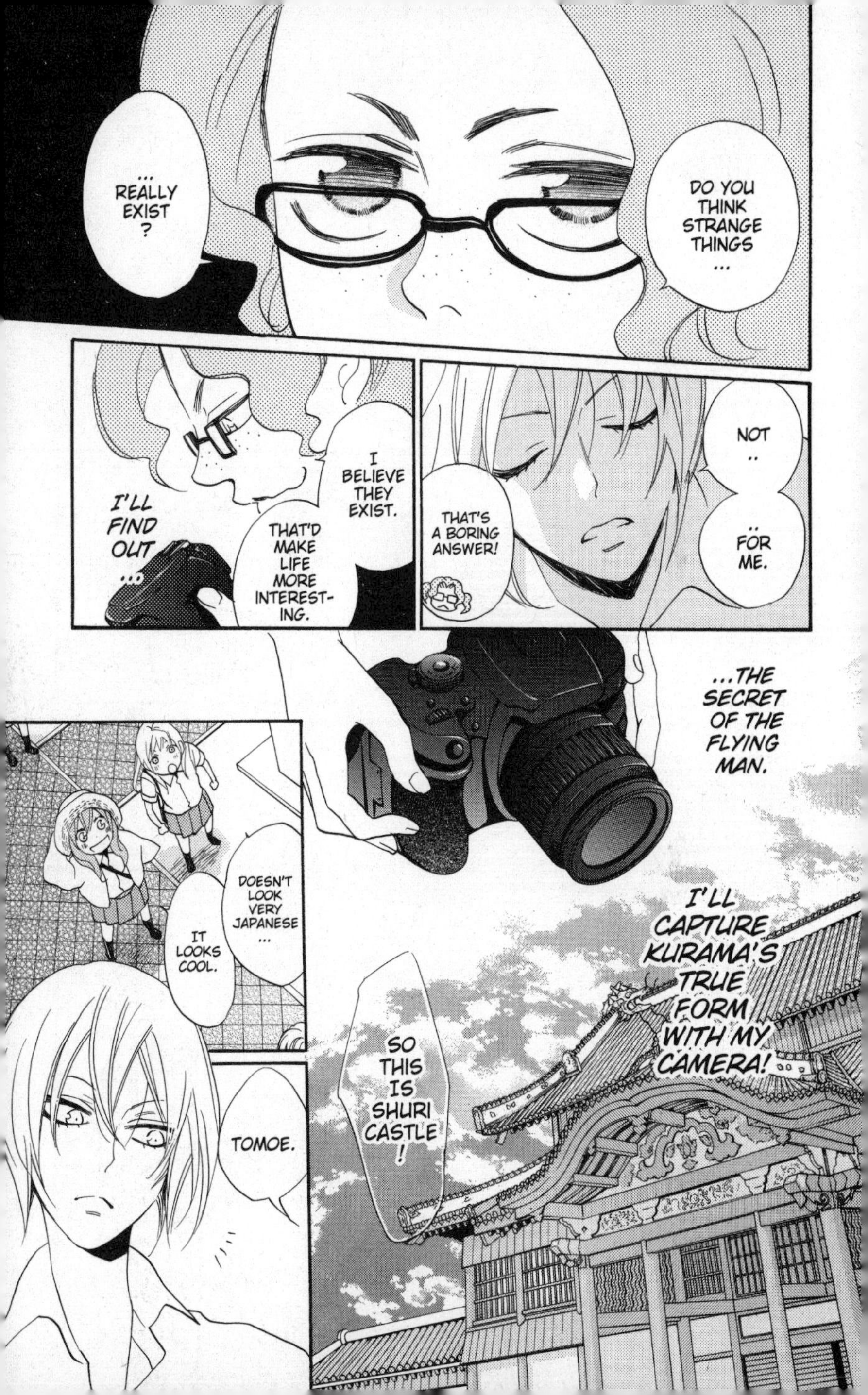
DO YOU THINK STRANGE THINGS ...
... REALLY EXIST ?
NOT ..
.. FOR ME.
THAT'S A BORING ANSWER!
I BELIEVE THEY EXIST.
THAT'D MAKE LIFE MORE INTEREST-ING.
I'LL FIND OUT ...
...THE SECRET OF THE FLYING MAN.
I'LL CAPTURE KURAMA'S TRUE FORM WITH MY CAMERA!
SO THIS IS SHURI CASTLE !
DOESN'T LOOK VERY JAPANESE ...
IT LOOKS COOL.
TOMOE.

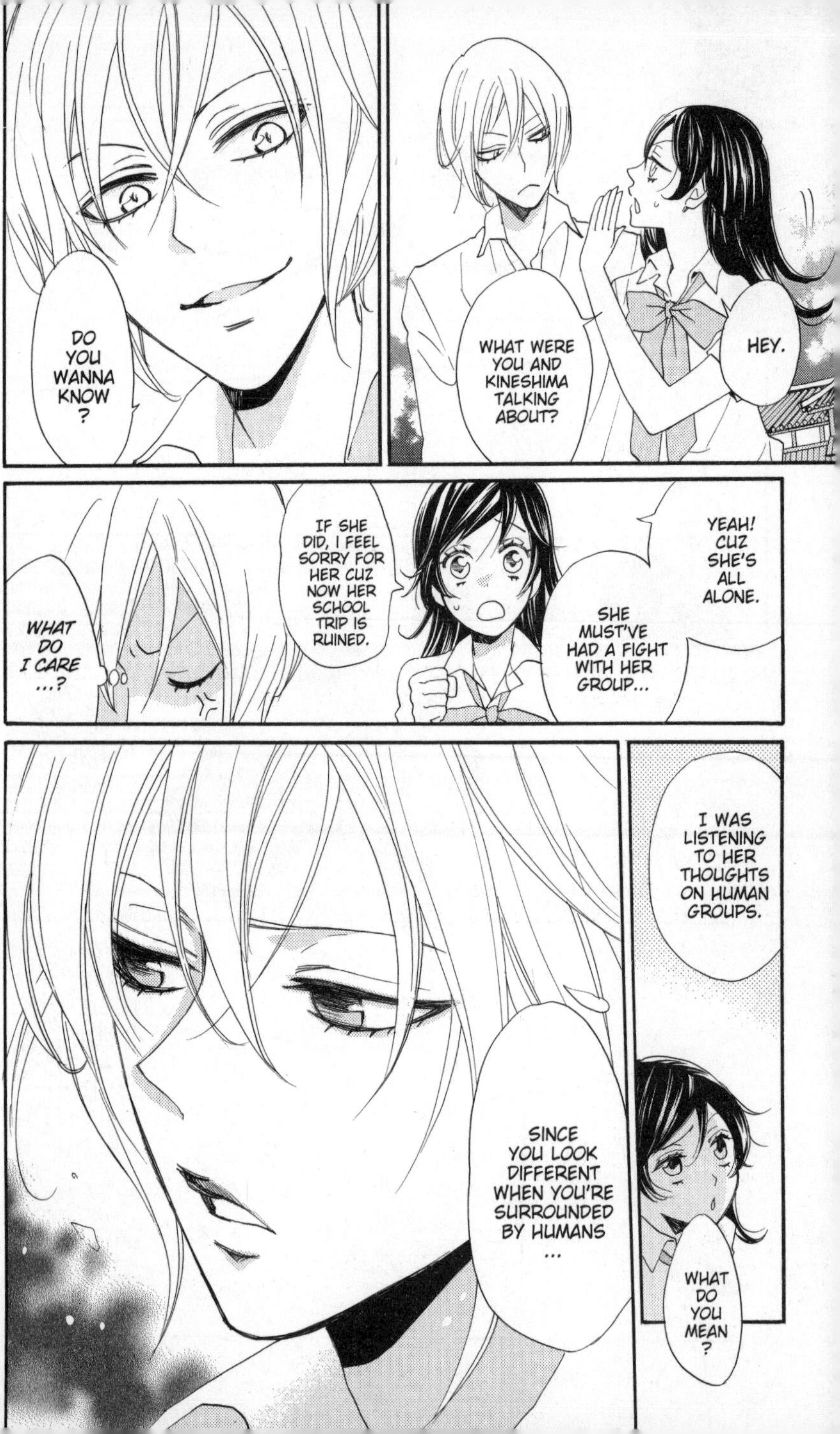
HEY.
WHAT WERE YOU AND KINESHIMA TALKING ABOUT?
DO YOU WANNA KNOW?
YEAH! CUZ SHE'S ALL ALONE.
SHE MUST'VE HAD A FIGHT WITH HER GROUP...
IF SHE DID, I FEEL SORRY FOR HER CUZ NOW HER SCHOOL TRIP IS RUINED.
WHAT DO I CARE ...?
I WAS LISTENING TO HER THOUGHTS ON HUMAN GROUPS.
WHAT DO YOU MEAN?
SINCE YOU LOOK DIFFERENT WHEN YOU'RE SURROUNDED BY HUMANS ...

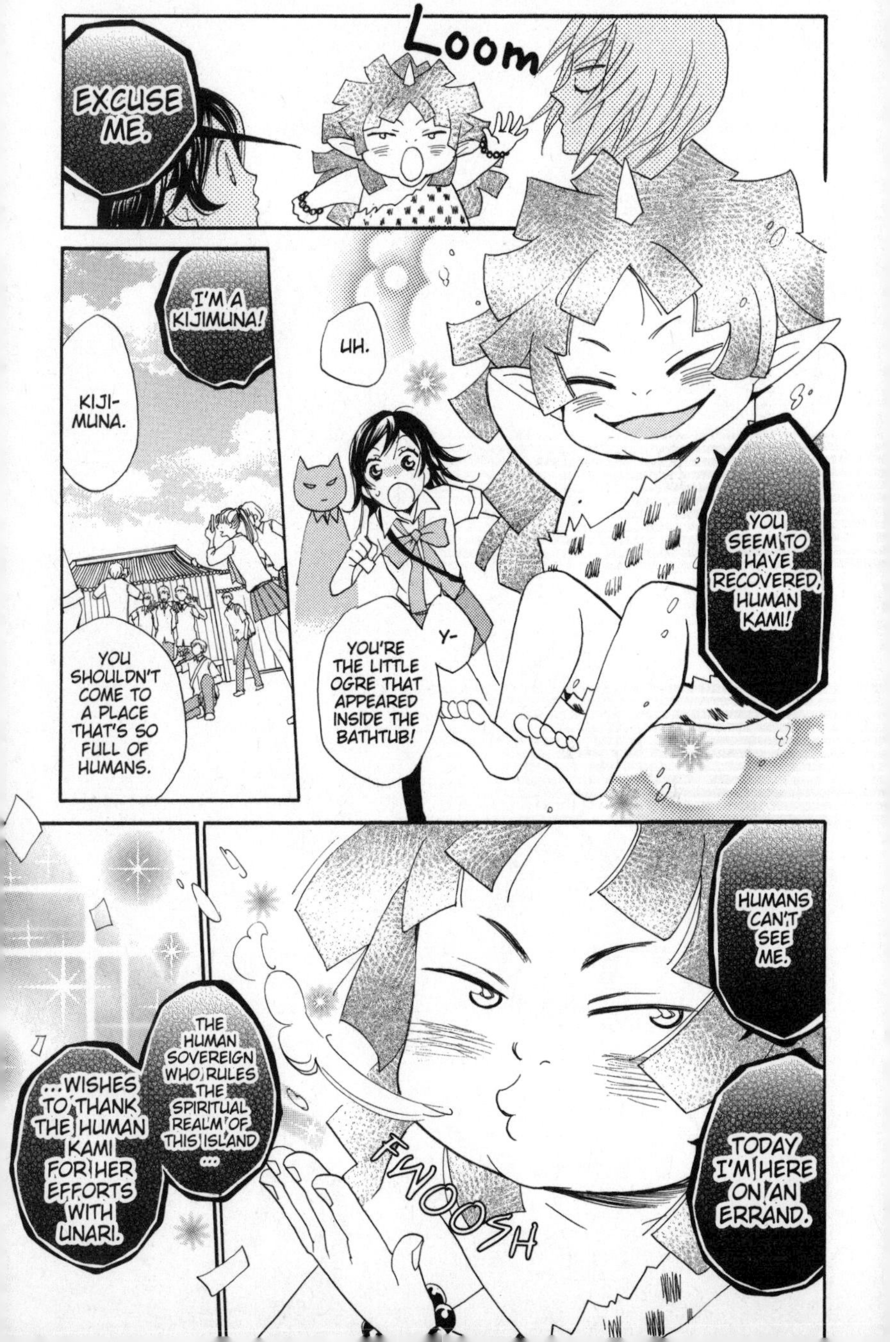
Loom
EXCUSE ME.
YOU SEEM TO HAVE RECOVERED, HUMAN KAMI!
UH.
Y-
YOU'RE THE LITTLE OGRE THAT APPEARED INSIDE THE BATHTUB!
I'M A KIJIMUNA!
KIJI-MUNA.
YOU SHOULDN'T COME TO A PLACE THAT'S SO FULL OF HUMANS.
HUMANS CAN'T SEE ME.
TODAY I'M HERE ON AN ERRAND.
FWOOSH
THE HUMAN SOVEREIGN WHO RULES THE SPIRITUAL REALM OF THIS ISLAND ...
...WISHES TO THANK THE HUMAN KAMI FOR HER EFFORTS WITH UNARI.

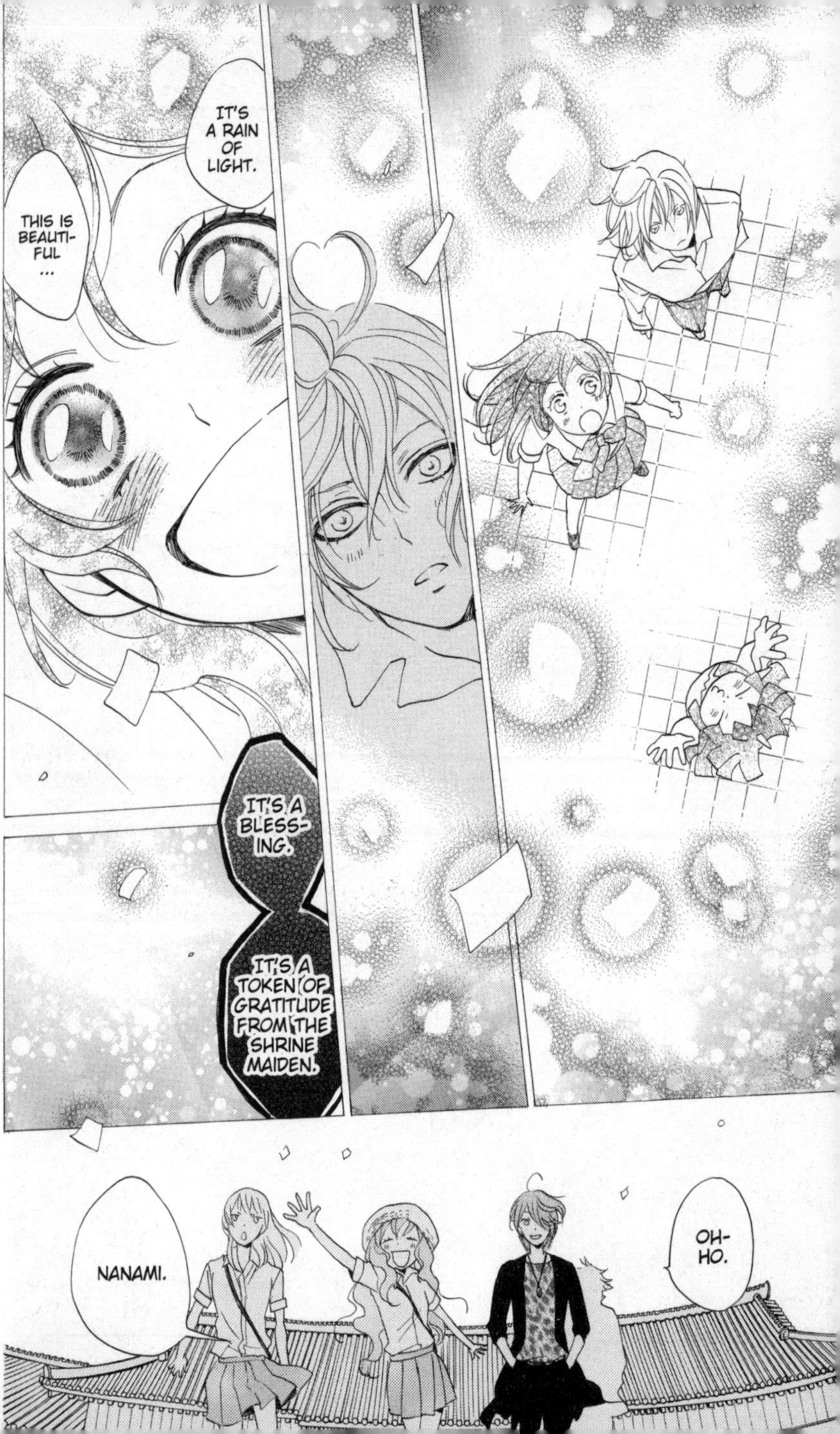
IT'S A RAIN OF LIGHT.
THIS IS BEAUTIFUL...
IT'S A BLESSING.
IT'S A TOKEN OF GRATITUDE FROM THE SHRINE MAIDEN.
OH-HO.
NANAMI.

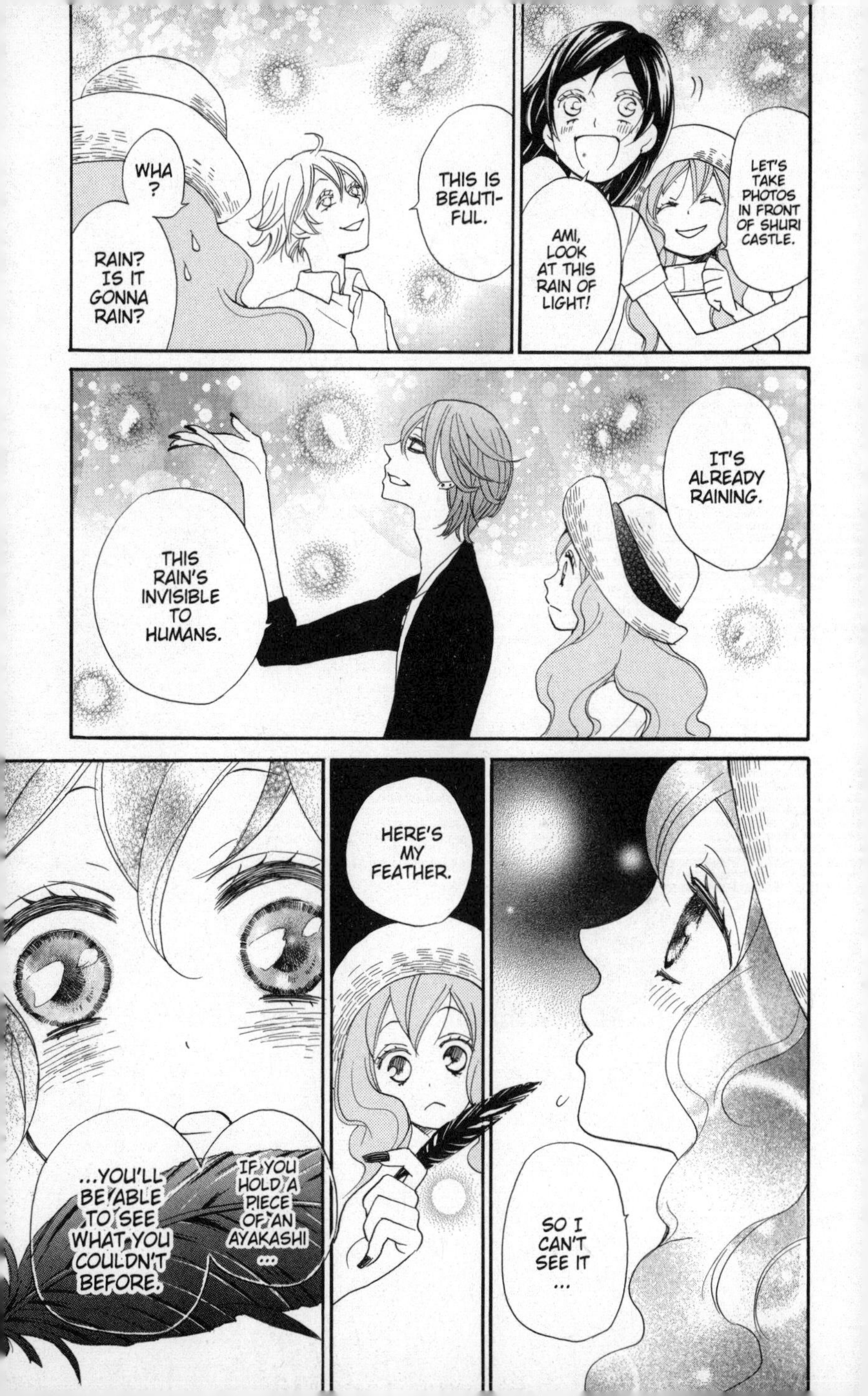
LET'S TAKE PHOTOS IN FRONT OF SHURI CASTLE.
AMI, LOOK AT THIS RAIN OF LIGHT!
THIS IS BEAUTI-FUL.
WHA?
RAIN? IS IT GONNA RAIN?
IT'S ALREADY RAINING.
THIS RAIN'S INVISIBLE TO HUMANS.
SO I CAN'T SEE IT ...
HERE'S MY FEATHER.
IF YOU HOLD A PIECE OF AN AYAKASHI ...
...YOU'LL BE ABLE TO SEE WHAT YOU COULDN'T BEFORE.

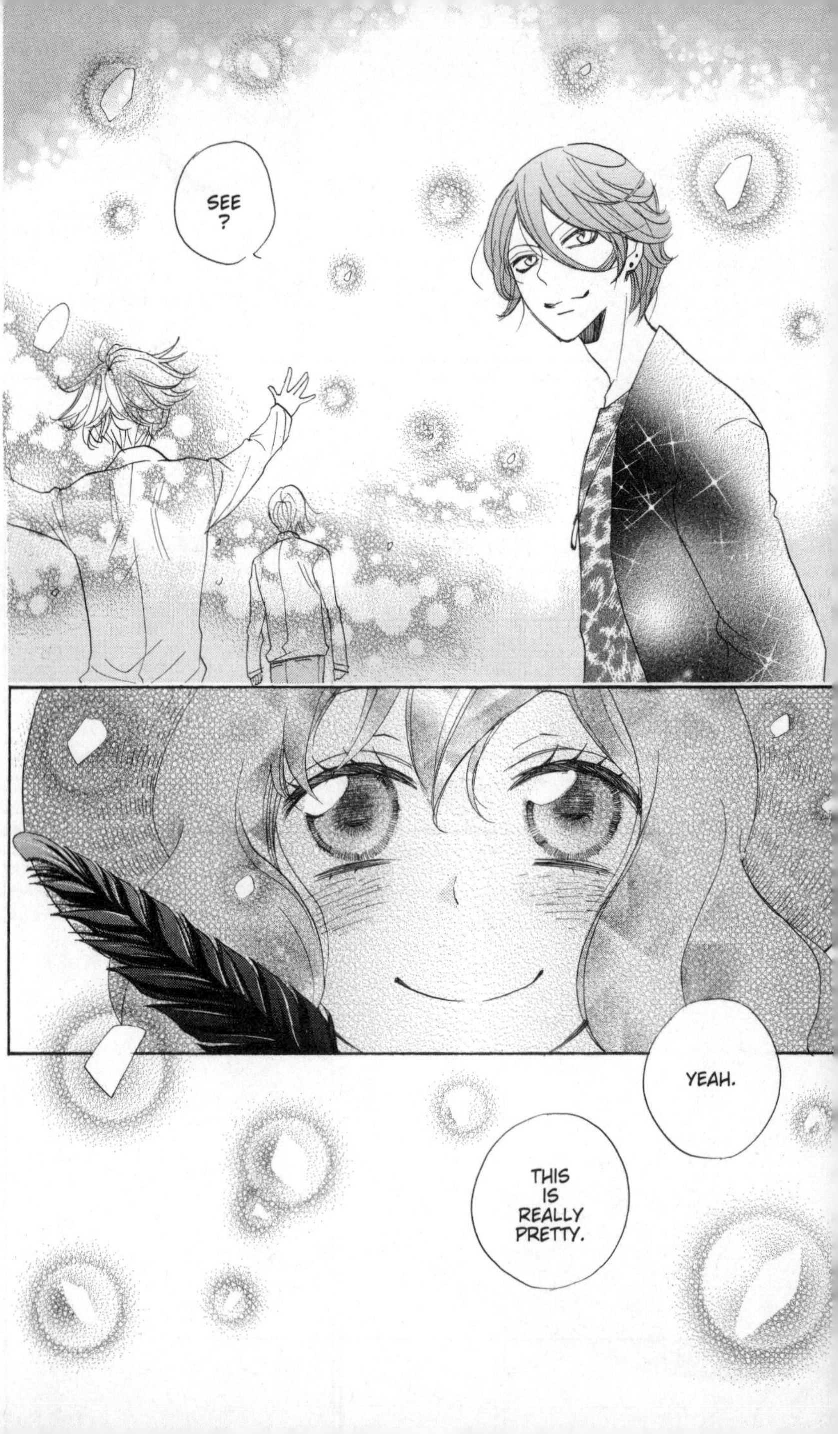
SEE?
YEAH.
THIS IS REALLY PRETTY.

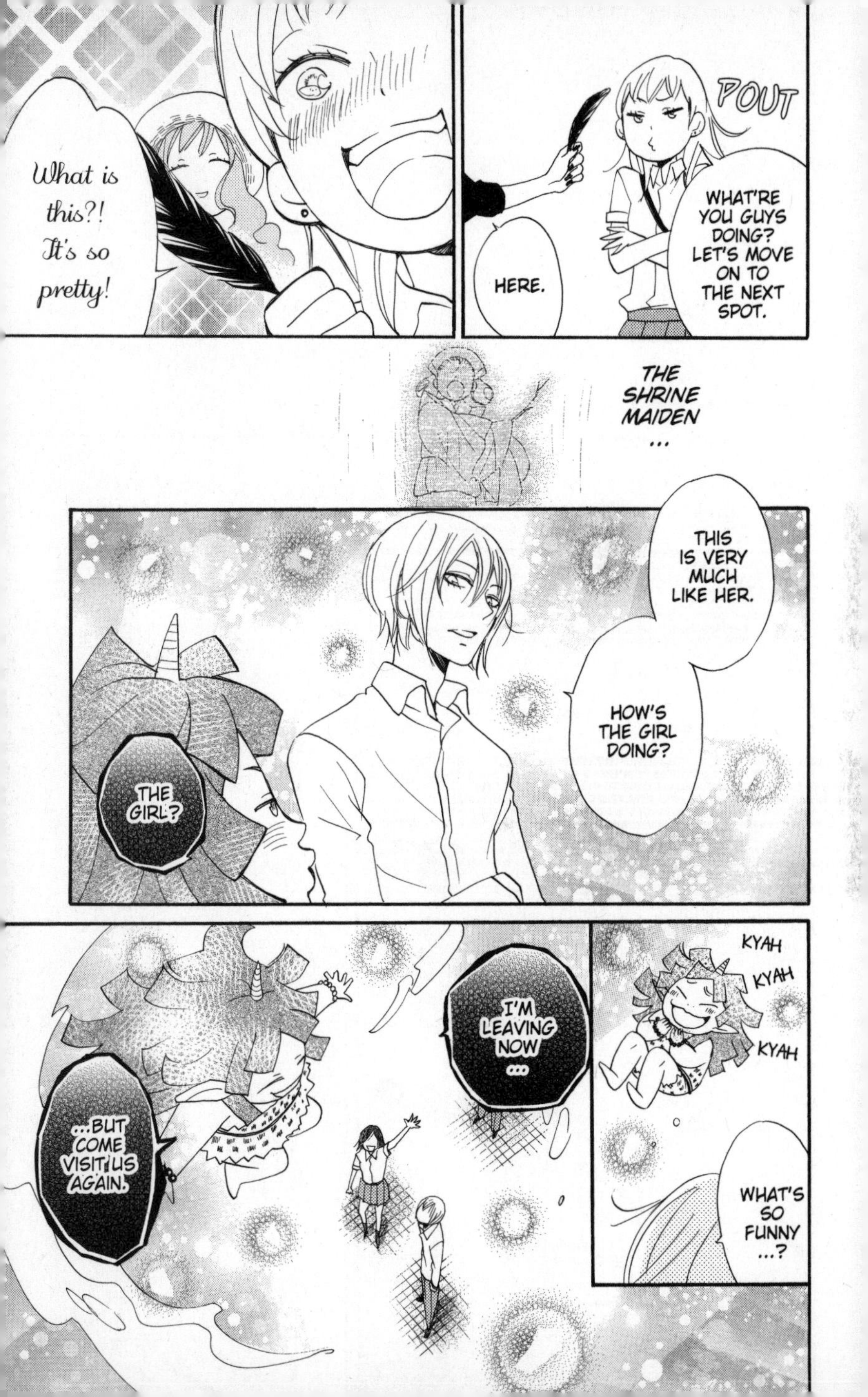
POUT
WHAT'RE YOU GUYS DOING? LET'S MOVE ON TO THE NEXT SPOT.
HERE.
What is this?! It's so pretty!
THE SHRINE MAIDEN ...
THIS IS VERY MUCH LIKE HER.
HOW'S THE GIRL DOING?
THE GIRL?
KYAH
KYAH
KYAH
WHAT'S SO FUNNY ...?
I'M LEAVING NOW ...
...BUT COME VISIT US AGAIN.

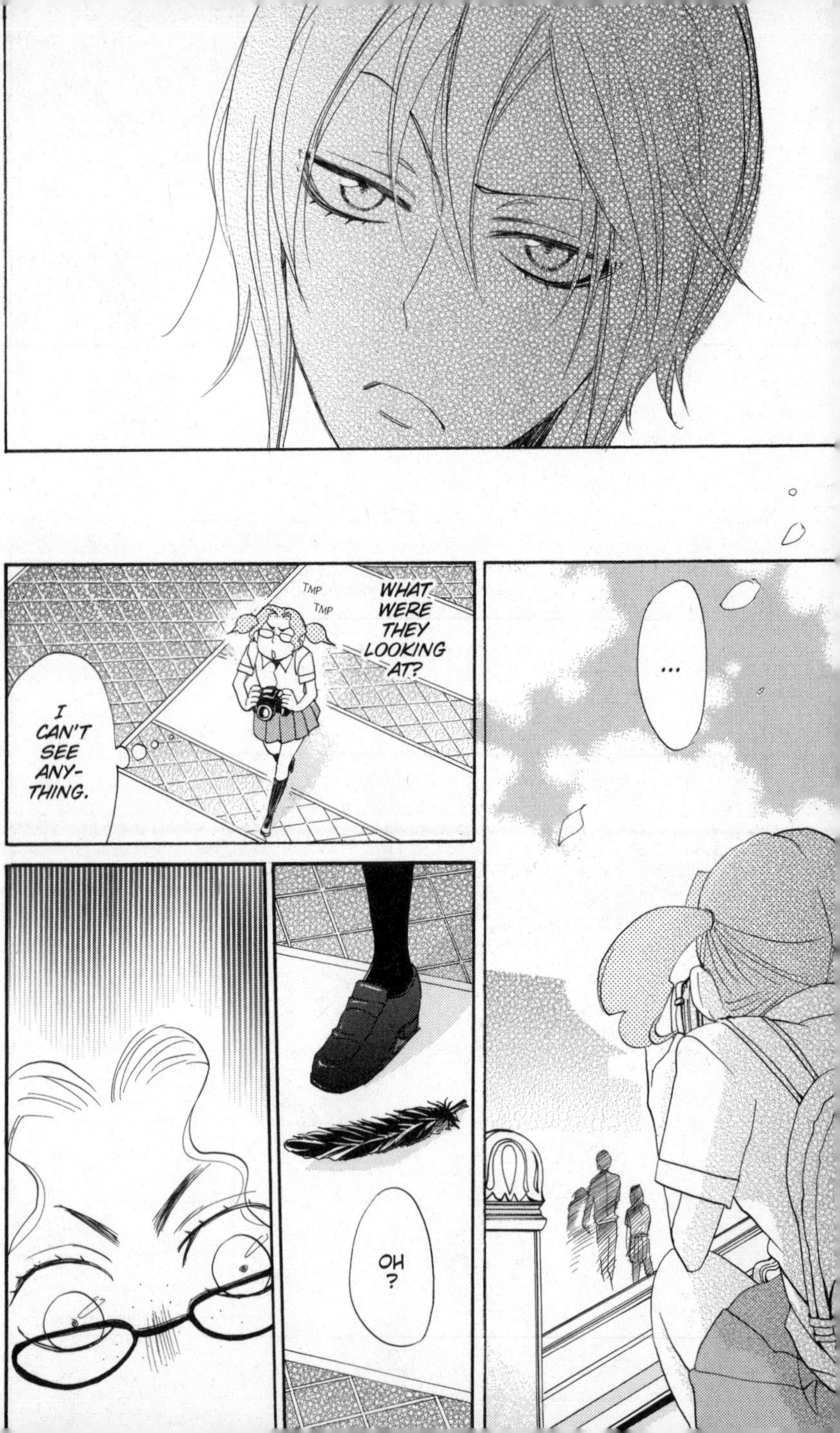
...
WHAT WERE THEY LOOKING AT?
TMP TMP
I CAN'T SEE ANY-THING.
OH ?

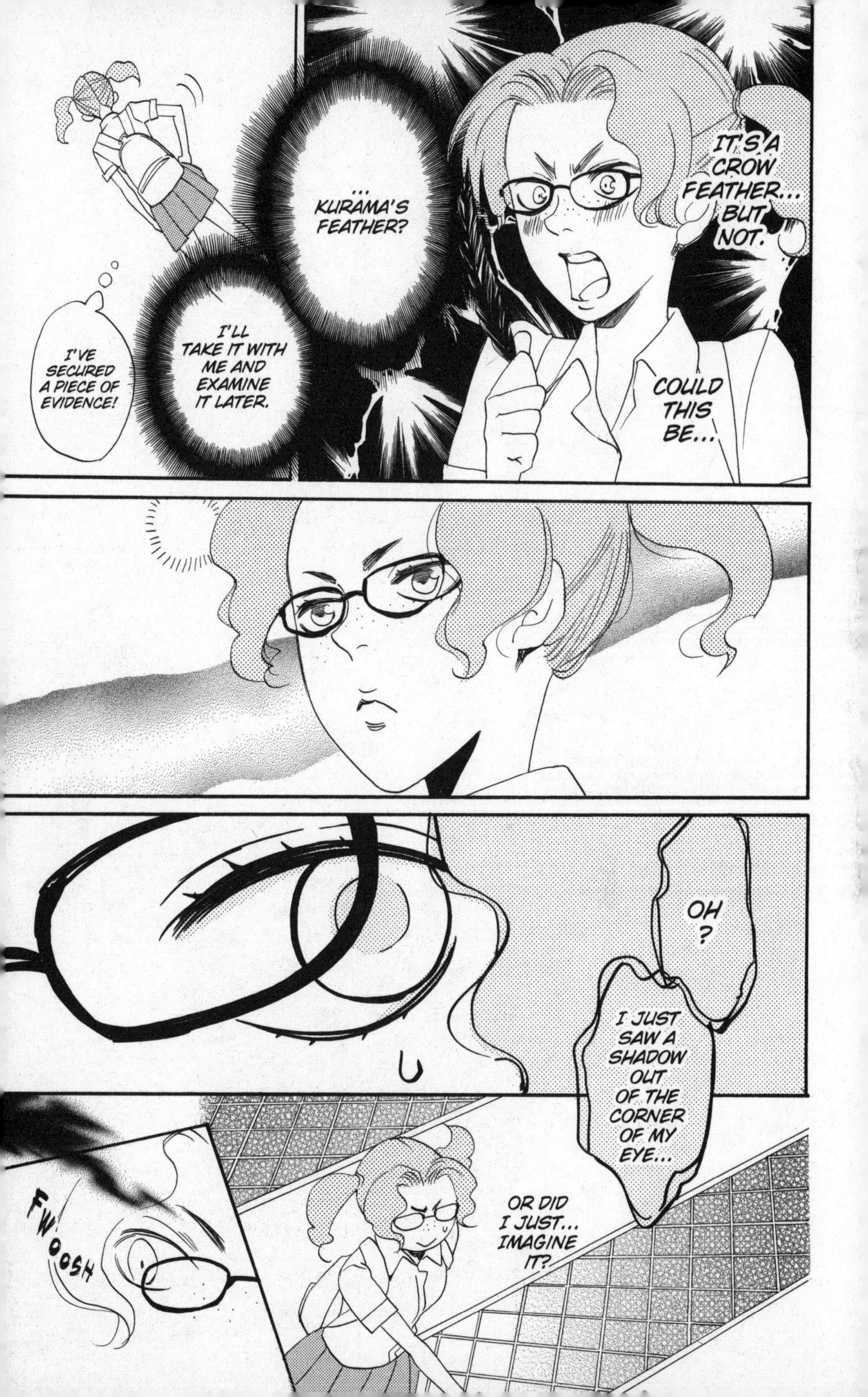
IT'S A CROW FEATHER... BUT NOT.
COULD THIS BE...
...KURAMA'S FEATHER?
I'LL TAKE IT WITH ME AND EXAMINE IT LATER.
I'VE SECURED A PIECE OF EVIDENCE!
OH?
I JUST SAW A SHADOW OUT OF THE CORNER OF MY EYE...
OR DID I JUST... IMAGINE IT?
FWOOSH

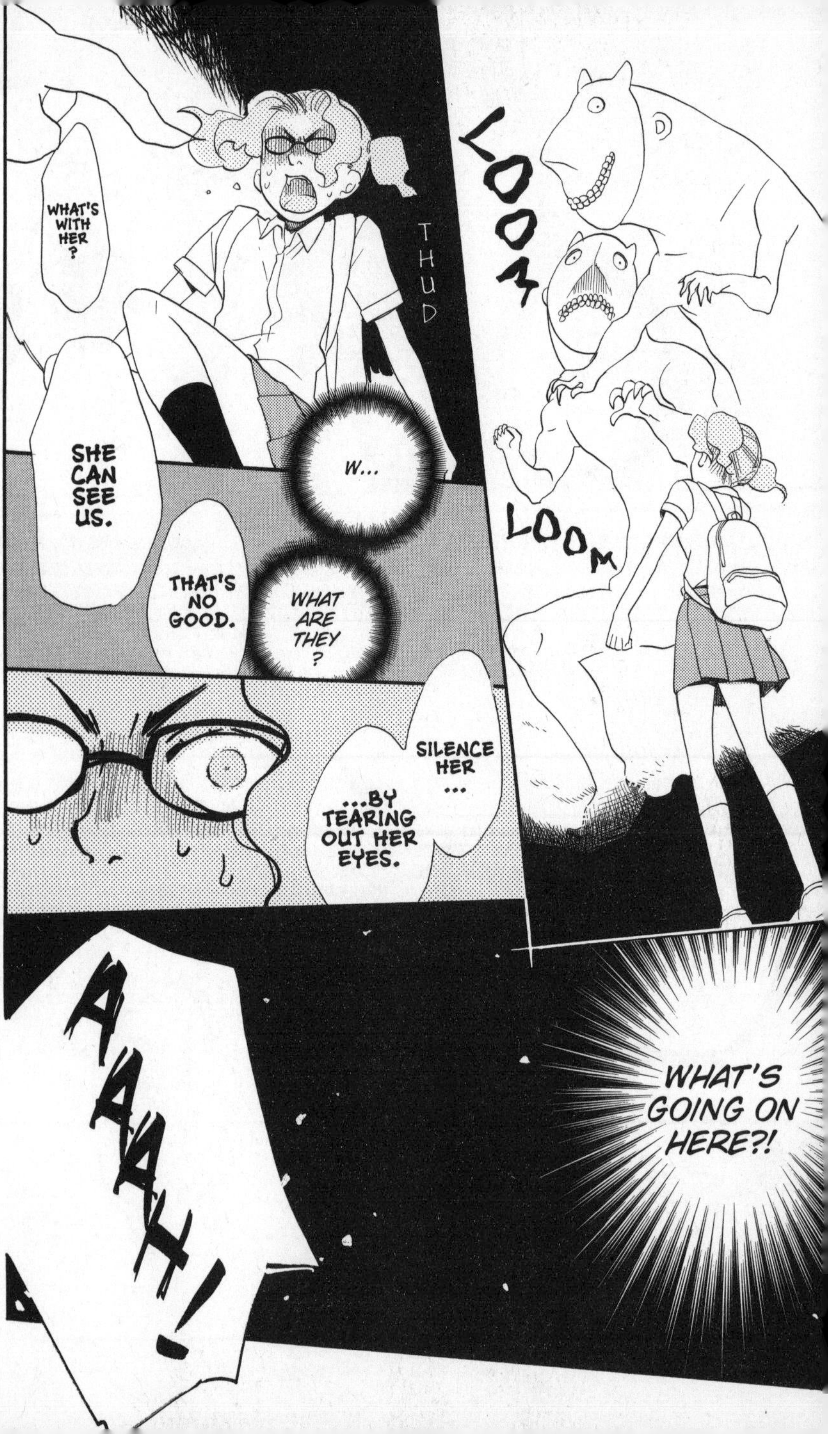
LOOM
LOOM
THUD
WHAT'S WITH HER?
W...
SHE CAN SEE US.
WHAT ARE THEY?
THAT'S NO GOOD.
SILENCE HER...
...BY TEARING OUT HER EYES.
WHAT'S GOING ON HERE?!
AAAH!

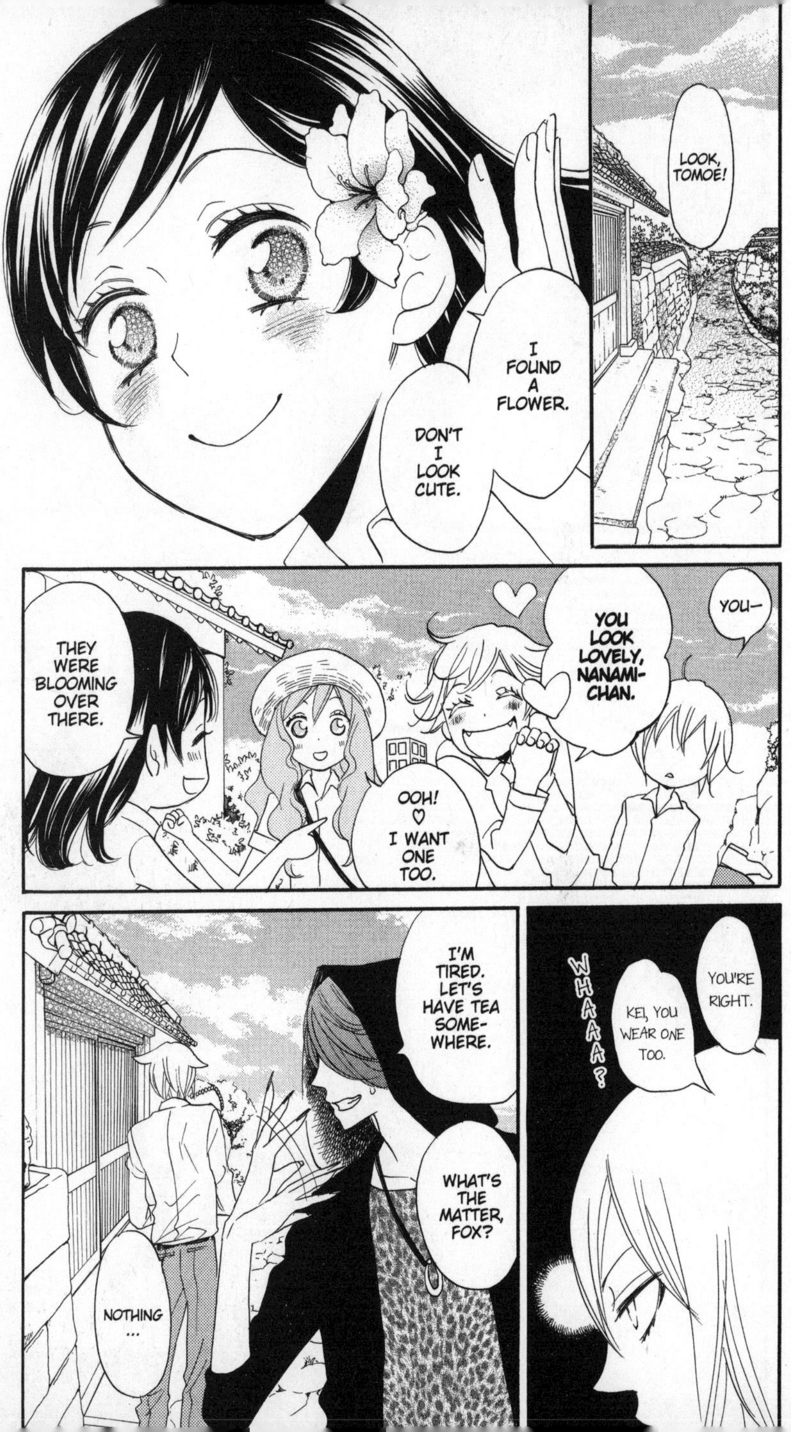
LOOK, TOMOE!
I FOUND A FLOWER.
DON'T I LOOK CUTE.
YOU—
YOU LOOK LOVELY, NANAMI-CHAN.
THEY WERE BLOOMING OVER THERE.
OOH! ♡ I WANT ONE TOO.
YOU'RE RIGHT.
KEI, YOU WEAR ONE TOO.
WHAAAA?
I'M TIRED. LET'S HAVE TEA SOME-WHERE.
WHAT'S THE MATTER, FOX?
NOTHING...

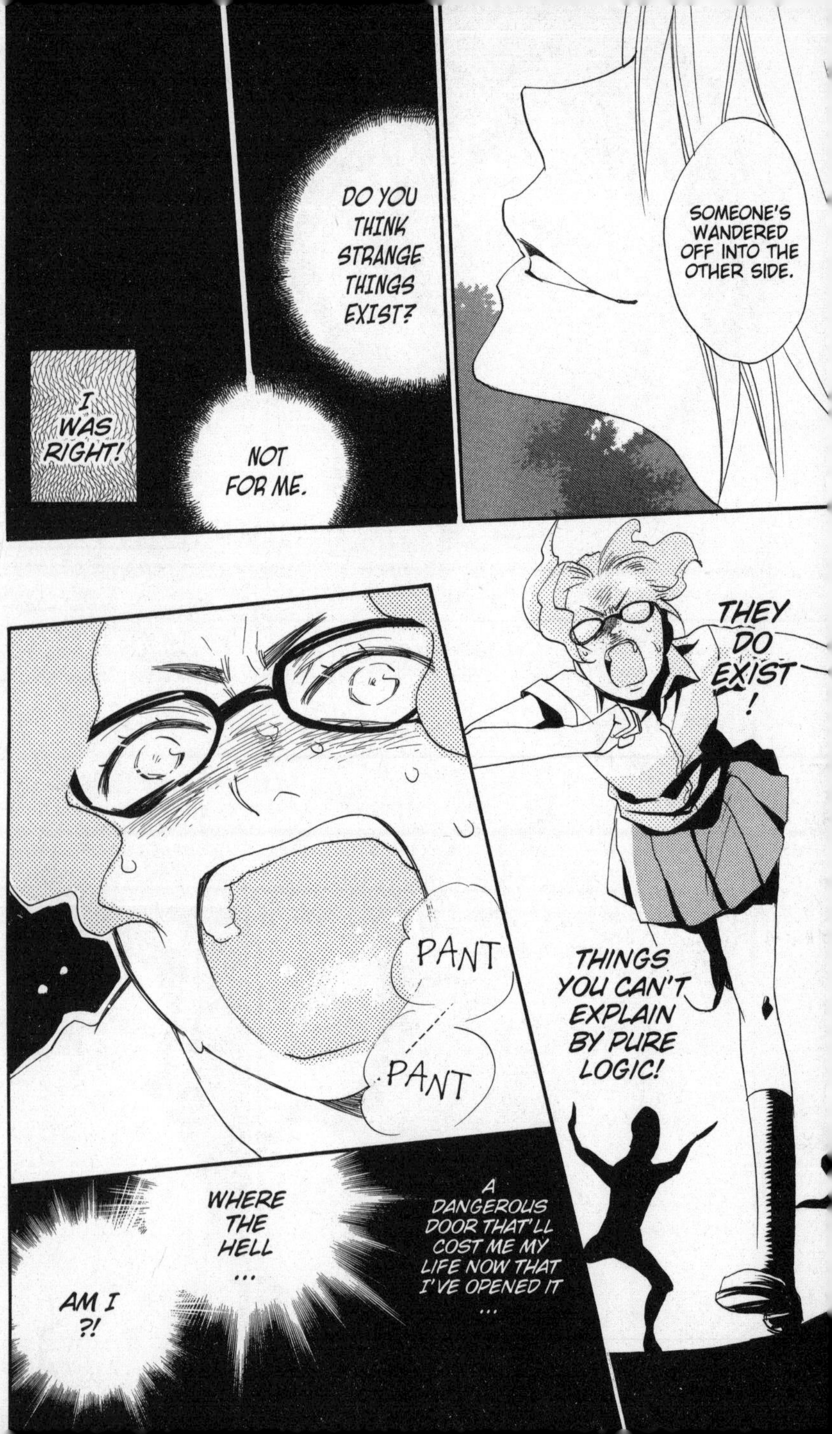
SOMEONE'S WANDERED OFF INTO THE OTHER SIDE.
DO YOU THINK STRANGE THINGS EXIST?
NOT FOR ME.
I WAS RIGHT!
THEY DO EXIST!
THINGS YOU CAN'T EXPLAIN BY PURE LOGIC!
PANT
PANT
A DANGEROUS DOOR THAT'LL COST ME MY LIFE NOW THAT I'VE OPENED IT...
WHERE THE HELL...
AM I ?!

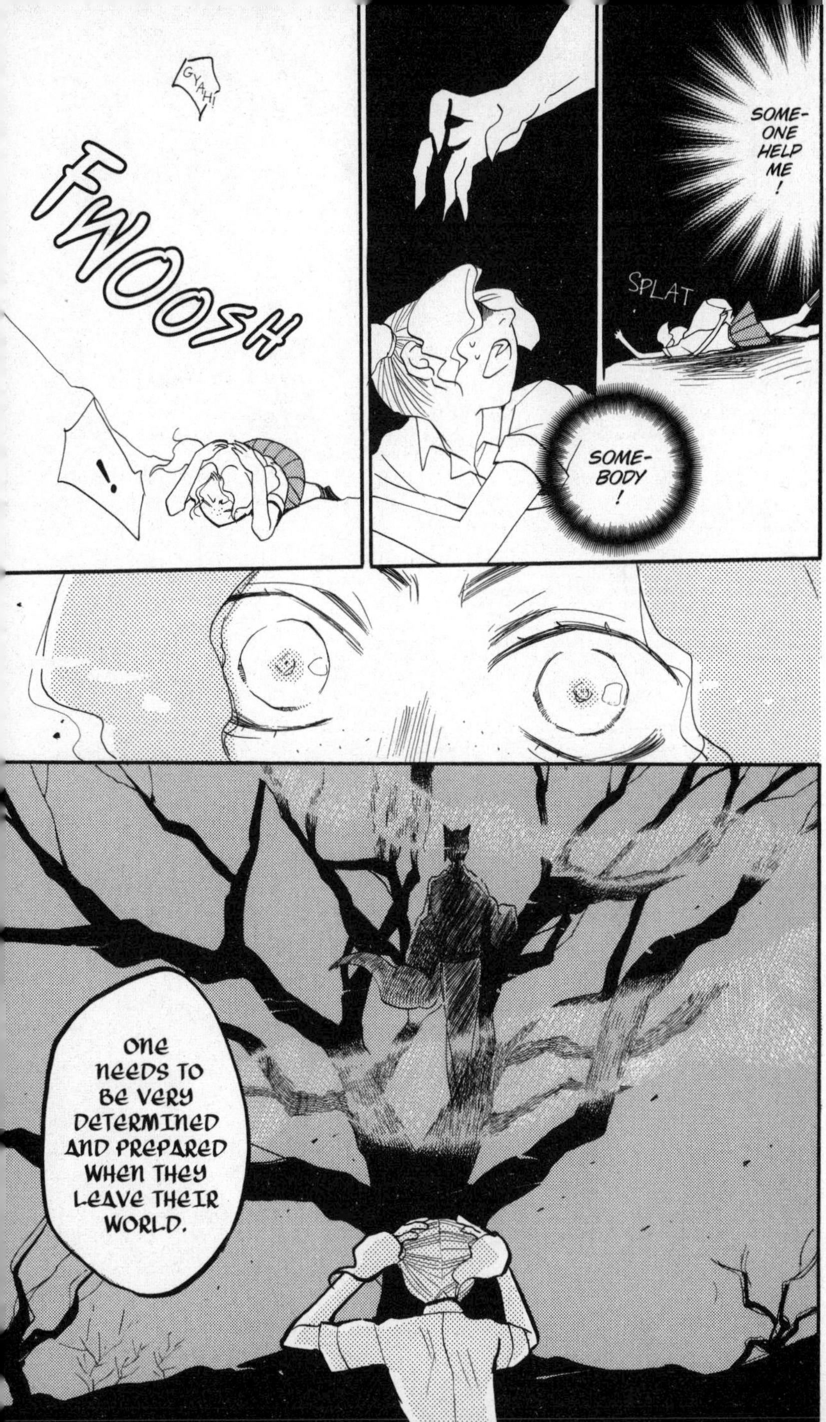
SOME-ONE HELP ME!
SPLAT
SOME-BODY!
GYAH!
FWOOSH
!
ONE NEEDS TO BE VERY DETERMINED AND PREPARED WHEN THEY LEAVE THEIR WORLD.

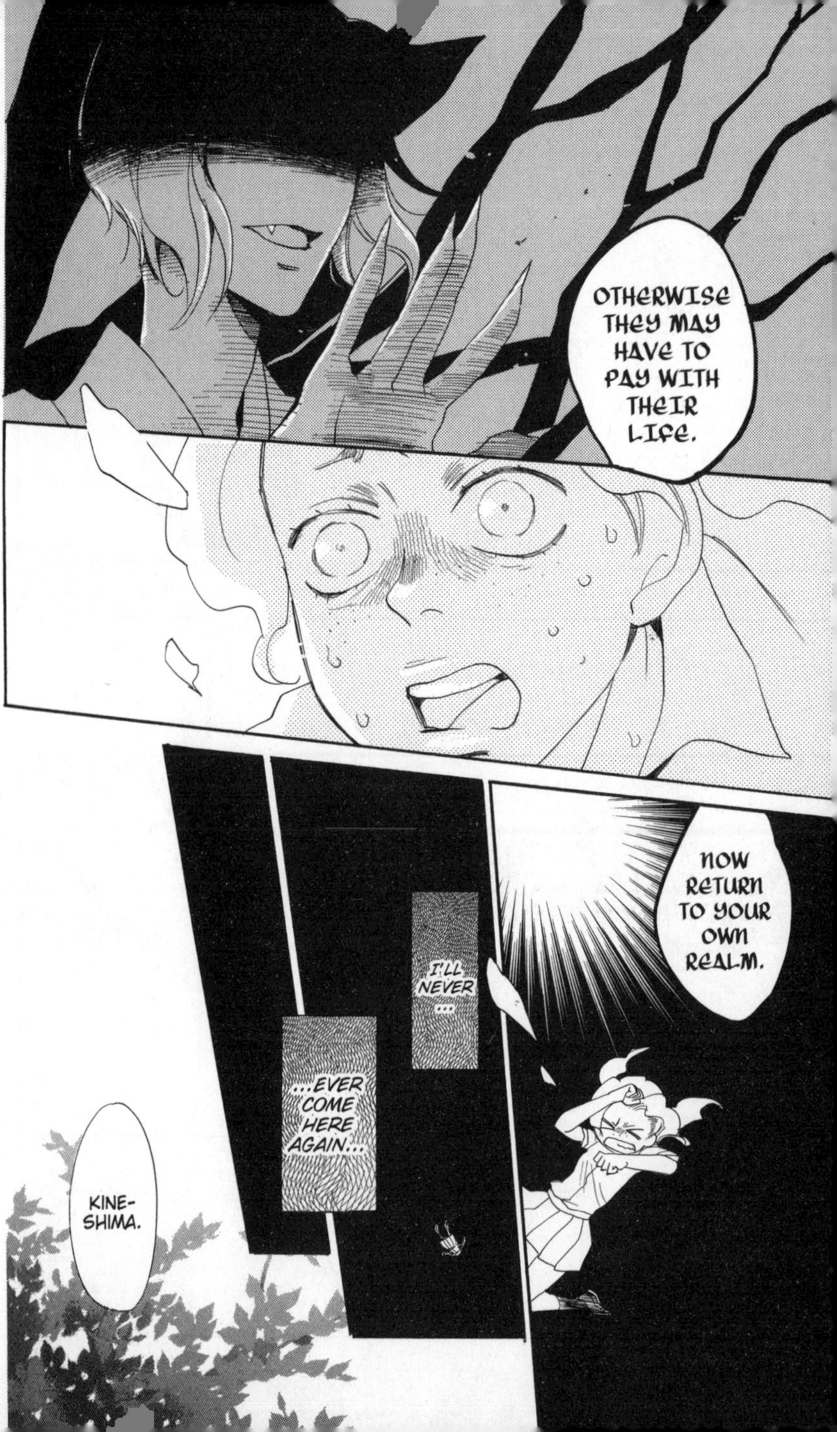
OTHERWISE THEY MAY HAVE TO PAY WITH THEIR LIFE.
NOW RETURN TO YOUR OWN REALM.
I'LL NEVER ...
...EVER COME HERE AGAIN...
KINE-SHIMA.

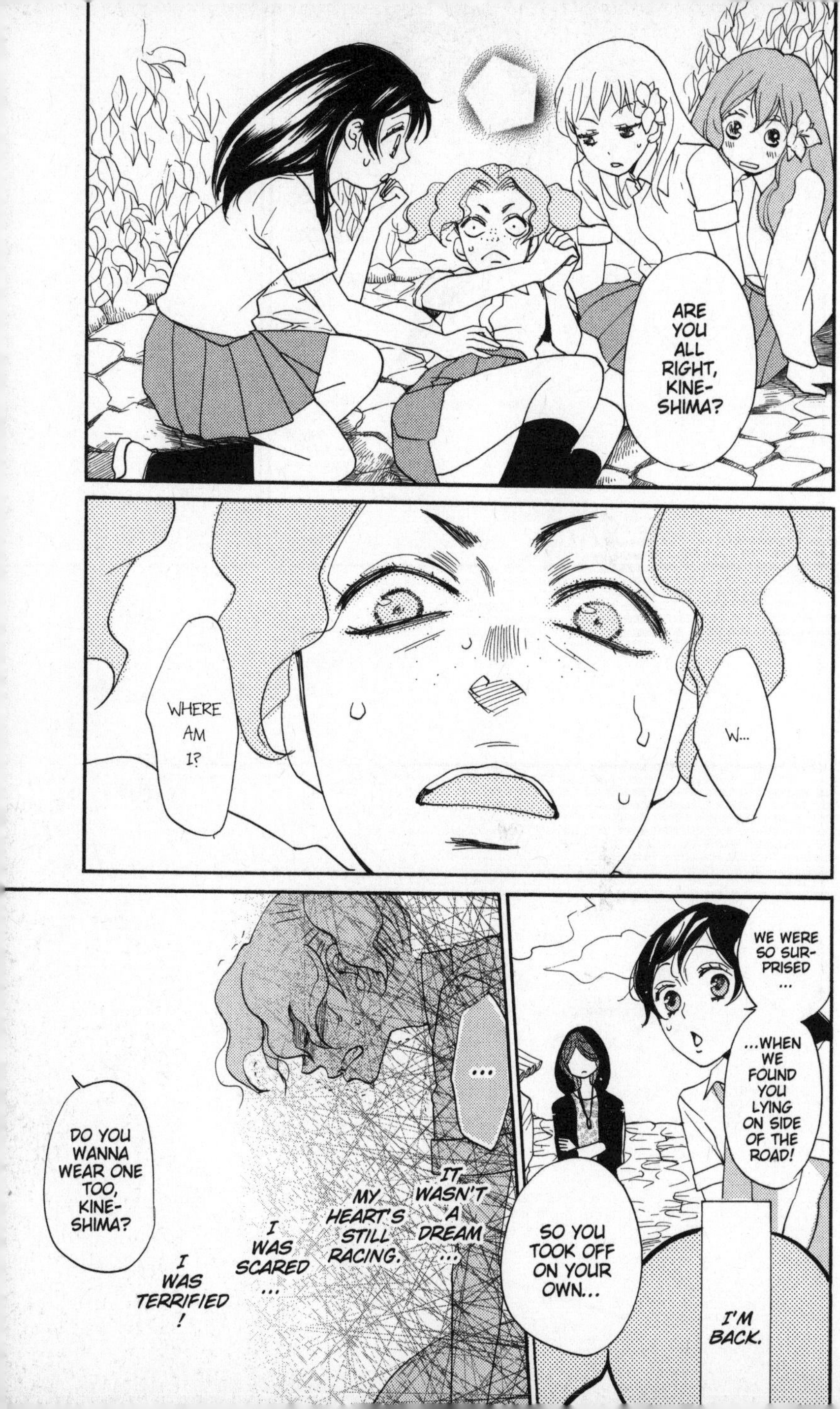
ARE YOU ALL RIGHT, KINE-SHIMA?
W...
WHERE AM I?
WE WERE SO SUR-PRISED...
...WHEN WE FOUND YOU LYING ON SIDE OF THE ROAD!
SO YOU TOOK OFF ON YOUR OWN...
I'M BACK.
...
IT WASN'T A DREAM...
MY HEART'S STILL RACING.
I WAS SCARED...
I WAS TERRIFIED!
DO YOU WANNA WEAR ONE TOO, KINE-SHIMA?

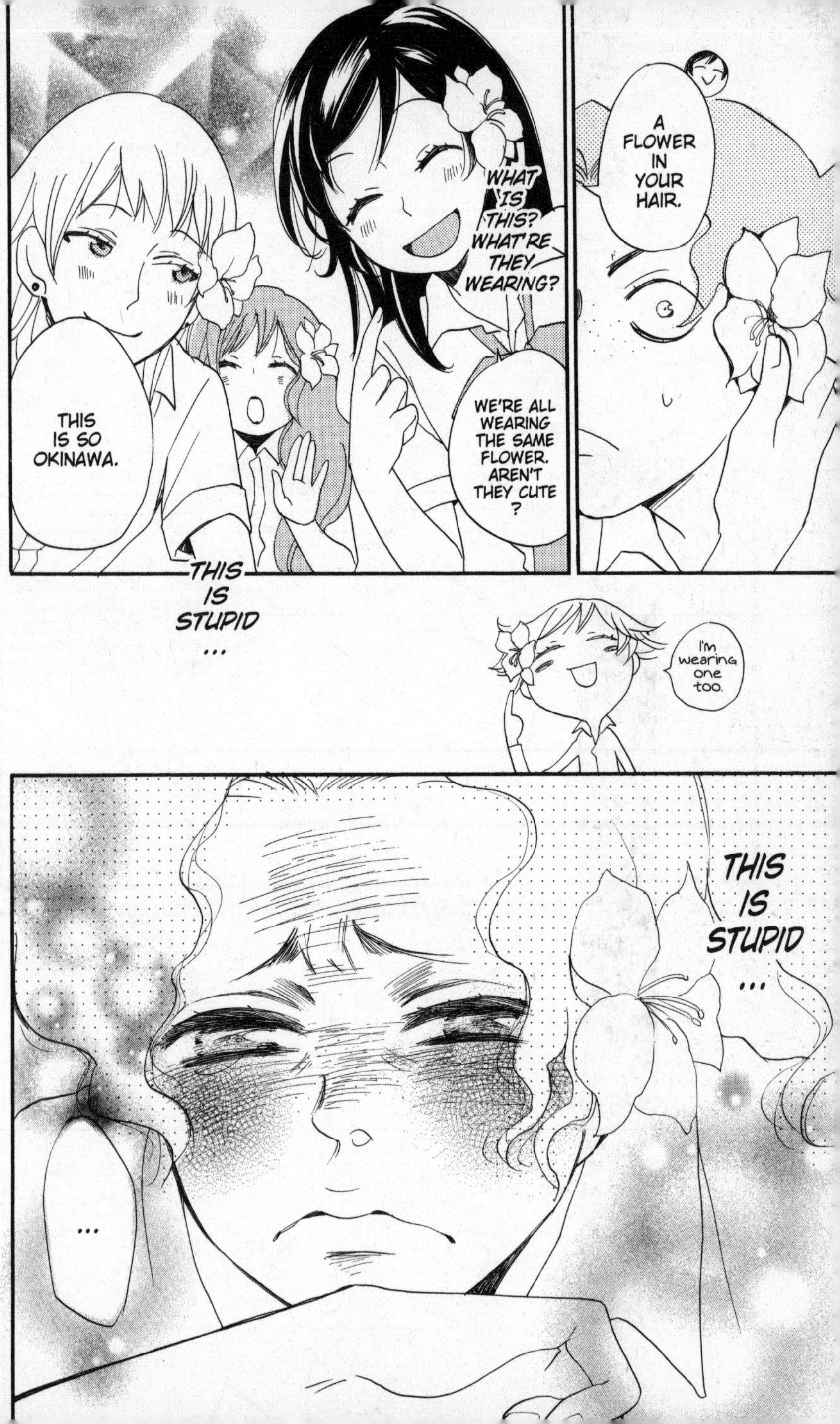
A FLOWER IN YOUR HAIR.
WHAT IS THIS? WHAT'RE THEY WEARING?
WE'RE ALL WEARING THE SAME FLOWER. AREN'T THEY CUTE?
THIS IS SO OKINAWA.
I'm wearing one too.
THIS IS STUPID...
THIS IS STUPID...
...

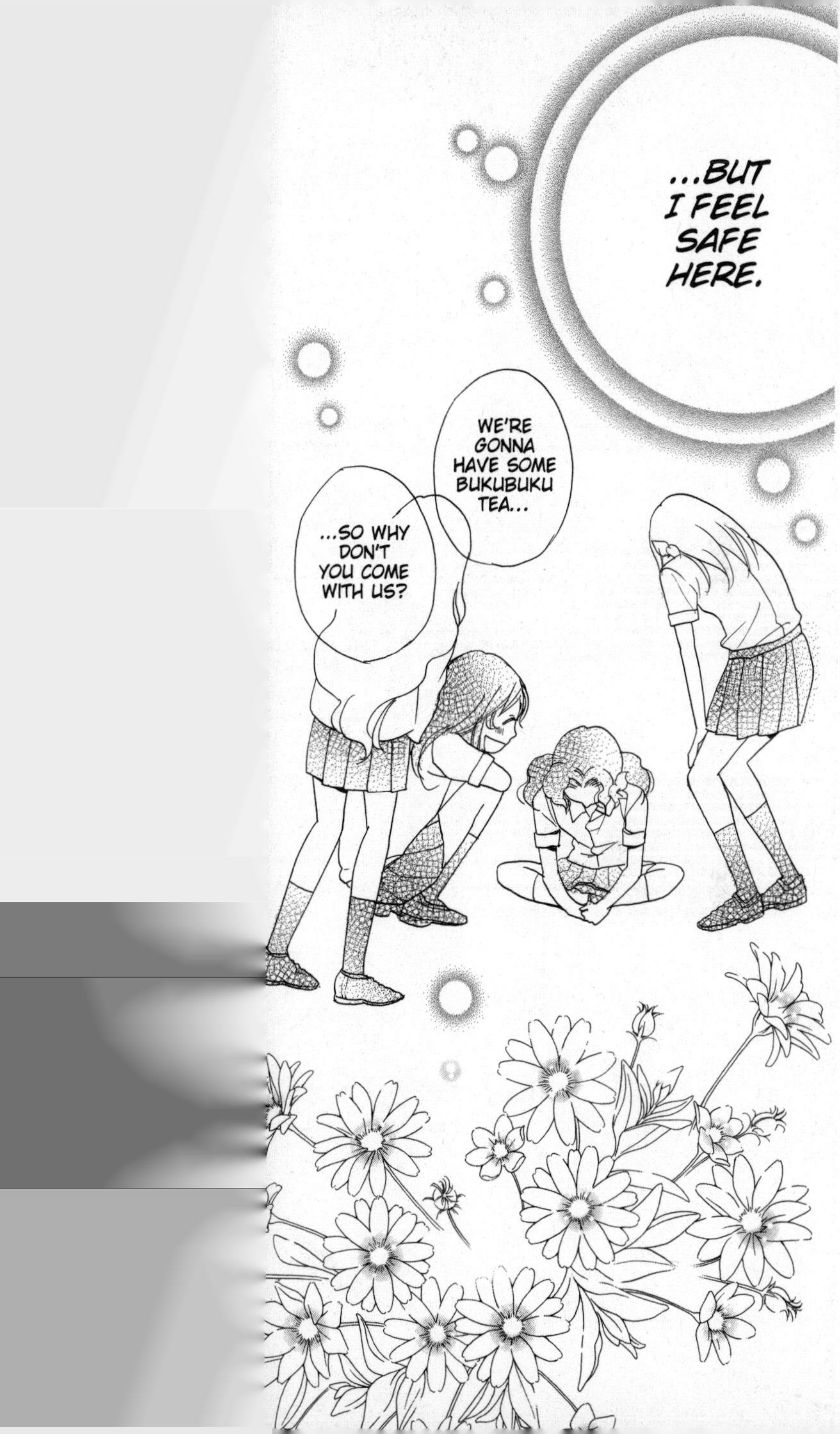
...BUT I FEEL SAFE HERE.
WE'RE GONNA HAVE SOME BUKUBUKU TEA...
...SO WHY DON'T YOU COME WITH US?

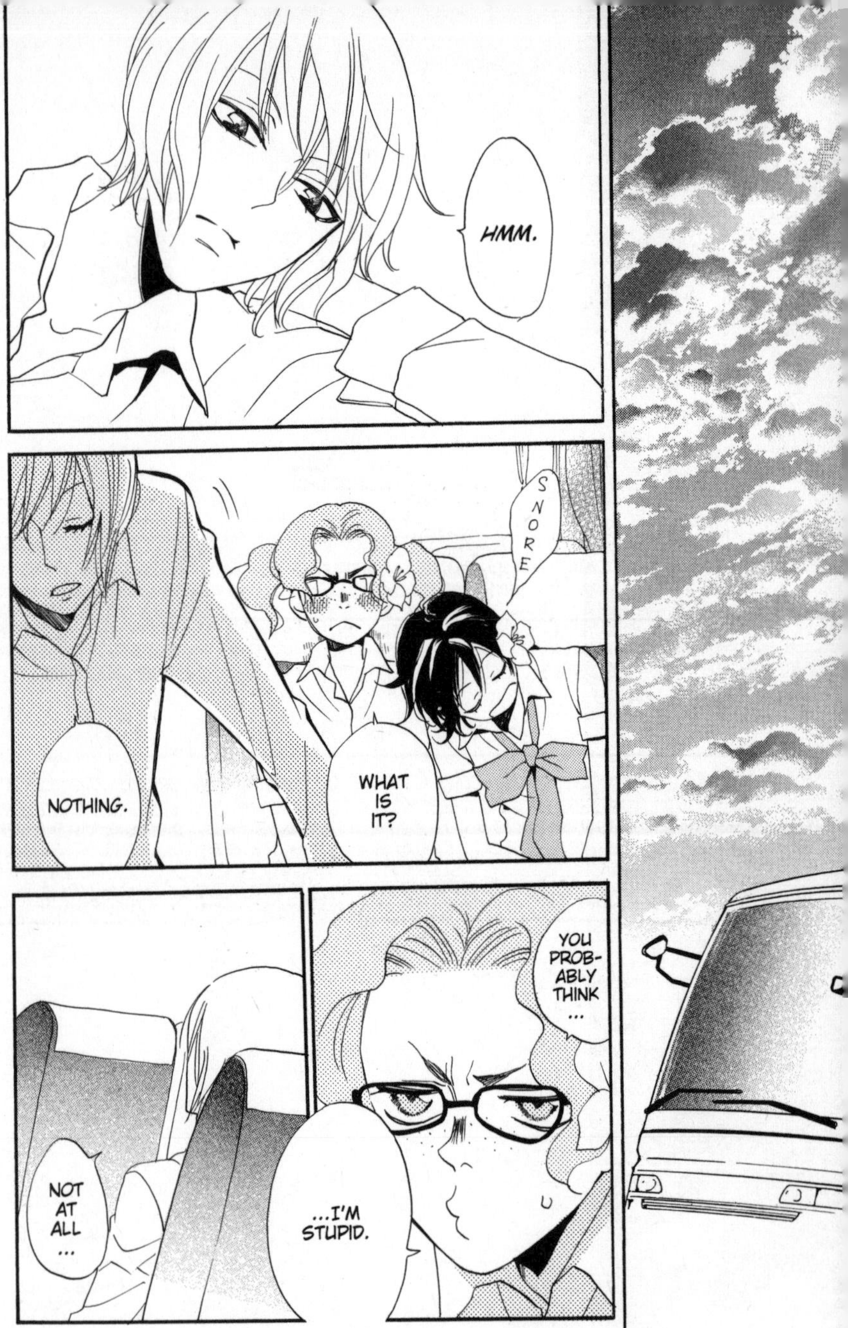
HMM.
SNORE
WHAT IS IT?
NOTHING.
YOU PROBABLY THINK...
...I'M STUPID.
NOT AT ALL...

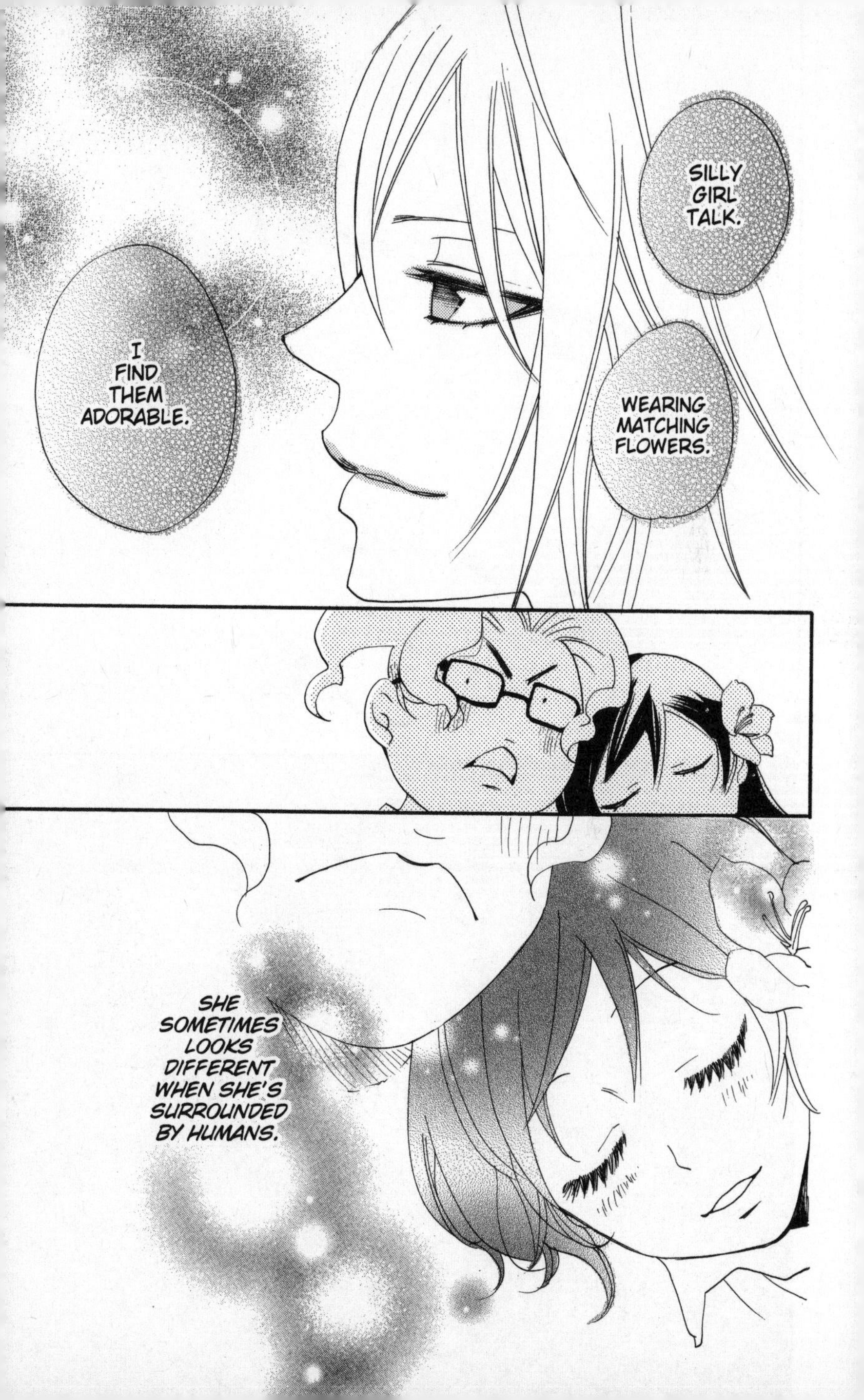
SILLY GIRL TALK.
WEARING MATCHING FLOWERS.
I FIND THEM ADORABLE.
SHE SOMETIMES LOOKS DIFFERENT WHEN SHE'S SURROUNDED BY HUMANS.

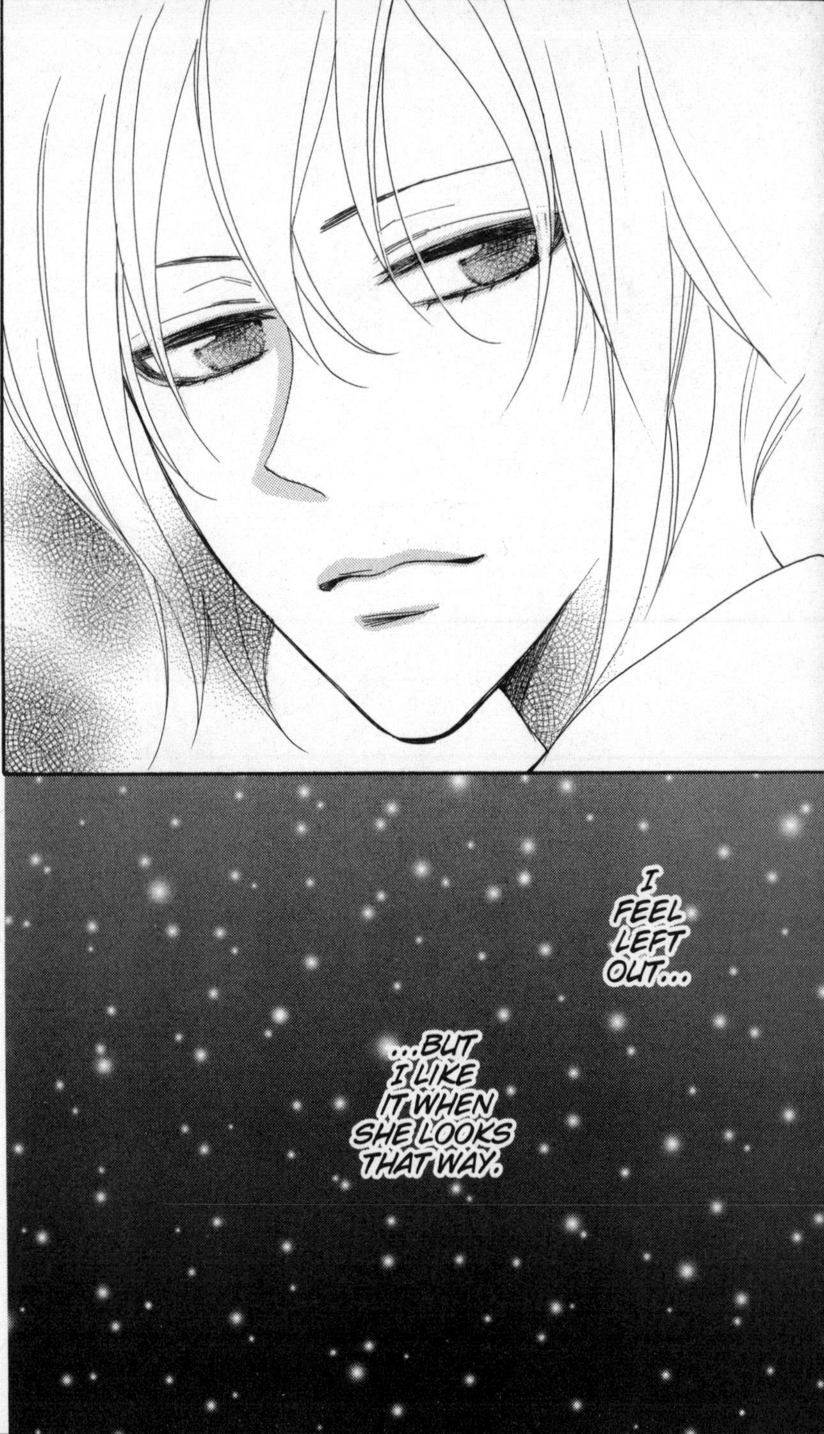
I FEEL LEFT OUT...
...BUT I LIKE IT WHEN SHE LOOKS THAT WAY.

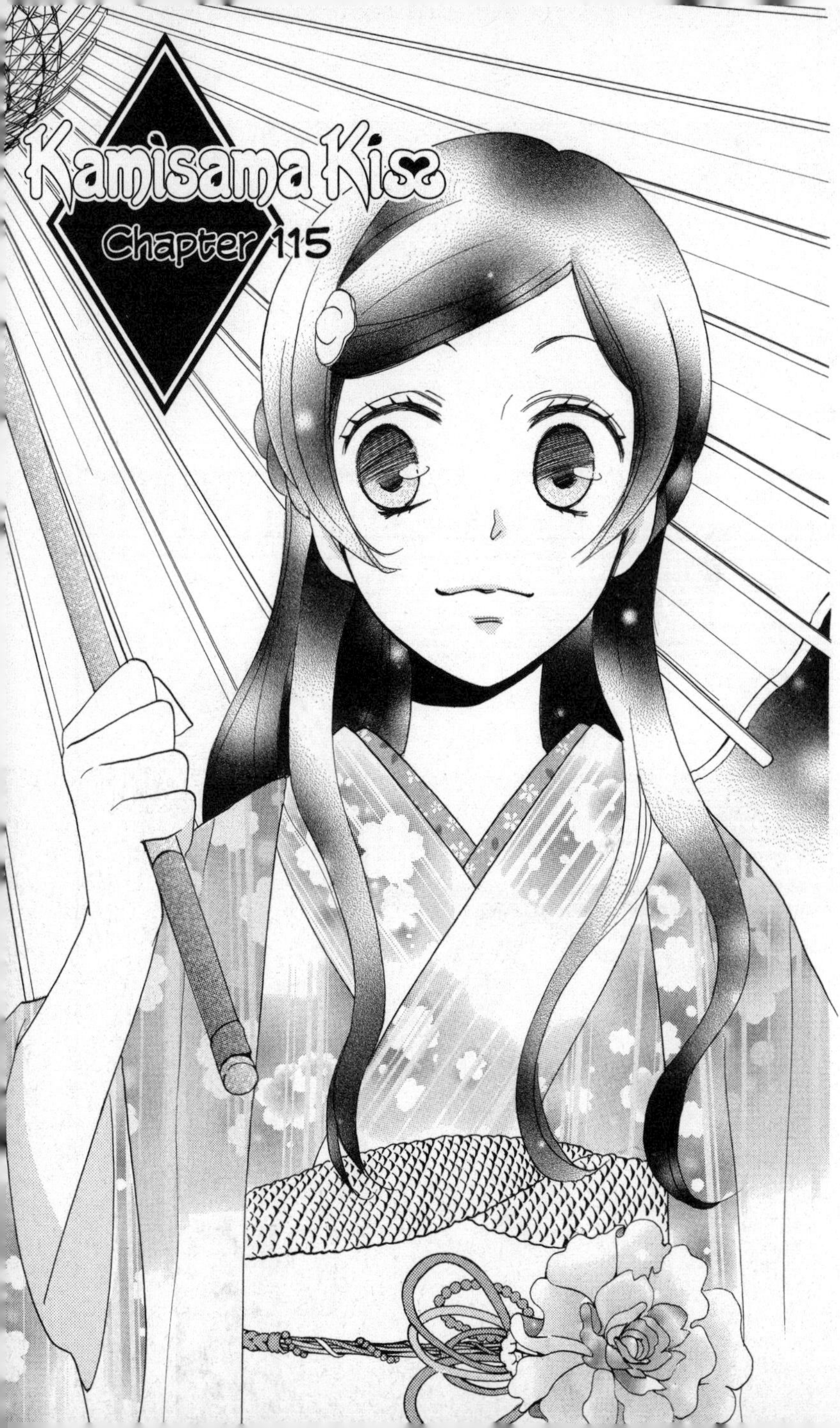
Kamisama Kiss
Chapter 115

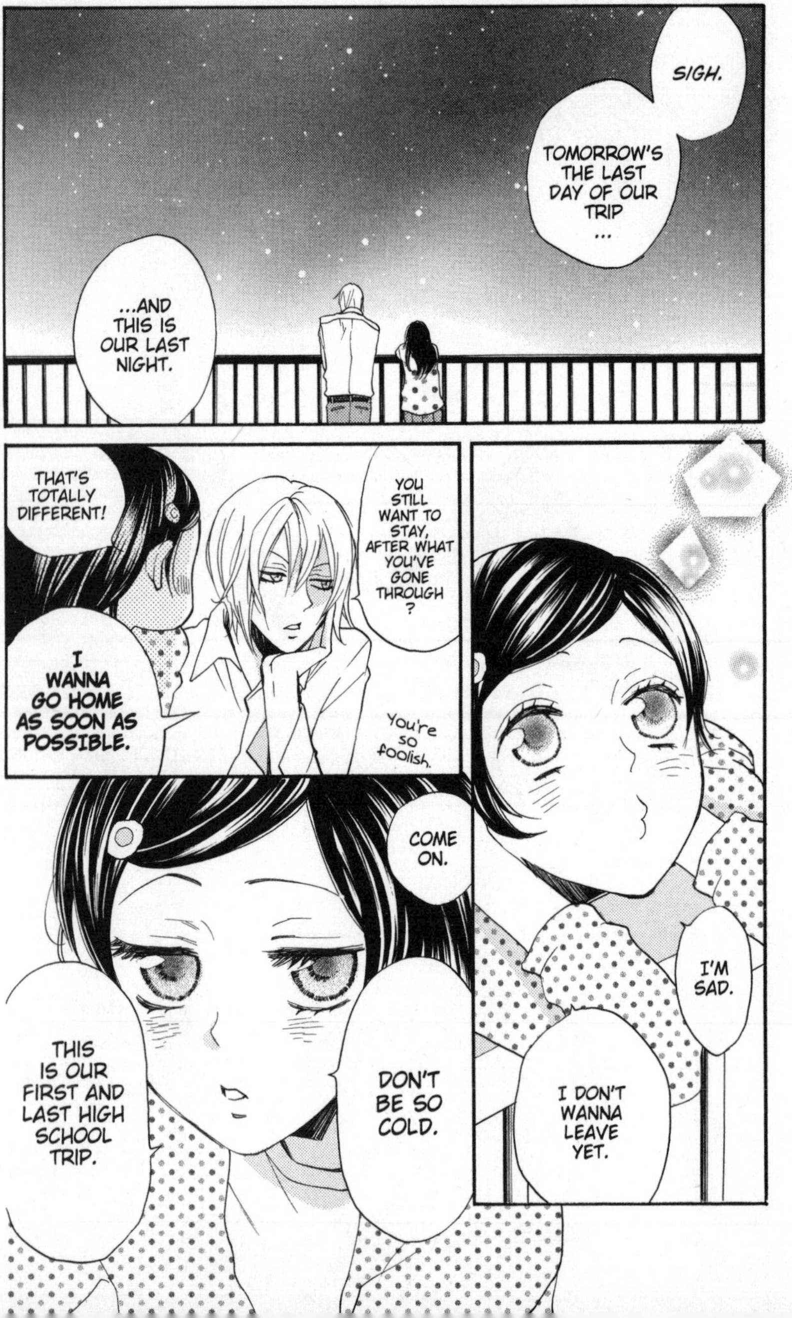
SIGH.
TOMORROW'S THE LAST DAY OF OUR TRIP ...
...AND THIS IS OUR LAST NIGHT.
I'M SAD.
I DON'T WANNA LEAVE YET.
YOU STILL WANT TO STAY, AFTER WHAT YOU'VE GONE THROUGH ?
You're so foolish.
THAT'S TOTALLY DIFFERENT!
I WANNA GO HOME AS SOON AS POSSIBLE.
COME ON.
DON'T BE SO COLD.
THIS IS OUR FIRST AND LAST HIGH SCHOOL TRIP.

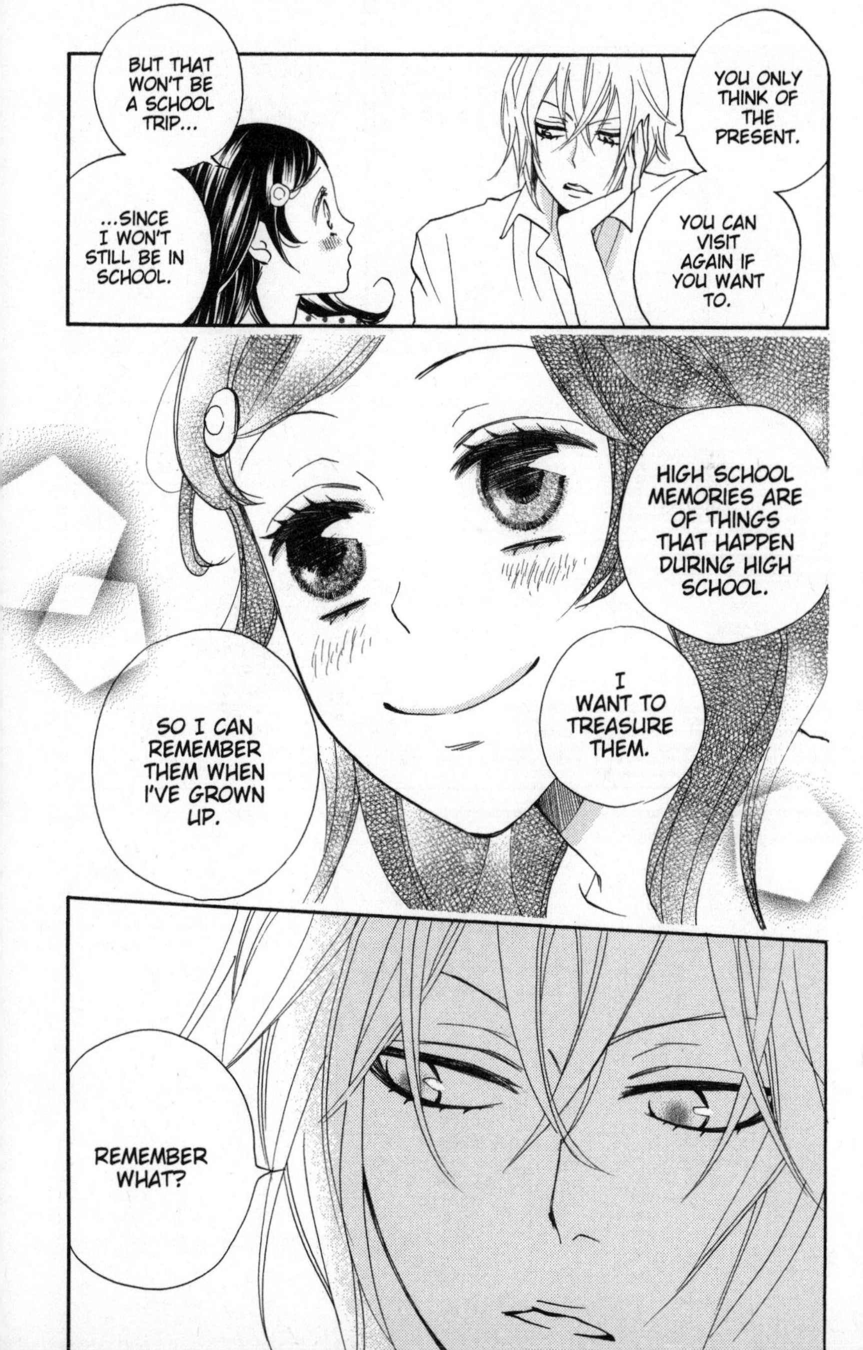
YOU ONLY THINK OF THE PRESENT.
YOU CAN VISIT AGAIN IF YOU WANT TO.
BUT THAT WON'T BE A SCHOOL TRIP...
...SINCE I WON'T STILL BE IN SCHOOL.
HIGH SCHOOL MEMORIES ARE OF THINGS THAT HAPPEN DURING HIGH SCHOOL.
I WANT TO TREASURE THEM.
SO I CAN REMEMBER THEM WHEN I'VE GROWN UP.
REMEMBER WHAT?

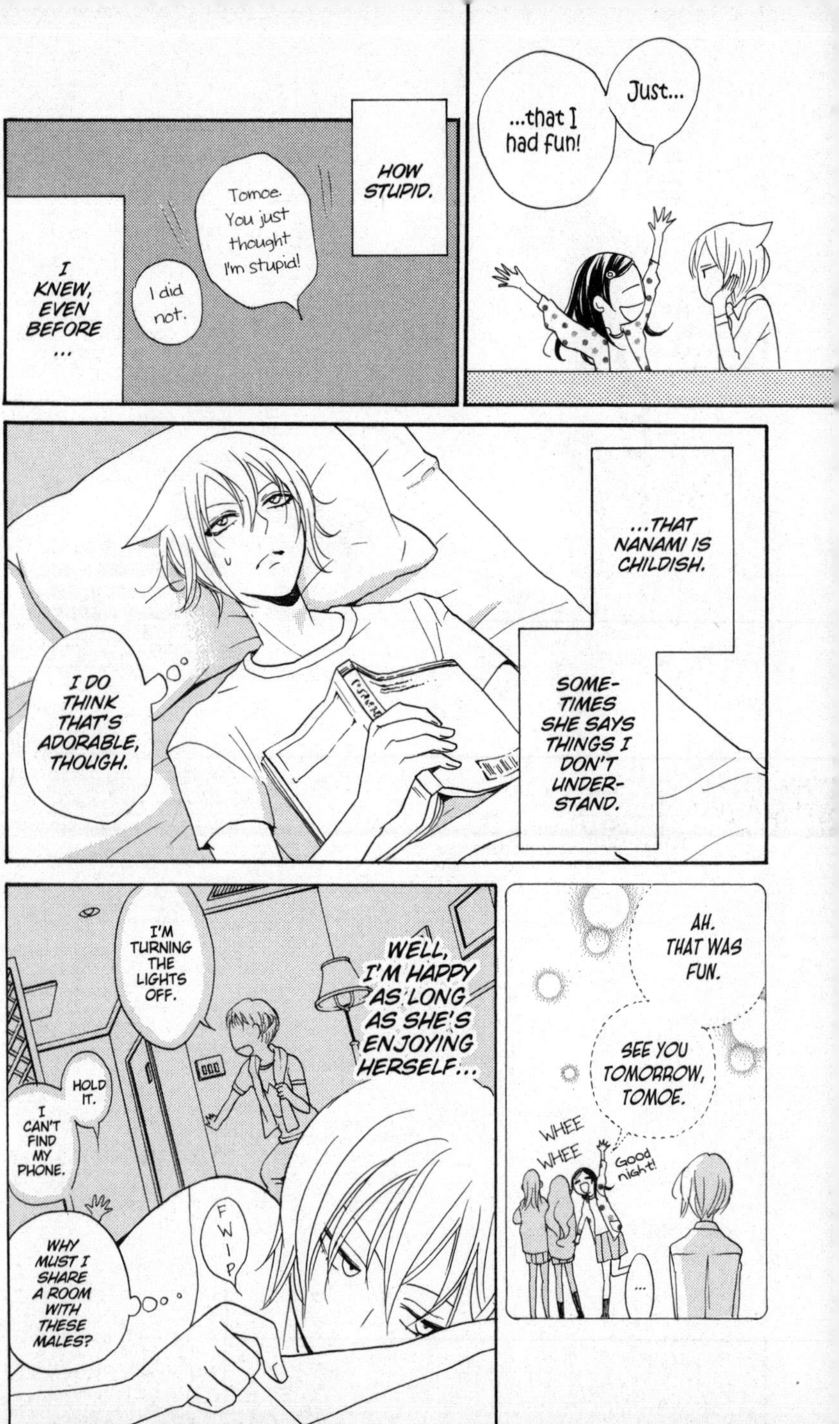
Just...
...that I had fun!
HOW STUPID.
Tomoe. You just thought I'm stupid!
I did not.
I KNEW, EVEN BEFORE...
...THAT NANAMI IS CHILDISH.
SOME-TIMES SHE SAYS THINGS I DON'T UNDER-STAND.
I DO THINK THAT'S ADORABLE, THOUGH.
AH. THAT WAS FUN.
SEE YOU TOMORROW, TOMOE.
Good night!
WHEE WHEE
...
WELL, I'M HAPPY AS LONG AS SHE'S ENJOYING HERSELF...
I'M TURNING THE LIGHTS OFF.
HOLD IT.
I CAN'T FIND MY PHONE.
FWIP
WHY MUST I SHARE A ROOM WITH THESE MALES?

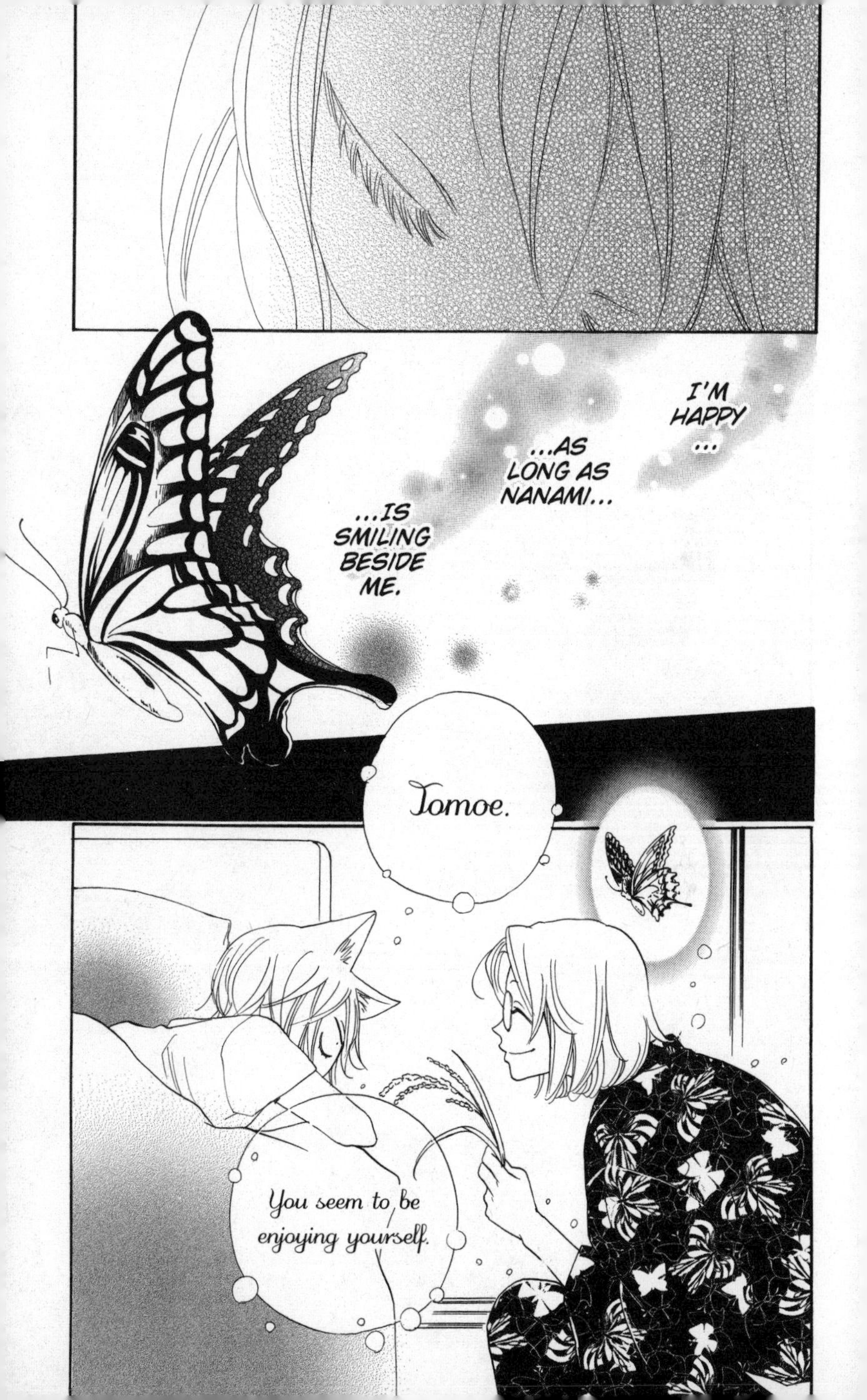
I'M HAPPY ...
...AS LONG AS NANAMI...
...IS SMILING BESIDE ME.
Tomoe.
You seem to be enjoying yourself.

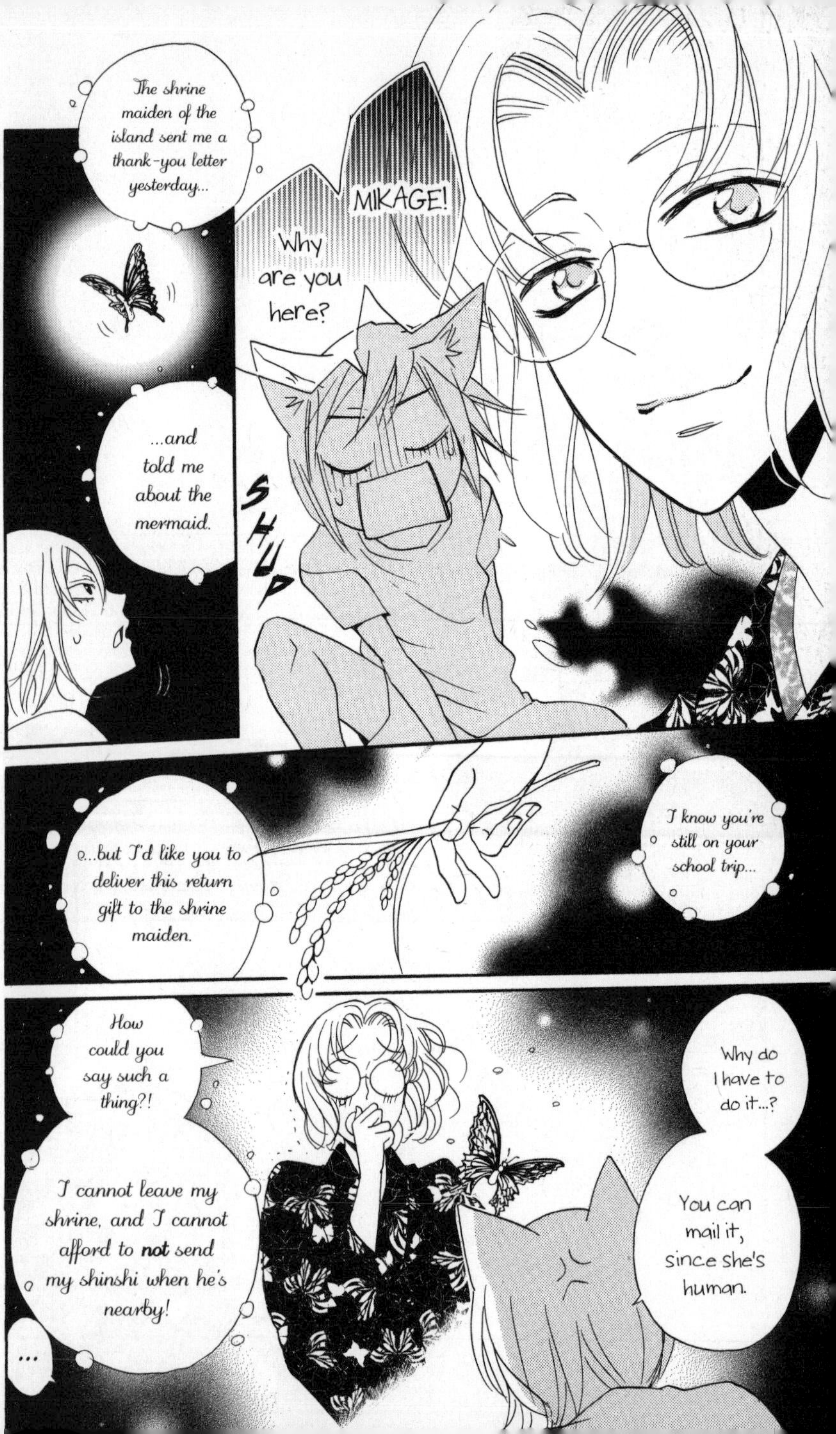
MIKAGE!
Why are you here?
SHUP
The shrine maiden of the island sent me a thank-you letter yesterday...
...and told me about the mermaid.
I know you're still on your school trip...
...but I'd like you to deliver this return gift to the shrine maiden.
Why do I have to do it...?
You can mail it, since she's human.
How could you say such a thing?!
I cannot leave my shrine, and I cannot afford to **not** send my shinshi when he's nearby!
...

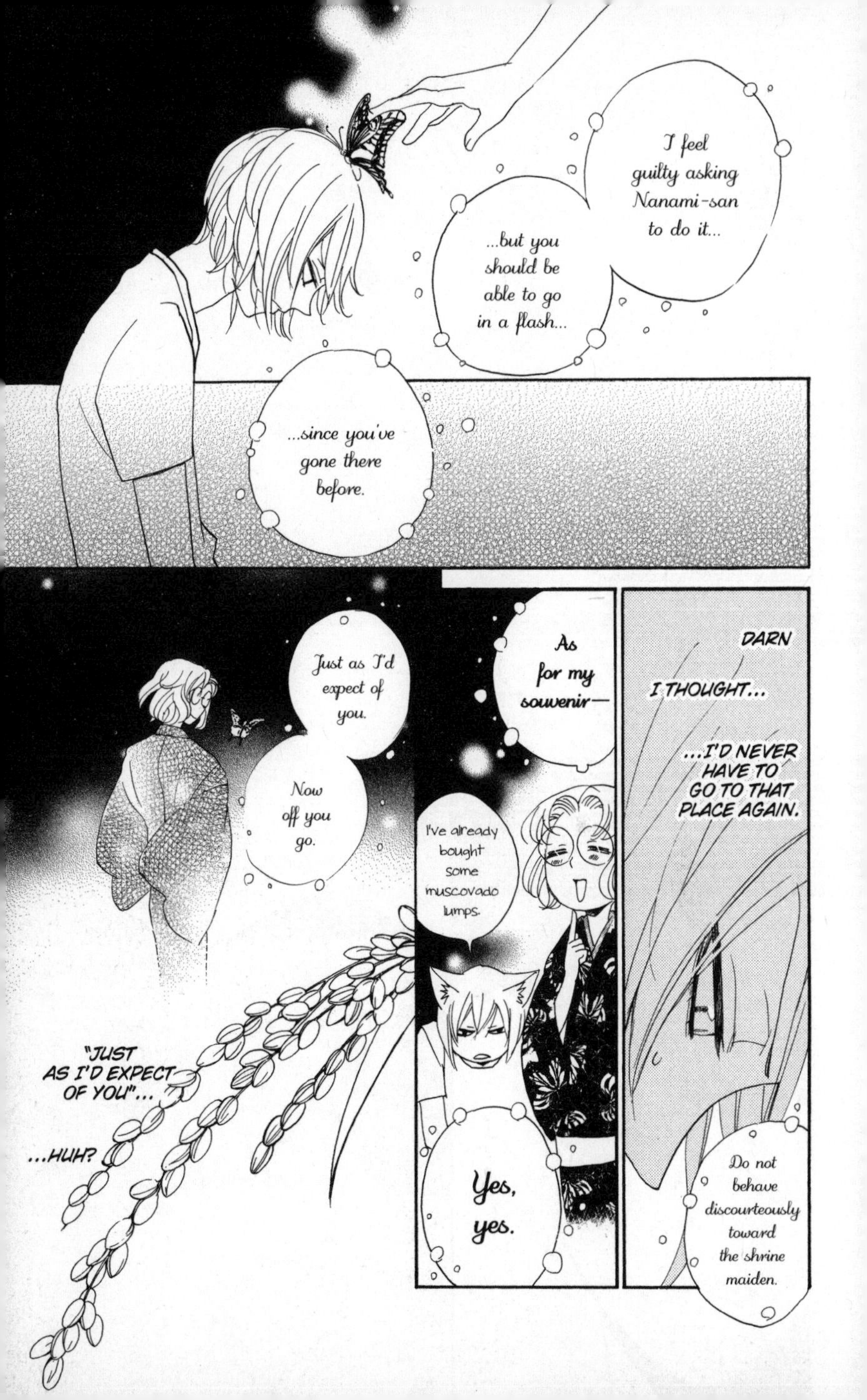
I feel guilty asking Nanami-san to do it...
...but you should be able to go in a flash...
...since you've gone there before.
DARN
I THOUGHT...
...I'D NEVER HAVE TO GO TO THAT PLACE AGAIN.
Do not behave discourteously toward the shrine maiden.
As for my souvenir—
I've already bought some muscovado lumps.
Yes, yes.
Just as I'd expect of you.
Now off you go.
"JUST AS I'D EXPECT OF YOU"...
...HUH?

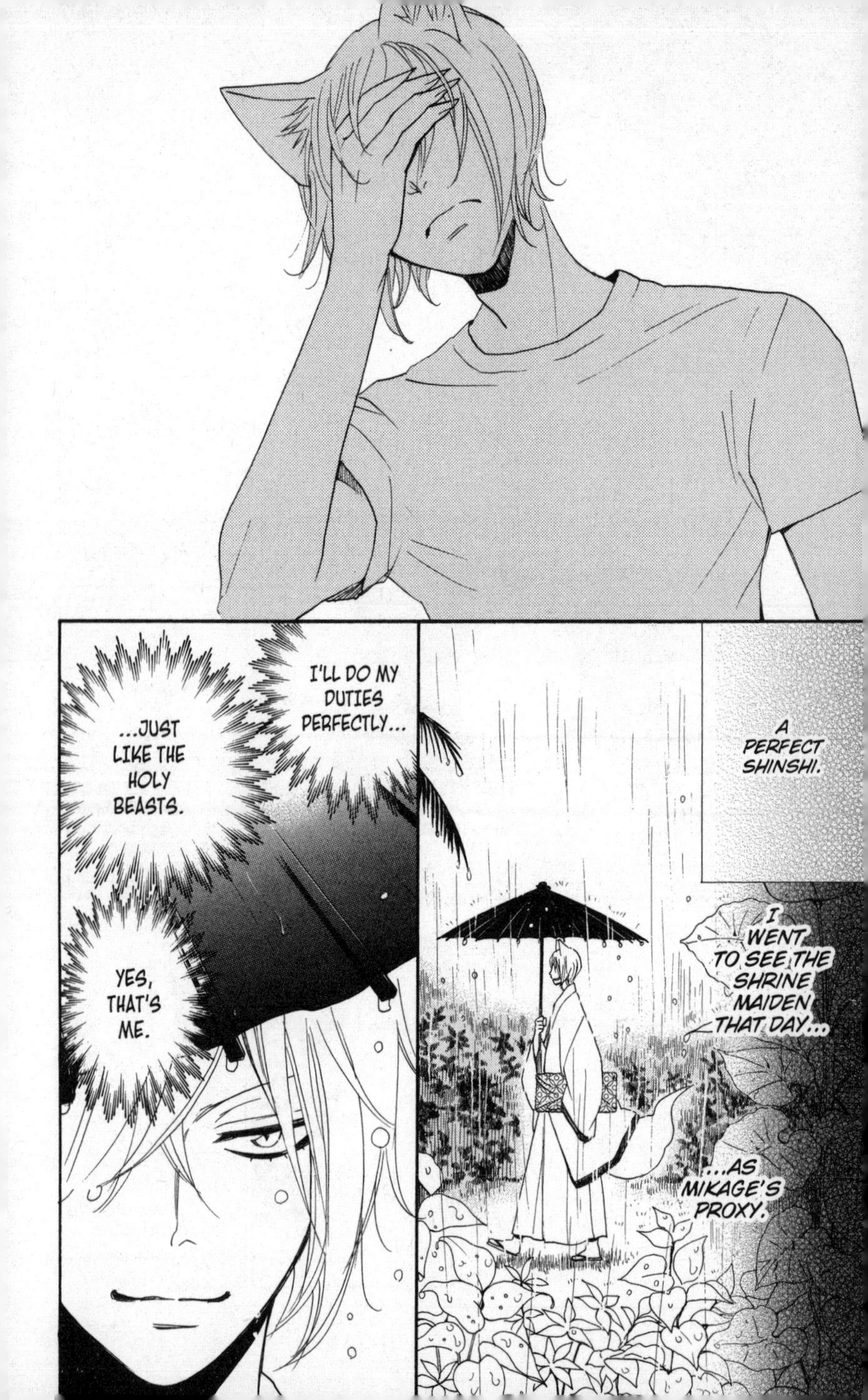
A PERFECT SHINSHI.
I WENT TO SEE THE SHRINE MAIDEN THAT DAY...
...AS MIKAGE'S PROXY.
I'LL DO MY DUTIES PERFECTLY...
...JUST LIKE THE HOLY BEASTS.
YES, THAT'S ME.

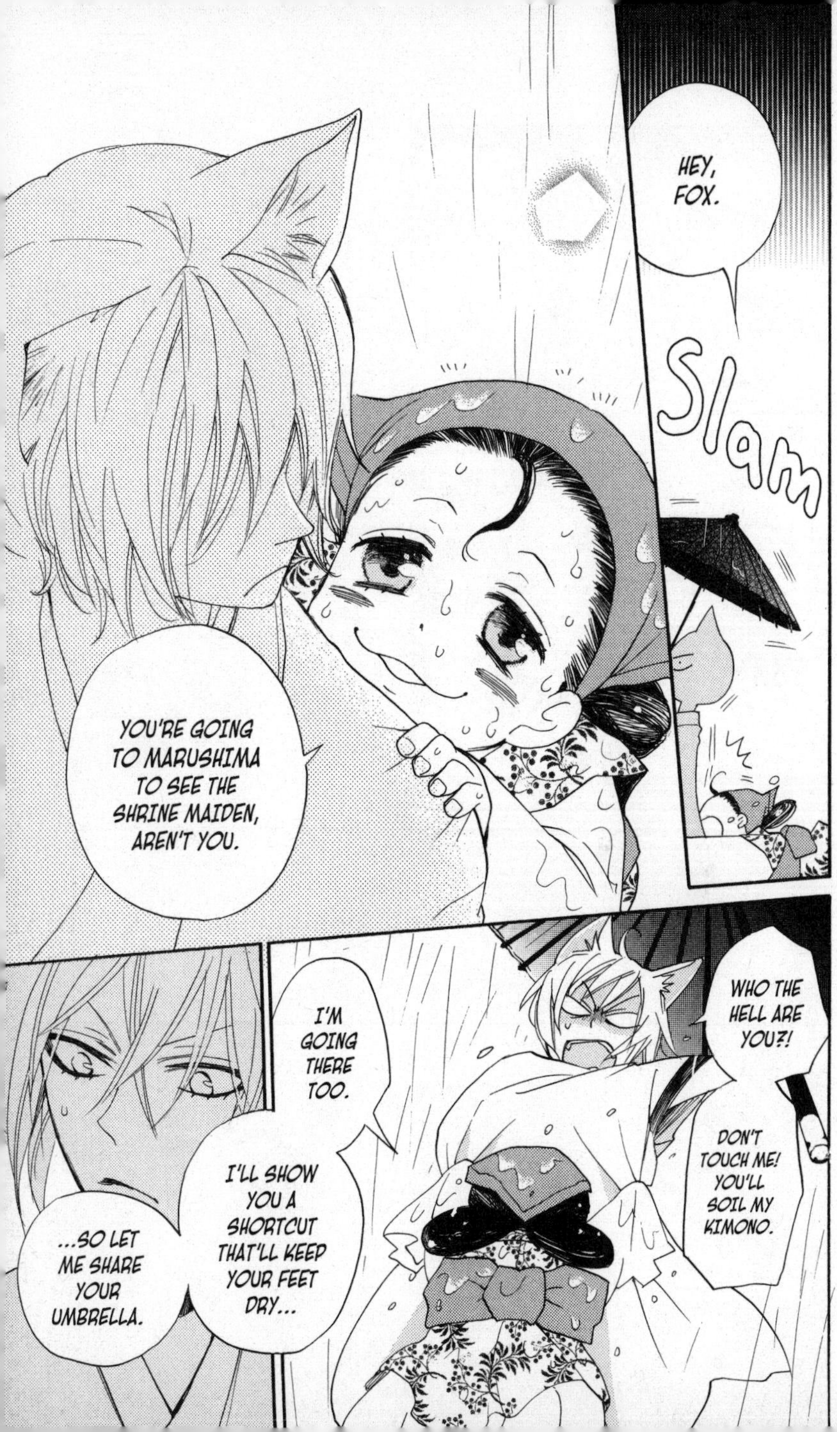
HEY, FOX.
Slam
YOU'RE GOING TO MARUSHIMA TO SEE THE SHRINE MAIDEN, AREN'T YOU.
WHO THE HELL ARE YOU?!
DON'T TOUCH ME! YOU'LL SOIL MY KIMONO.
I'M GOING THERE TOO.
I'LL SHOW YOU A SHORTCUT THAT'LL KEEP YOUR FEET DRY...
...SO LET ME SHARE YOUR UMBRELLA.

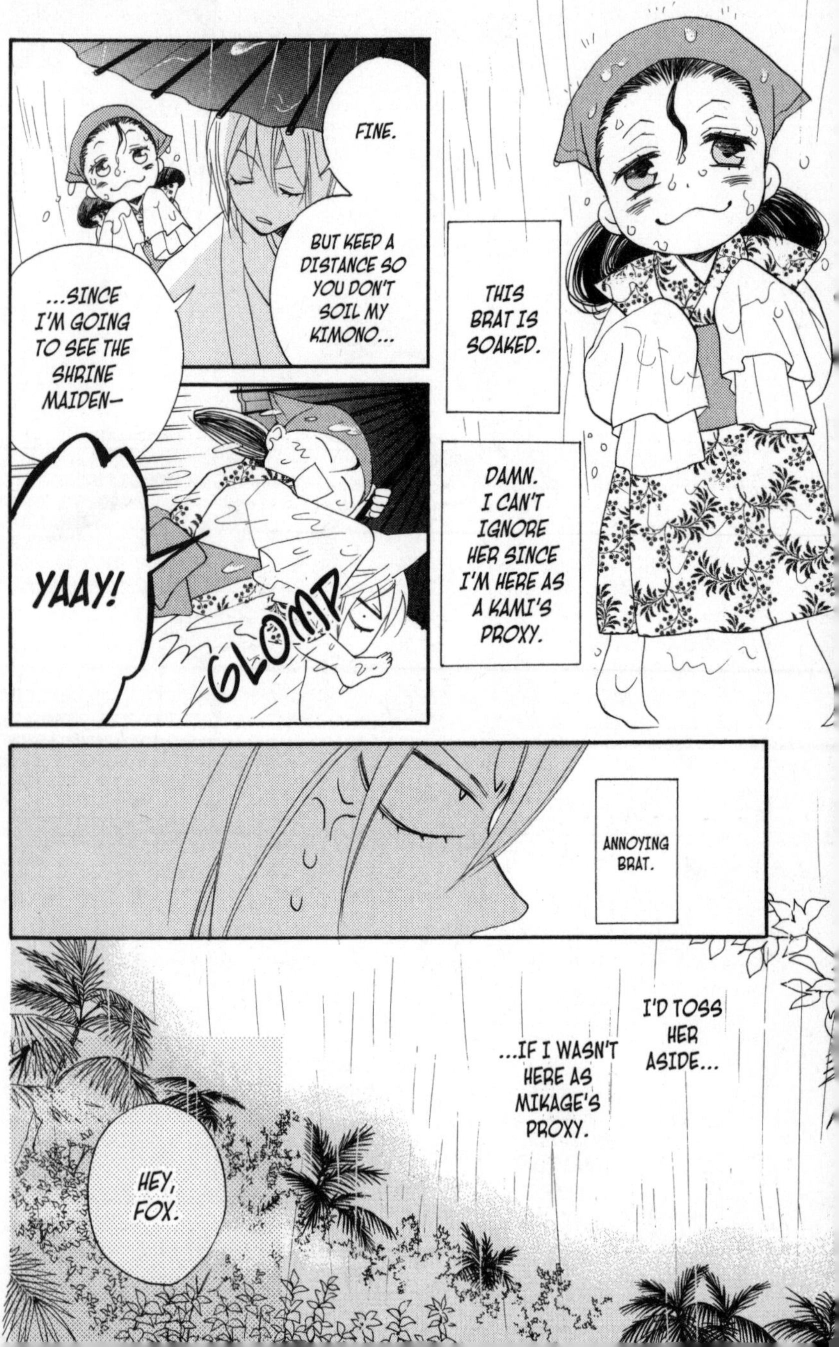
THIS BRAT IS SOAKED.
DAMN. I CAN'T IGNORE HER SINCE I'M HERE AS A KAMI'S PROXY.
FINE.
BUT KEEP A DISTANCE SO YOU DON'T SOIL MY KIMONO...
...SINCE I'M GOING TO SEE THE SHRINE MAIDEN—
YAAY!
GLOMP
ANNOYING BRAT.
I'D TOSS HER ASIDE...
...IF I WASN'T HERE AS MIKAGE'S PROXY.
HEY, FOX.

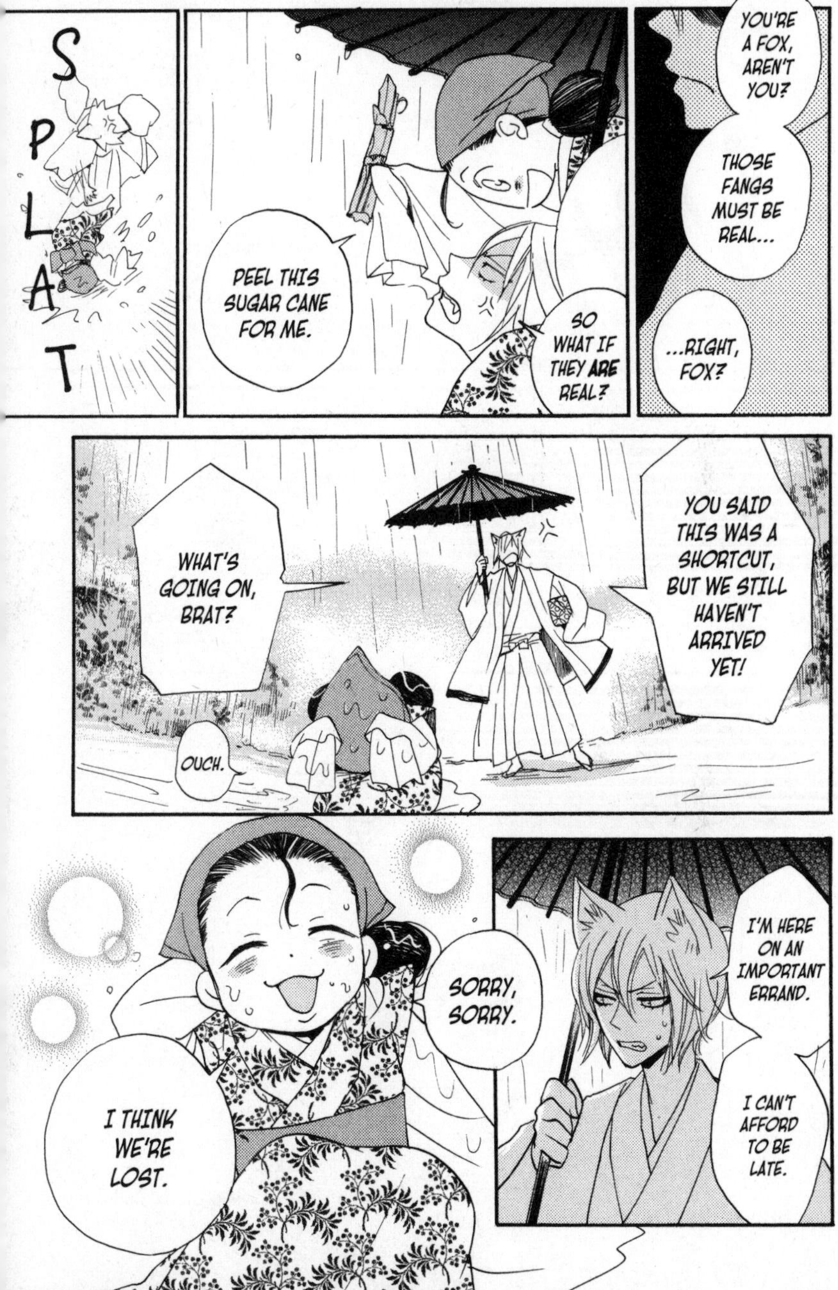
YOU'RE A FOX, AREN'T YOU?
THOSE FANGS MUST BE REAL...
...RIGHT, FOX?
SO WHAT IF THEY **ARE** REAL?
PEEL THIS SUGAR CANE FOR ME.
SPLAT
YOU SAID THIS WAS A SHORTCUT, BUT WE STILL HAVEN'T ARRIVED YET!
WHAT'S GOING ON, BRAT?
OUCH.
I'M HERE ON AN IMPORTANT ERRAND.
I CAN'T AFFORD TO BE LATE.
SORRY, SORRY.
I THINK WE'RE LOST.

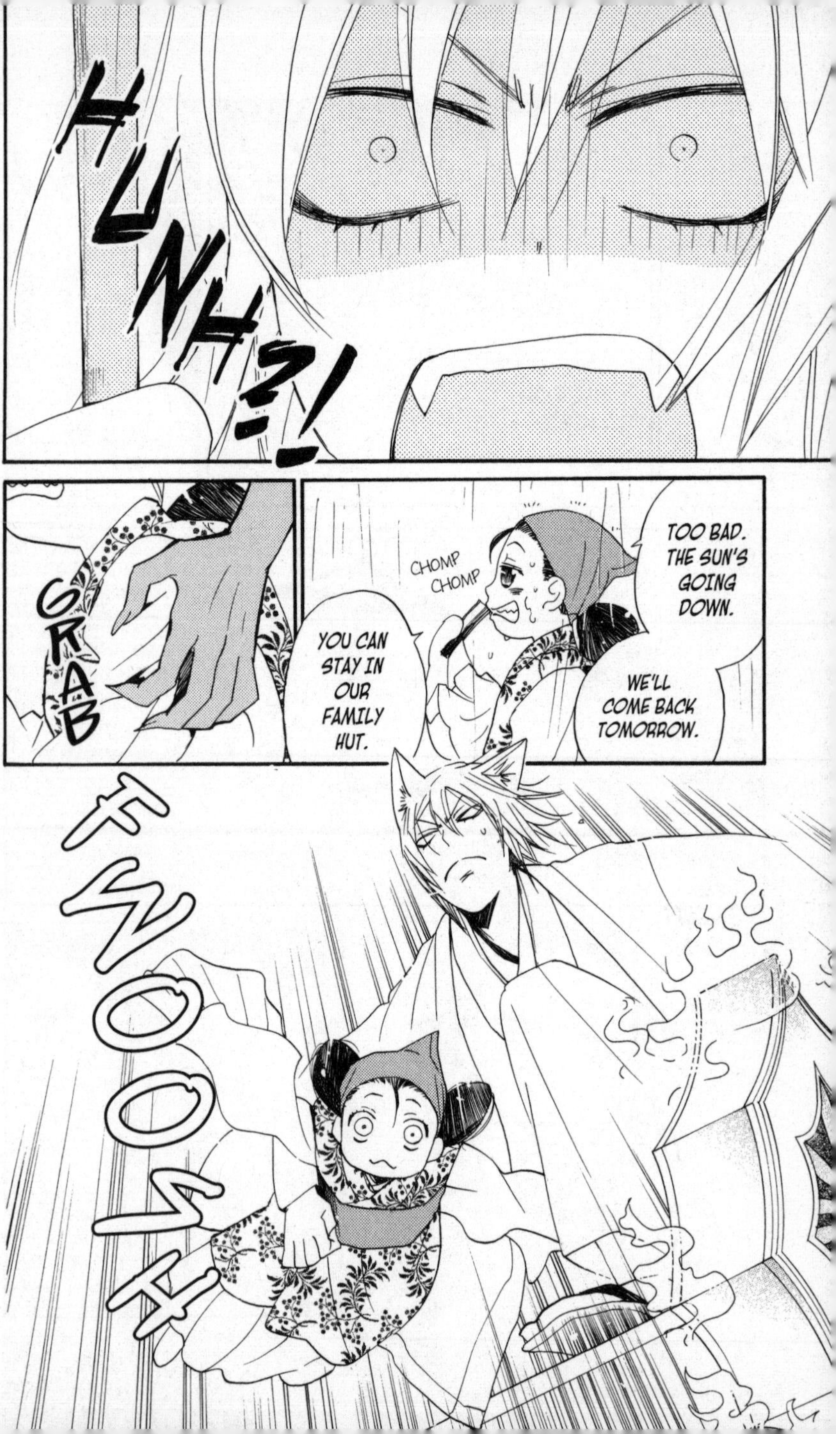
HUNH?!
TOO BAD. THE SUN'S GOING DOWN.
CHOMP CHOMP
WE'LL COME BACK TOMORROW.
YOU CAN STAY IN OUR FAMILY HUT.
GRAB
FWOOSH

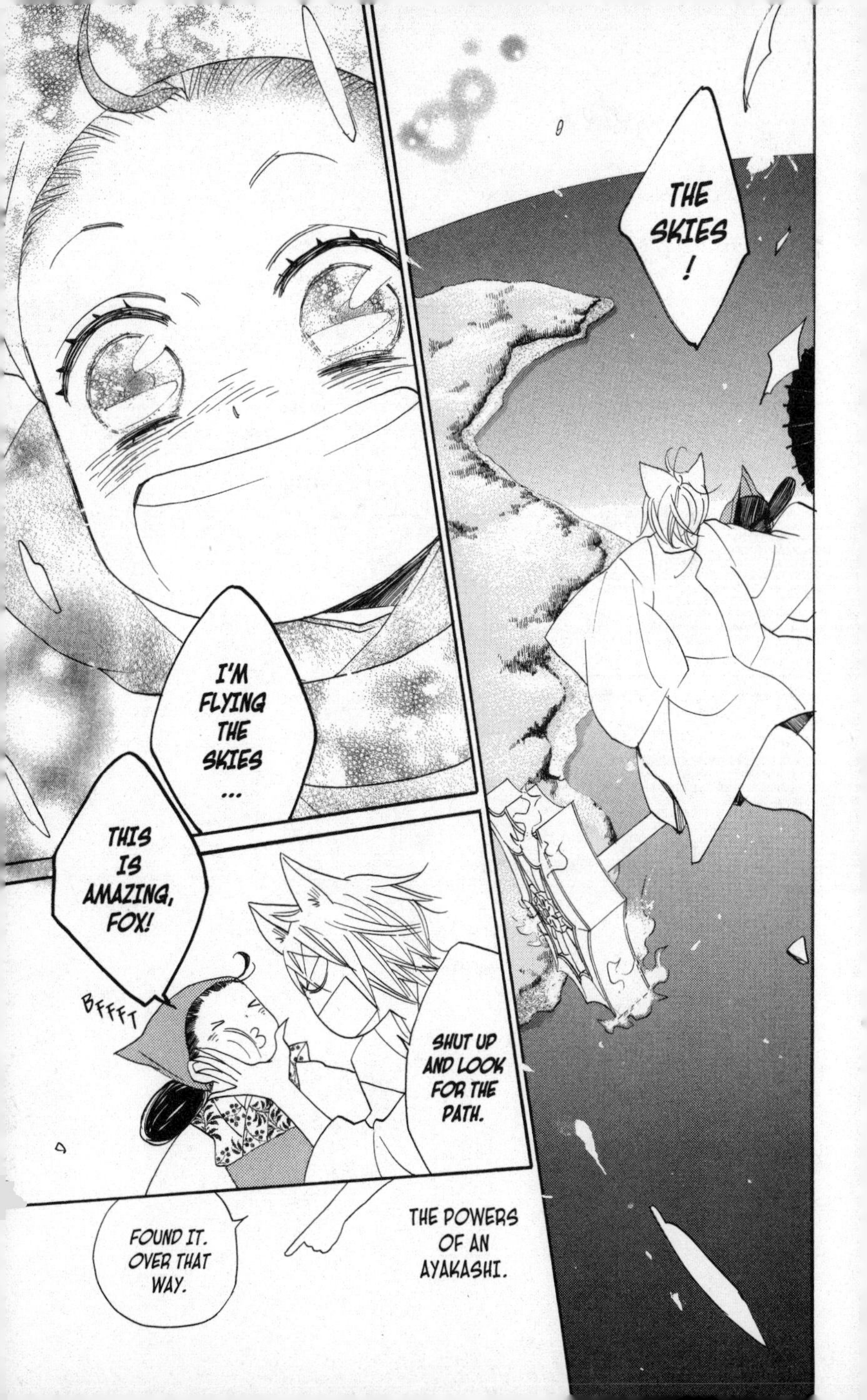
THE SKIES!
THE POWERS OF AN AYAKASHI.
I'M FLYING THE SKIES...
THIS IS AMAZING, FOX!
BFFFT
SHUT UP AND LOOK FOR THE PATH.
FOUND IT. OVER THAT WAY.

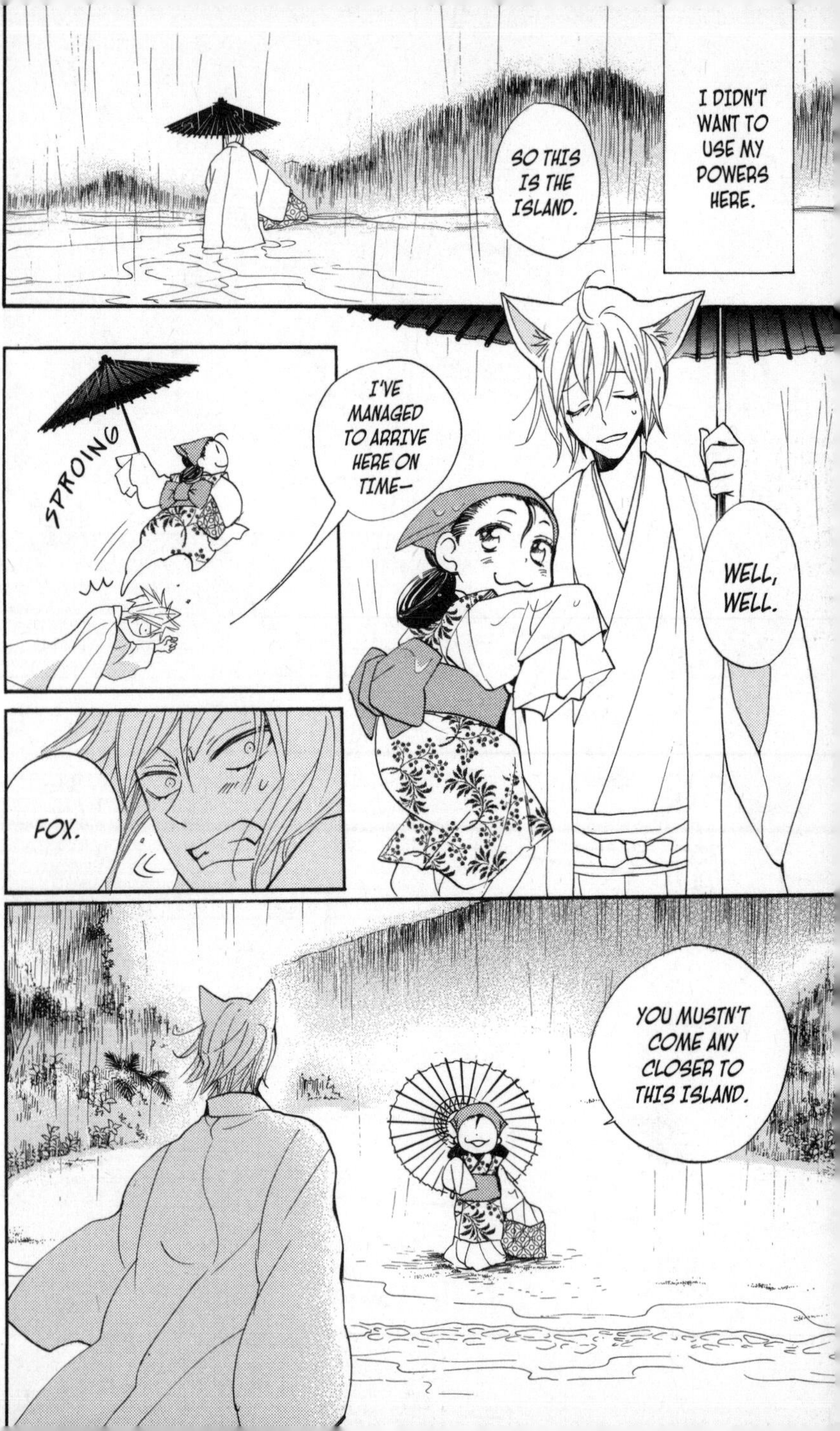
I DIDN'T WANT TO USE MY POWERS HERE.
SO THIS IS THE ISLAND.
I'VE MANAGED TO ARRIVE HERE ON TIME—
WELL, WELL.
SPROING
FOX.
YOU MUSTN'T COME ANY CLOSER TO THIS ISLAND.

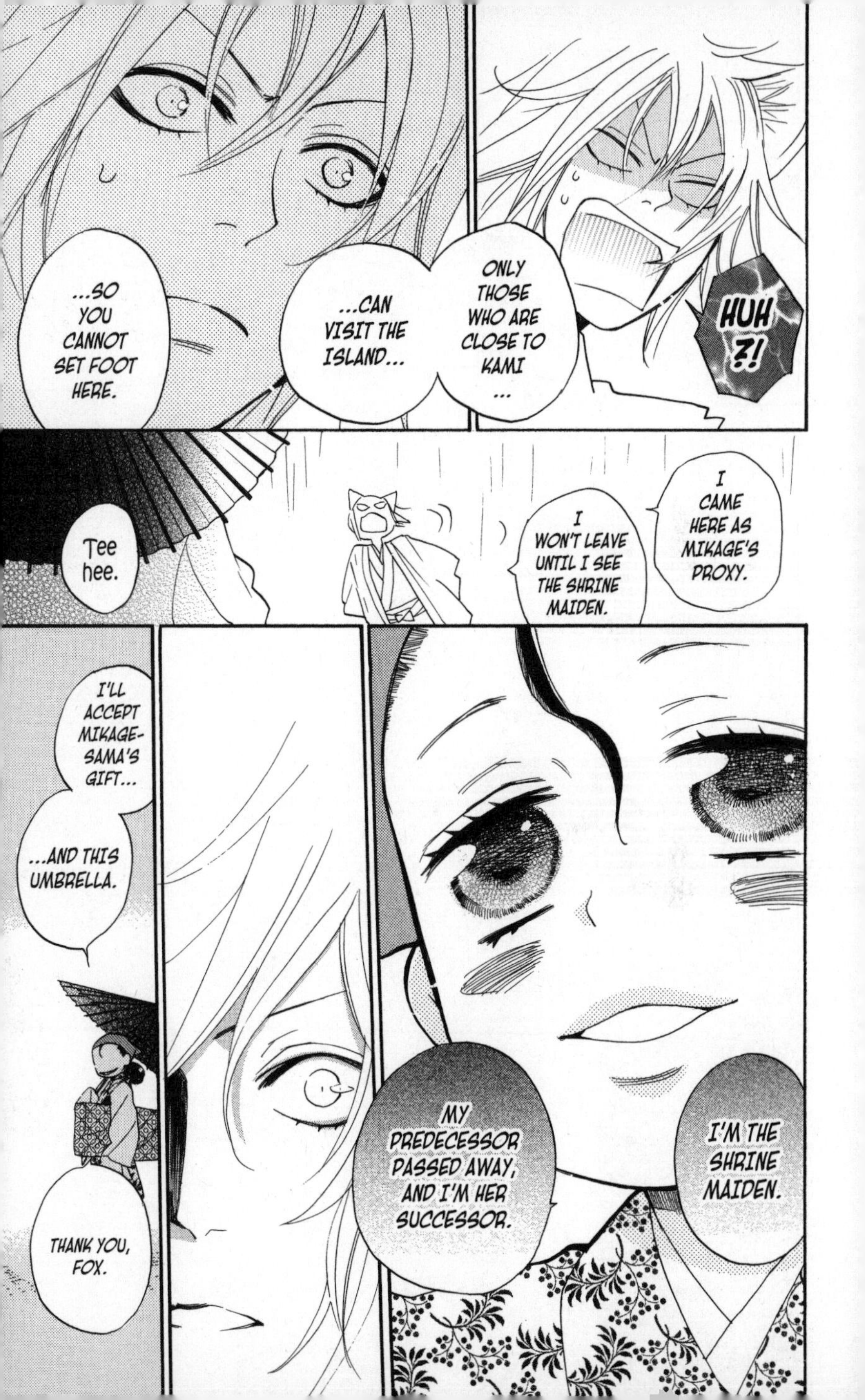
ONLY THOSE WHO ARE CLOSE TO KAMI ...
...CAN VISIT THE ISLAND...
...SO YOU CANNOT SET FOOT HERE.
HUH ?!
I CAME HERE AS MIKAGE'S PROXY.
I WON'T LEAVE UNTIL I SEE THE SHRINE MAIDEN.
Tee hee.
I'M THE SHRINE MAIDEN.
MY PREDECESSOR PASSED AWAY, AND I'M HER SUCCESSOR.
I'LL ACCEPT MIKAGE-SAMA'S GIFT...
...AND THIS UMBRELLA.
THANK YOU, FOX.

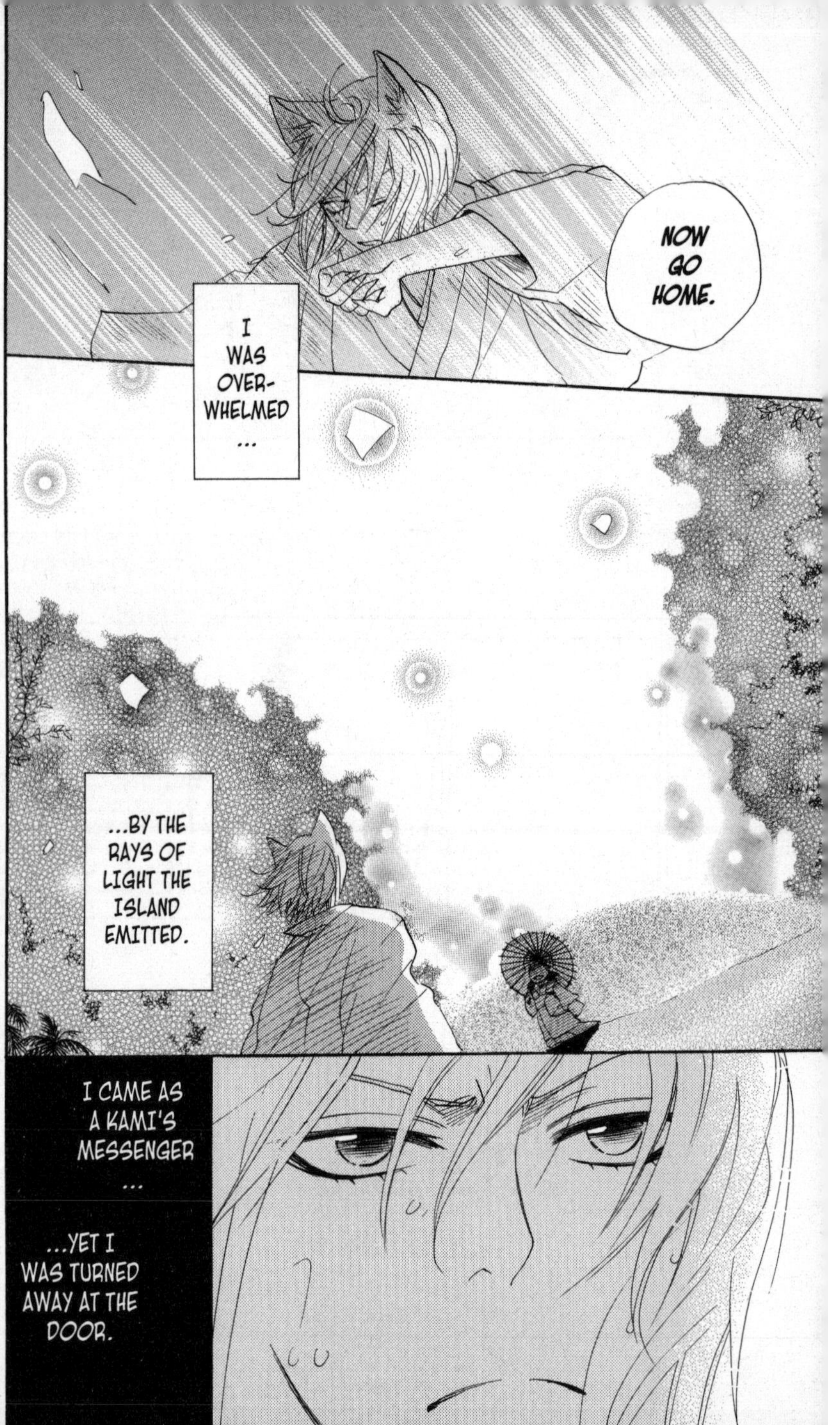
NOW GO HOME.
I WAS OVER-WHELMED...
...BY THE RAYS OF LIGHT THE ISLAND EMITTED.
I CAME AS A KAMI'S MESSENGER...
...YET I WAS TURNED AWAY AT THE DOOR.

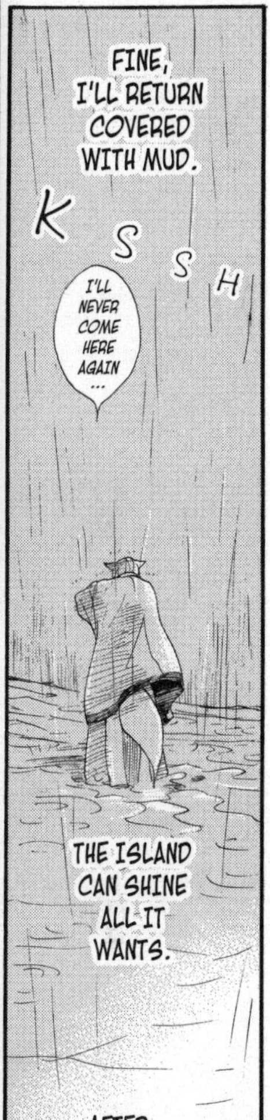
FINE, I'LL RETURN COVERED WITH MUD.
KSSH
I'LL NEVER COME HERE AGAIN...
THE ISLAND CAN SHINE ALL IT WANTS.
AFTER ALL...

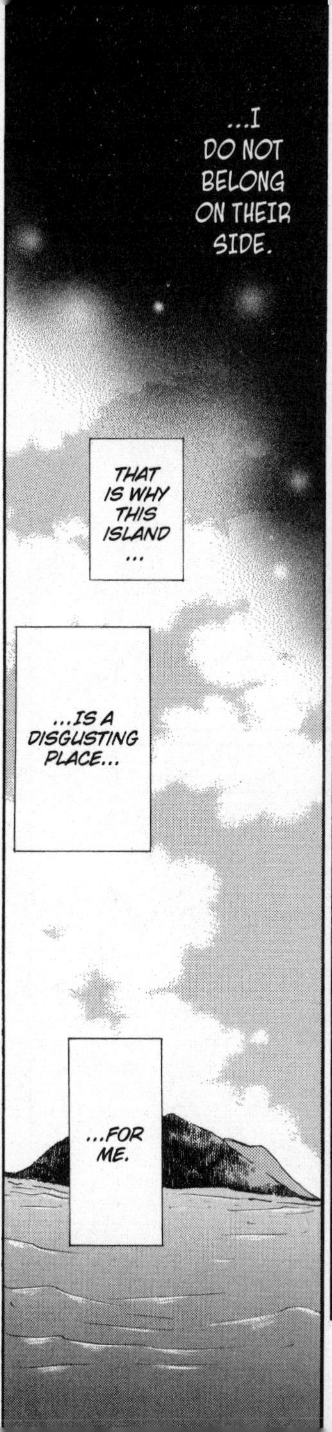
...I DO NOT BELONG ON THEIR SIDE.
THAT IS WHY THIS ISLAND...
...IS A DISGUSTING PLACE...
...FOR ME.

I now have one empty room, so I thought I'd have a huge bookcase attached to a wall like I've always wanted! So I came up with various designs.

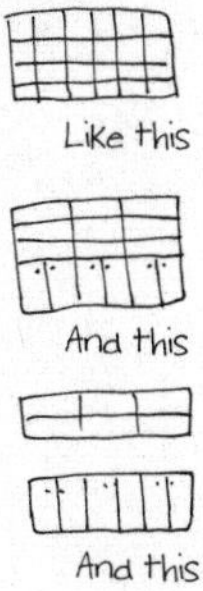
Like this
And this
And this

In the end I didn't get them made, but I still dream of big bookcases. I'd like to be able to buy lots of books without worrying about where I'll store them.

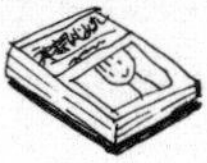

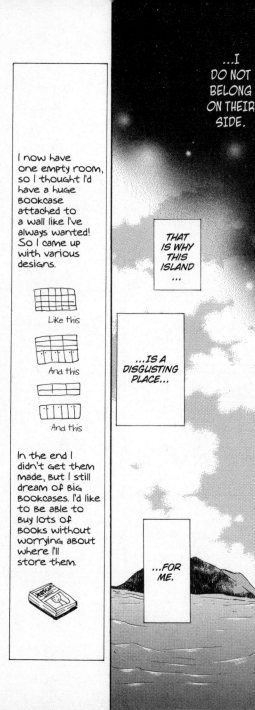

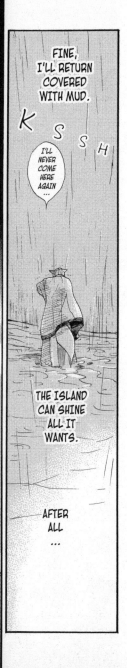

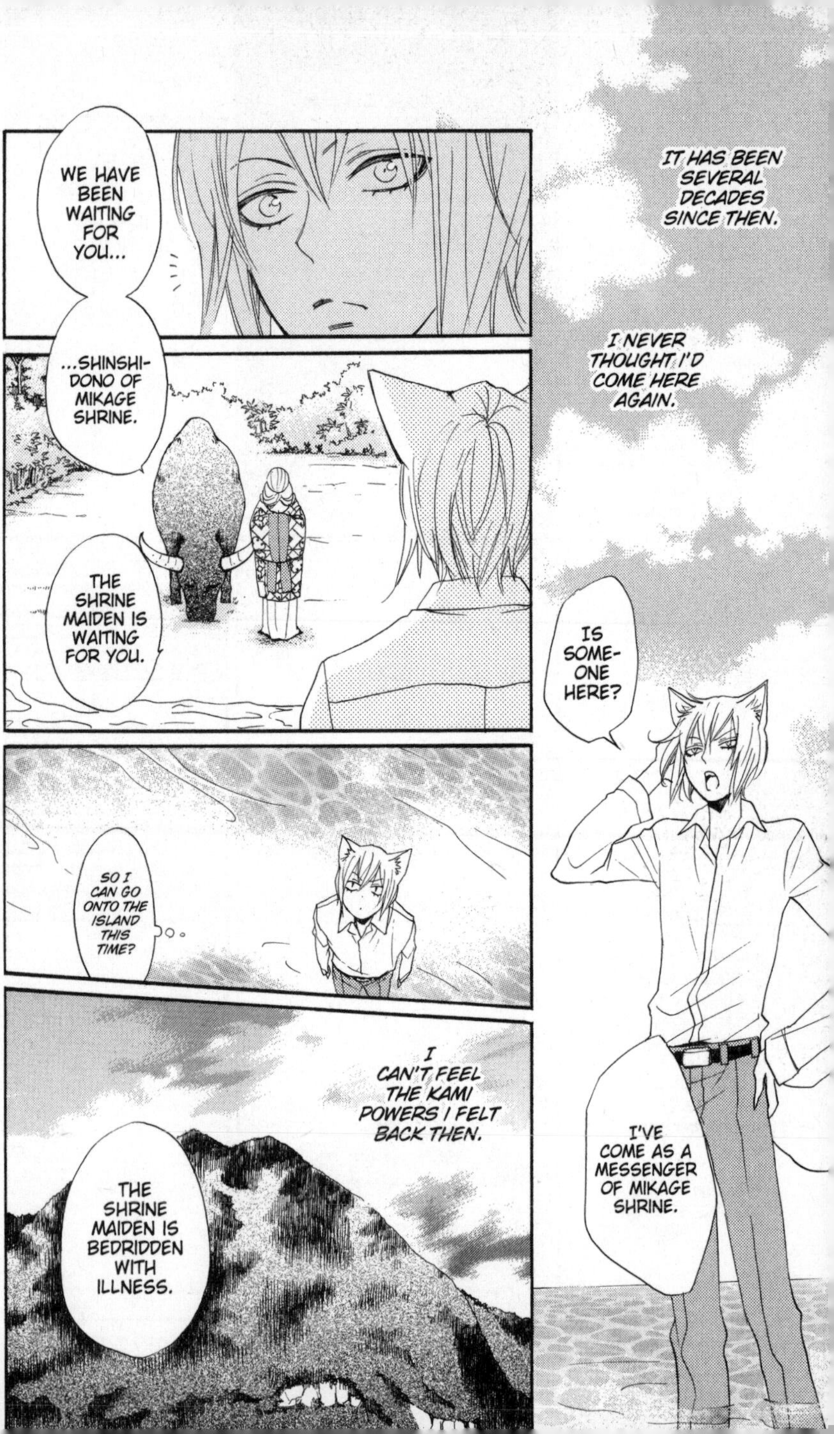
IT HAS BEEN SEVERAL DECADES SINCE THEN.
I NEVER THOUGHT I'D COME HERE AGAIN.
IS SOME-ONE HERE?
I'VE COME AS A MESSENGER OF MIKAGE SHRINE.
WE HAVE BEEN WAITING FOR YOU...
...SHINSHI-DONO OF MIKAGE SHRINE.
THE SHRINE MAIDEN IS WAITING FOR YOU.
SO I CAN GO ONTO THE ISLAND THIS TIME?
I CAN'T FEEL THE KAMI POWERS I FELT BACK THEN.
THE SHRINE MAIDEN IS BEDRIDDEN WITH ILLNESS.

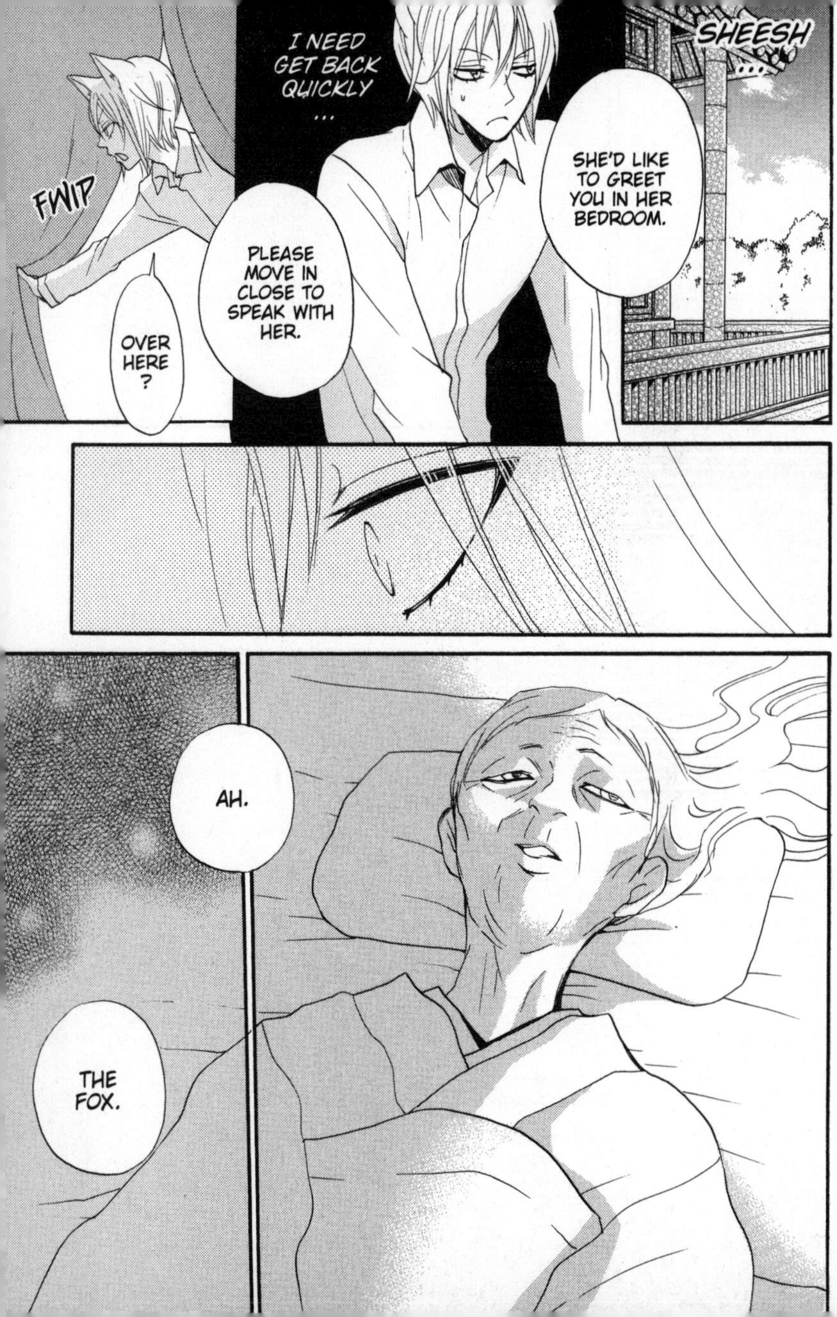
SHEESH...
SHE'D LIKE TO GREET YOU IN HER BEDROOM.
I NEED GET BACK QUICKLY ...
PLEASE MOVE IN CLOSE TO SPEAK WITH HER.
FWIP
OVER HERE ?
AH.
THE FOX.

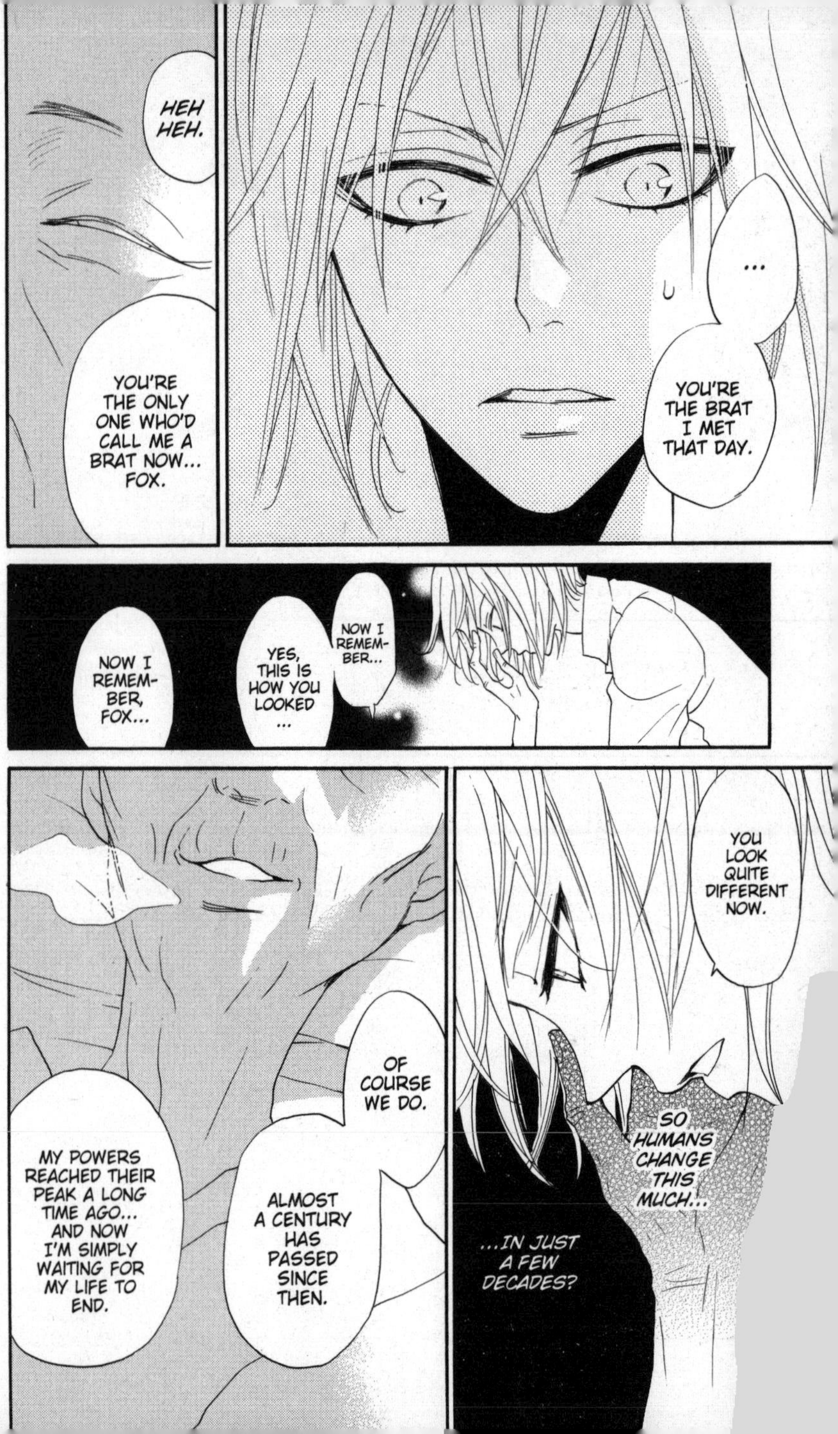
...
YOU'RE THE BRAT I MET THAT DAY.
HEH HEH.
YOU'RE THE ONLY ONE WHO'D CALL ME A BRAT NOW... FOX.
NOW I REMEM-BER...
YES, THIS IS HOW YOU LOOKED...
NOW I REMEM-BER, FOX...
YOU LOOK QUITE DIFFERENT NOW.
SO HUMANS CHANGE THIS MUCH...
...IN JUST A FEW DECADES?
OF COURSE WE DO.
ALMOST A CENTURY HAS PASSED SINCE THEN.
MY POWERS REACHED THEIR PEAK A LONG TIME AGO... AND NOW I'M SIMPLY WAITING FOR MY LIFE TO END.

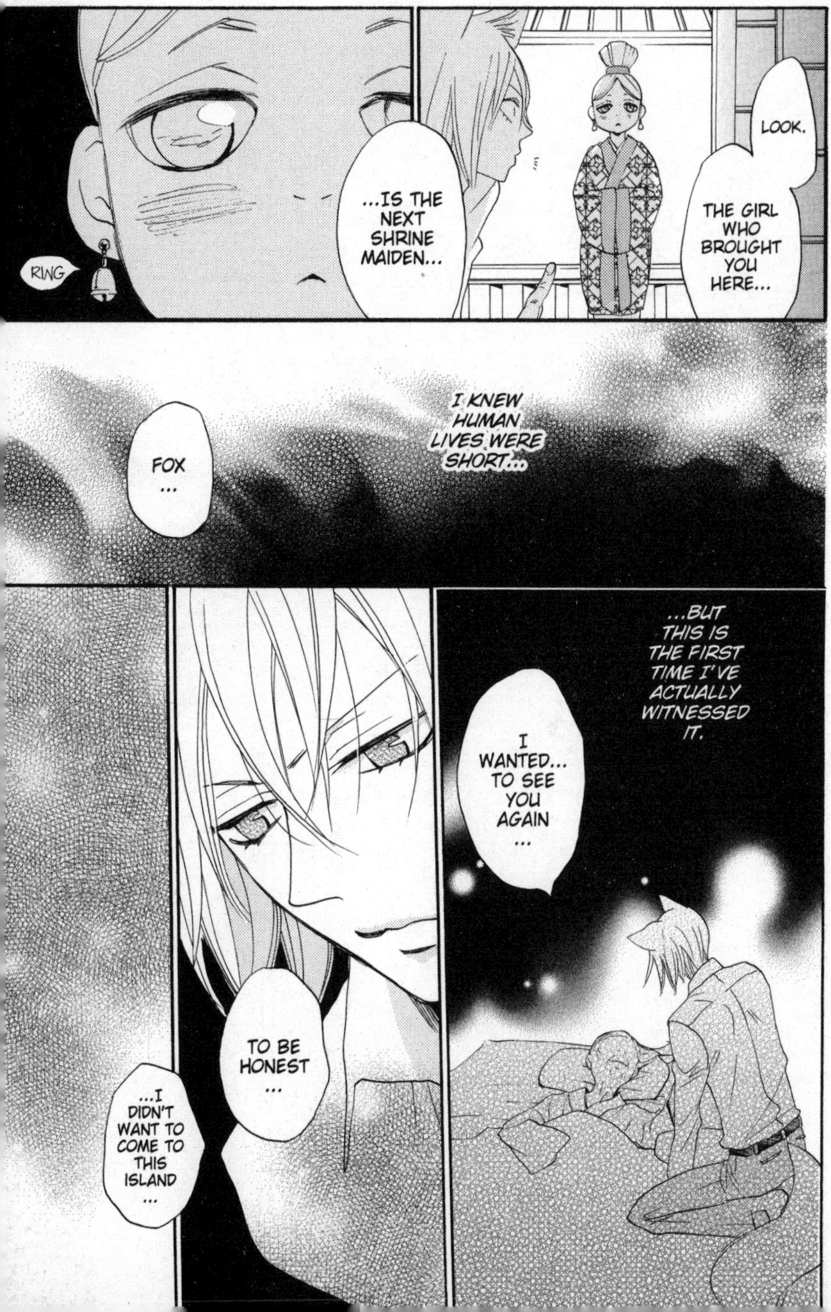
LOOK.
THE GIRL WHO BROUGHT YOU HERE...
...IS THE NEXT SHRINE MAIDEN...
RING
I KNEW HUMAN LIVES WERE SHORT...
FOX ...
...BUT THIS IS THE FIRST TIME I'VE ACTUALLY WITNESSED IT.
I WANTED... TO SEE YOU AGAIN ...
TO BE HONEST ...
...I DIDN'T WANT TO COME TO THIS ISLAND ...

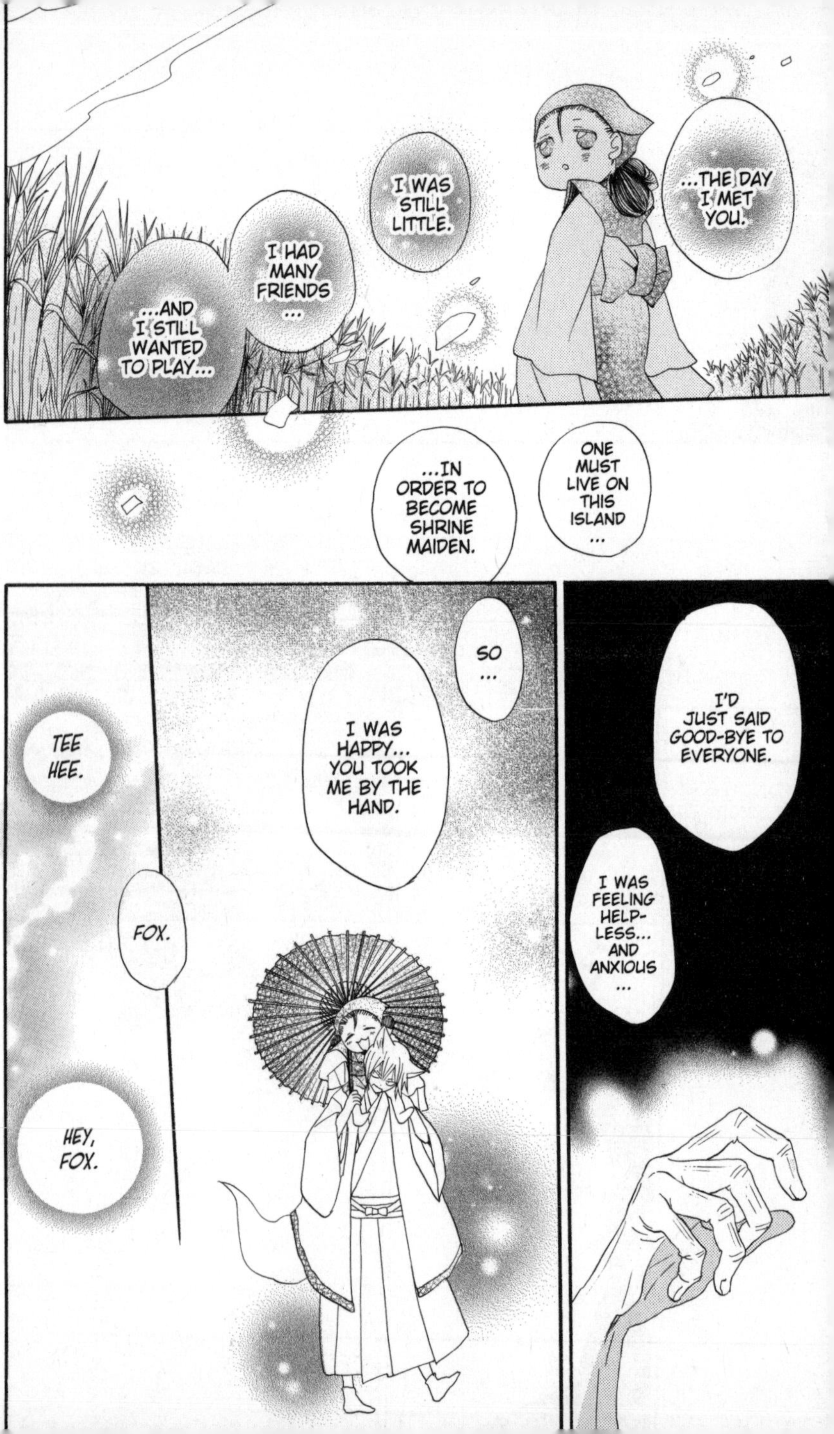
...THE DAY I MET YOU.
I WAS STILL LITTLE.
I HAD MANY FRIENDS...
...AND I STILL WANTED TO PLAY...
ONE MUST LIVE ON THIS ISLAND...
...IN ORDER TO BECOME SHRINE MAIDEN.
I'D JUST SAID GOOD-BYE TO EVERYONE.
I WAS FEELING HELP-LESS... AND ANXIOUS...
SO...
I WAS HAPPY... YOU TOOK ME BY THE HAND.
TEE HEE.
FOX.
HEY, FOX.

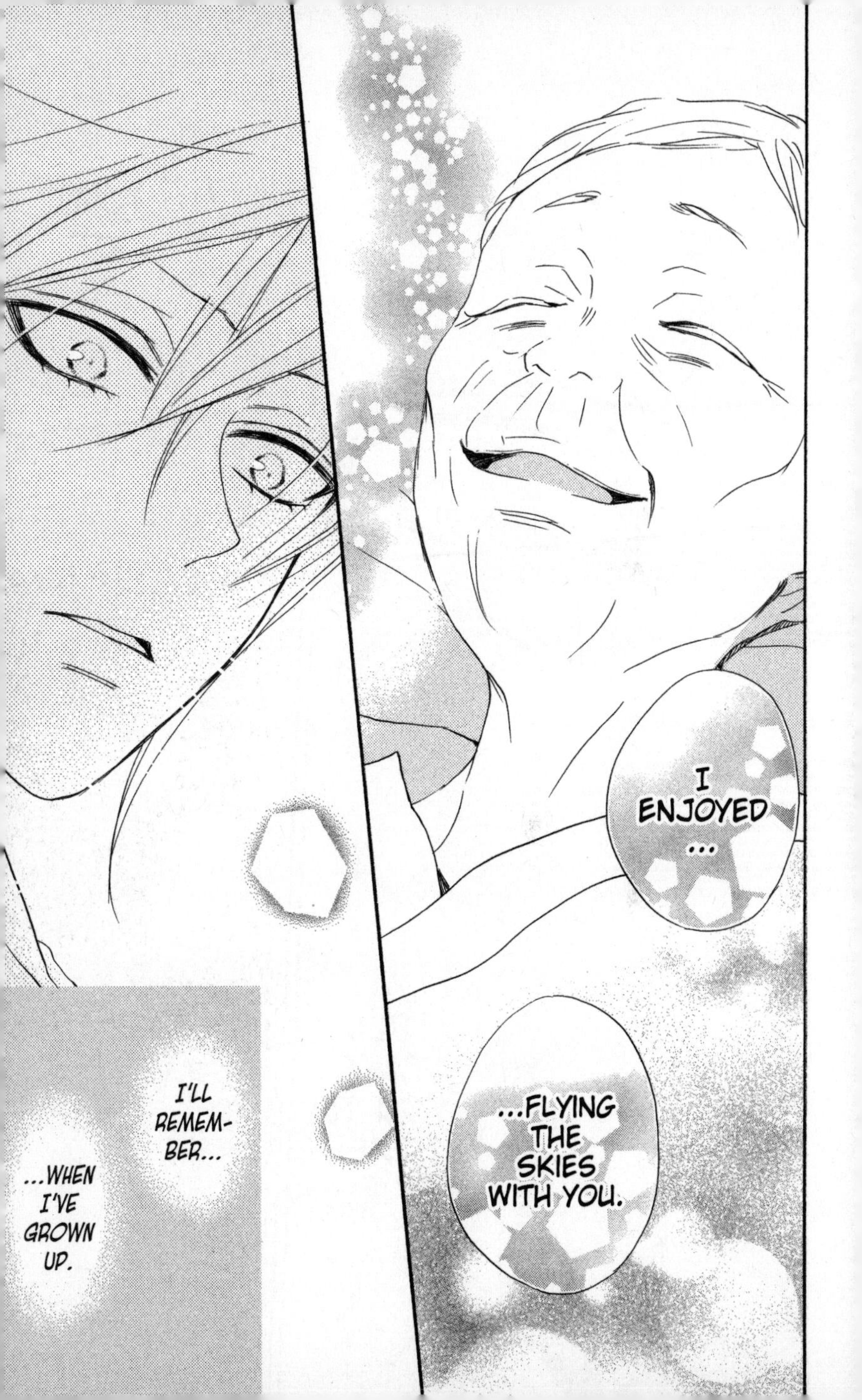
I ENJOYED ...
...FLYING THE SKIES WITH YOU.
I'LL REMEMBER...
...WHEN I'VE GROWN UP.

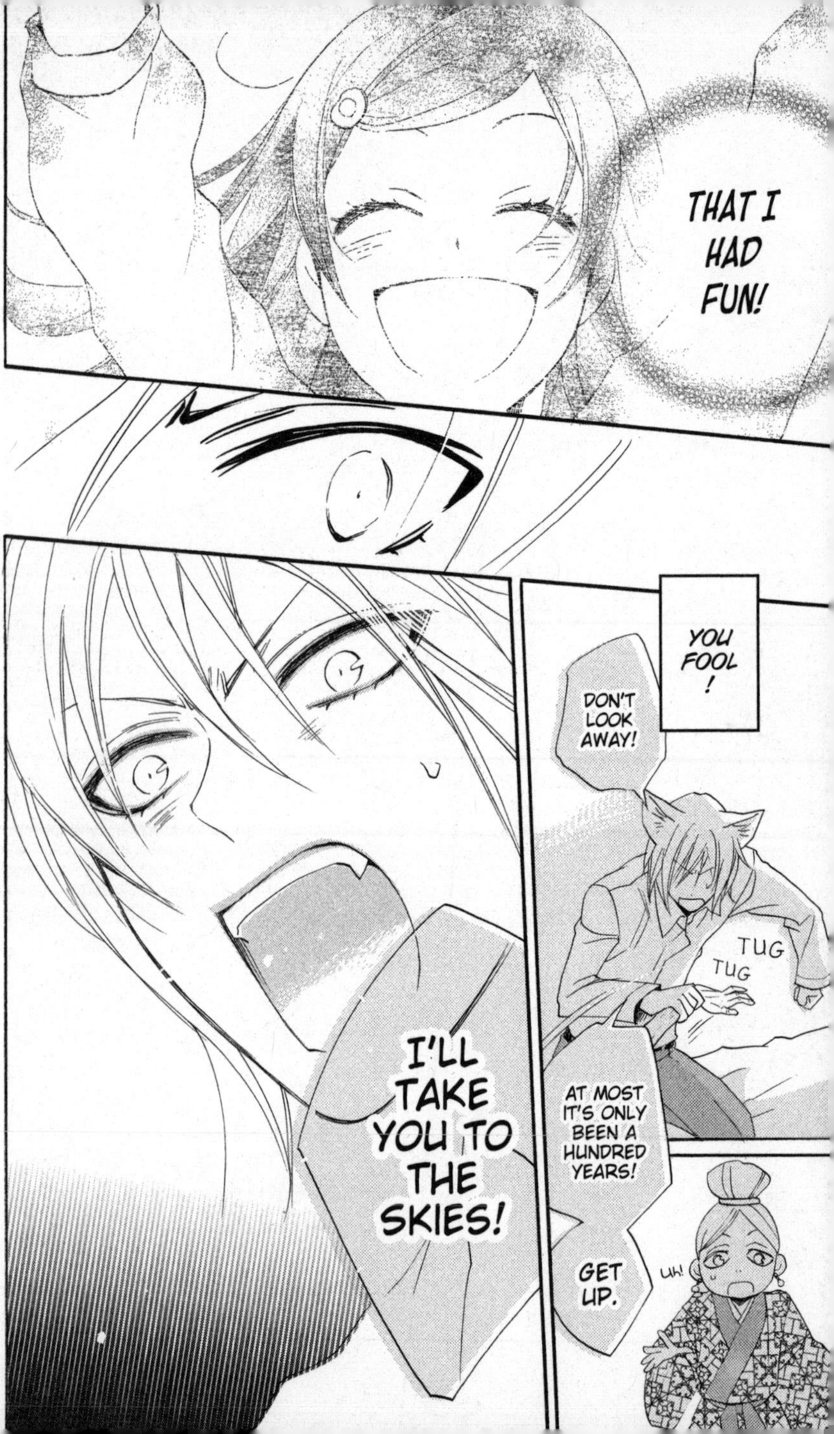
THAT I HAD FUN!
YOU FOOL!
DON'T LOOK AWAY!
TUG TUG
AT MOST IT'S ONLY BEEN A HUNDRED YEARS!
Uh!
GET UP.
I'LL TAKE YOU TO THE SKIES!

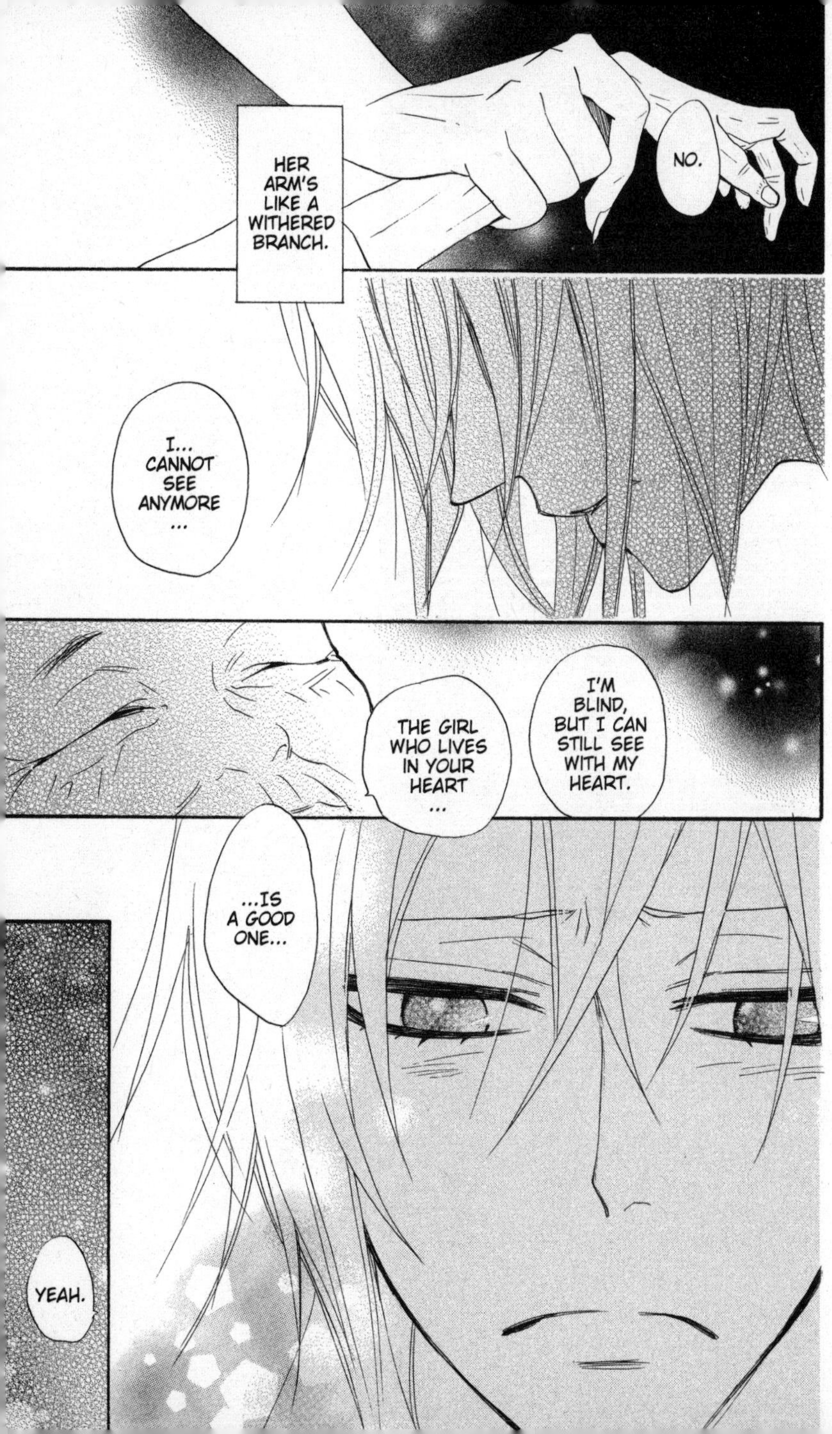
NO.
HER ARM'S LIKE A WITHERED BRANCH.
I... CANNOT SEE ANYMORE...
I'M BLIND, BUT I CAN STILL SEE WITH MY HEART.
THE GIRL WHO LIVES IN YOUR HEART...
...IS A GOOD ONE...
YEAH.

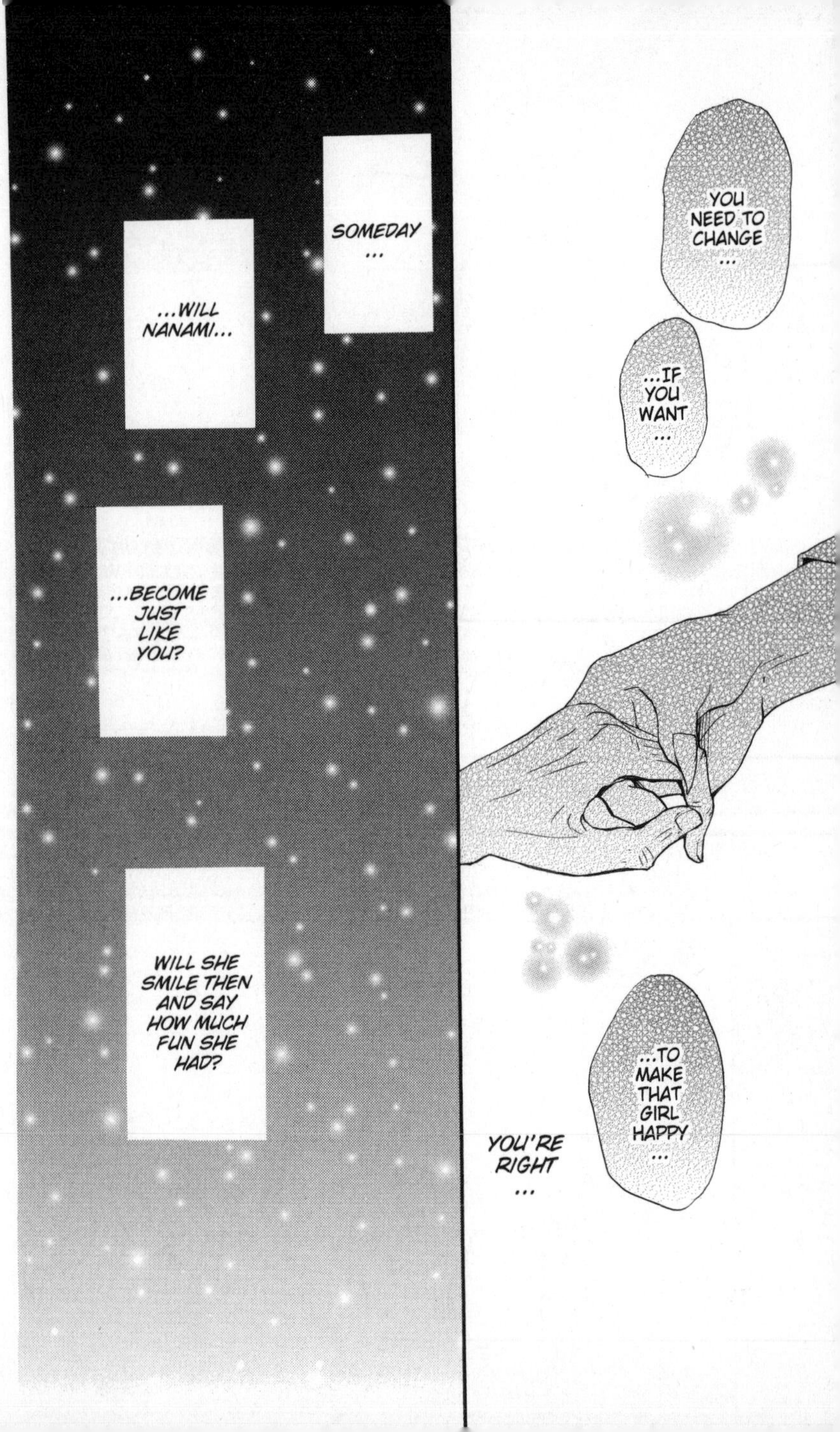
YOU NEED TO CHANGE...
...IF YOU WANT...
...TO MAKE THAT GIRL HAPPY...
YOU'RE RIGHT...
SOMEDAY...
...WILL NANAMI...
...BECOME JUST LIKE YOU?
WILL SHE SMILE THEN AND SAY HOW MUCH FUN SHE HAD?

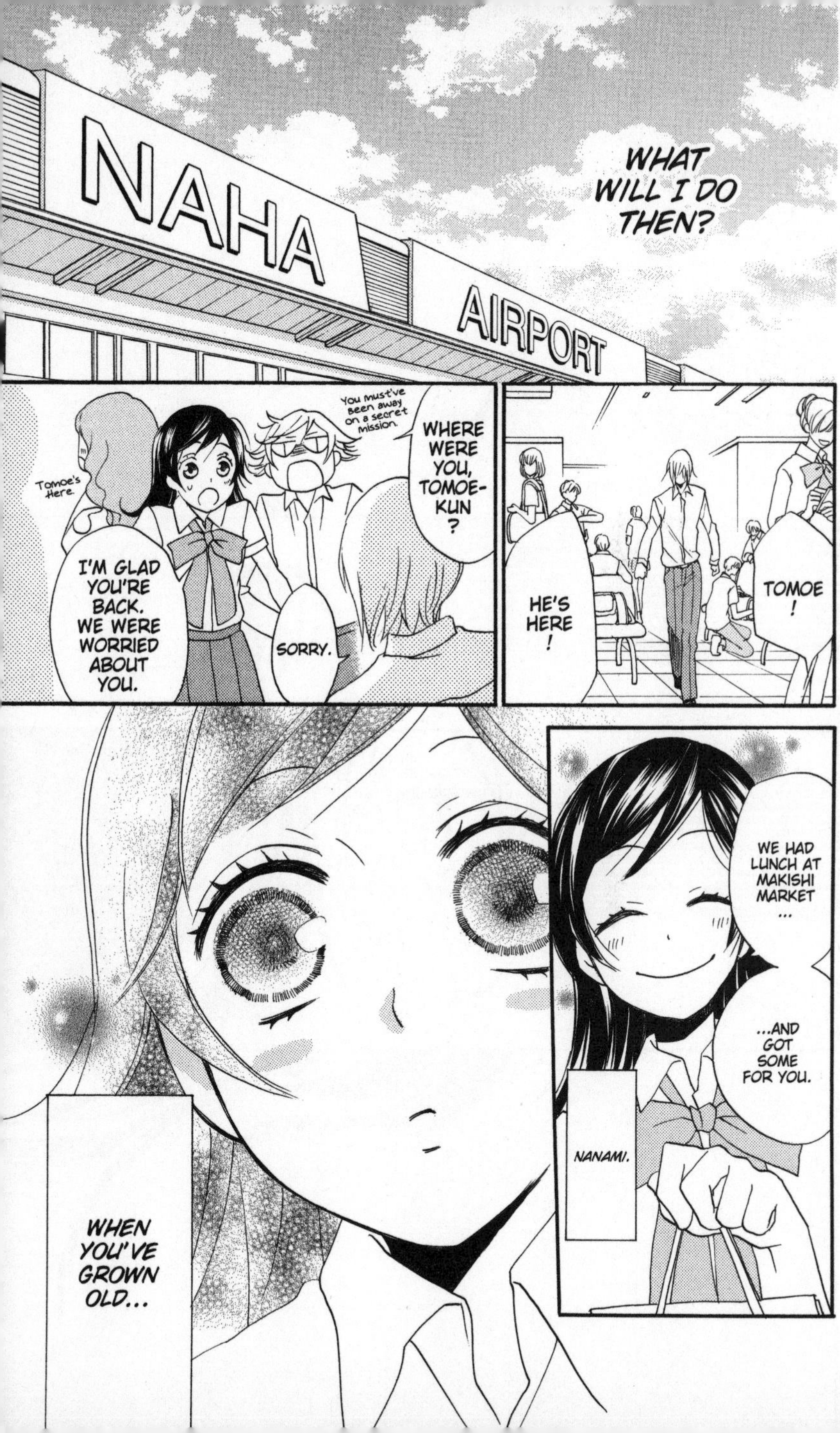
NAHA AIRPORT
WHAT WILL I DO THEN?
TOMOE!
HE'S HERE!
WHERE WERE YOU, TOMOE-KUN?
You must've been away on a secret mission.
SORRY.
Tomoe's here.
I'M GLAD YOU'RE BACK. WE WERE WORRIED ABOUT YOU.
WE HAD LUNCH AT MAKISHI MARKET...
...AND GOT SOME FOR YOU.
NANAMI.
WHEN YOU'VE GROWN OLD...

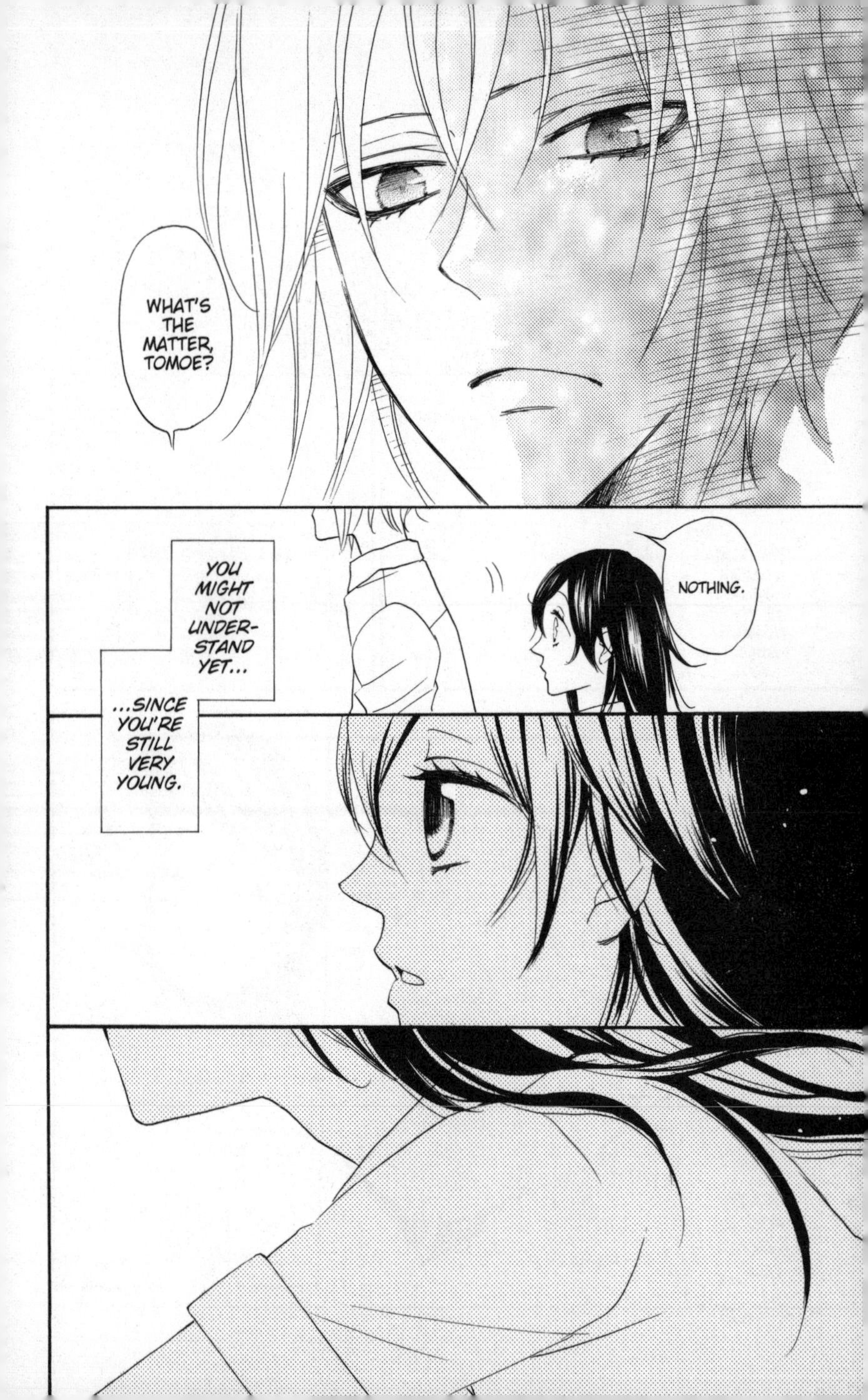
WHAT'S THE MATTER, TOMOE?
NOTHING.
YOU MIGHT NOT UNDER-STAND YET...
...SINCE YOU'RE STILL VERY YOUNG.

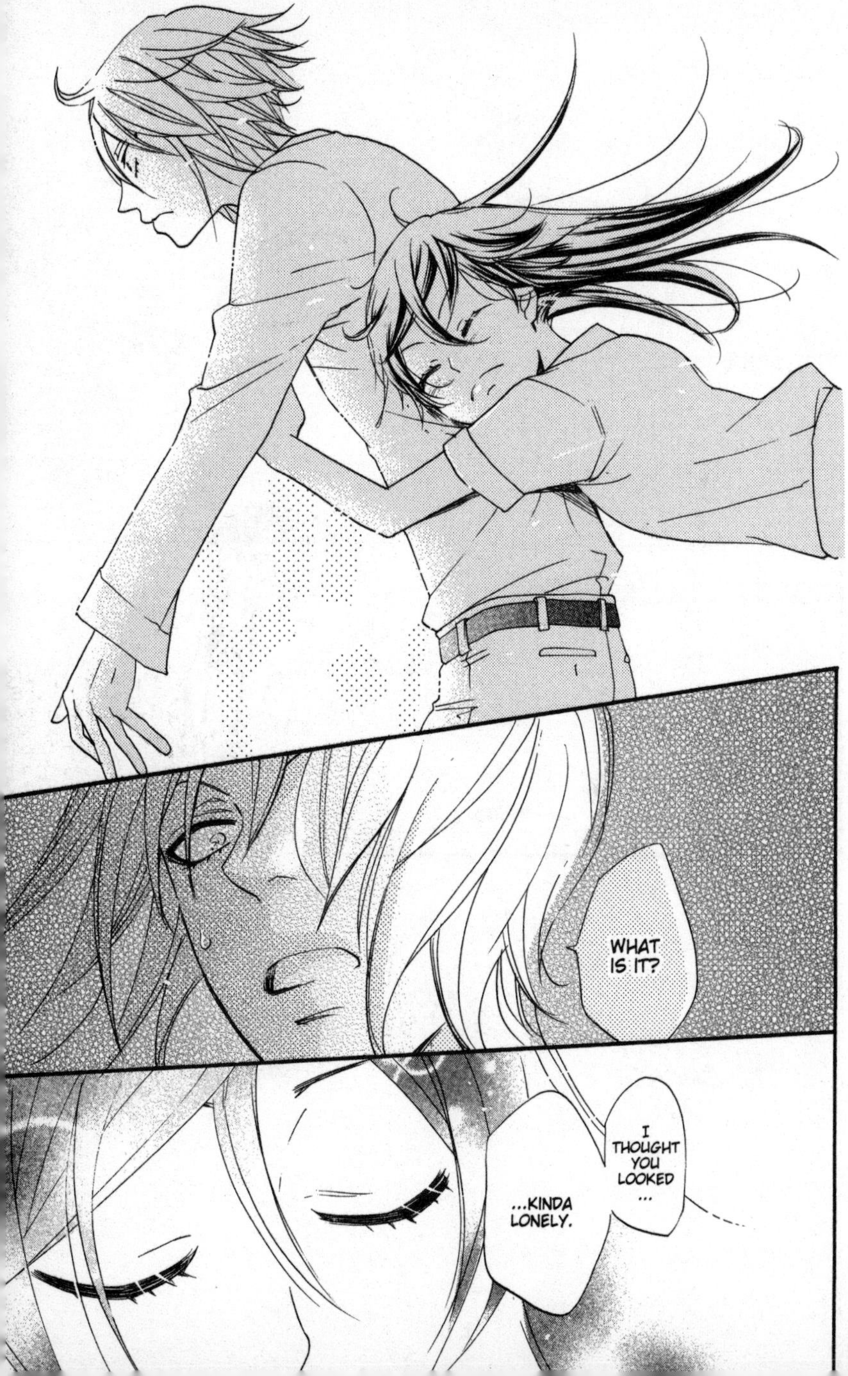
WHAT IS IT?
I THOUGHT YOU LOOKED ...
...KINDA LONELY.

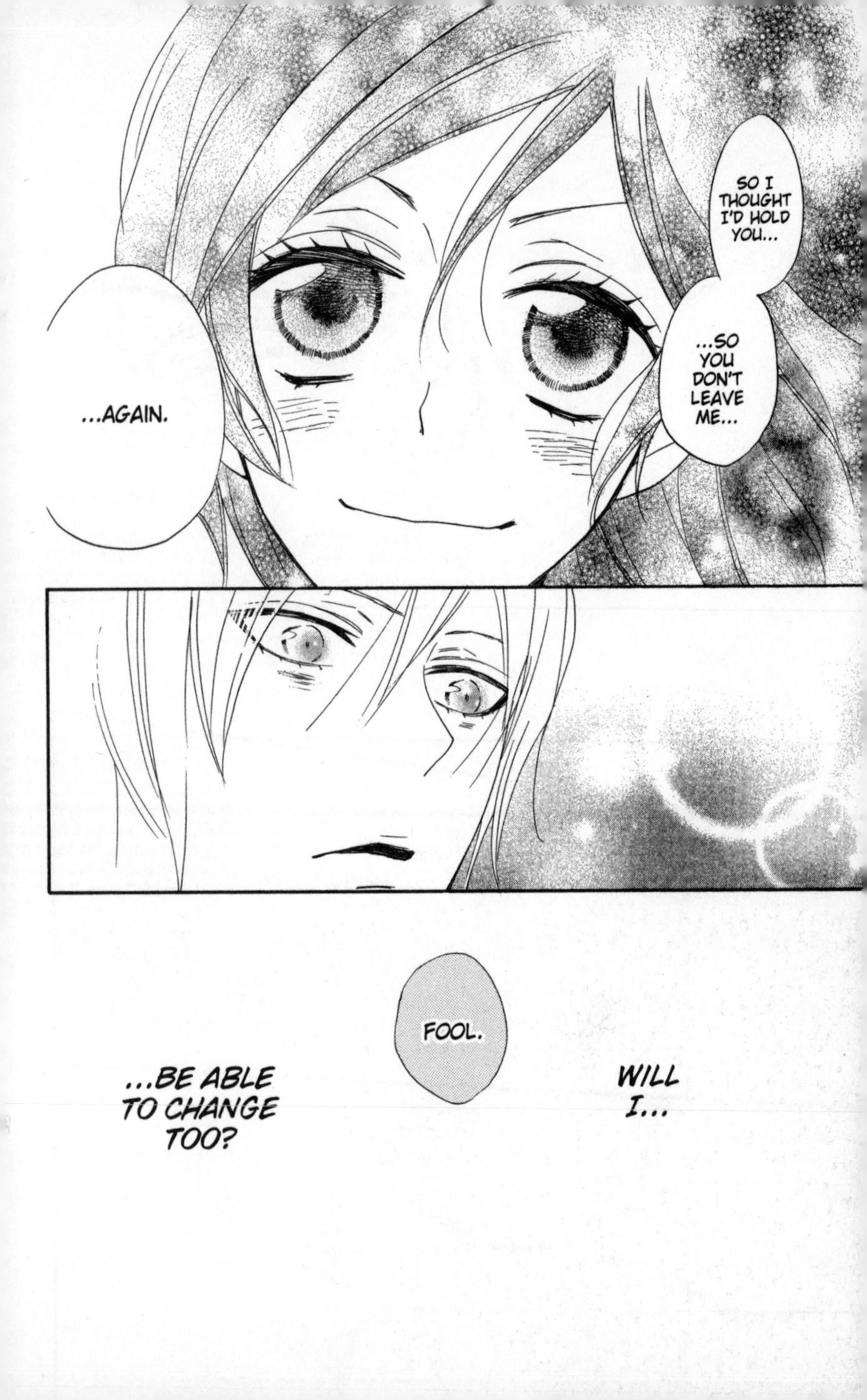
SO I THOUGHT I'D HOLD YOU...
...SO YOU DON'T LEAVE ME...
...AGAIN.
FOOL.
WILL I...
...BE ABLE TO CHANGE TOO?

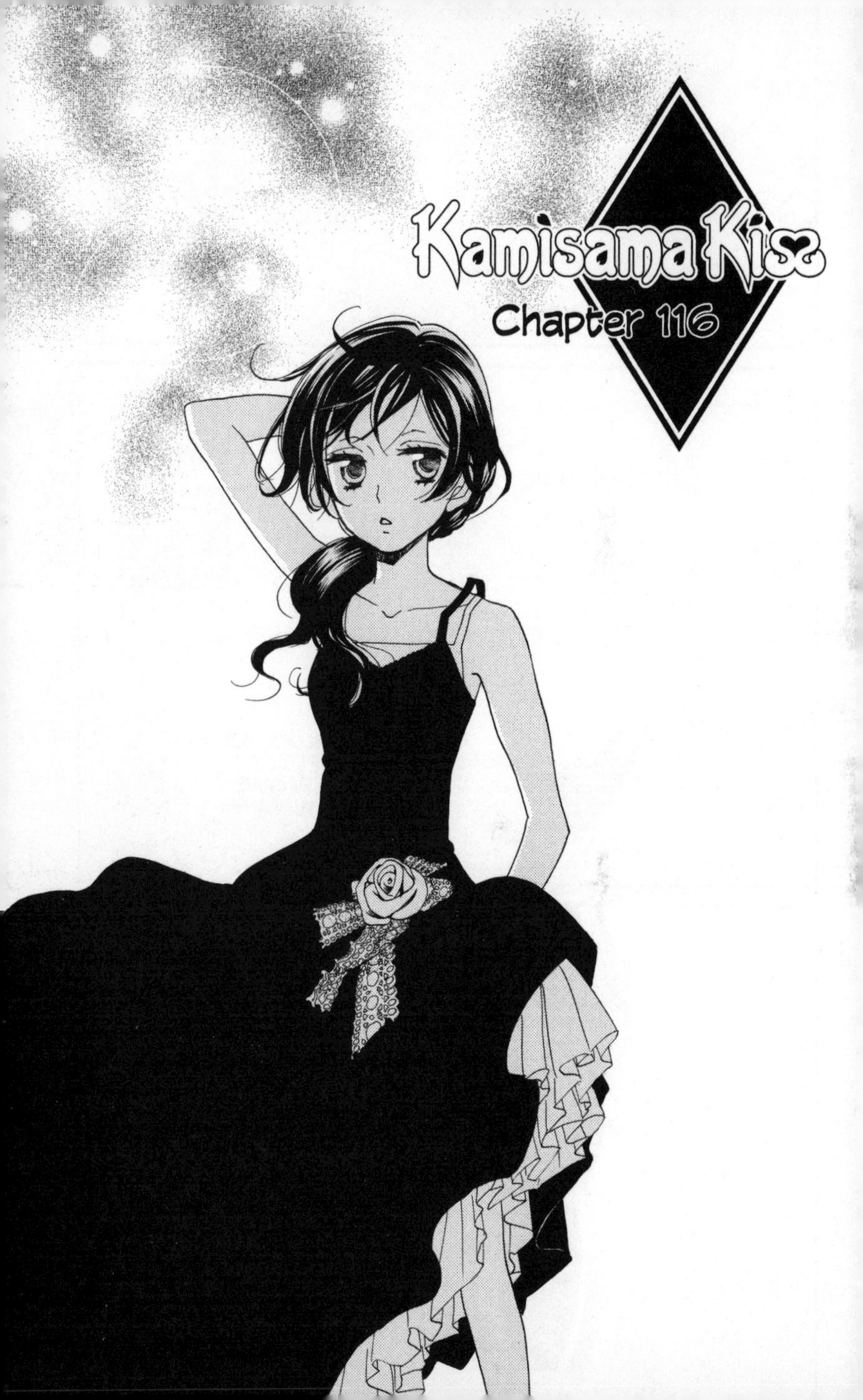
Kamisama Kiss
Chapter 116

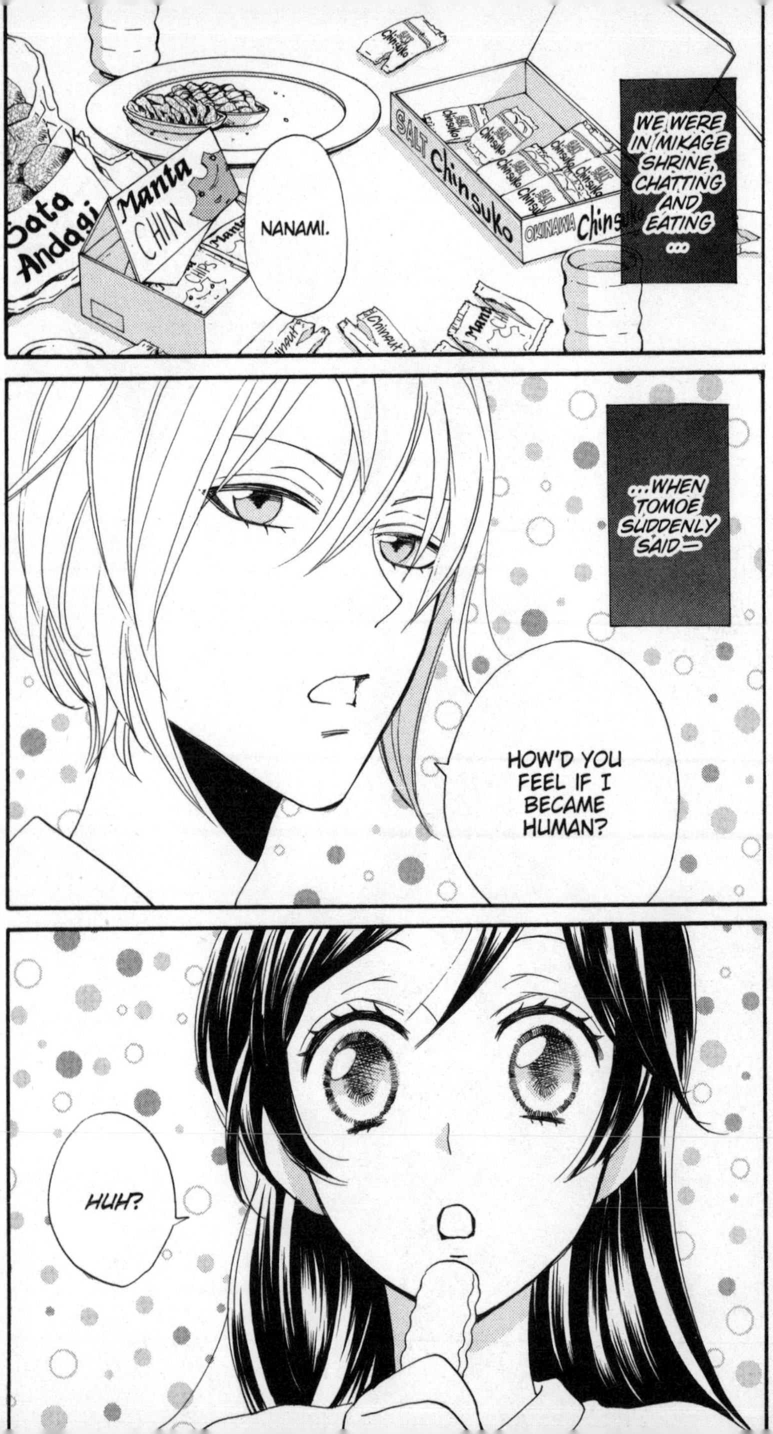
WE WERE IN MIKAGE SHRINE, CHATTING AND EATING ...
NANAMI.
SALT Chinsuko
OKINAWA Chinsuko
Manta CHIN
Sata Andagi
...WHEN TOMOE SUDDENLY SAID—
HOW'D YOU FEEL IF I BECAME HUMAN?
HUH?

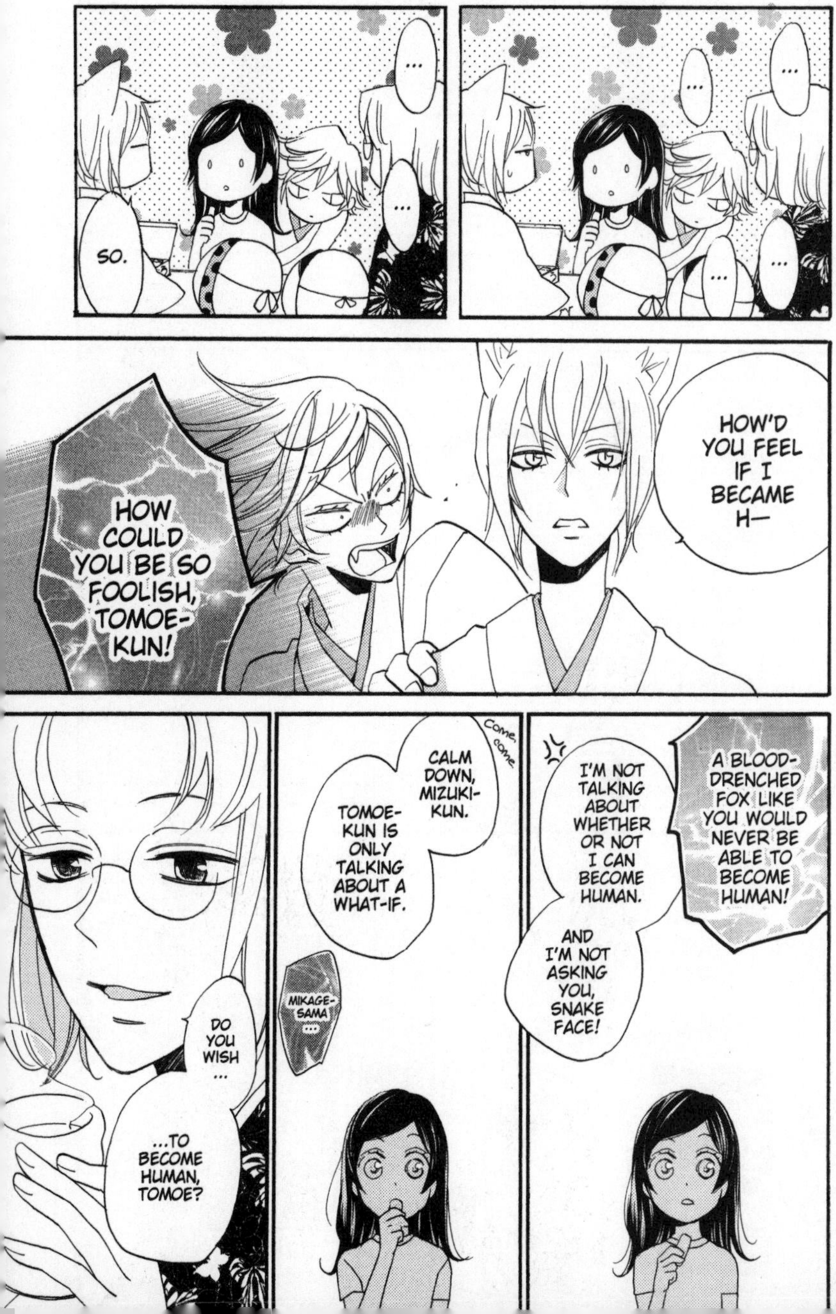
...
...
...
...
...
...
SO.
HOW'D YOU FEEL IF I BECAME H—
HOW COULD YOU BE SO FOOLISH, TOMOE-KUN!
A BLOOD-DRENCHED FOX LIKE YOU WOULD NEVER BE ABLE TO BECOME HUMAN!
I'M NOT TALKING ABOUT WHETHER OR NOT I CAN BECOME HUMAN.
AND I'M NOT ASKING YOU, SNAKE FACE!
Come, come
CALM DOWN, MIZUKI-KUN.
TOMOE-KUN IS ONLY TALKING ABOUT A WHAT-IF.
MIKAGE-SAMA ...
DO YOU WISH ...
...TO BECOME HUMAN, TOMOE?

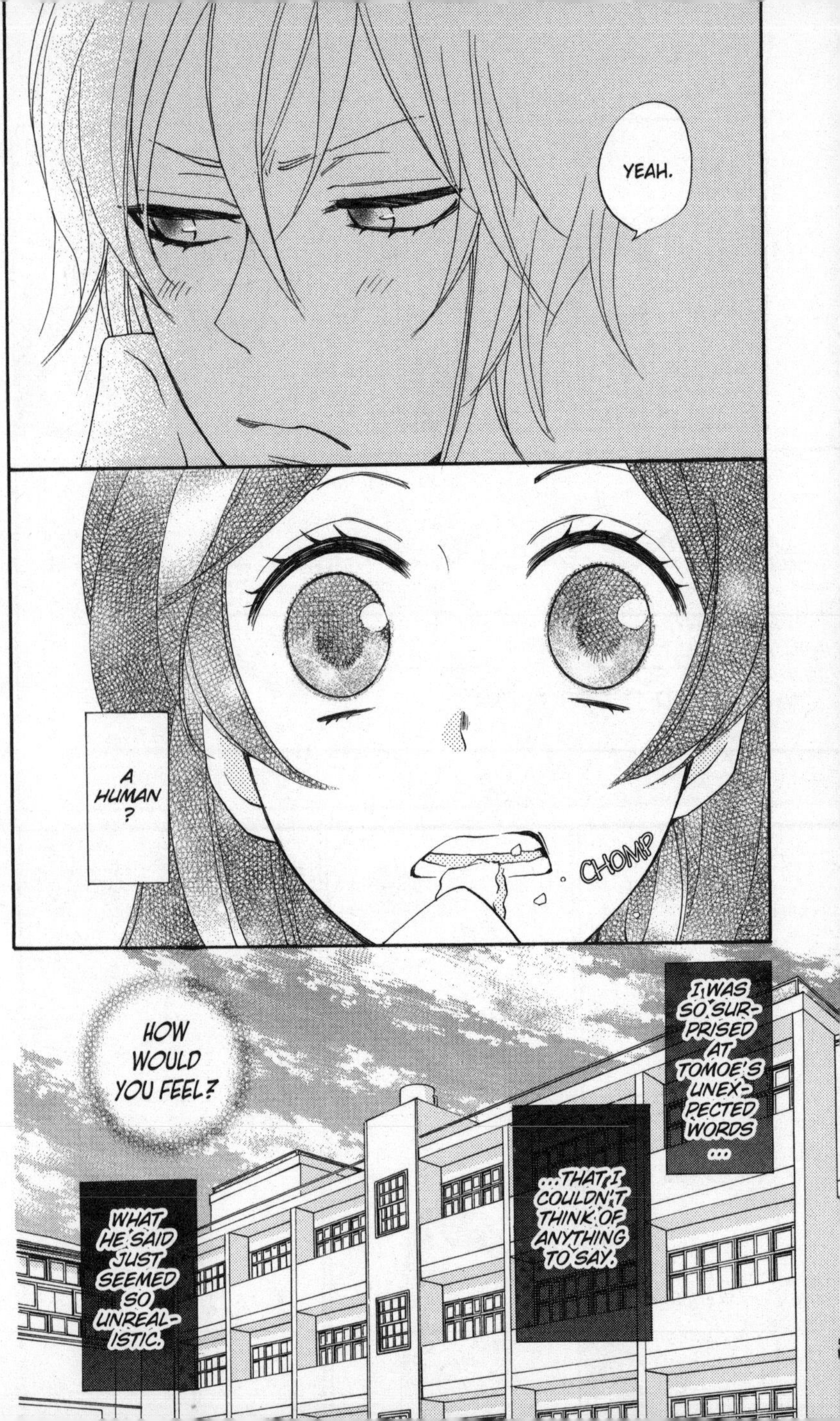
YEAH.
A HUMAN?
CHOMP
I WAS SO SURPRISED AT TOMOE'S UNEXPECTED WORDS...
...THAT I COULDN'T THINK OF ANYTHING TO SAY.
HOW WOULD YOU FEEL?
WHAT HE SAID JUST SEEMED SO UNREALISTIC.

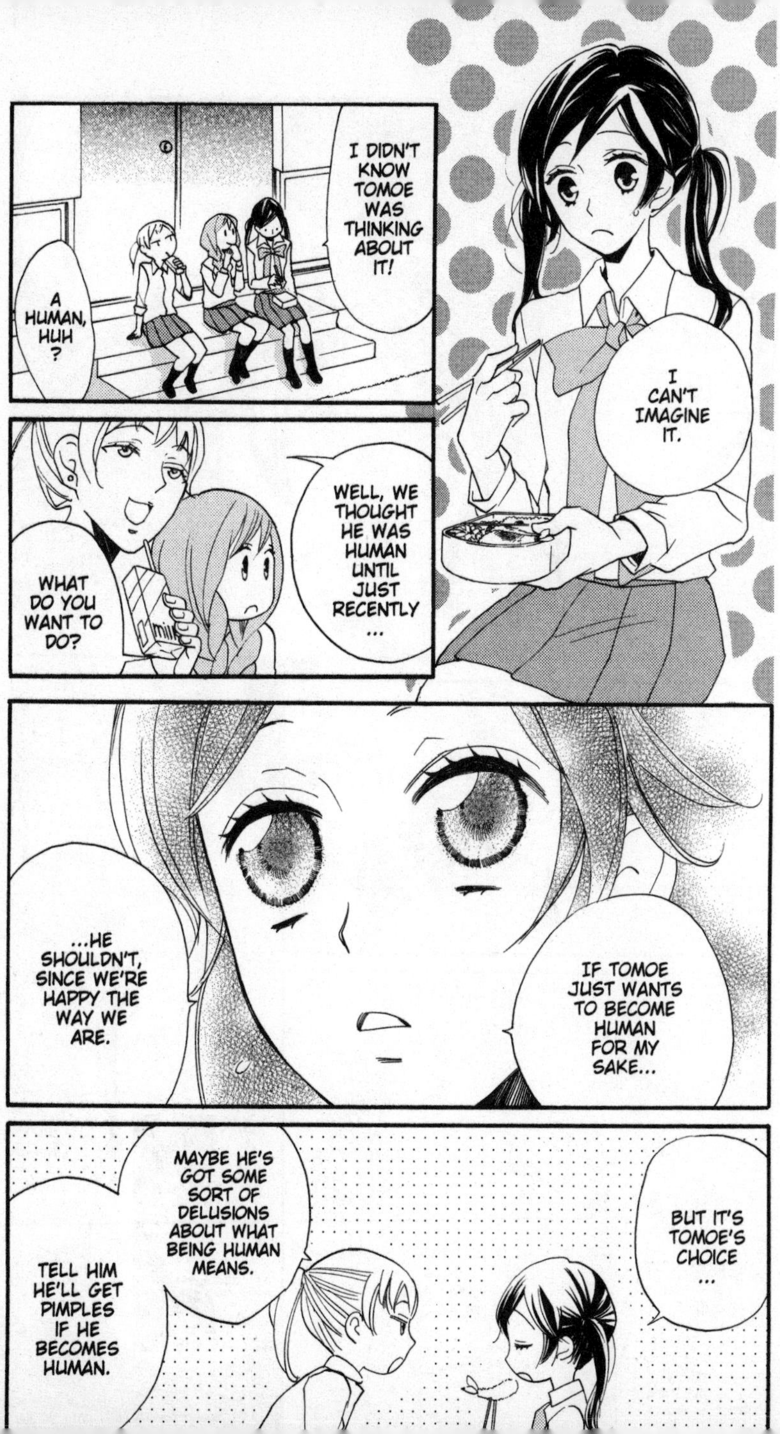
I CAN'T IMAGINE IT.
I DIDN'T KNOW TOMOE WAS THINKING ABOUT IT!
A HUMAN, HUH?
WELL, WE THOUGHT HE WAS HUMAN UNTIL JUST RECENTLY...
WHAT DO YOU WANT TO DO?
IF TOMOE JUST WANTS TO BECOME HUMAN FOR MY SAKE...
...HE SHOULDN'T, SINCE WE'RE HAPPY THE WAY WE ARE.
BUT IT'S TOMOE'S CHOICE...
MAYBE HE'S GOT SOME SORT OF DELUSIONS ABOUT WHAT BEING HUMAN MEANS.
TELL HIM HE'LL GET PIMPLES IF HE BECOMES HUMAN.

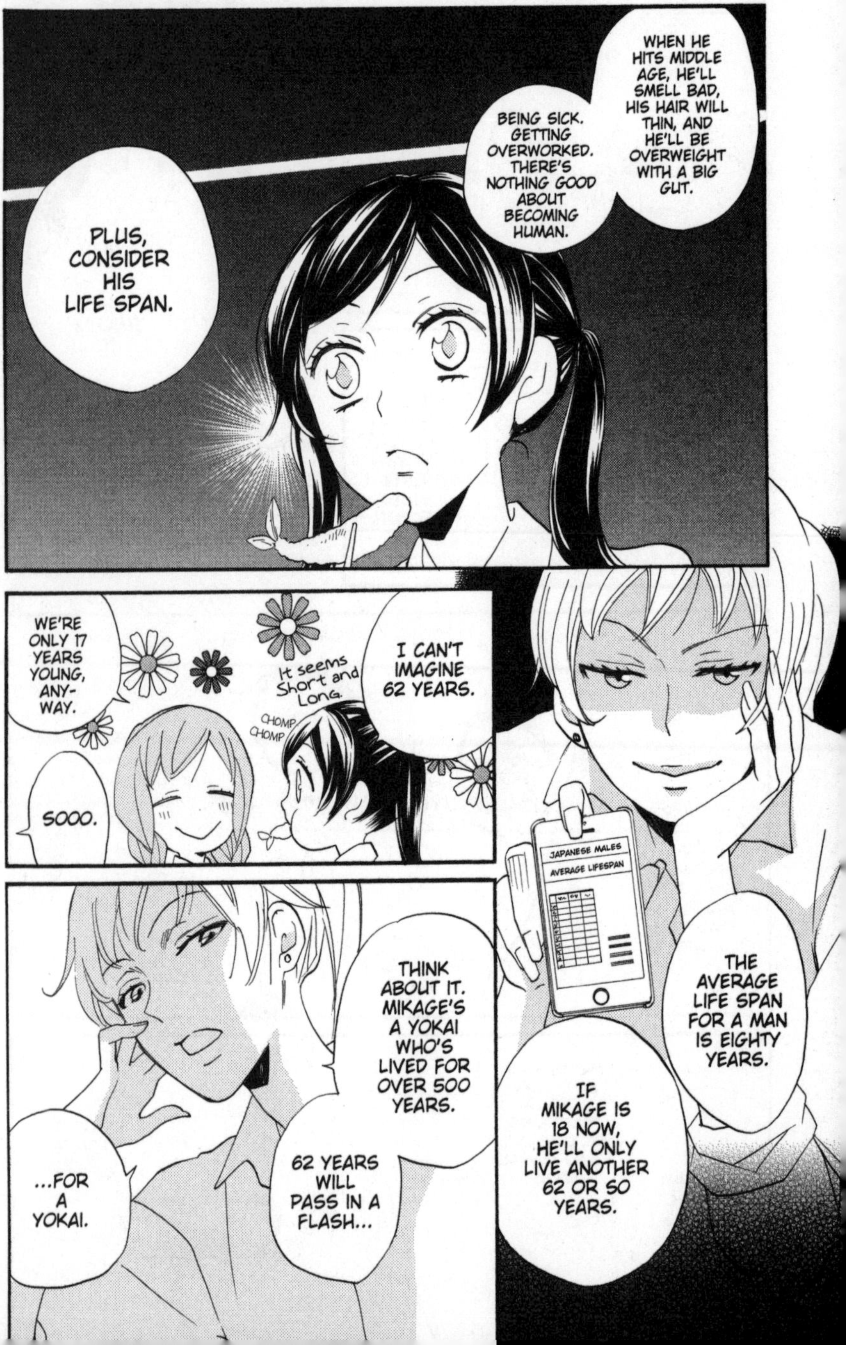
WHEN HE HITS MIDDLE AGE, HE'LL SMELL BAD, HIS HAIR WILL THIN, AND HE'LL BE OVERWEIGHT WITH A BIG GUT.
BEING SICK. GETTING OVERWORKED. THERE'S NOTHING GOOD ABOUT BECOMING HUMAN.
PLUS, CONSIDER HIS LIFE SPAN.
JAPANESE MALES
AVERAGE LIFESPAN
THE AVERAGE LIFE SPAN FOR A MAN IS EIGHTY YEARS.
IF MIKAGE IS 18 NOW, HE'LL ONLY LIVE ANOTHER 62 OR SO YEARS.
I CAN'T IMAGINE 62 YEARS.
It seems Short and Long.
CHOMP CHOMP
WE'RE ONLY 17 YEARS YOUNG, ANYWAY.
SOOO.
THINK ABOUT IT. MIKAGE'S A YOKAI WHO'S LIVED FOR OVER 500 YEARS.
62 YEARS WILL PASS IN A FLASH...
...FOR A YOKAI.

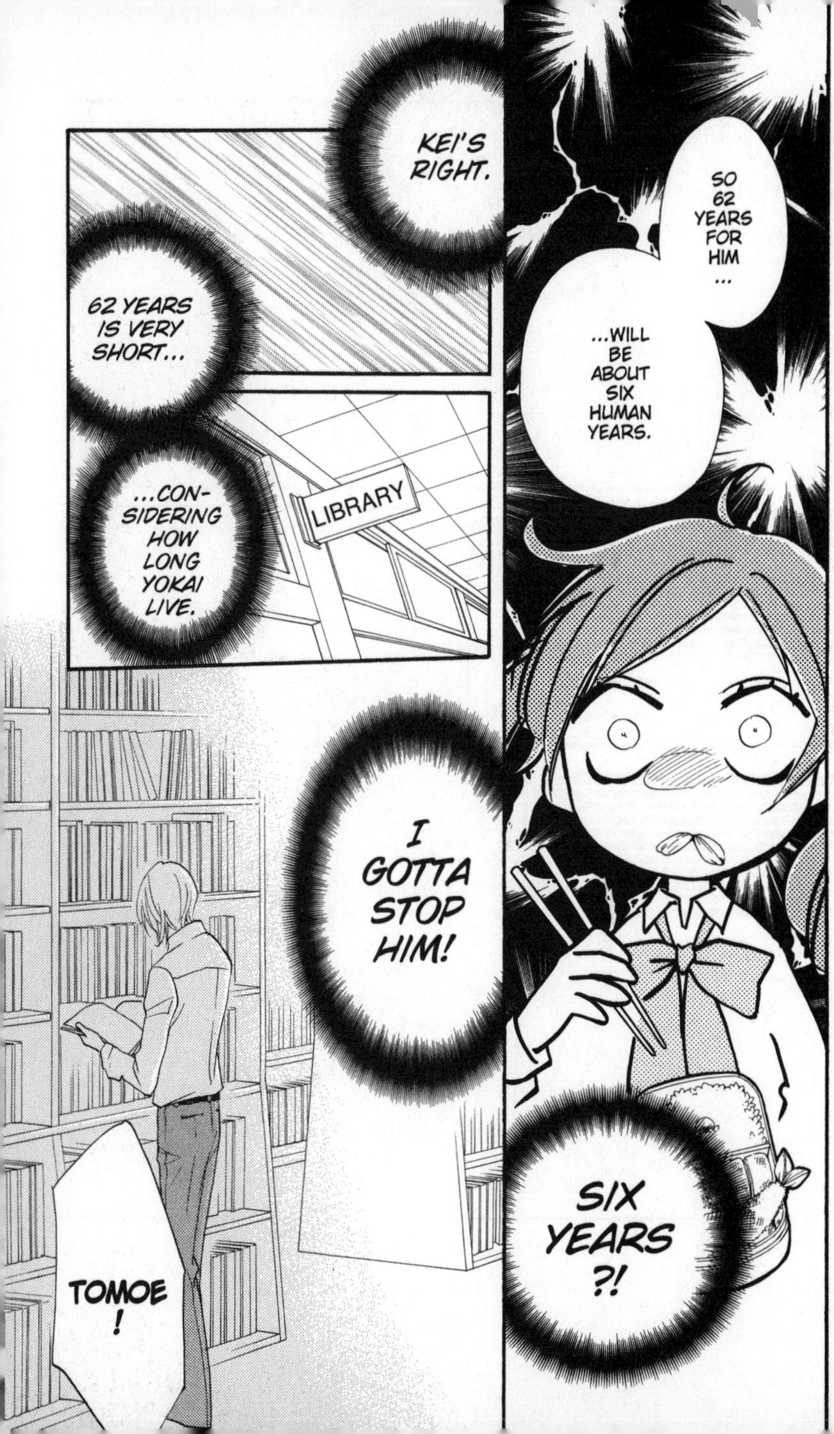
SO 62 YEARS FOR HIM...
...WILL BE ABOUT SIX HUMAN YEARS.
SIX YEARS?!
KEI'S RIGHT.
62 YEARS IS VERY SHORT...
...CON-SIDERING HOW LONG YOKAI LIVE.
LIBRARY
I GOTTA STOP HIM!
TOMOE!

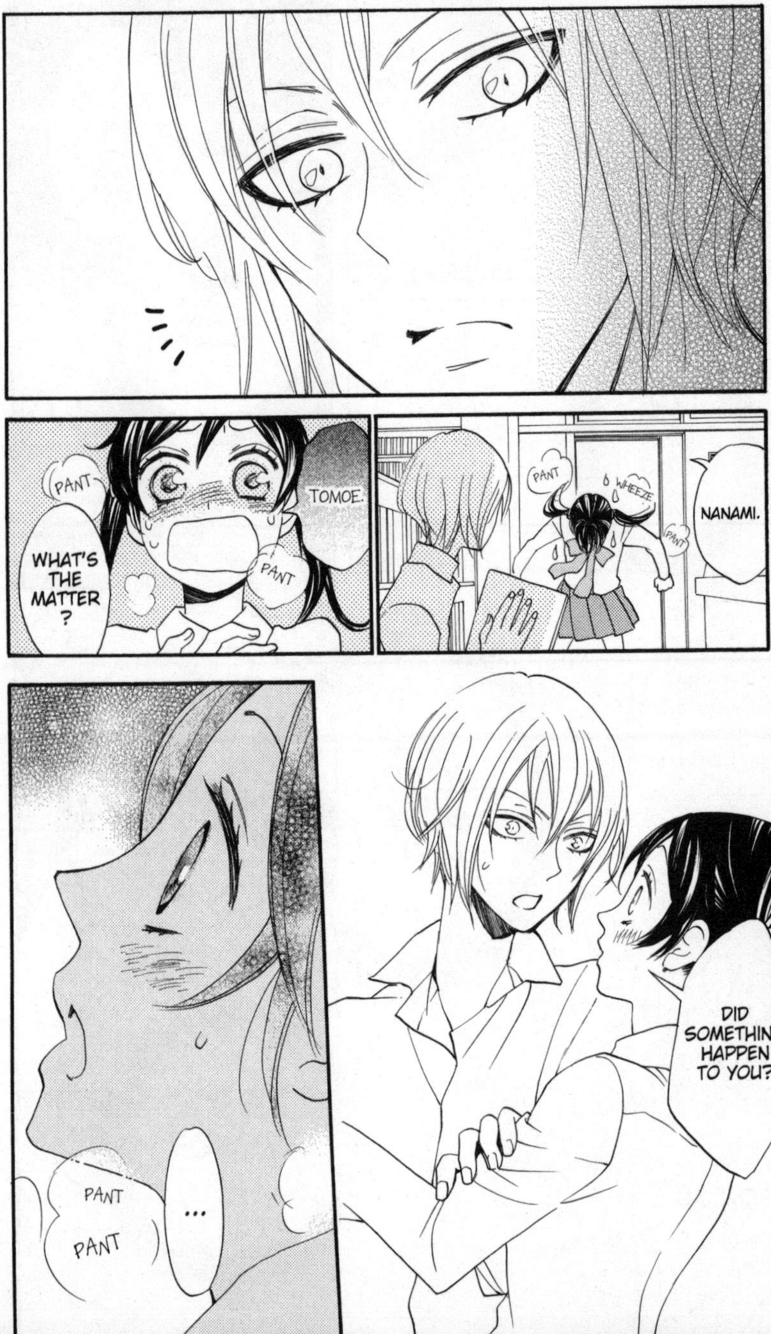
PANT
WHEEZE
PANT
NANAMI.
TOMOE.
PANT
PANT
WHAT'S THE MATTER?
DID SOMETHING HAPPEN TO YOU?
...
PANT
PANT

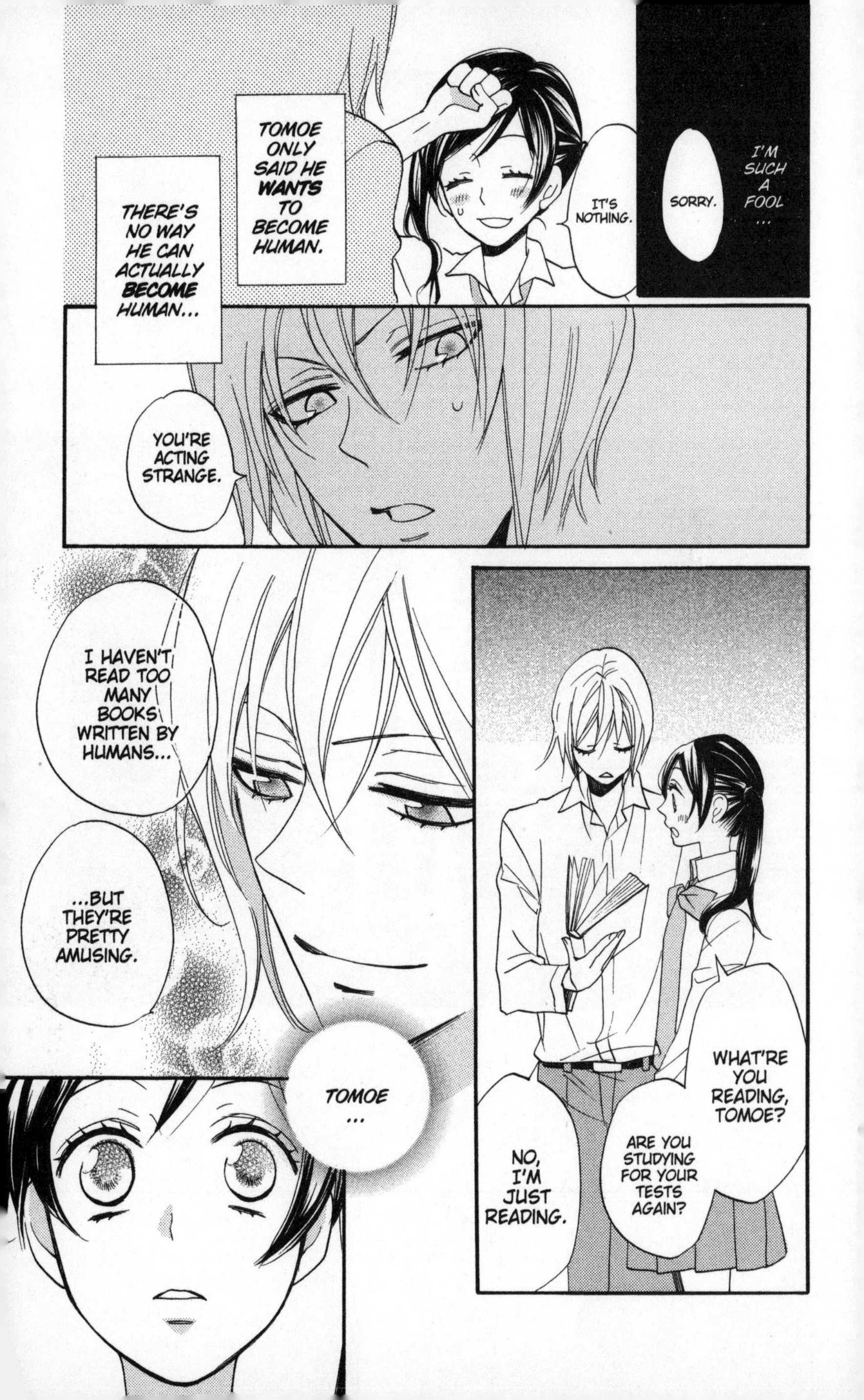

I'M SUCH A FOOL...
SORRY.
IT'S NOTHING.
TOMOE ONLY SAID HE **WANTS** TO BECOME HUMAN.
THERE'S NO WAY HE CAN ACTUALLY **BECOME** HUMAN...
YOU'RE ACTING STRANGE.
WHAT'RE YOU READING, TOMOE?
ARE YOU STUDYING FOR YOUR TESTS AGAIN?
NO, I'M JUST READING.
I HAVEN'T READ TOO MANY BOOKS WRITTEN BY HUMANS...
...BUT THEY'RE PRETTY AMUSING.
TOMOE...

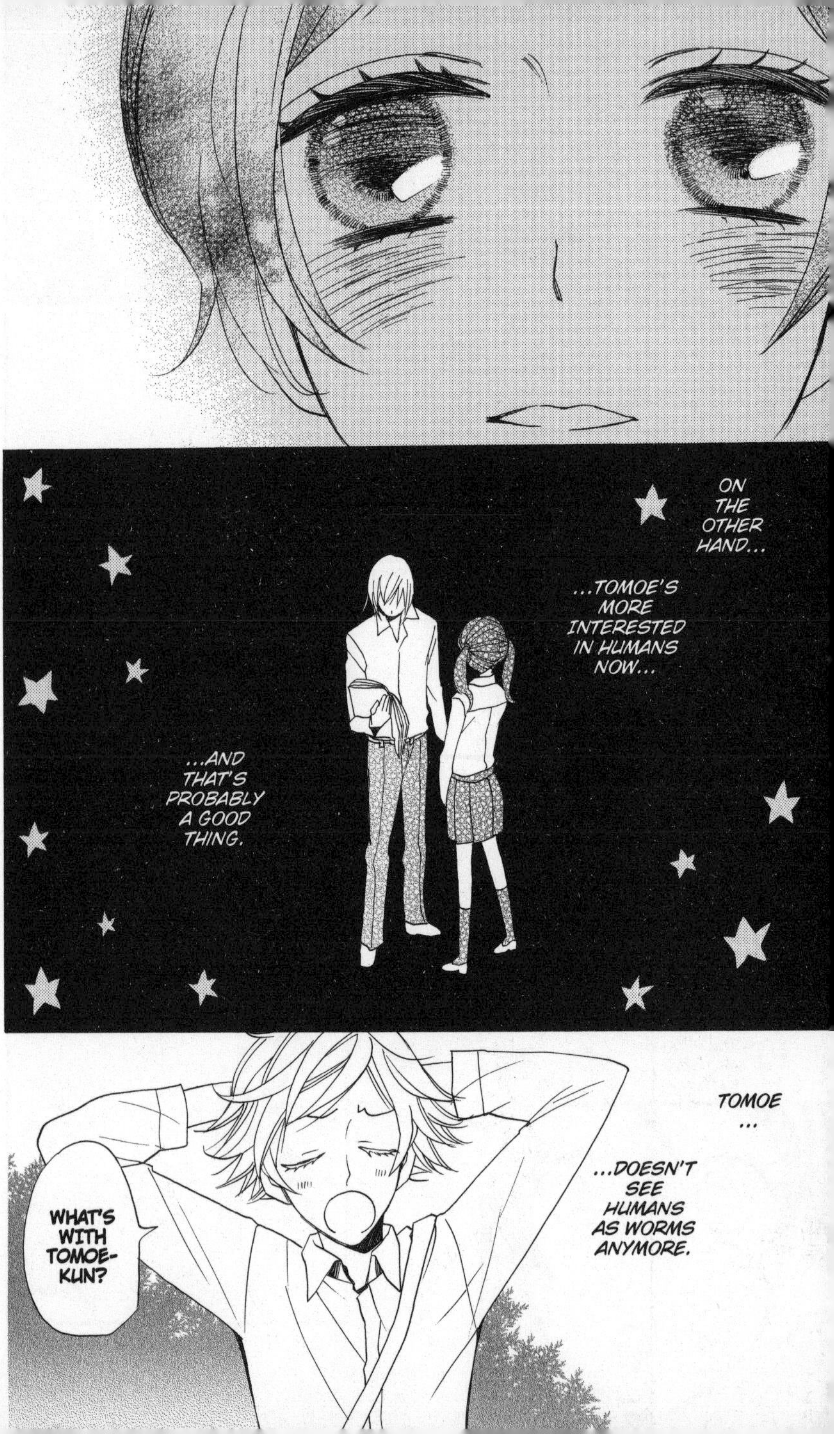
ON THE OTHER HAND...
...TOMOE'S MORE INTERESTED IN HUMANS NOW...
...AND THAT'S PROBABLY A GOOD THING.
TOMOE...
...DOESN'T SEE HUMANS AS WORMS ANYMORE.
WHAT'S WITH TOMOE-KUN?

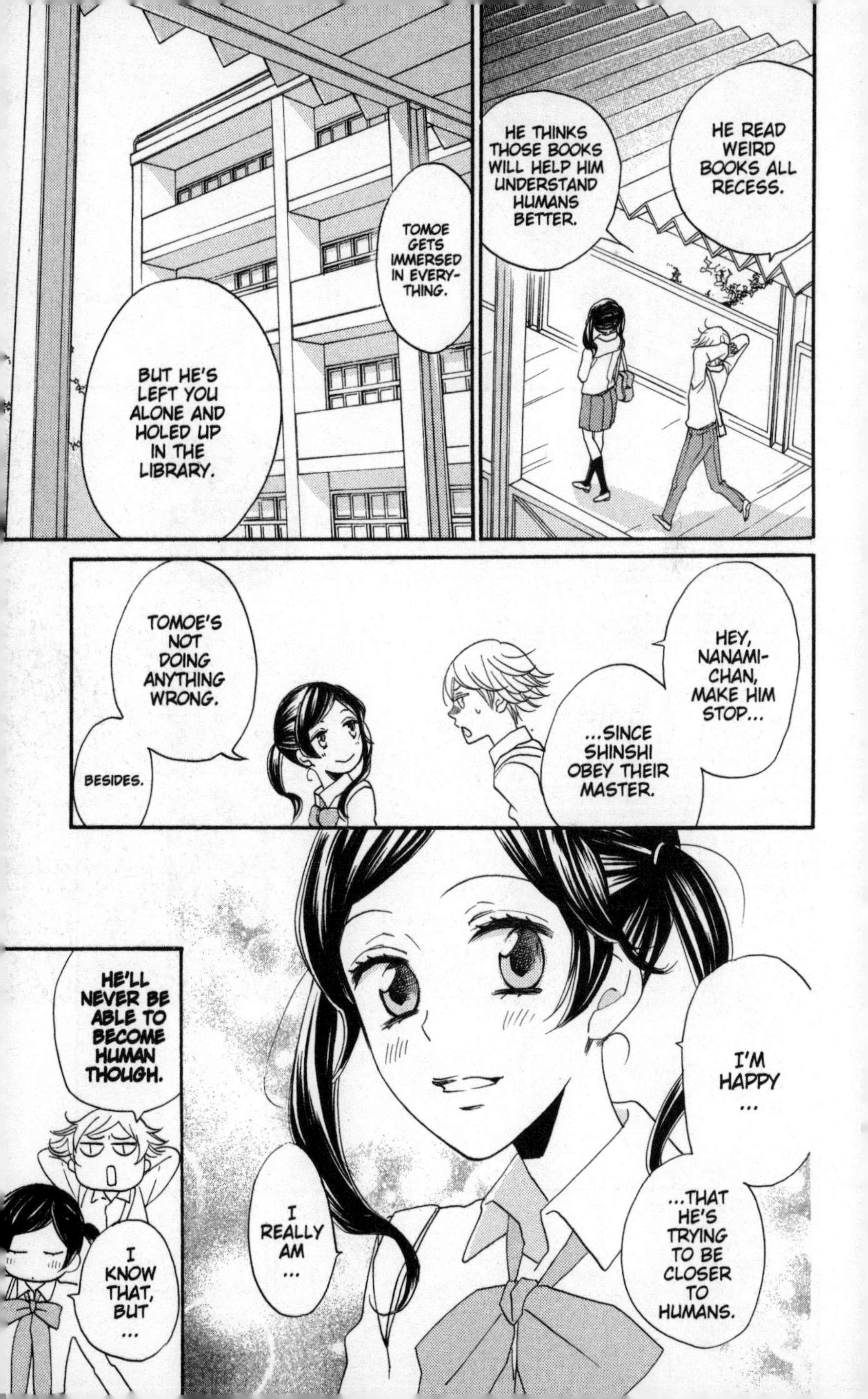
HE READ WEIRD BOOKS ALL RECESS.
HE THINKS THOSE BOOKS WILL HELP HIM UNDERSTAND HUMANS BETTER.
TOMOE GETS IMMERSED IN EVERY-THING.
BUT HE'S LEFT YOU ALONE AND HOLED UP IN THE LIBRARY.
HEY, NANAMI-CHAN, MAKE HIM STOP...
...SINCE SHINSHI OBEY THEIR MASTER.
TOMOE'S NOT DOING ANYTHING WRONG.
BESIDES.
I'M HAPPY ...
...THAT HE'S TRYING TO BE CLOSER TO HUMANS.
I REALLY AM ...
HE'LL NEVER BE ABLE TO BECOME HUMAN THOUGH.
I KNOW THAT, BUT ...

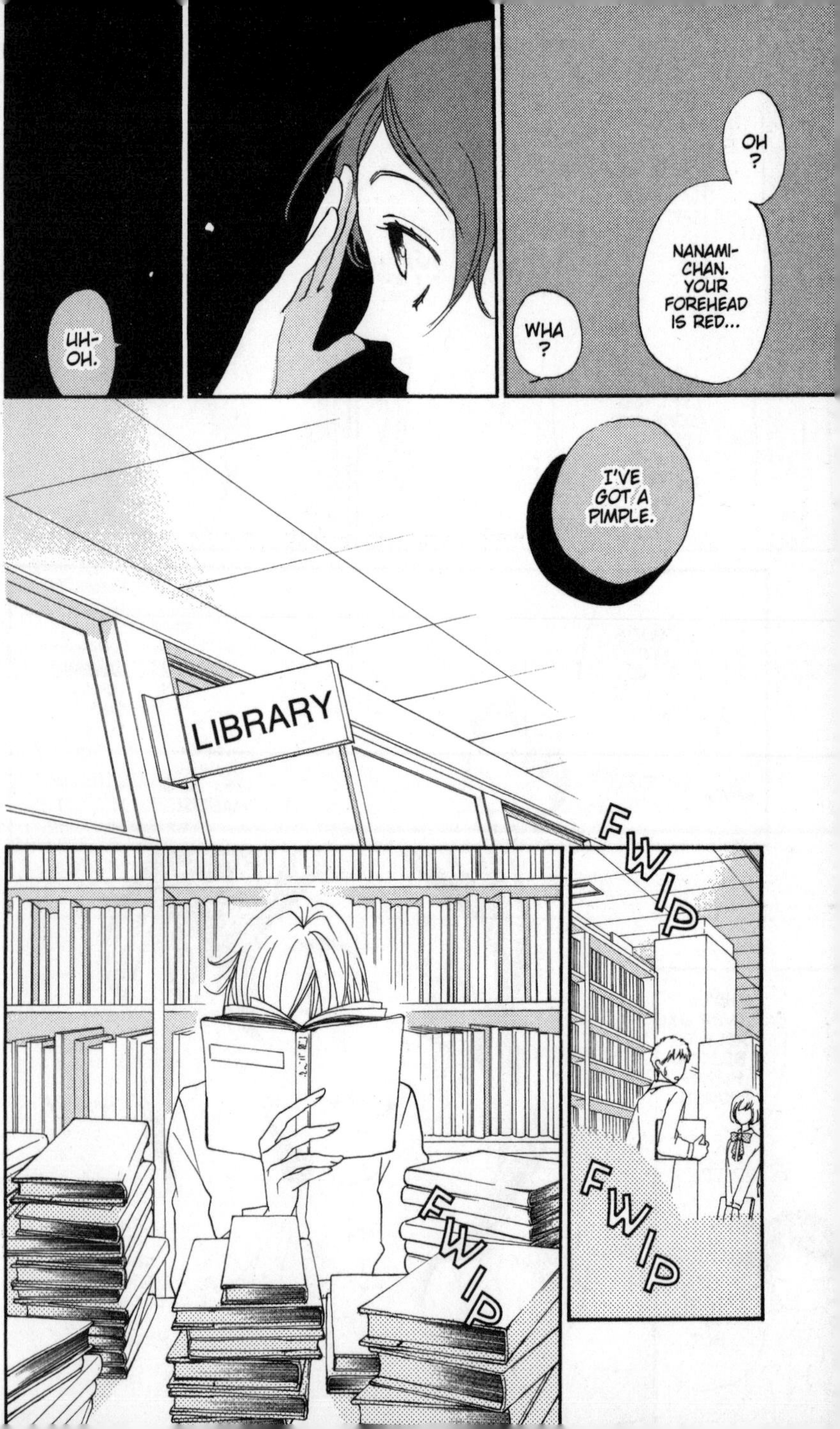
OH?
NANAMI-CHAN. YOUR FOREHEAD IS RED...
WHA?
UH-OH.
I'VE GOT A PIMPLE.
LIBRARY
FWIP
FWIP
FWIP

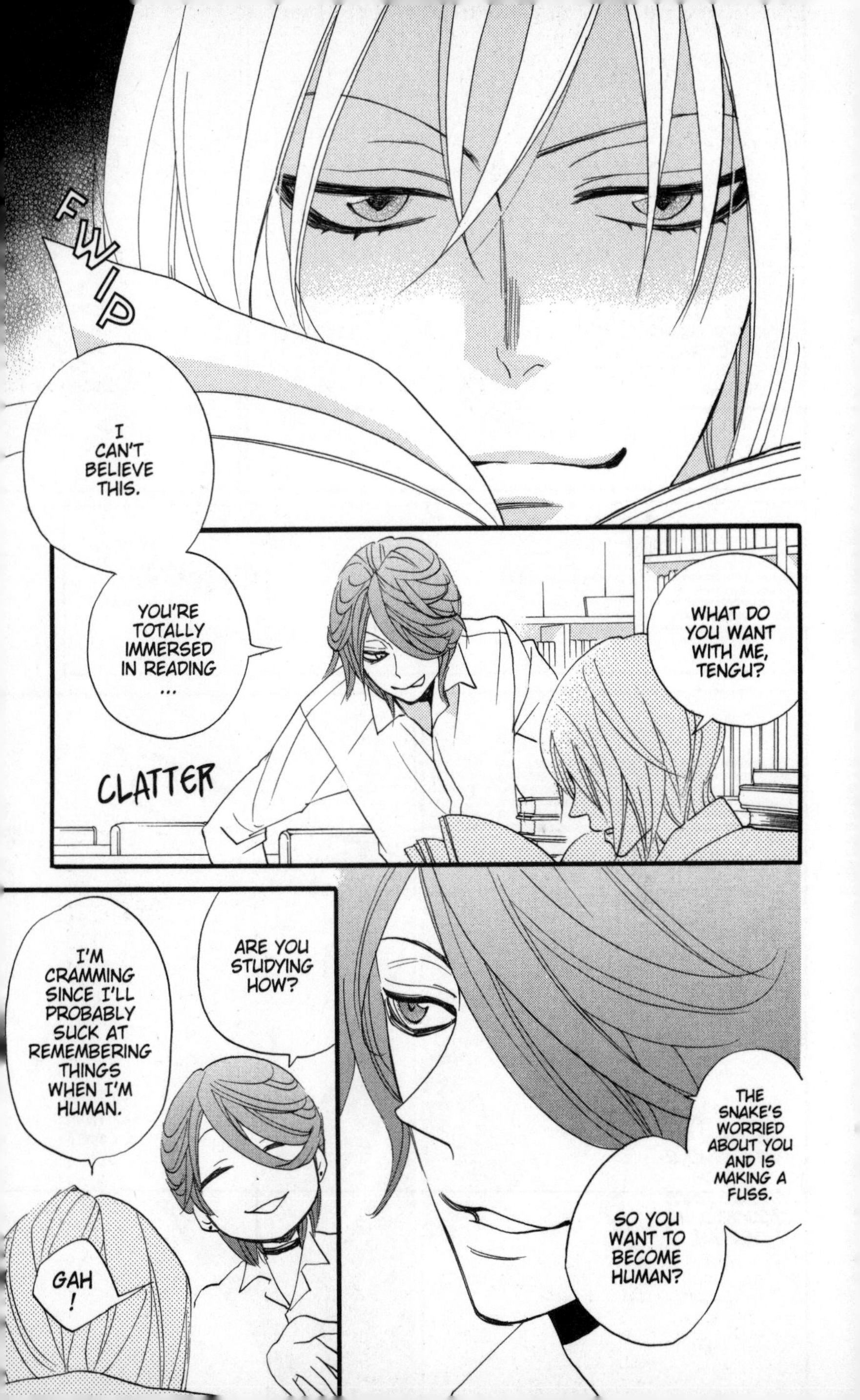
FWIP
I CAN'T BELIEVE THIS.
YOU'RE TOTALLY IMMERSED IN READING...
CLATTER
WHAT DO YOU WANT WITH ME, TENGU?
THE SNAKE'S WORRIED ABOUT YOU AND IS MAKING A FUSS.
SO YOU WANT TO BECOME HUMAN?
ARE YOU STUDYING HOW?
I'M CRAMMING SINCE I'LL PROBABLY SUCK AT REMEMBERING THINGS WHEN I'M HUMAN.
GAH!

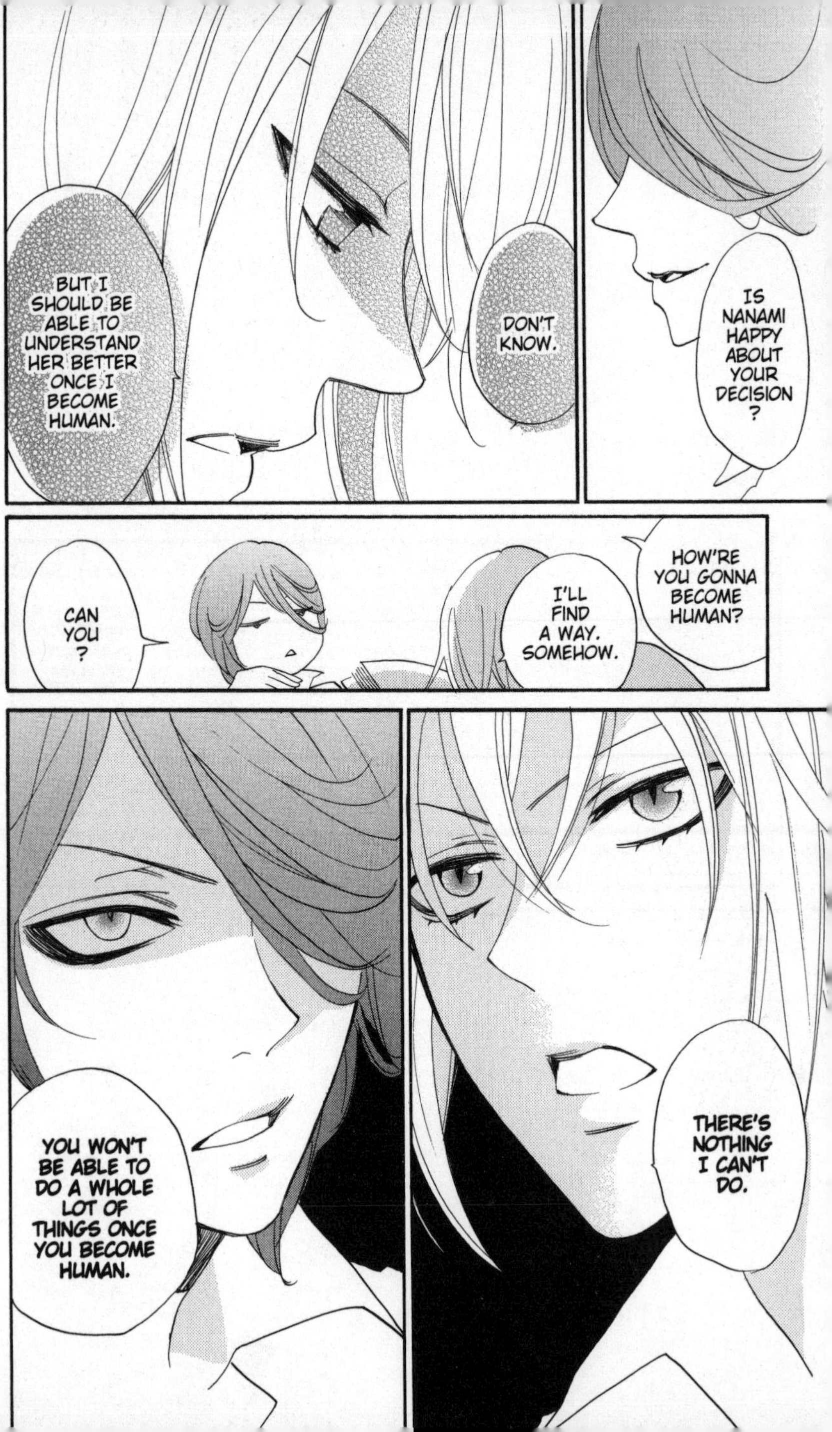
IS NANAMI HAPPY ABOUT YOUR DECISION?
DON'T KNOW.
BUT I SHOULD BE ABLE TO UNDERSTAND HER BETTER ONCE I BECOME HUMAN.
HOW'RE YOU GONNA BECOME HUMAN?
I'LL FIND A WAY. SOMEHOW.
CAN YOU?
THERE'S NOTHING I CAN'T DO.
YOU WON'T BE ABLE TO DO A WHOLE LOT OF THINGS ONCE YOU BECOME HUMAN.

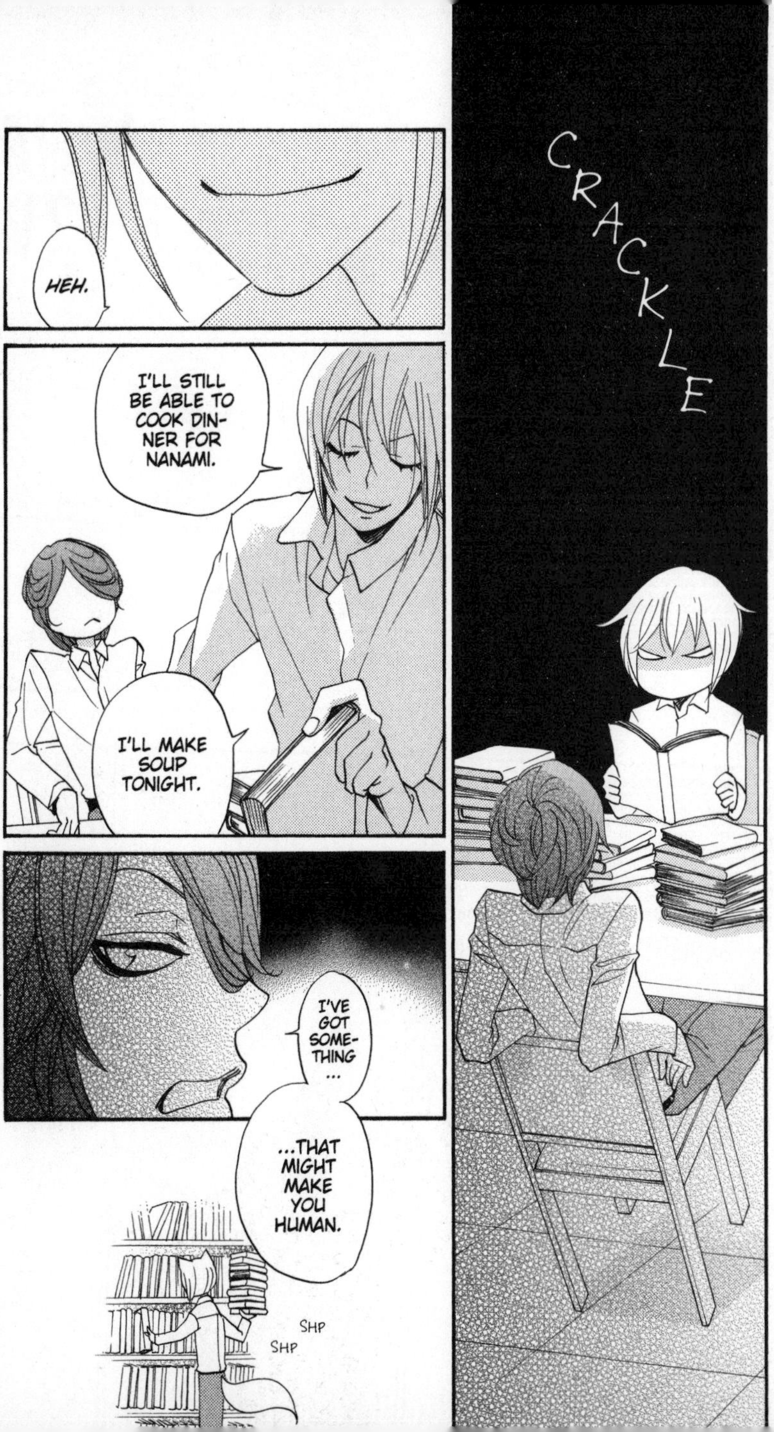
CRACKLE
HEH.
I'LL STILL BE ABLE TO COOK DIN-NER FOR NANAMI.
I'LL MAKE SOUP TONIGHT.
I'VE GOT SOME-THING...
...THAT MIGHT MAKE YOU HUMAN.
SHP
SHP

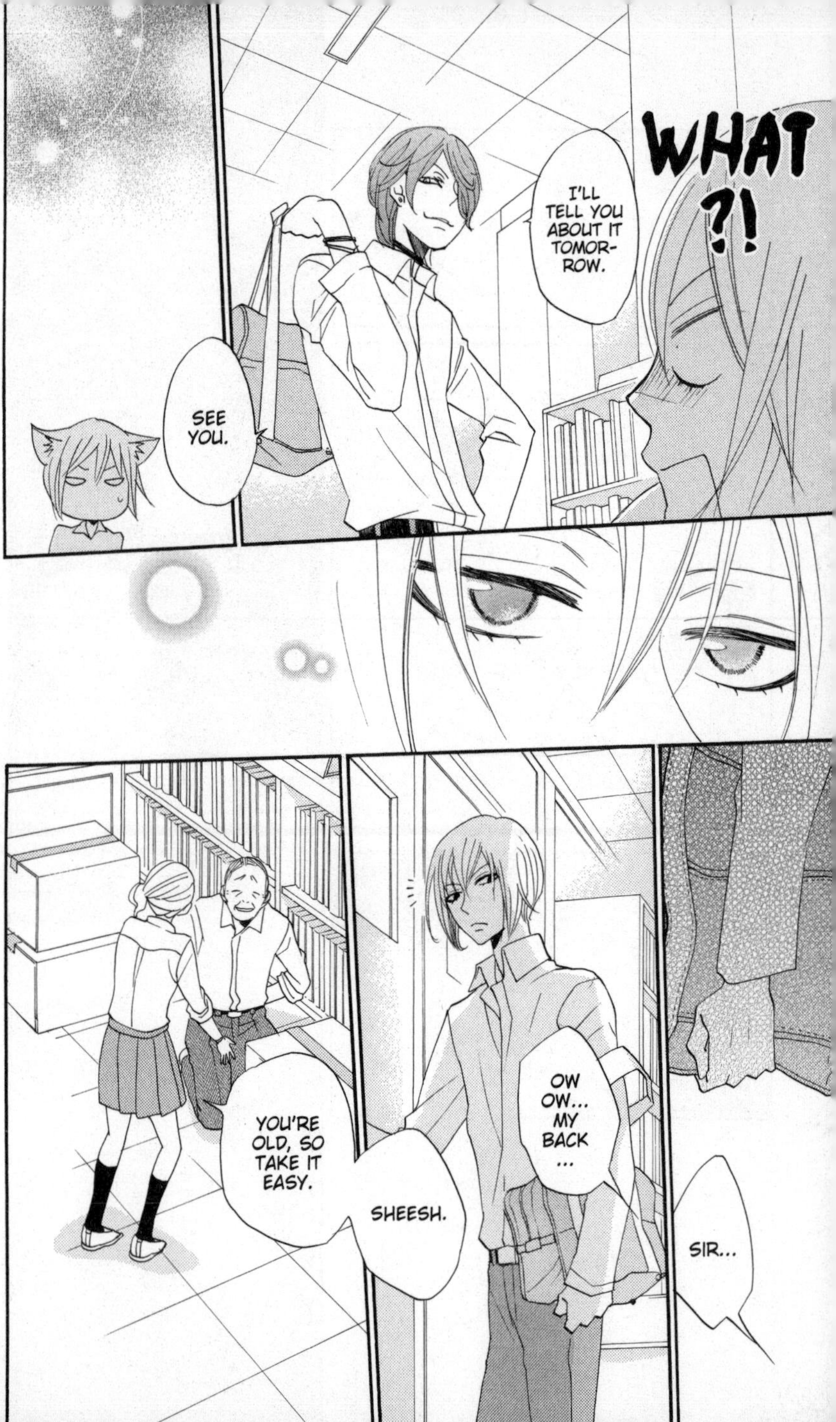
WHAT?!
I'LL TELL YOU ABOUT IT TOMORROW.
SEE YOU.
SIR...
OW OW... MY BACK ...
YOU'RE OLD, SO TAKE IT EASY.
SHEESH.

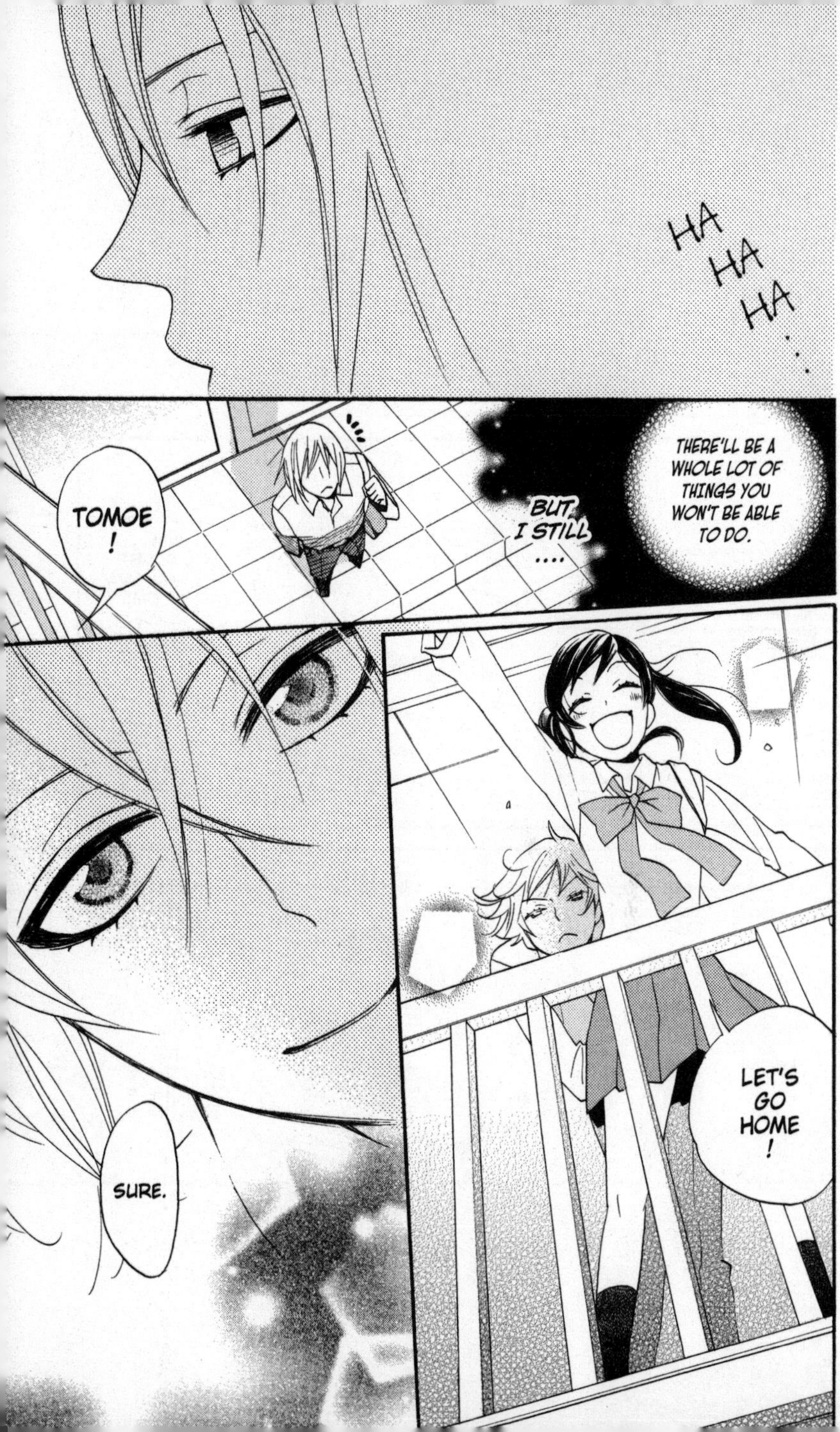
HA HA HA...
THERE'LL BE A WHOLE LOT OF THINGS YOU WON'T BE ABLE TO DO.
BUT I STILL....
TOMOE!
LET'S GO HOME!
SURE.

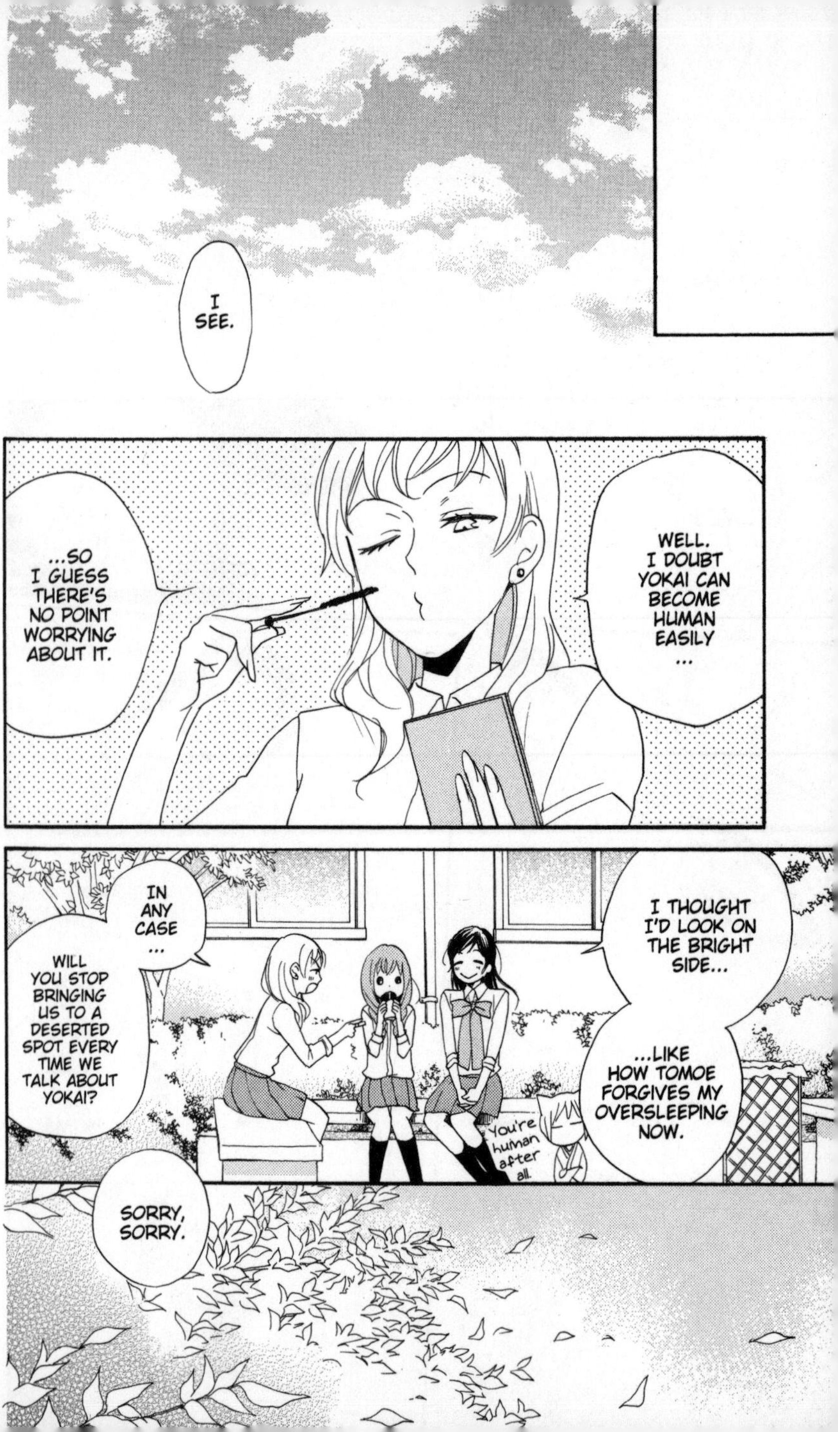
I SEE.
WELL. I DOUBT YOKAI CAN BECOME HUMAN EASILY ...
...SO I GUESS THERE'S NO POINT WORRYING ABOUT IT.
I THOUGHT I'D LOOK ON THE BRIGHT SIDE...
...LIKE HOW TOMOE FORGIVES MY OVERSLEEPING NOW.
You're human after all.
IN ANY CASE ...
WILL YOU STOP BRINGING US TO A DESERTED SPOT EVERY TIME WE TALK ABOUT YOKAI?
SORRY, SORRY.

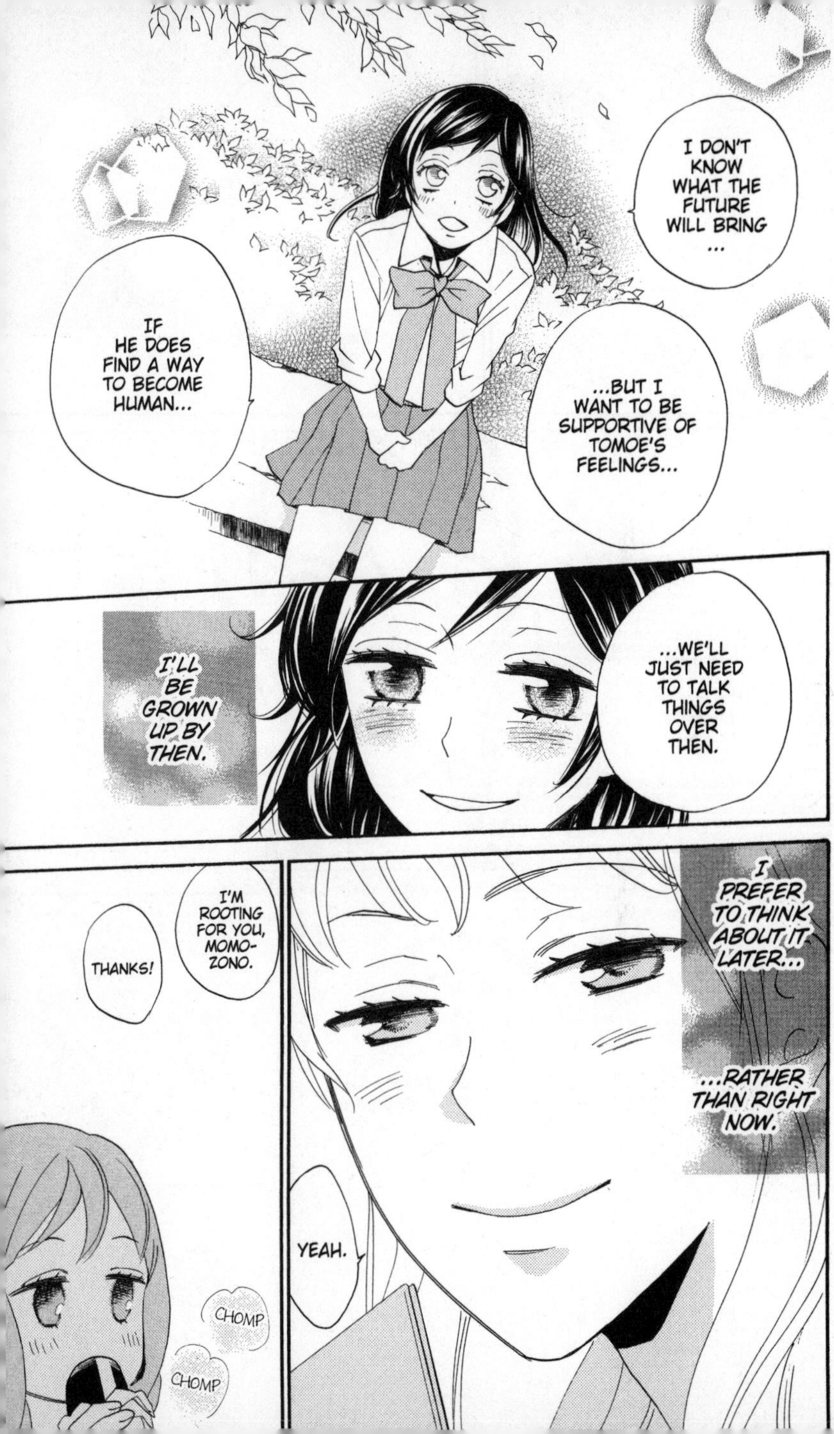
I DON'T KNOW WHAT THE FUTURE WILL BRING ...
...BUT I WANT TO BE SUPPORTIVE OF TOMOE'S FEELINGS...
IF HE DOES FIND A WAY TO BECOME HUMAN...
...WE'LL JUST NEED TO TALK THINGS OVER THEN.
I'LL BE GROWN UP BY THEN.
I PREFER TO THINK ABOUT IT LATER...
...RATHER THAN RIGHT NOW.
YEAH.
I'M ROOTING FOR YOU, MOMO-ZONO.
THANKS!
CHOMP
CHOMP

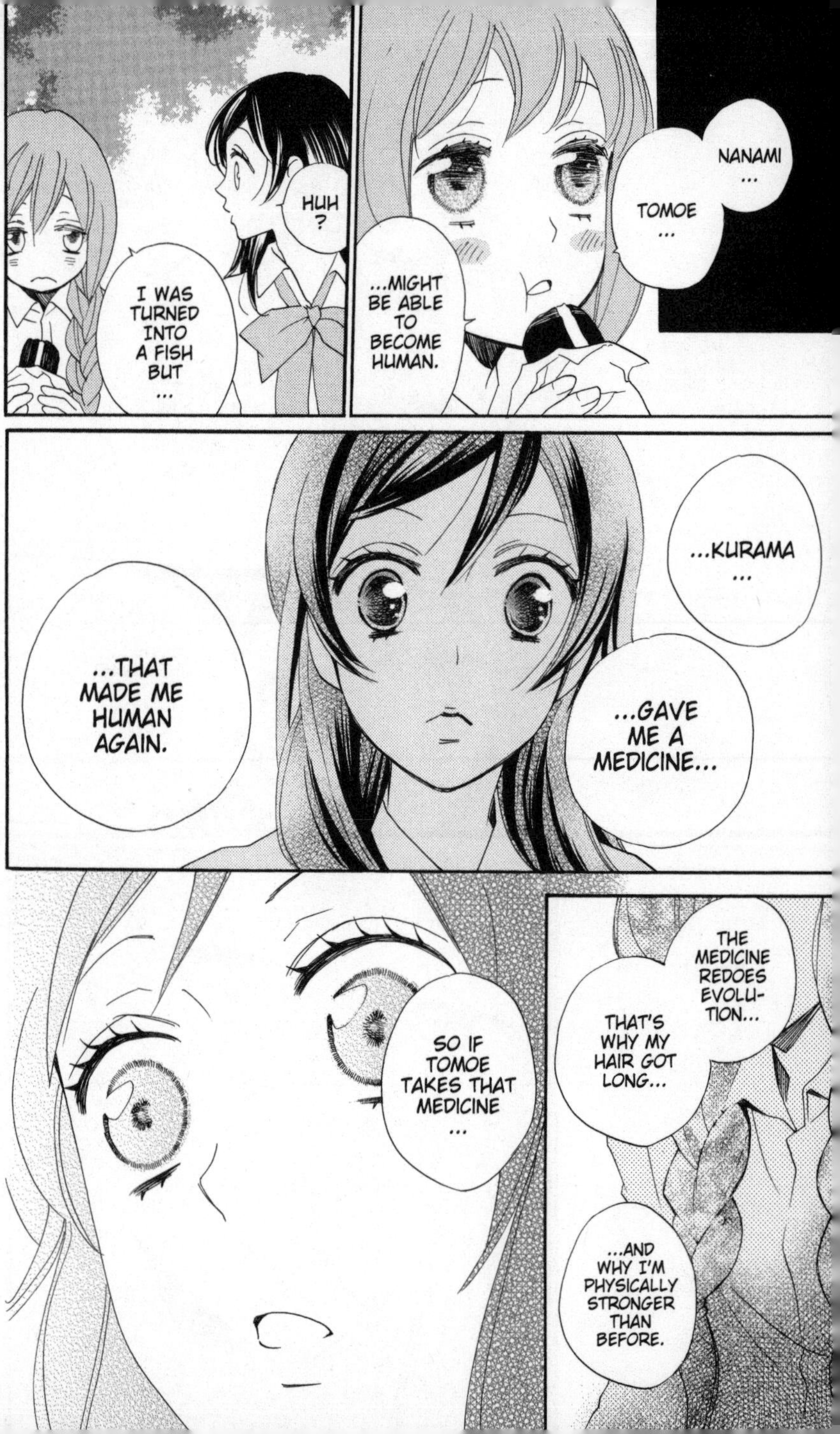
NANAMI ...
TOMOE ...
...MIGHT BE ABLE TO BECOME HUMAN.
HUH ?
I WAS TURNED INTO A FISH BUT ...
...KURAMA ...
...GAVE ME A MEDICINE...
...THAT MADE ME HUMAN AGAIN.
THE MEDICINE REDOES EVOLU-TION...
THAT'S WHY MY HAIR GOT LONG...
...AND WHY I'M PHYSICALLY STRONGER THAN BEFORE.
SO IF TOMOE TAKES THAT MEDICINE ...

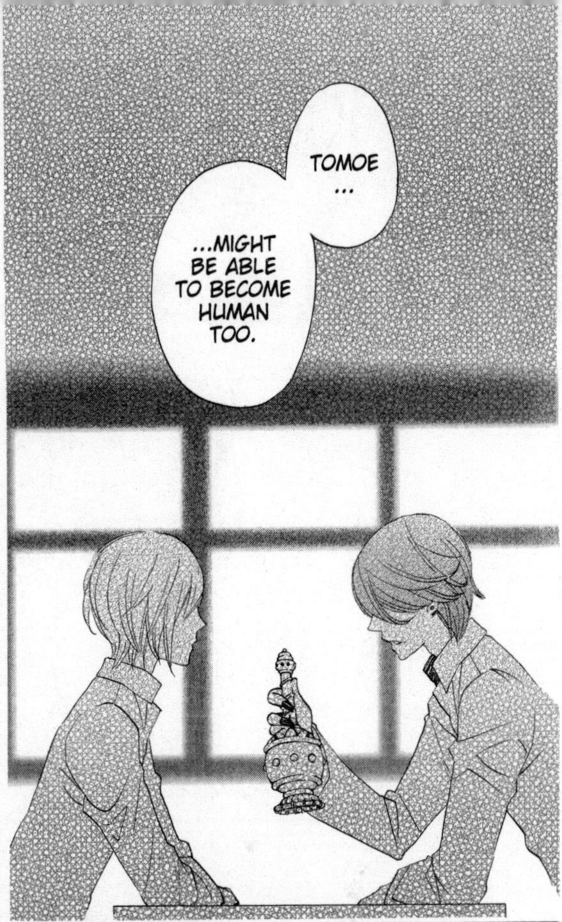
TOMOE ...
...MIGHT BE ABLE TO BECOME HUMAN TOO.
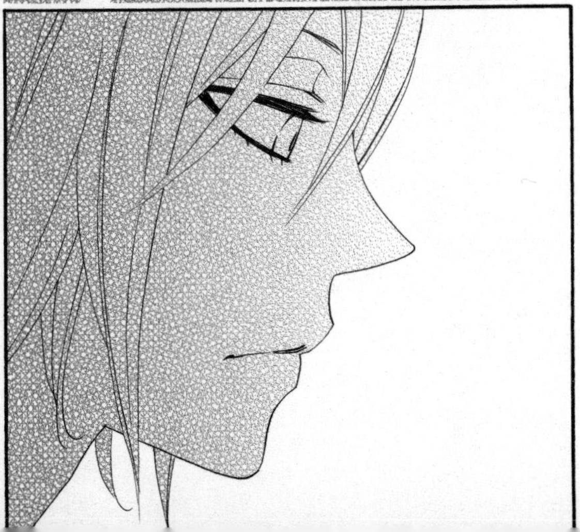
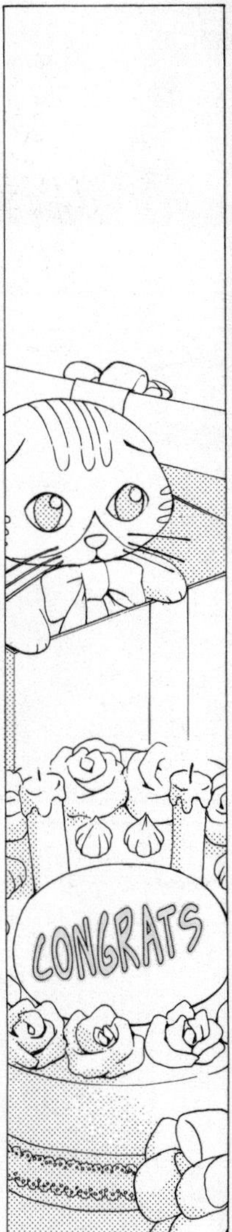
CONGRATS
By OKazaKi

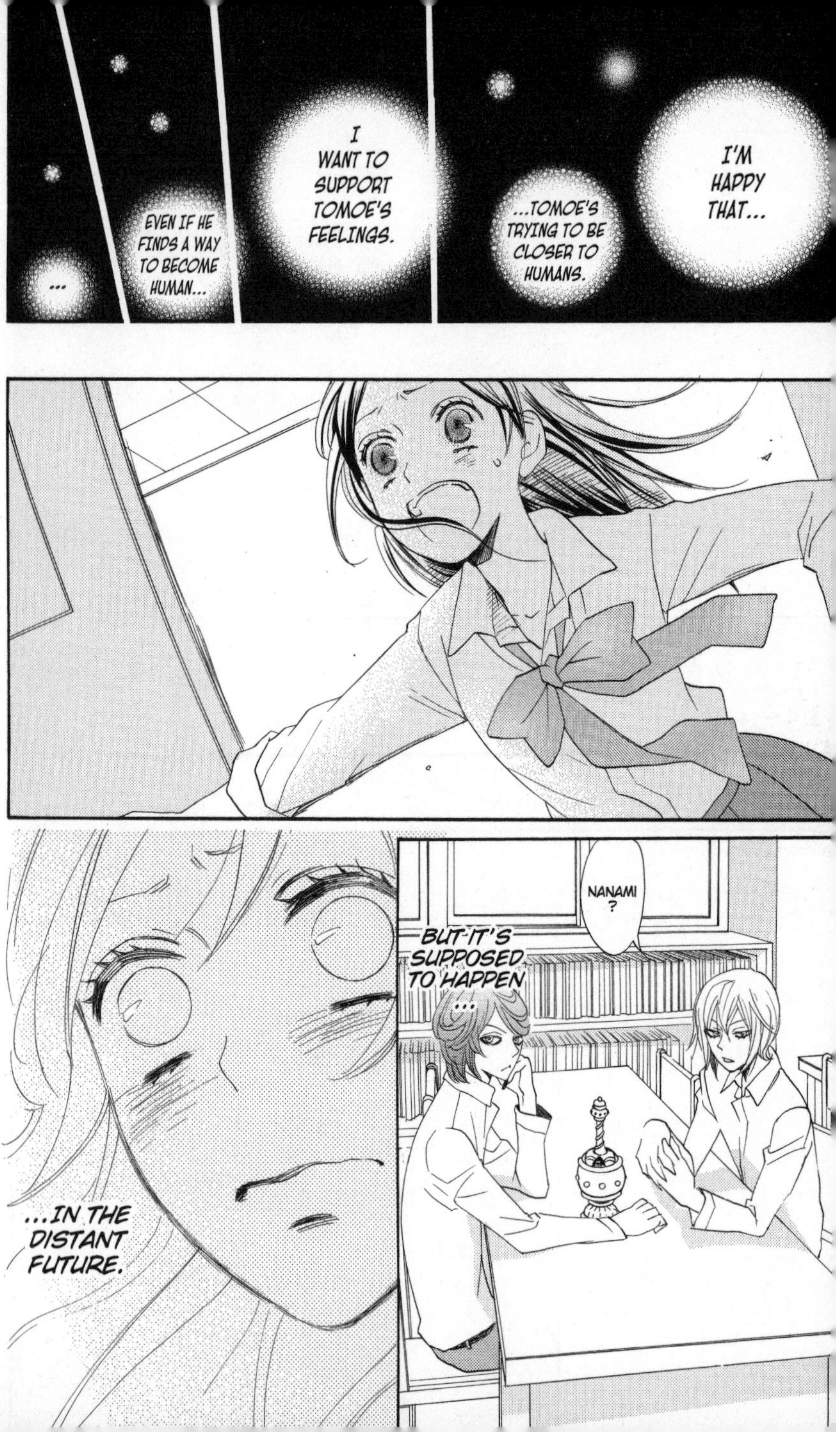
I'M HAPPY THAT...
...TOMOE'S TRYING TO BE CLOSER TO HUMANS.
I WANT TO SUPPORT TOMOE'S FEELINGS.
EVEN IF HE FINDS A WAY TO BECOME HUMAN...
...
NANAMI?
BUT IT'S SUPPOSED TO HAPPEN
...
...IN THE DISTANT FUTURE.

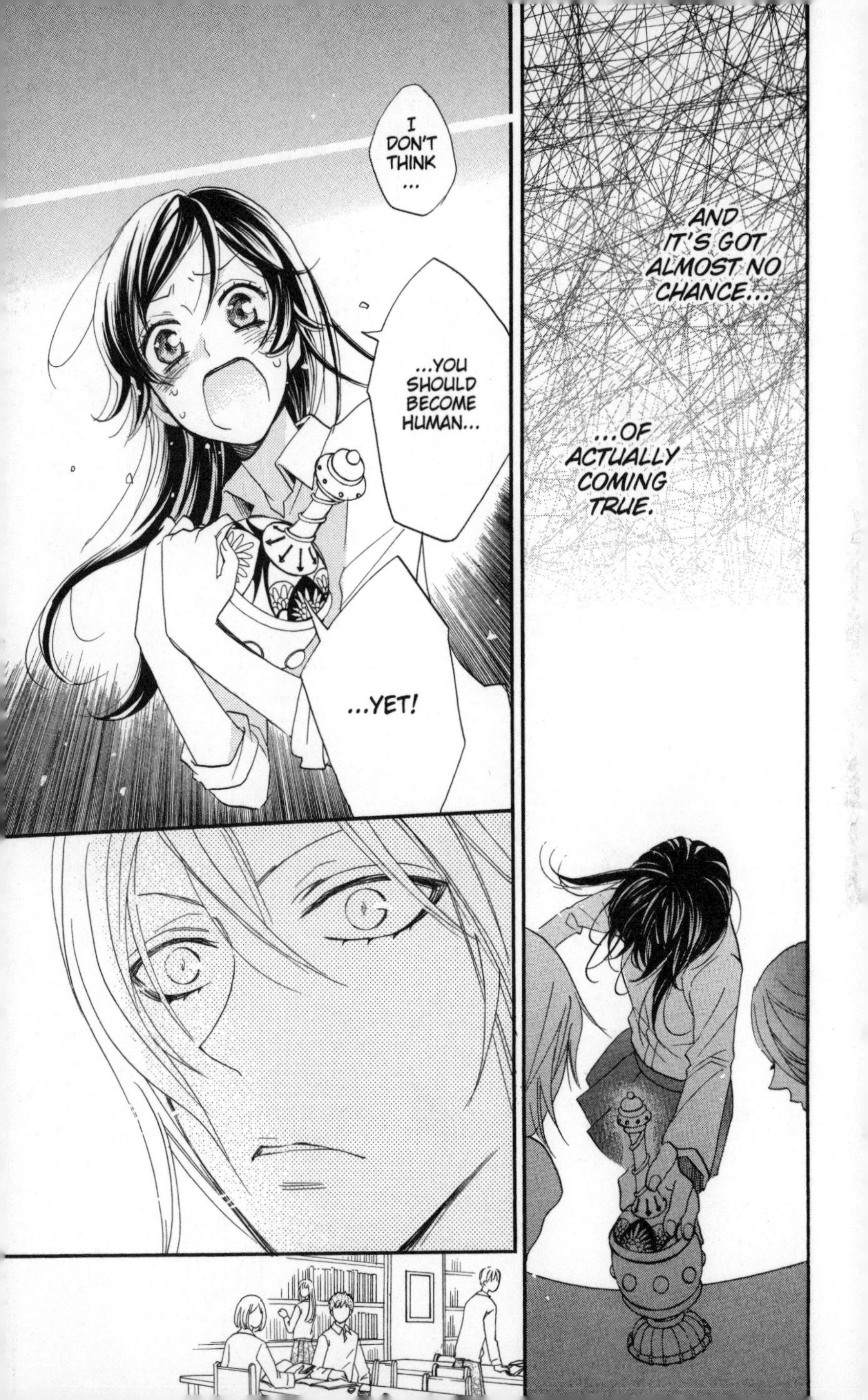
AND IT'S GOT ALMOST NO CHANCE...
...OF ACTUALLY COMING TRUE.
I DON'T THINK ...
...YOU SHOULD BECOME HUMAN...
...YET!

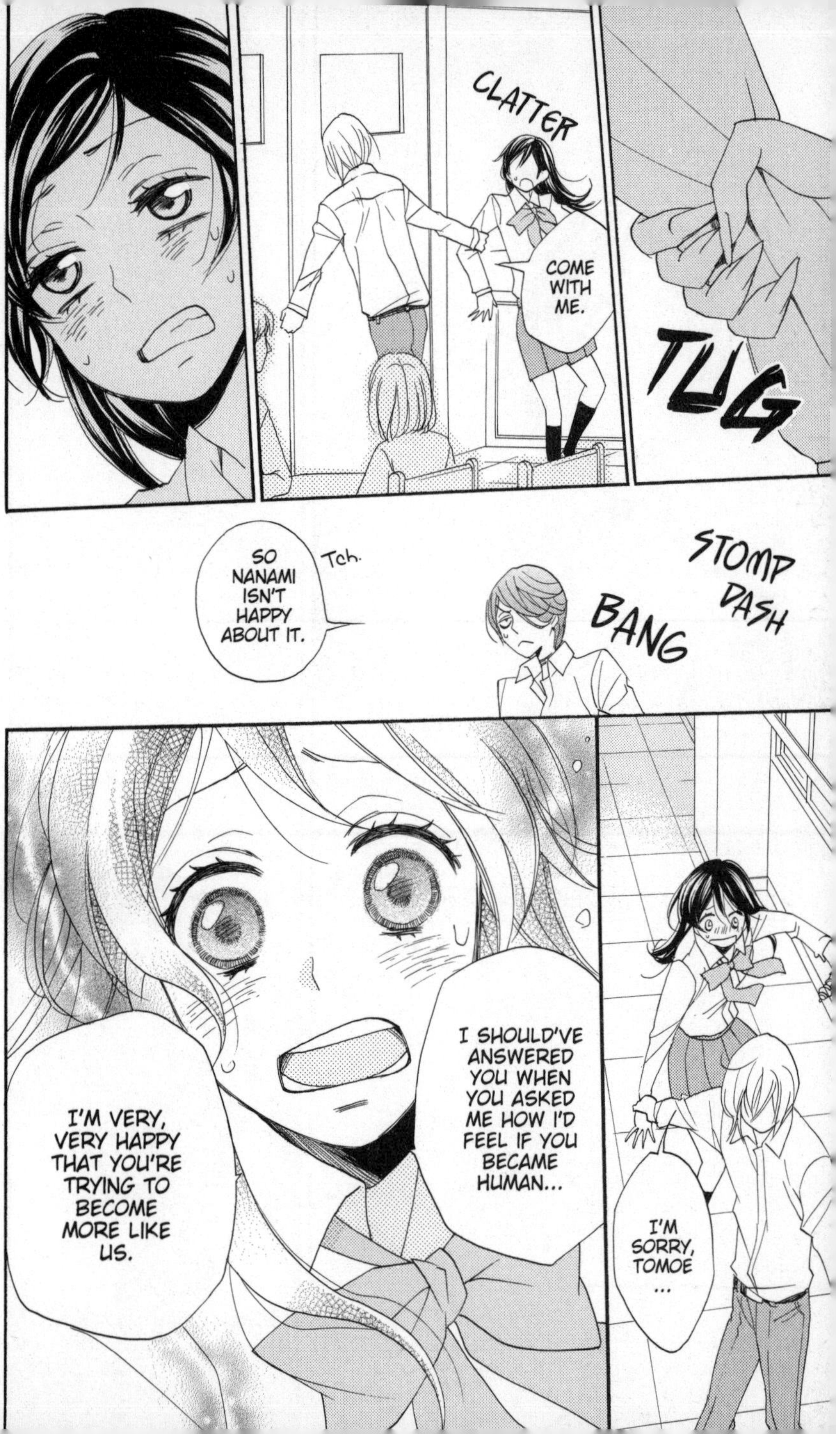
TUG
CLATTER
COME WITH ME.
STOMP
DASH
BANG
Tch.
SO NANAMI ISN'T HAPPY ABOUT IT.
I'M SORRY, TOMOE...
I SHOULD'VE ANSWERED YOU WHEN YOU ASKED ME HOW I'D FEEL IF YOU BECAME HUMAN...
I'M VERY, VERY HAPPY THAT YOU'RE TRYING TO BECOME MORE LIKE US.

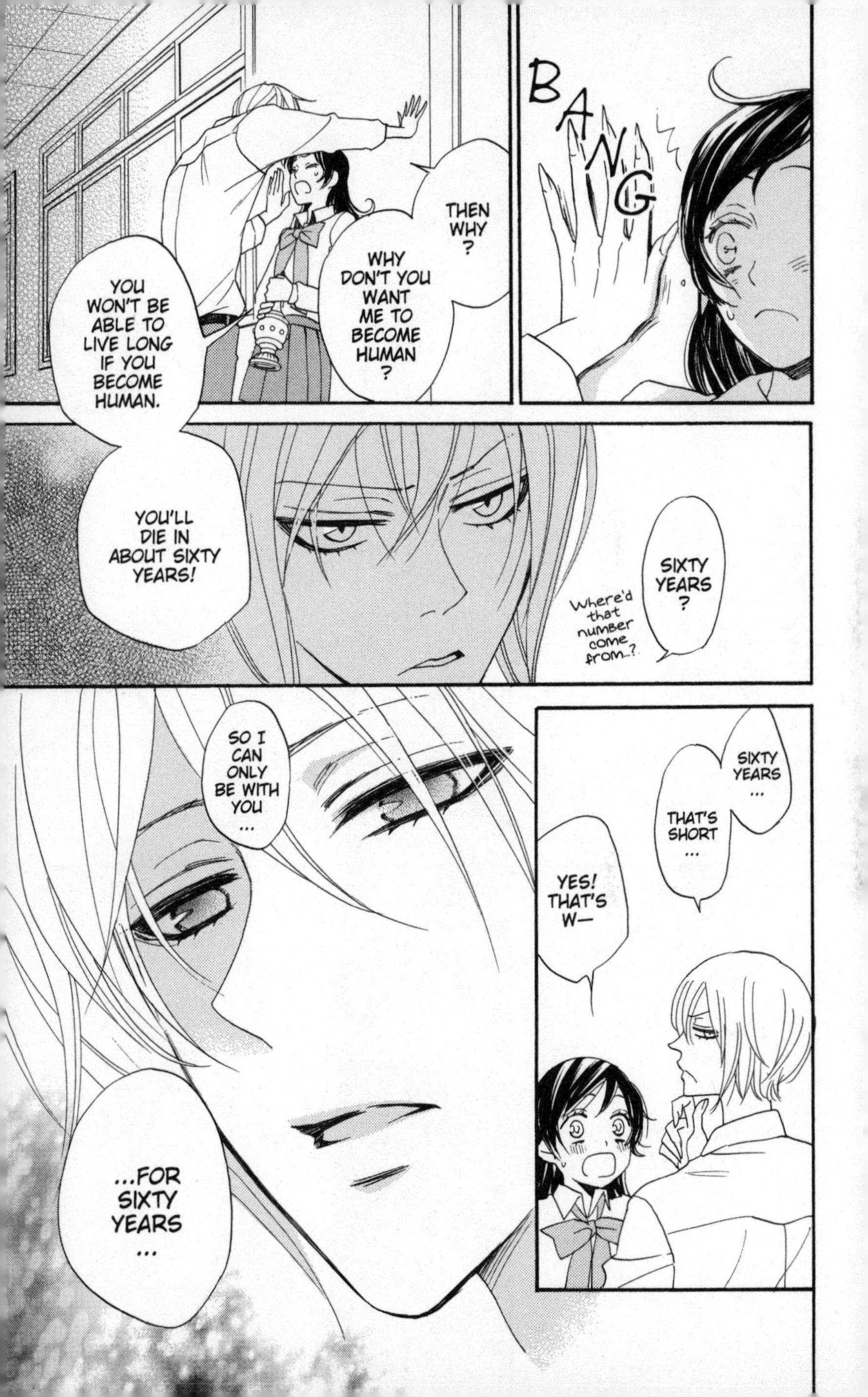
BANG
THEN WHY?
WHY DON'T YOU WANT ME TO BECOME HUMAN?
YOU WON'T BE ABLE TO LIVE LONG IF YOU BECOME HUMAN.
YOU'LL DIE IN ABOUT SIXTY YEARS!
SIXTY YEARS?
Where'd that number come from...?
SIXTY YEARS... THAT'S SHORT...
YES! THAT'S W—
SO I CAN ONLY BE WITH YOU...
...FOR SIXTY YEARS...

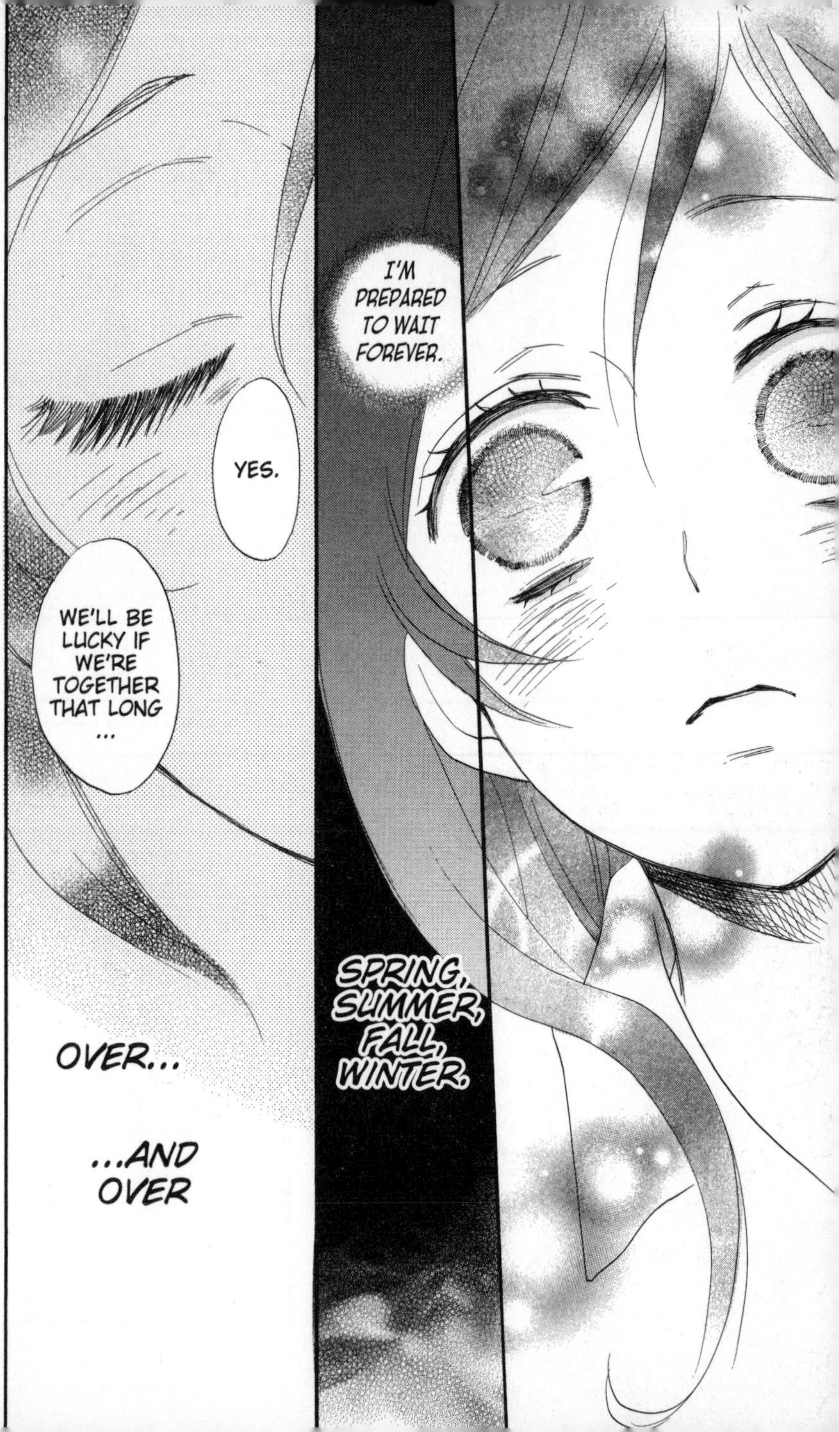
I'M PREPARED TO WAIT FOREVER.
SPRING, SUMMER, FALL, WINTER.
YES.
WE'LL BE LUCKY IF WE'RE TOGETHER THAT LONG ...
OVER...
...AND OVER

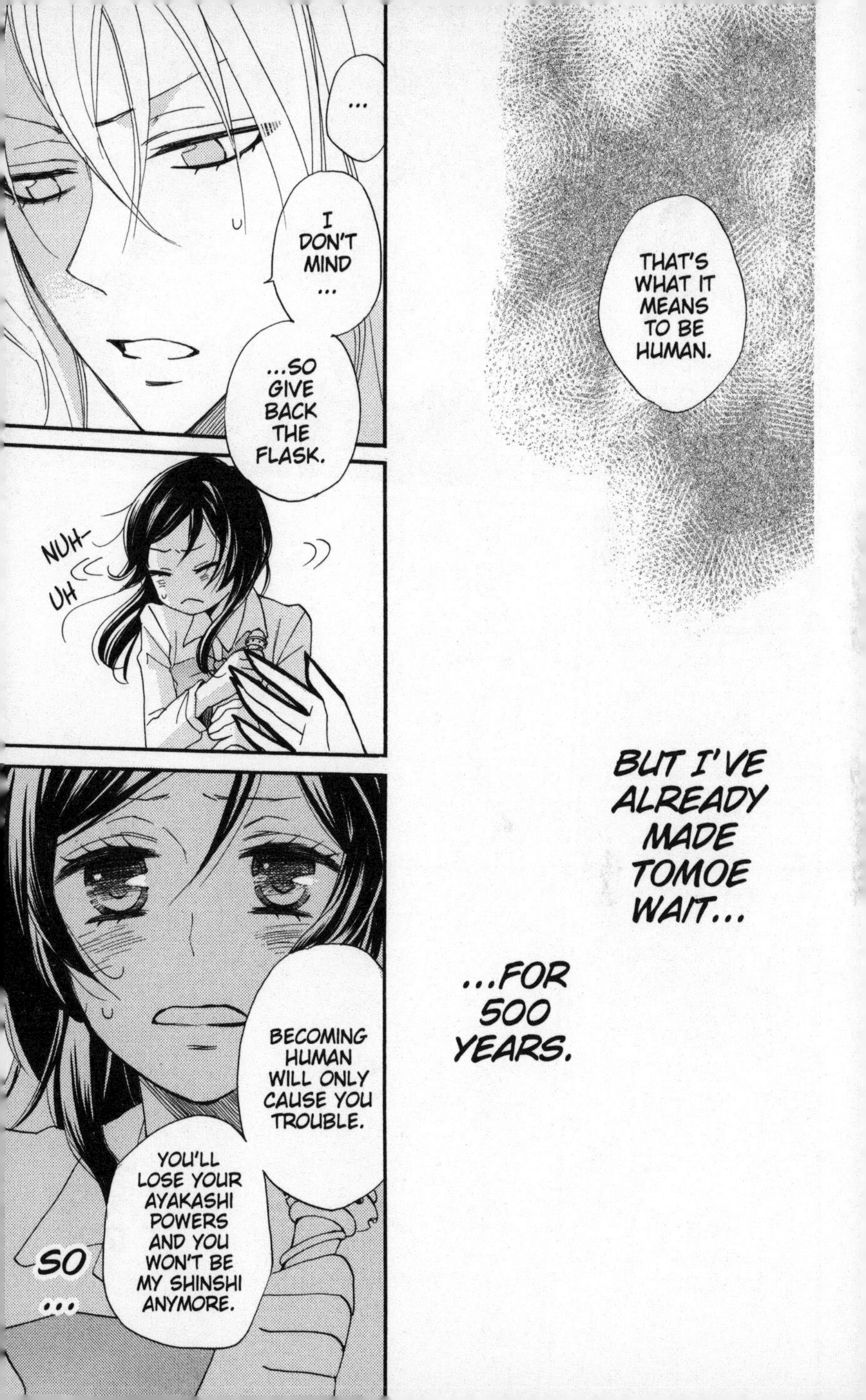
THAT'S WHAT IT MEANS TO BE HUMAN.
BUT I'VE ALREADY MADE TOMOE WAIT...
...FOR 500 YEARS.
...
I DON'T MIND ...
...SO GIVE BACK THE FLASK.
NUH-UH
BECOMING HUMAN WILL ONLY CAUSE YOU TROUBLE.
YOU'LL LOSE YOUR AYAKASHI POWERS AND YOU WON'T BE MY SHINSHI ANYMORE.
SO ...

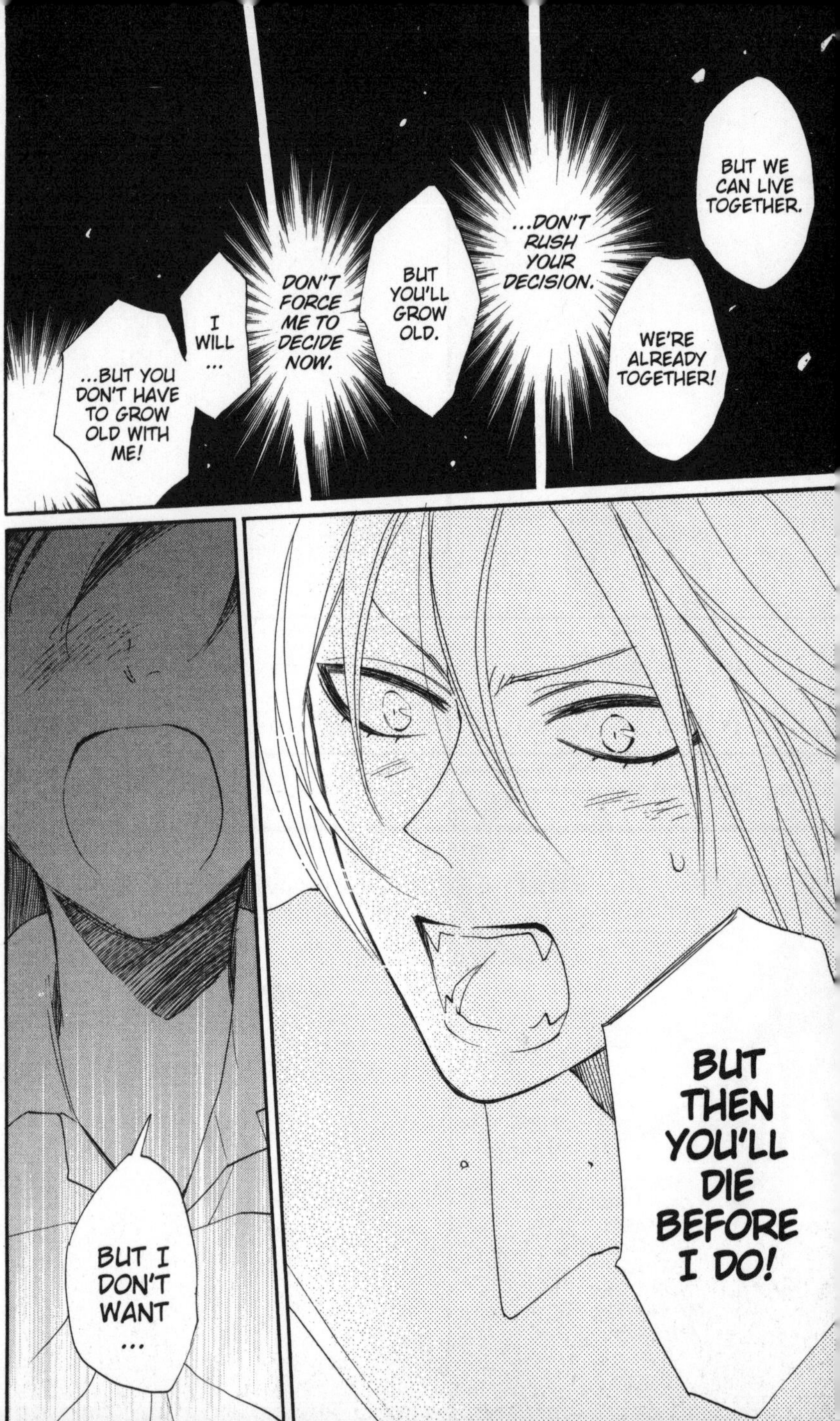
BUT WE CAN LIVE TOGETHER.
WE'RE ALREADY TOGETHER!
...DON'T RUSH YOUR DECISION.
BUT YOU'LL GROW OLD.
DON'T FORCE ME TO DECIDE NOW.
I WILL ...
...BUT YOU DON'T HAVE TO GROW OLD WITH ME!
BUT THEN YOU'LL DIE BEFORE I DO!
BUT I DON'T WANT ...

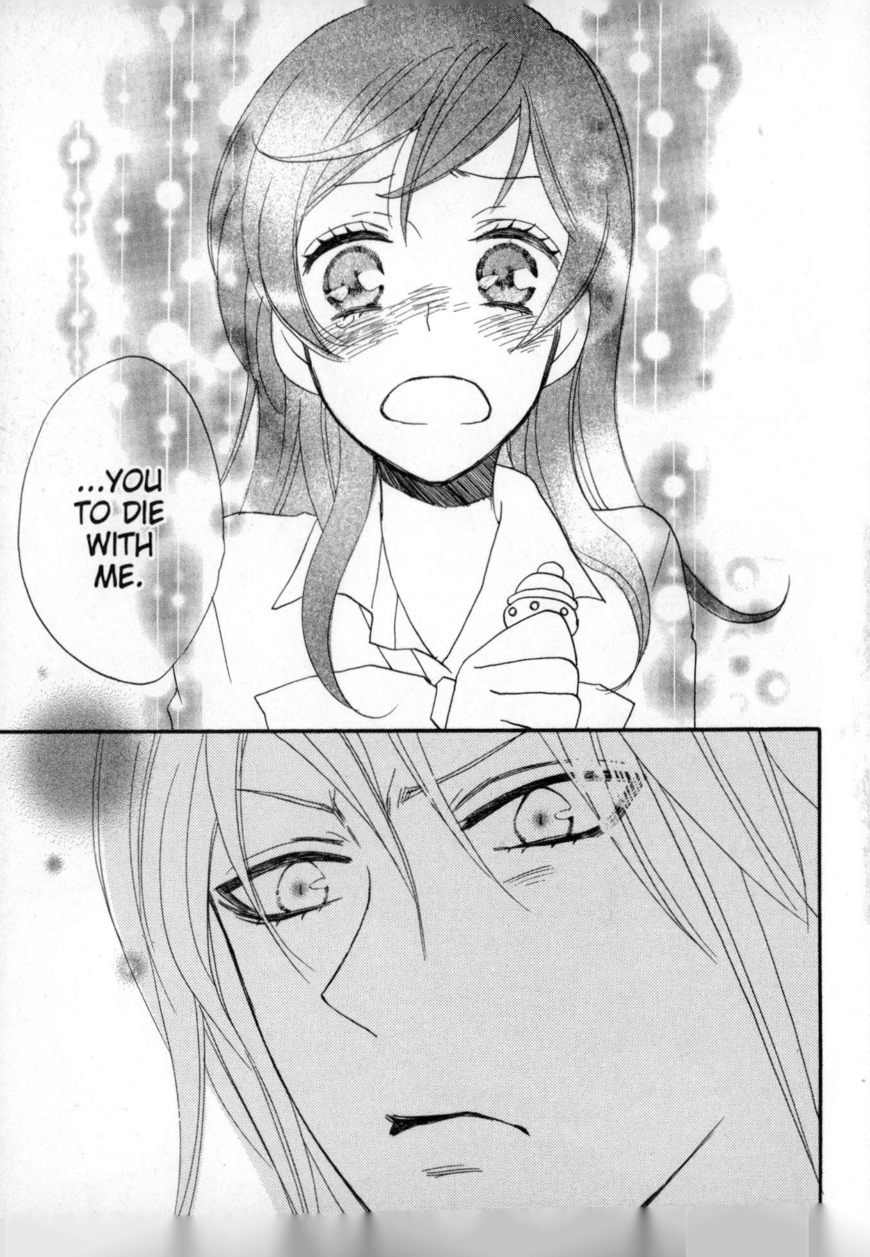
...YOU TO DIE WITH ME.

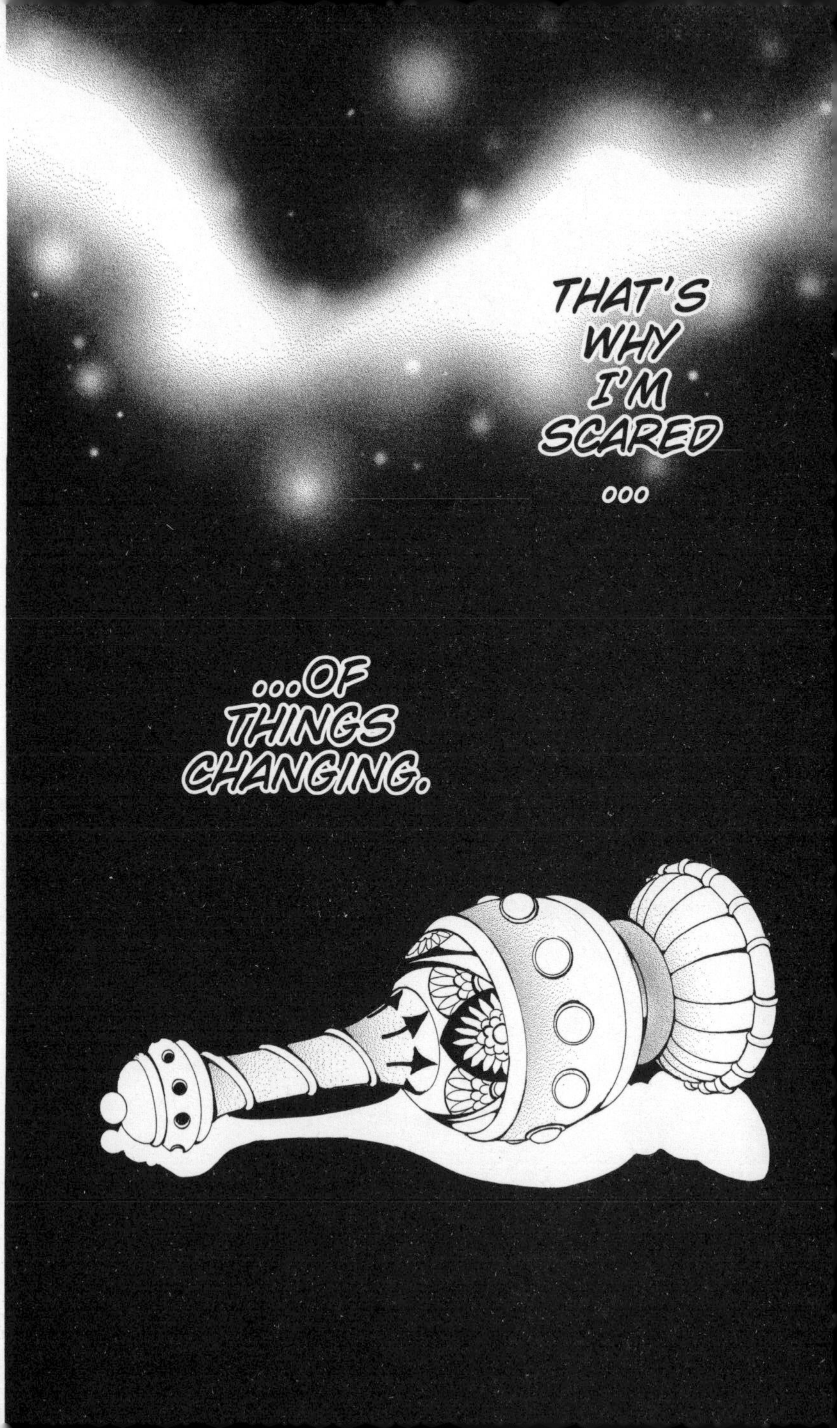
THAT'S WHY I'M SCARED...
...OF THINGS CHANGING.

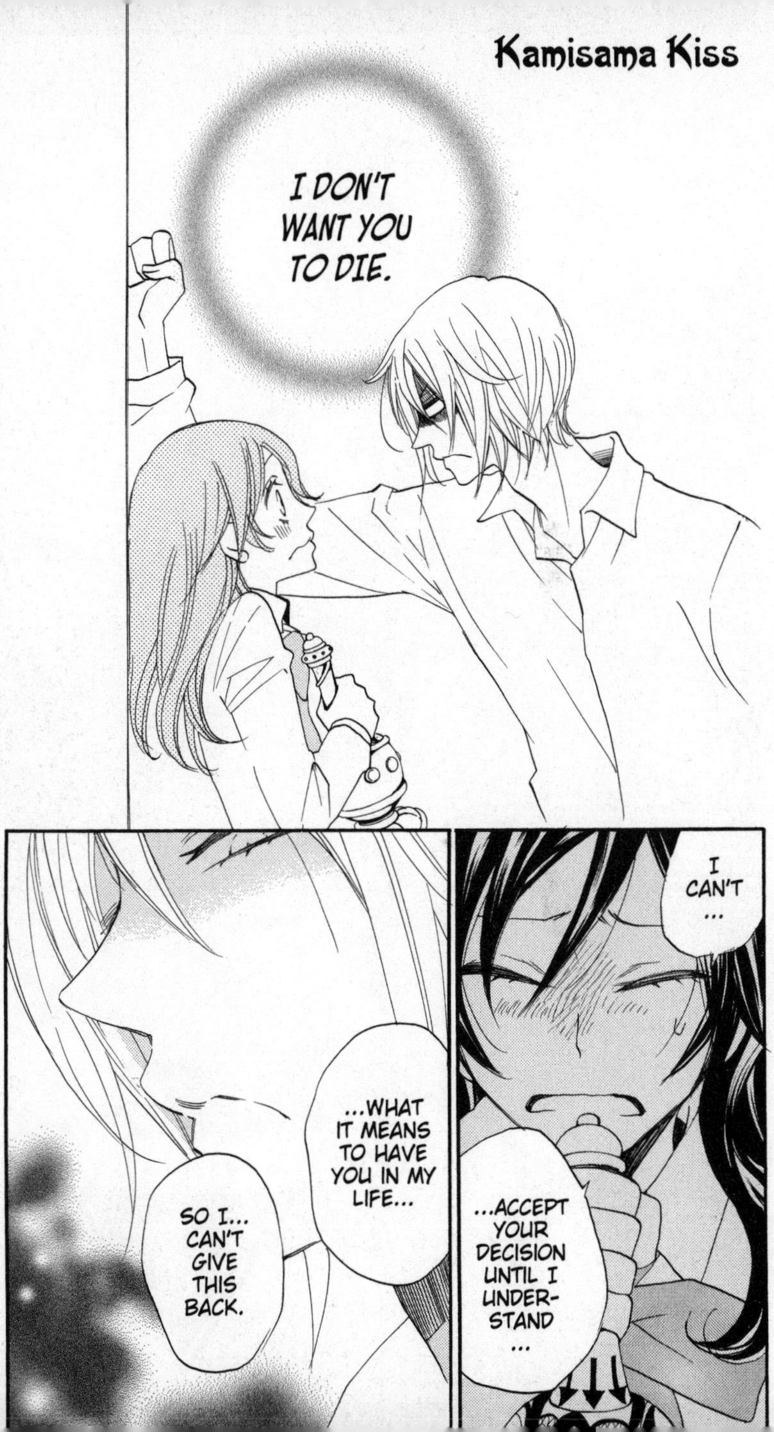
I DON'T WANT YOU TO DIE.
I CAN'T ...
...ACCEPT YOUR DECISION UNTIL I UNDER-STAND ...
...WHAT IT MEANS TO HAVE YOU IN MY LIFE...
SO I... CAN'T GIVE THIS BACK.

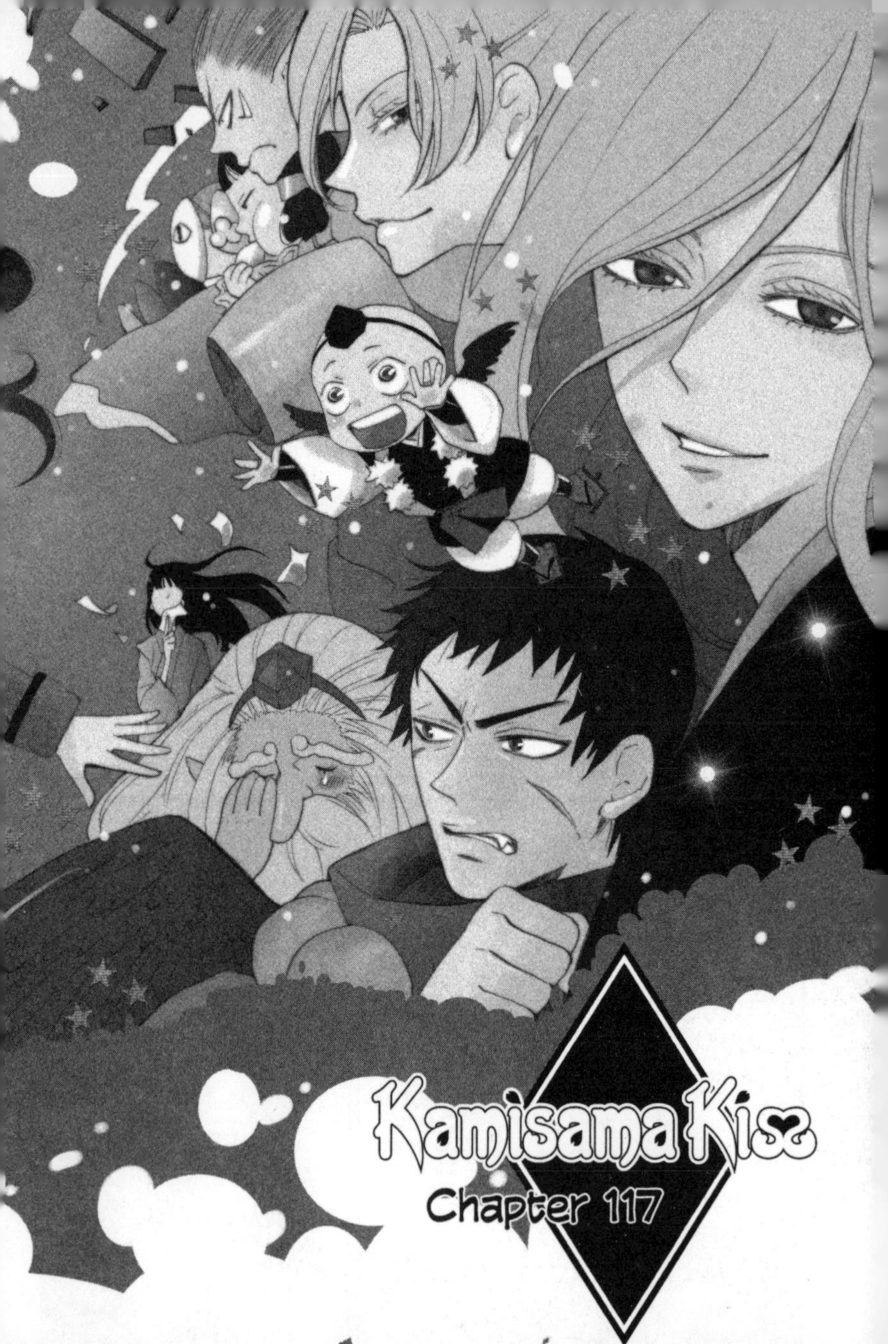
Kamisama Kiss
Chapter 117

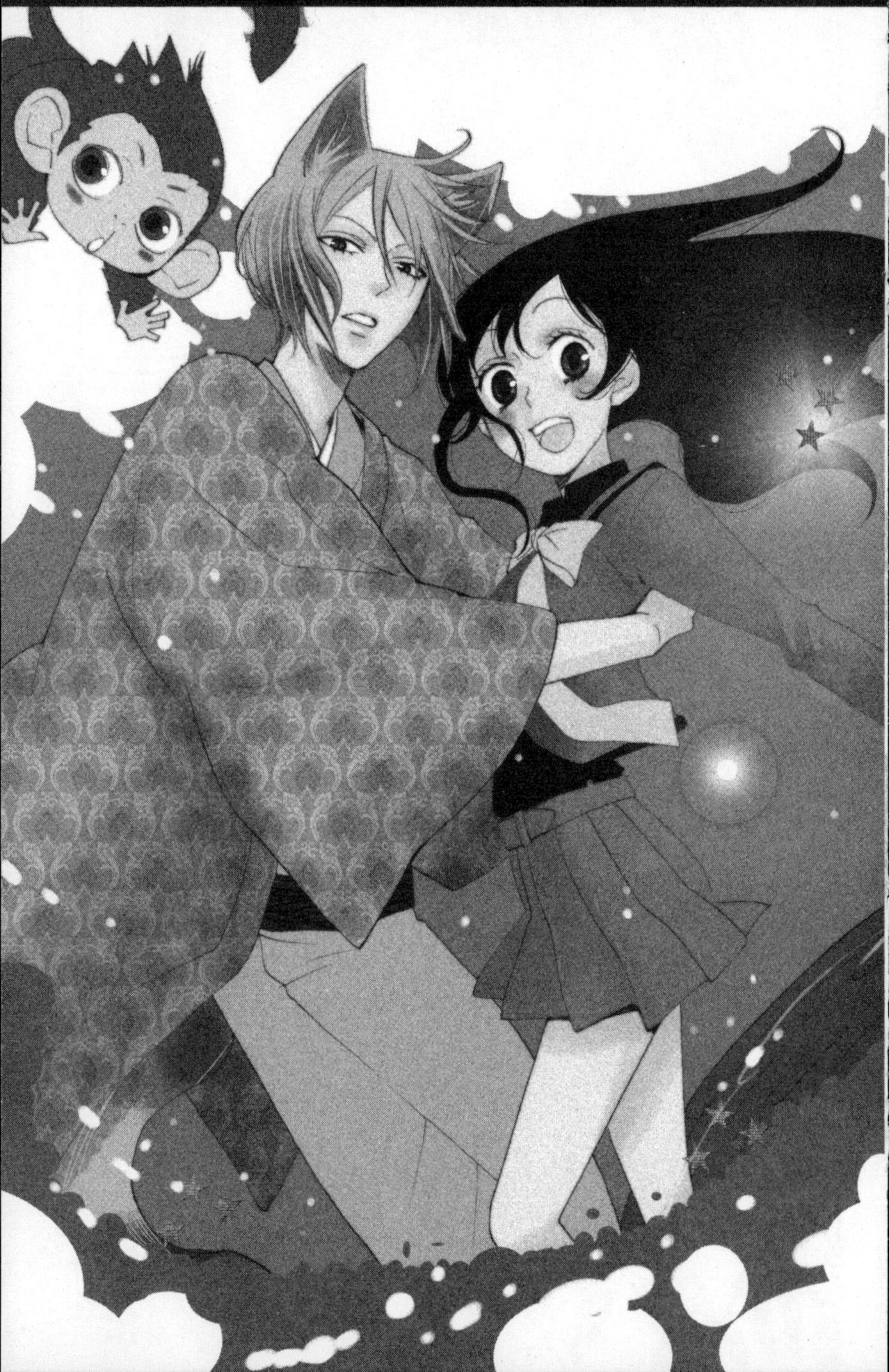

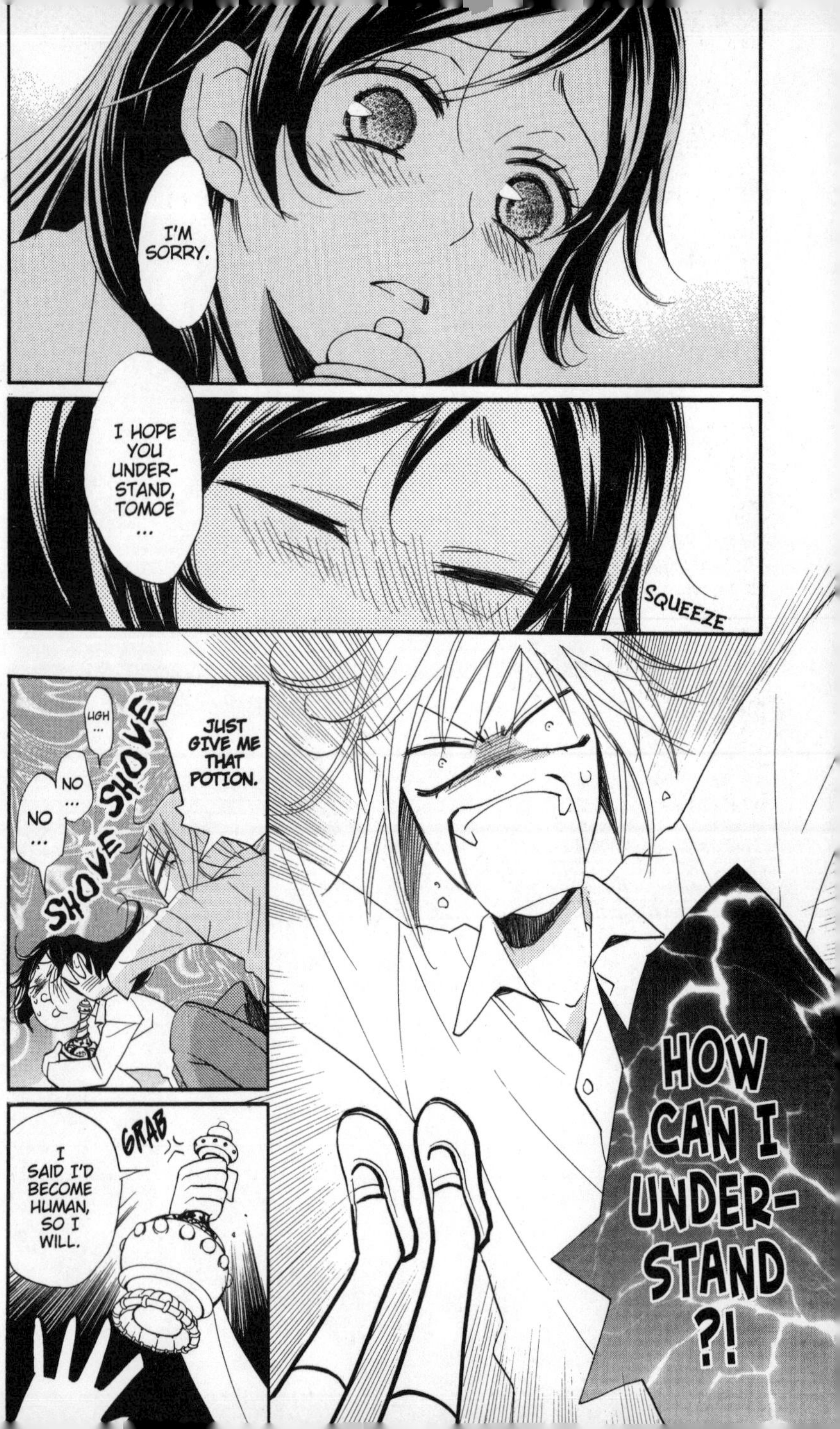
I'M SORRY.
I HOPE YOU UNDER-STAND, TOMOE...
SQUEEZE
HOW CAN I UNDER-STAND?!
JUST GIVE ME THAT POTION.
UGH...
NO...
NO...
SHOVE SHOVE
GRAB
I SAID I'D BECOME HUMAN, SO I WILL.

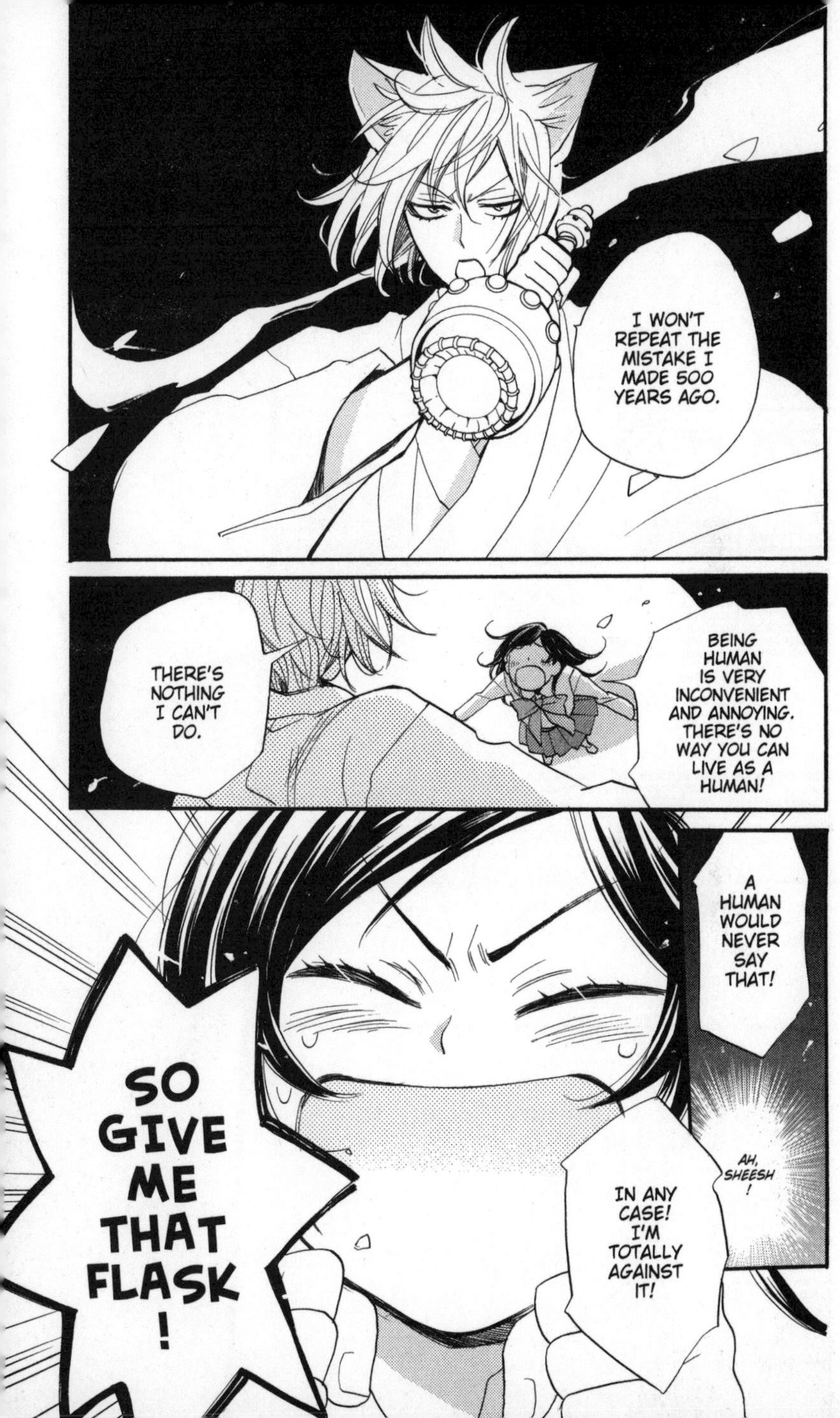
I WON'T REPEAT THE MISTAKE I MADE 500 YEARS AGO.
BEING HUMAN IS VERY INCONVENIENT AND ANNOYING. THERE'S NO WAY YOU CAN LIVE AS A HUMAN!
THERE'S NOTHING I CAN'T DO.
A HUMAN WOULD NEVER SAY THAT!
AH, SHEESH!
IN ANY CASE! I'M TOTALLY AGAINST IT!
SO GIVE ME THAT FLASK!

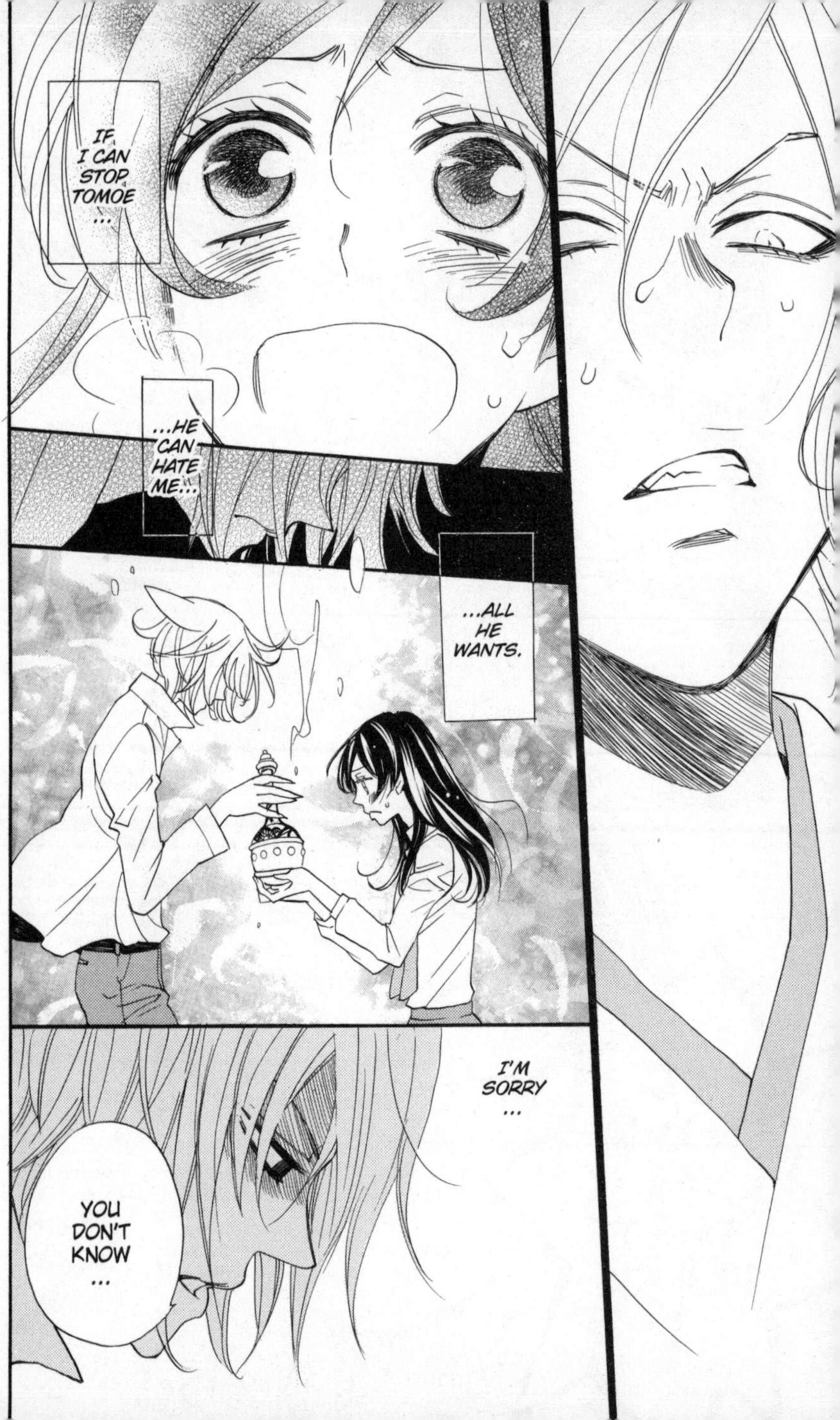
IF I CAN STOP TOMOE ...
...HE CAN HATE ME...
...ALL HE WANTS.
I'M SORRY ...
YOU DON'T KNOW ...

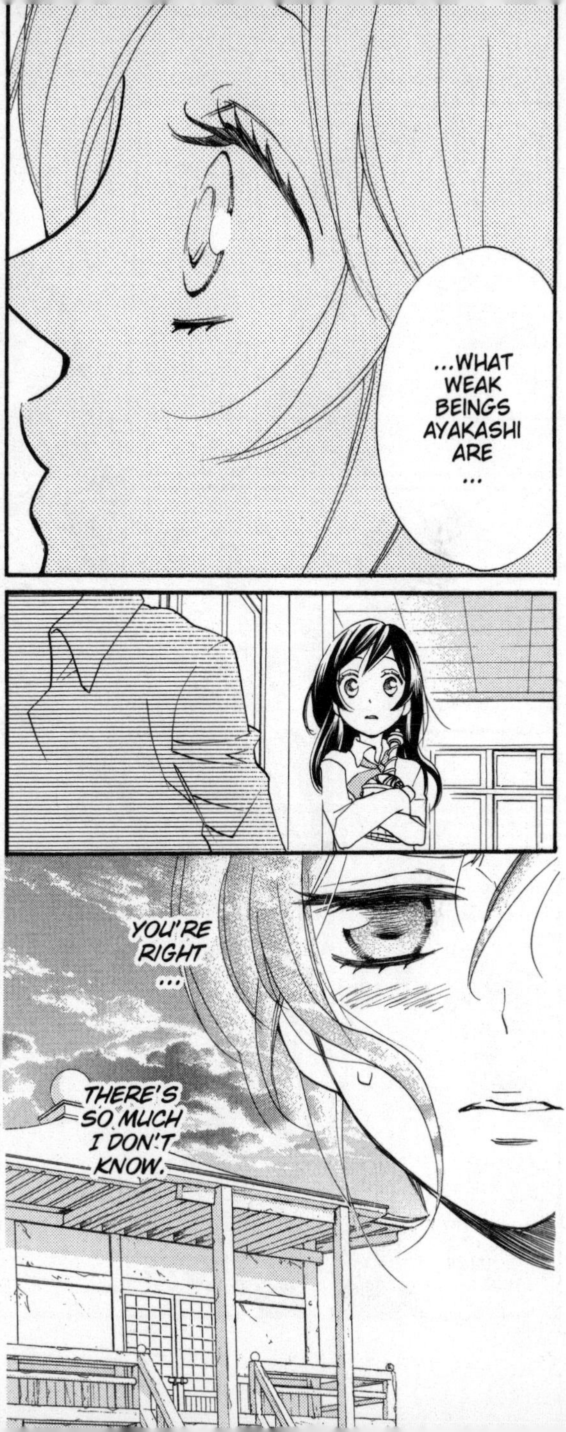
...WHAT WEAK BEINGS AYAKASHI ARE ...
YOU'RE RIGHT ...
THERE'S SO MUCH I DON'T KNOW.

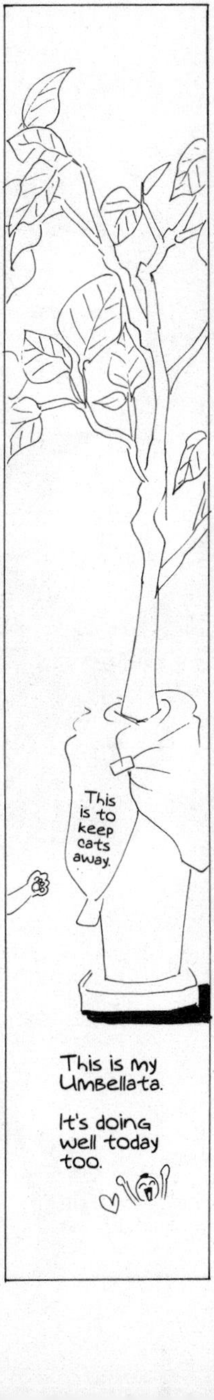
This is to keep cats away.
This is my Umbellata.
It's doing well today too.

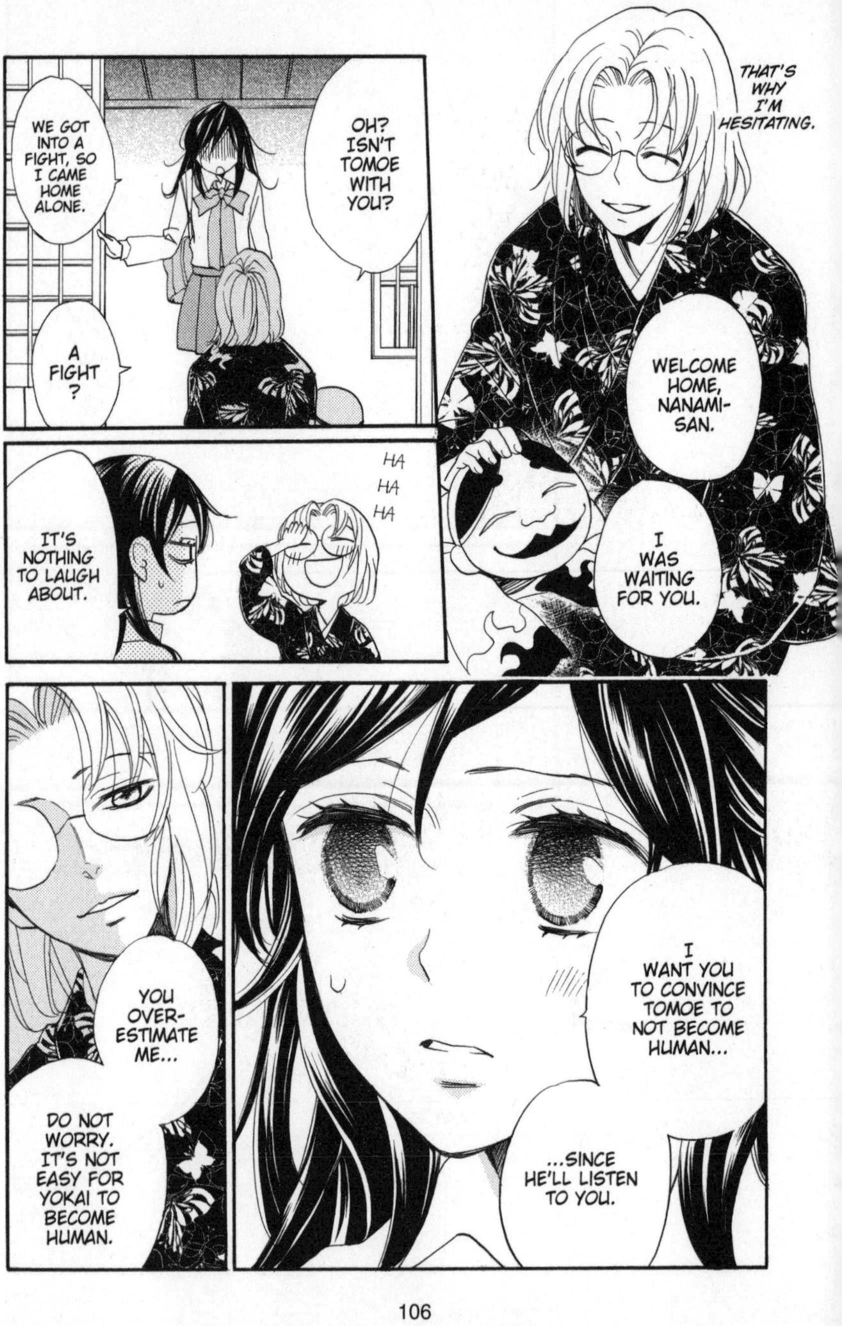
THAT'S WHY I'M HESITATING.
WELCOME HOME, NANAMI-SAN.
I WAS WAITING FOR YOU.
OH? ISN'T TOMOE WITH YOU?
WE GOT INTO A FIGHT, SO I CAME HOME ALONE.
A FIGHT?
HA HA HA
IT'S NOTHING TO LAUGH ABOUT.
I WANT YOU TO CONVINCE TOMOE TO NOT BECOME HUMAN...
...SINCE HE'LL LISTEN TO YOU.
YOU OVER-ESTIMATE ME...
DO NOT WORRY. IT'S NOT EASY FOR YOKAI TO BECOME HUMAN.

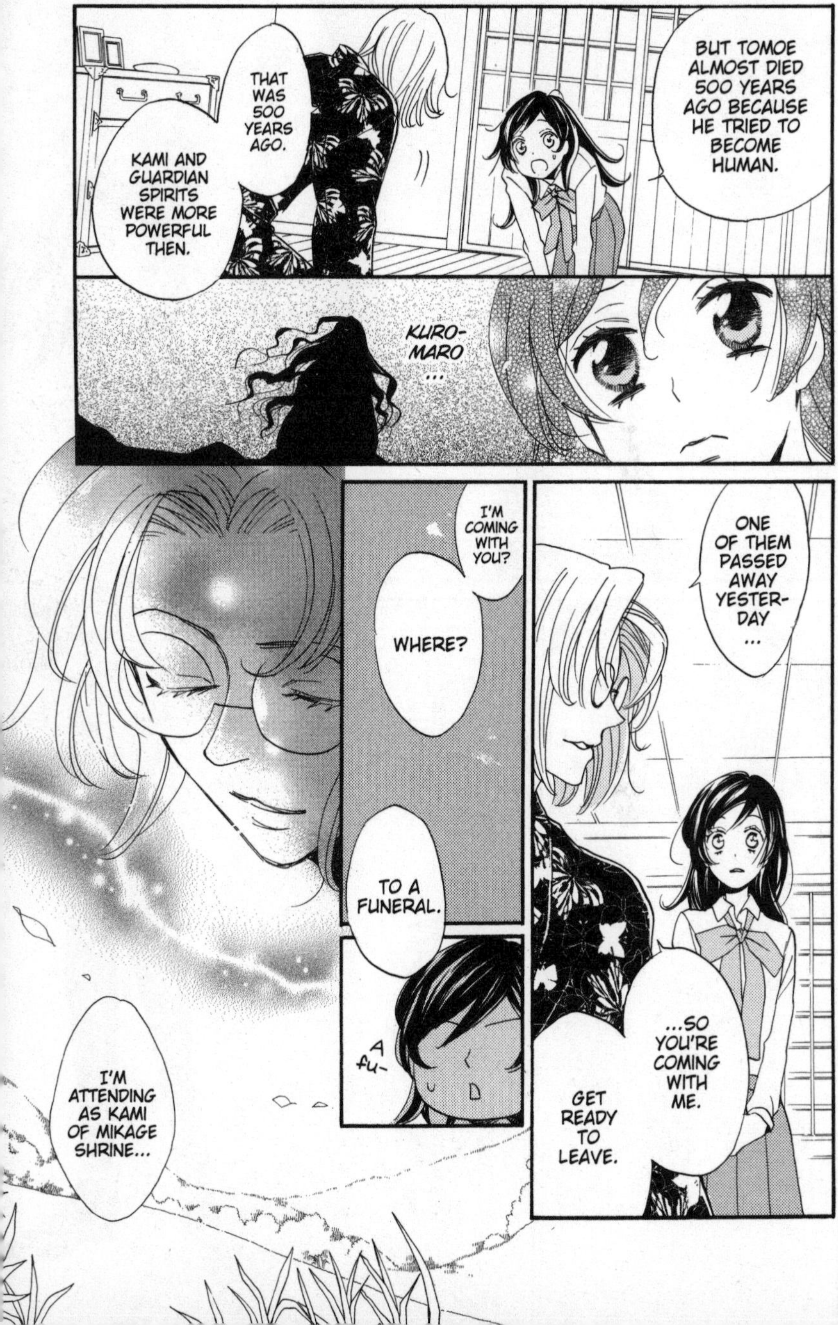
BUT TOMOE ALMOST DIED 500 YEARS AGO BECAUSE HE TRIED TO BECOME HUMAN.
THAT WAS 500 YEARS AGO.
KAMI AND GUARDIAN SPIRITS WERE MORE POWERFUL THEN.
KURO-MARO ...
ONE OF THEM PASSED AWAY YESTER-DAY ...
I'M ATTENDING AS KAMI OF MIKAGE SHRINE...
...SO YOU'RE COMING WITH ME.
GET READY TO LEAVE.
I'M COMING WITH YOU?
WHERE?
TO A FUNERAL.
A fu-

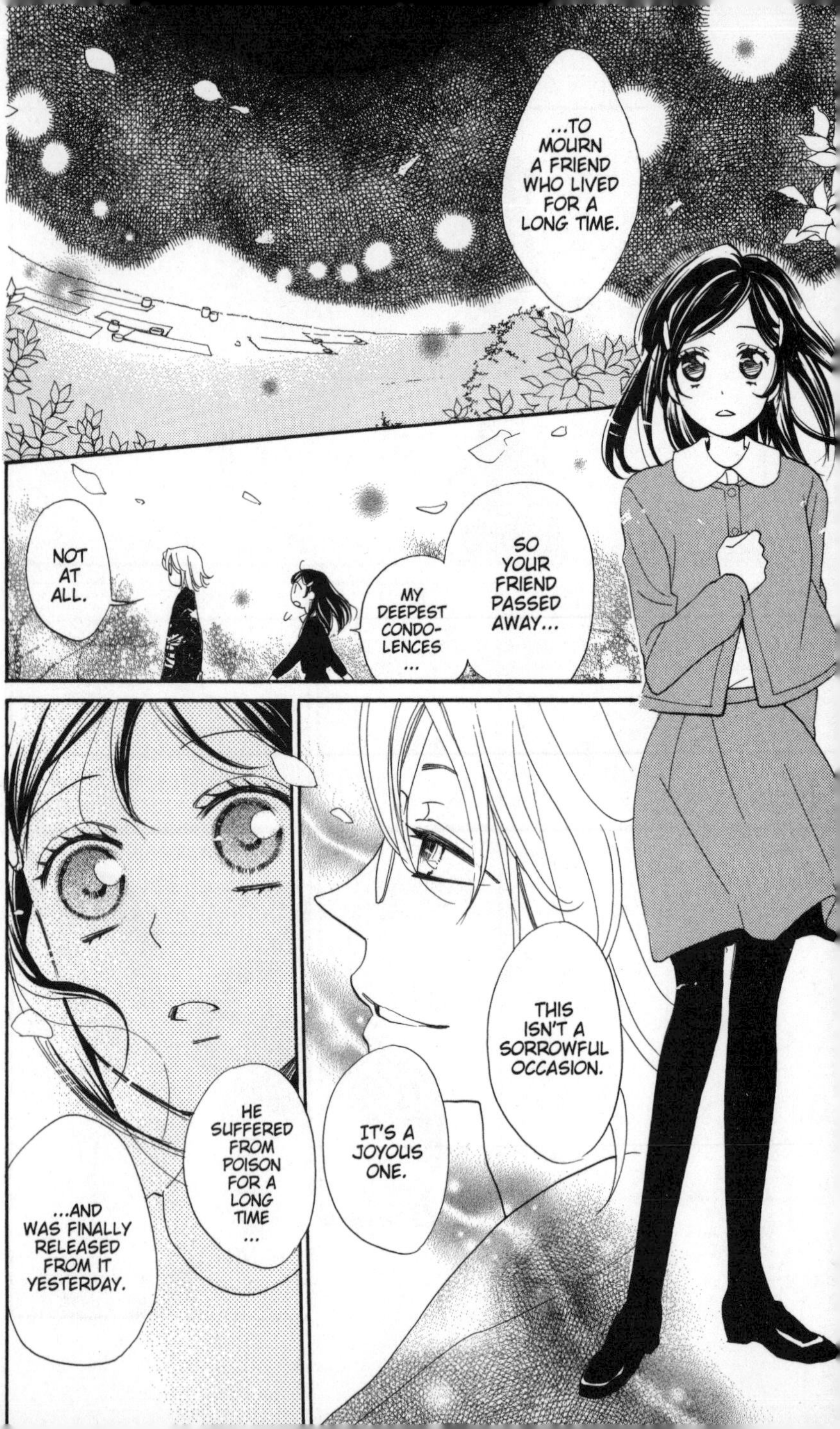
...TO MOURN A FRIEND WHO LIVED FOR A LONG TIME.
SO YOUR FRIEND PASSED AWAY...
MY DEEPEST CONDO-LENCES...
NOT AT ALL.
THIS ISN'T A SORROWFUL OCCASION.
IT'S A JOYOUS ONE.
HE SUFFERED FROM POISON FOR A LONG TIME...
...AND WAS FINALLY RELEASED FROM IT YESTERDAY.

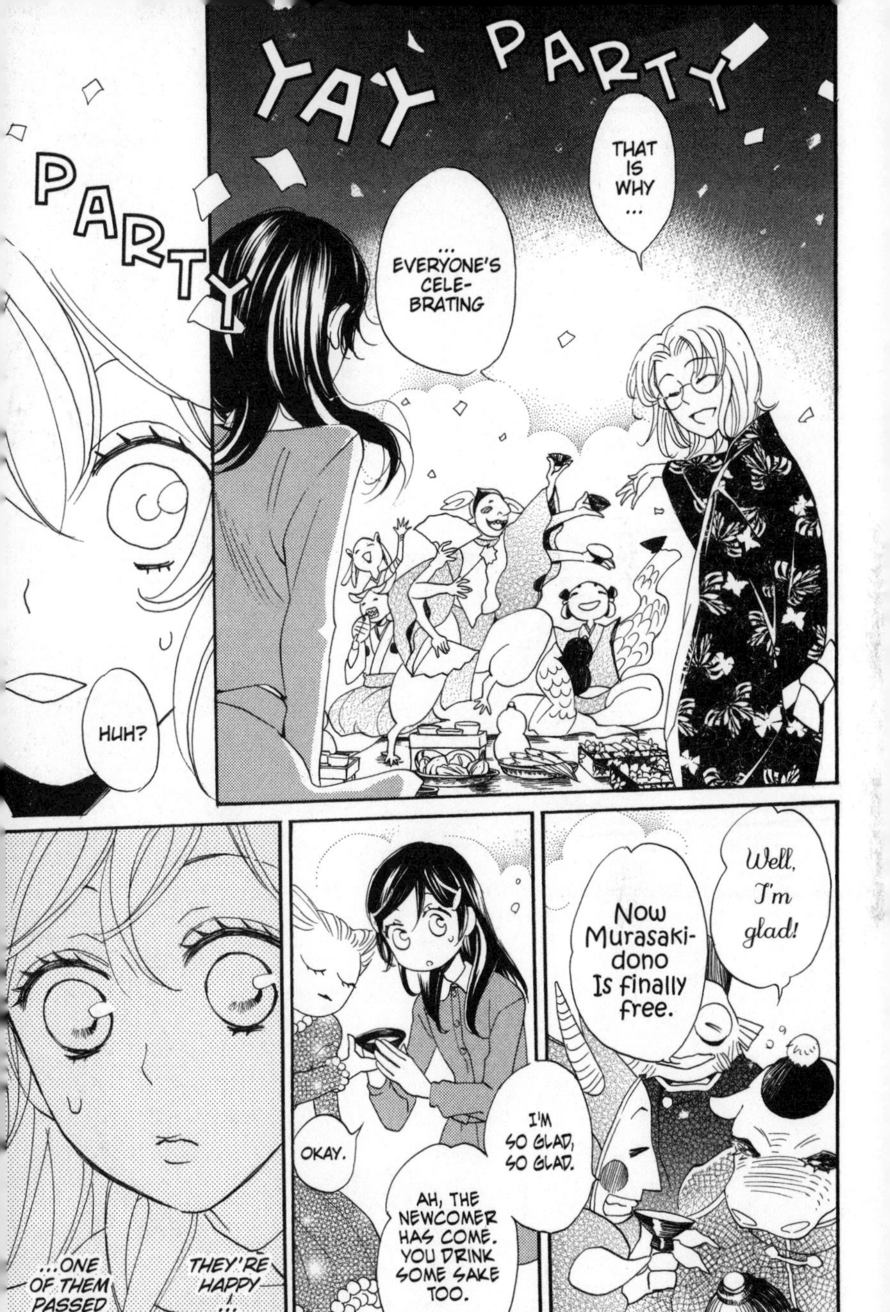
YAY PARTY
PARTY PARTY
THAT IS WHY...
...EVERYONE'S CELE-BRATING
HUH?
Well, I'm glad!
Now Murasaki-dono Is finally free.
I'M SO GLAD, SO GLAD.
AH, THE NEWCOMER HAS COME. YOU DRINK SOME SAKE TOO.
OKAY.
THEY'RE HAPPY...
...ONE OF THEM PASSED AWAY?

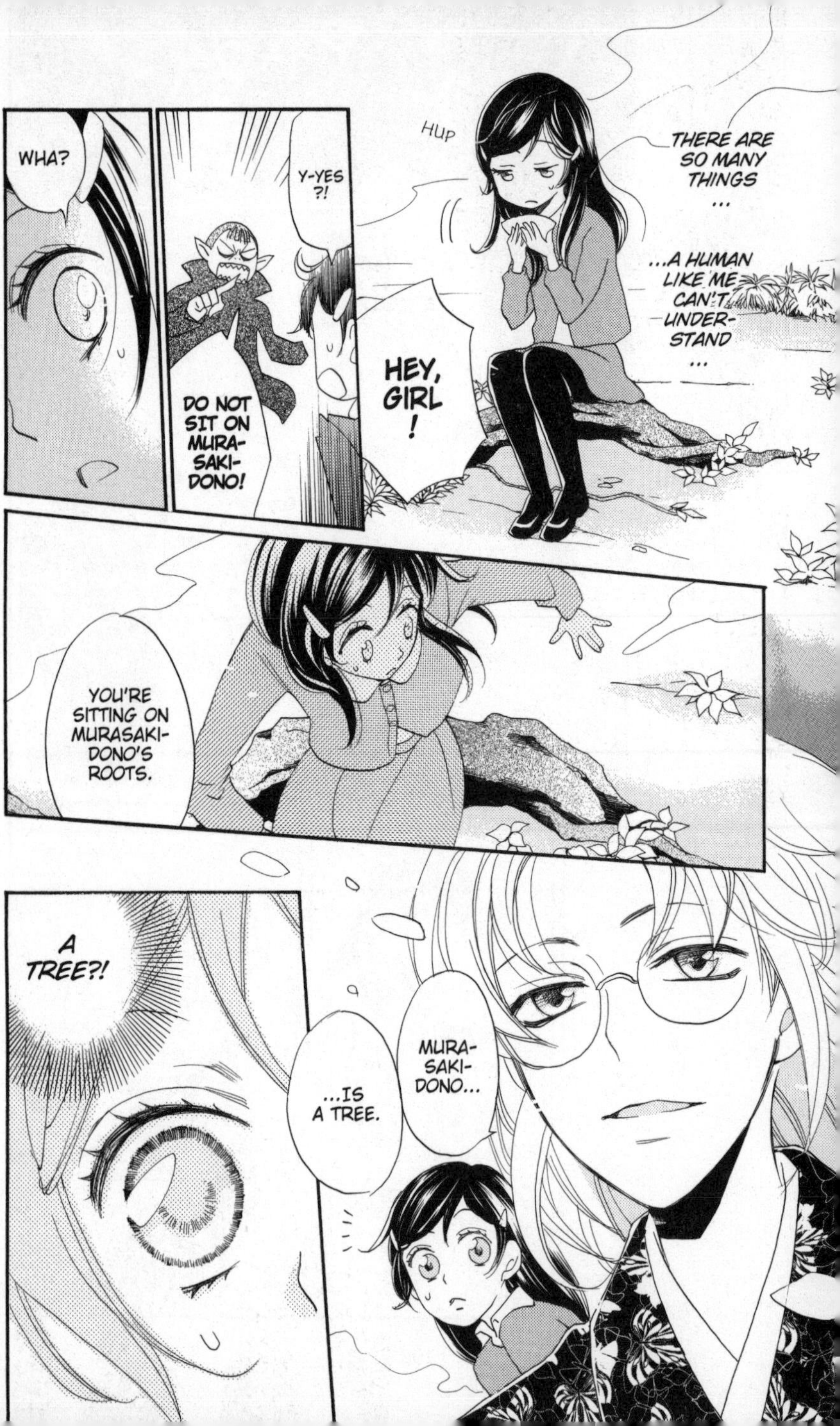
THERE ARE SO MANY THINGS ...
HUP
...A HUMAN LIKE ME CAN'T UNDERSTAND ...
HEY, GIRL!
Y-YES ?!
DO NOT SIT ON MURA-SAKI-DONO!
WHA?
YOU'RE SITTING ON MURASAKI-DONO'S ROOTS.
MURA-SAKI-DONO...
...IS A TREE.
A TREE?!

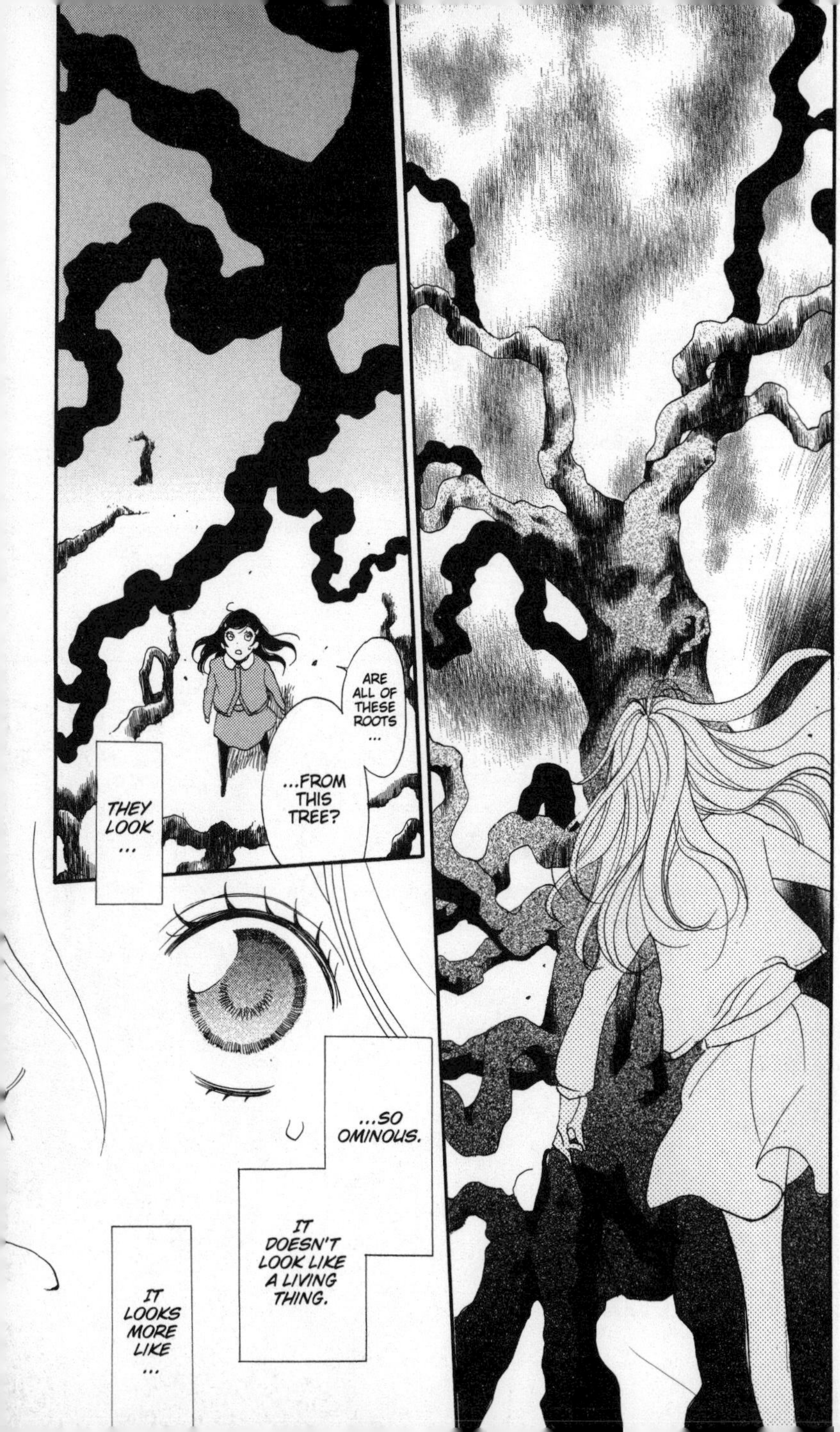
ARE ALL OF THESE ROOTS ...
...FROM THIS TREE?
THEY LOOK ...
...SO OMINOUS.
IT DOESN'T LOOK LIKE A LIVING THING.
IT LOOKS MORE LIKE ...

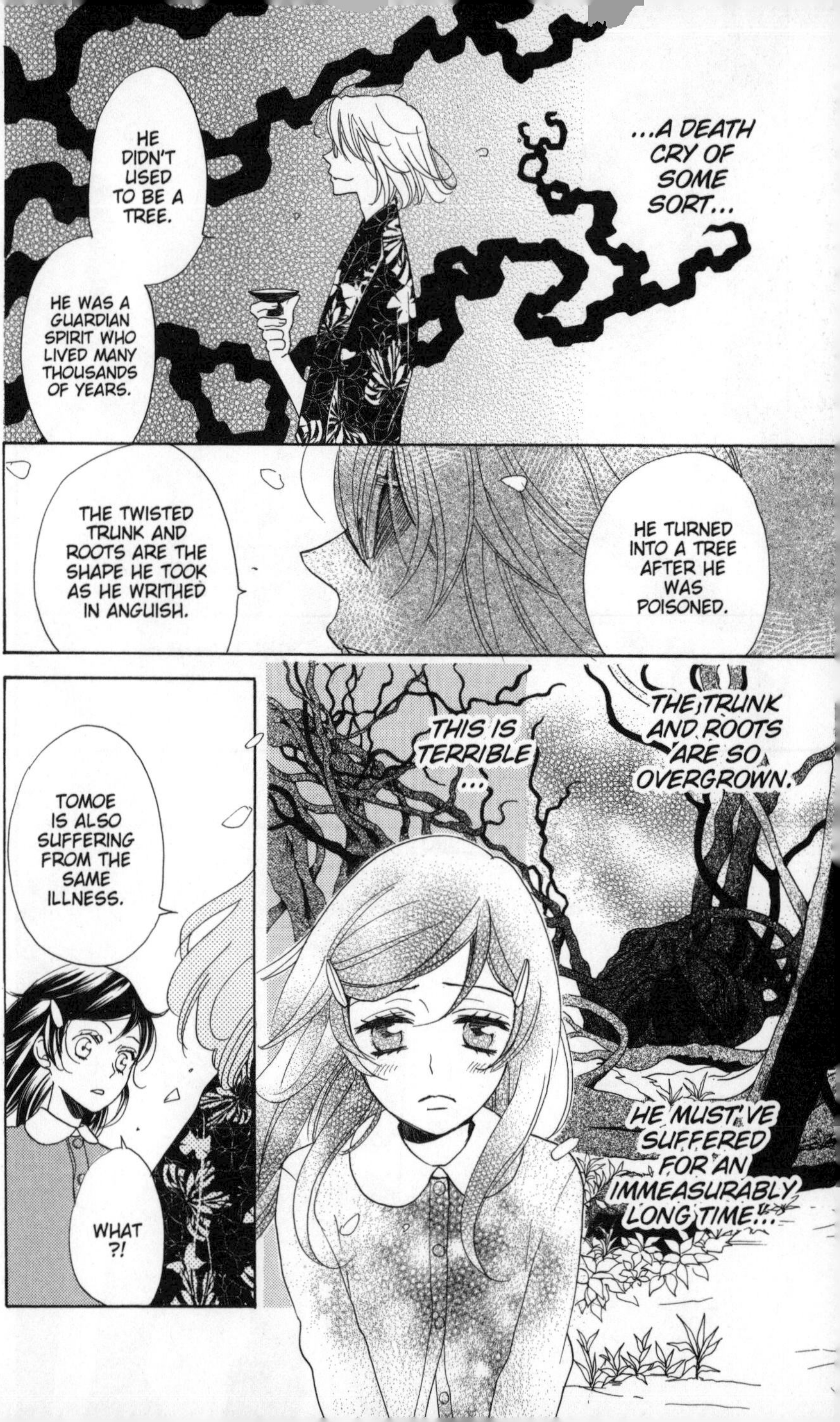
...A DEATH CRY OF SOME SORT...
HE DIDN'T USED TO BE A TREE.
HE WAS A GUARDIAN SPIRIT WHO LIVED MANY THOUSANDS OF YEARS.
HE TURNED INTO A TREE AFTER HE WAS POISONED.
THE TWISTED TRUNK AND ROOTS ARE THE SHAPE HE TOOK AS HE WRITHED IN ANGUISH.
THE TRUNK AND ROOTS ARE SO OVERGROWN.
THIS IS TERRIBLE...
HE MUST'VE SUFFERED FOR AN IMMEASURABLY LONG TIME...
TOMOE IS ALSO SUFFERING FROM THE SAME ILLNESS.
WHAT?!

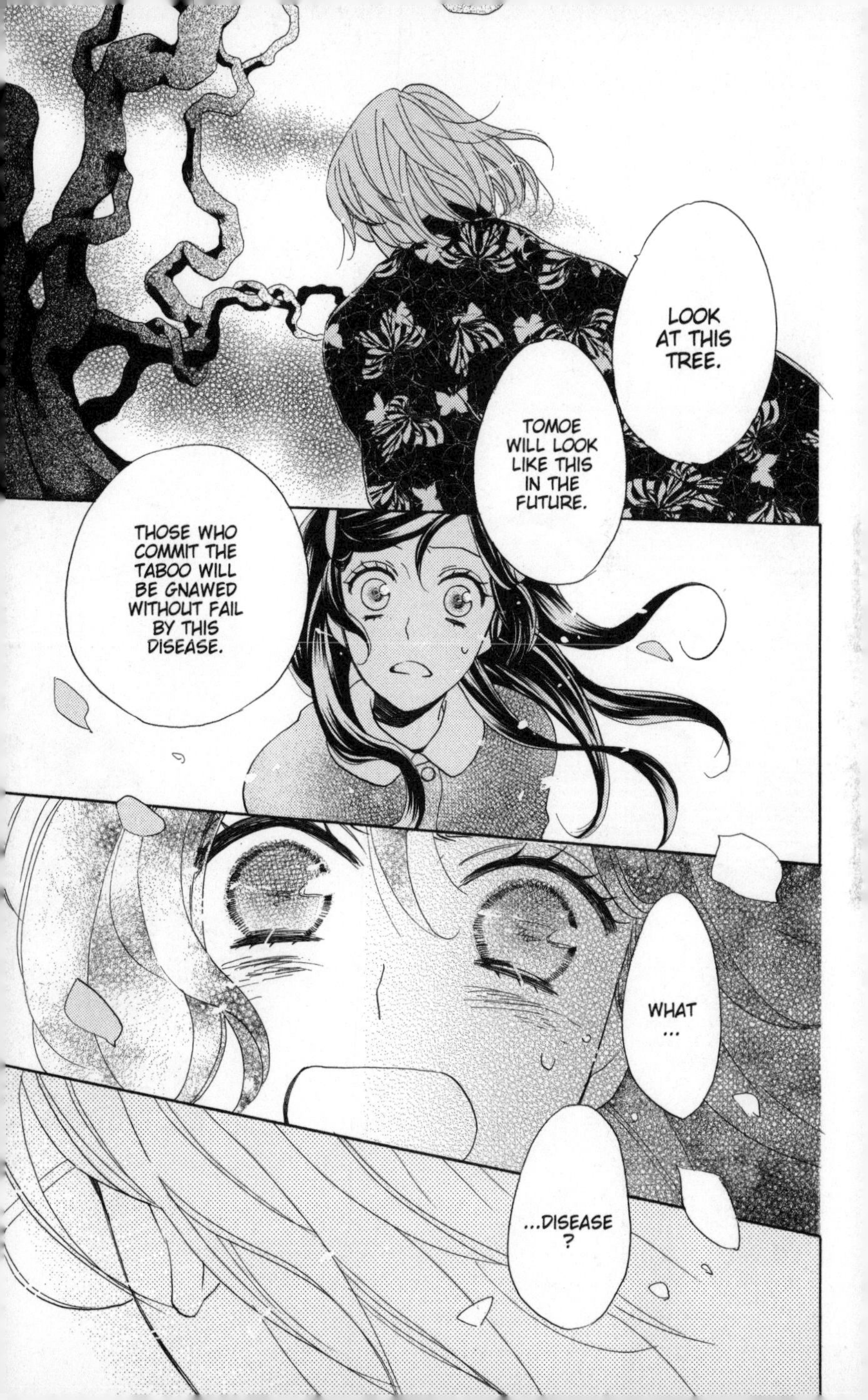
LOOK AT THIS TREE.
TOMOE WILL LOOK LIKE THIS IN THE FUTURE.
THOSE WHO COMMIT THE TABOO WILL BE GNAWED WITHOUT FAIL BY THIS DISEASE.
WHAT...
...DISEASE?

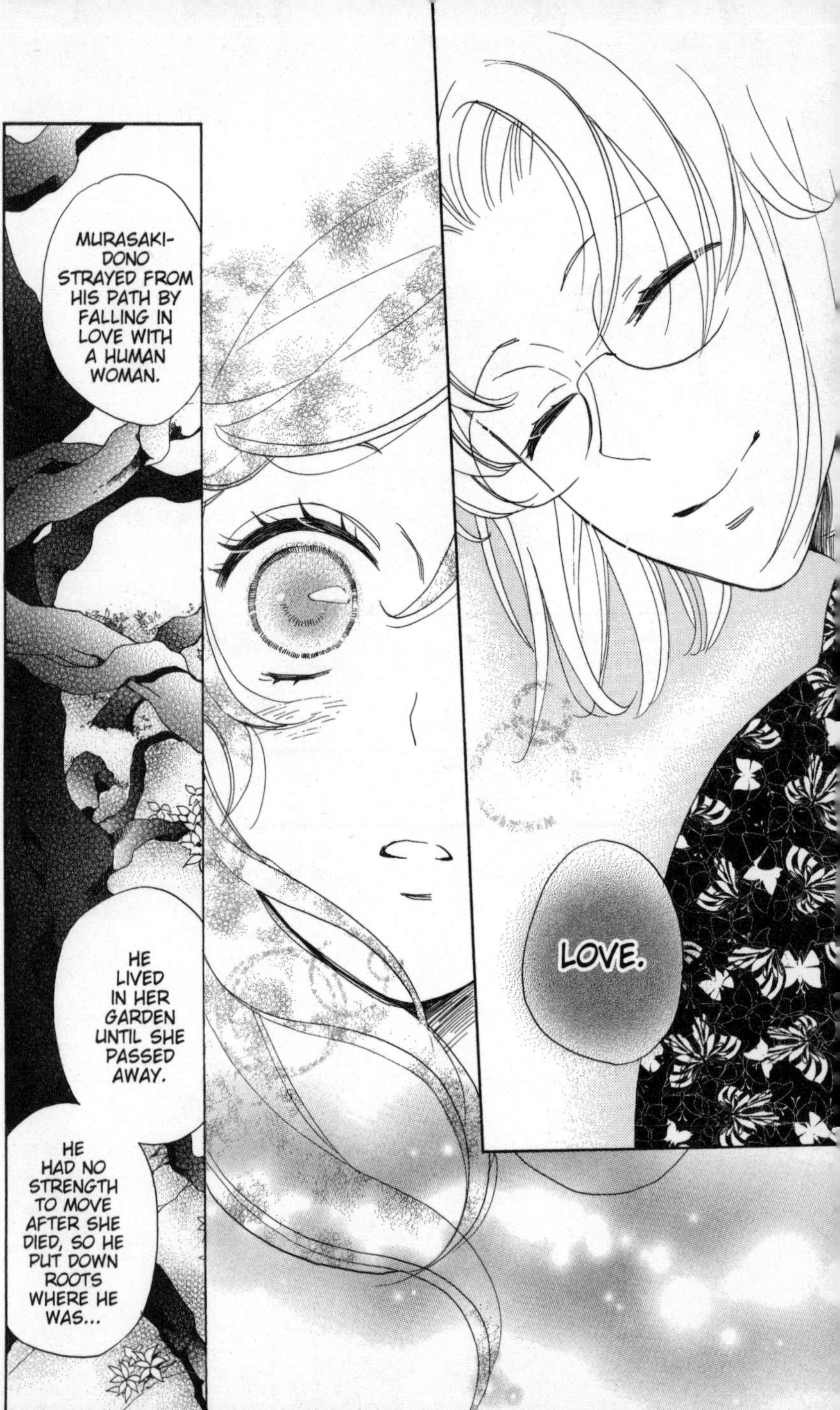
LOVE.
MURASAKI-DONO STRAYED FROM HIS PATH BY FALLING IN LOVE WITH A HUMAN WOMAN.
HE LIVED IN HER GARDEN UNTIL SHE PASSED AWAY.
HE HAD NO STRENGTH TO MOVE AFTER SHE DIED, SO HE PUT DOWN ROOTS WHERE HE WAS...

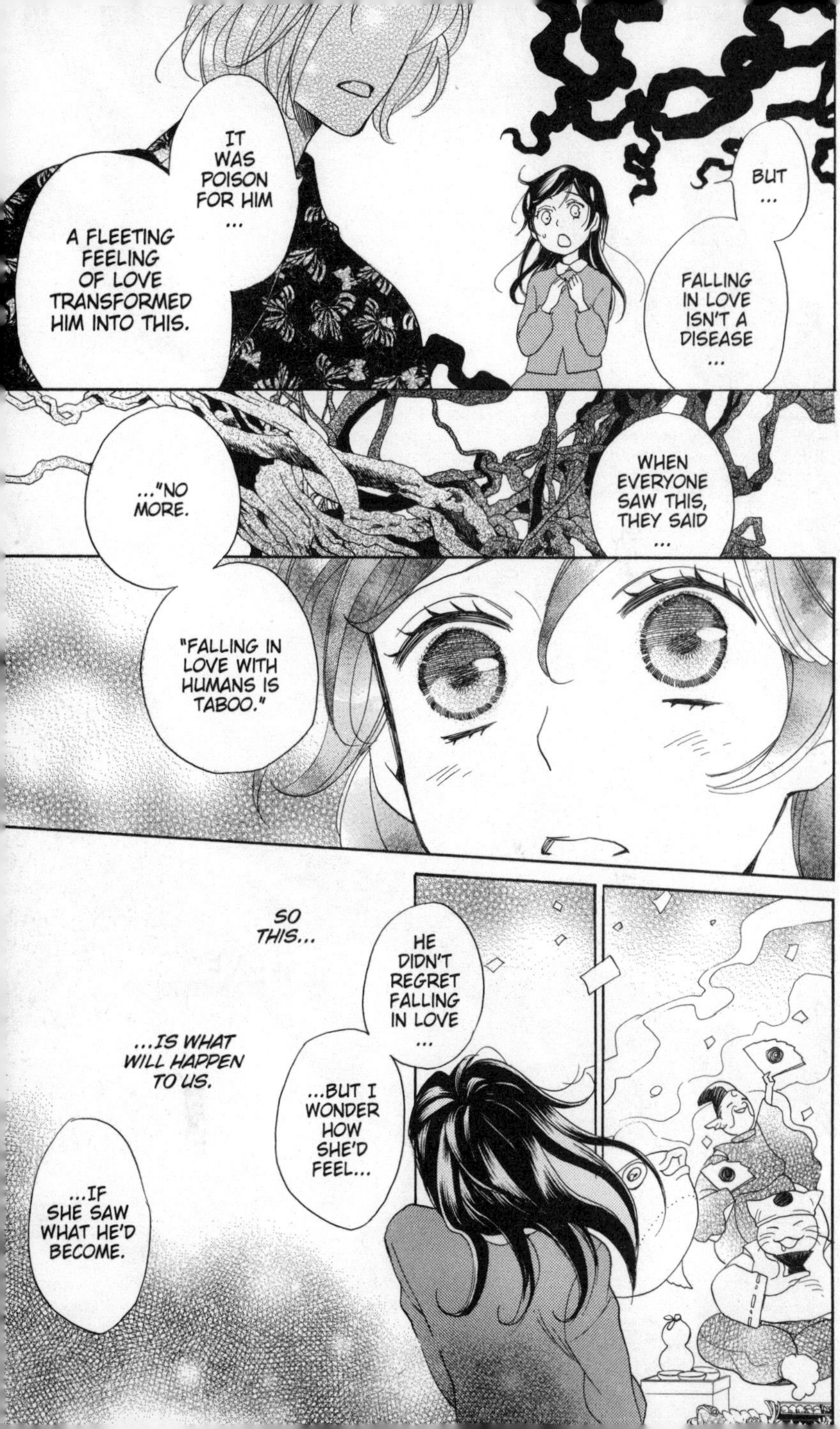

BUT... FALLING IN LOVE ISN'T A DISEASE...
IT WAS POISON FOR HIM...
A FLEETING FEELING OF LOVE TRANSFORMED HIM INTO THIS.
WHEN EVERYONE SAW THIS, THEY SAID...
..."NO MORE.
"FALLING IN LOVE WITH HUMANS IS TABOO."
HE DIDN'T REGRET FALLING IN LOVE...
...BUT I WONDER HOW SHE'D FEEL...
...IF SHE SAW WHAT HE'D BECOME.
SO THIS...
...IS WHAT WILL HAPPEN TO US.

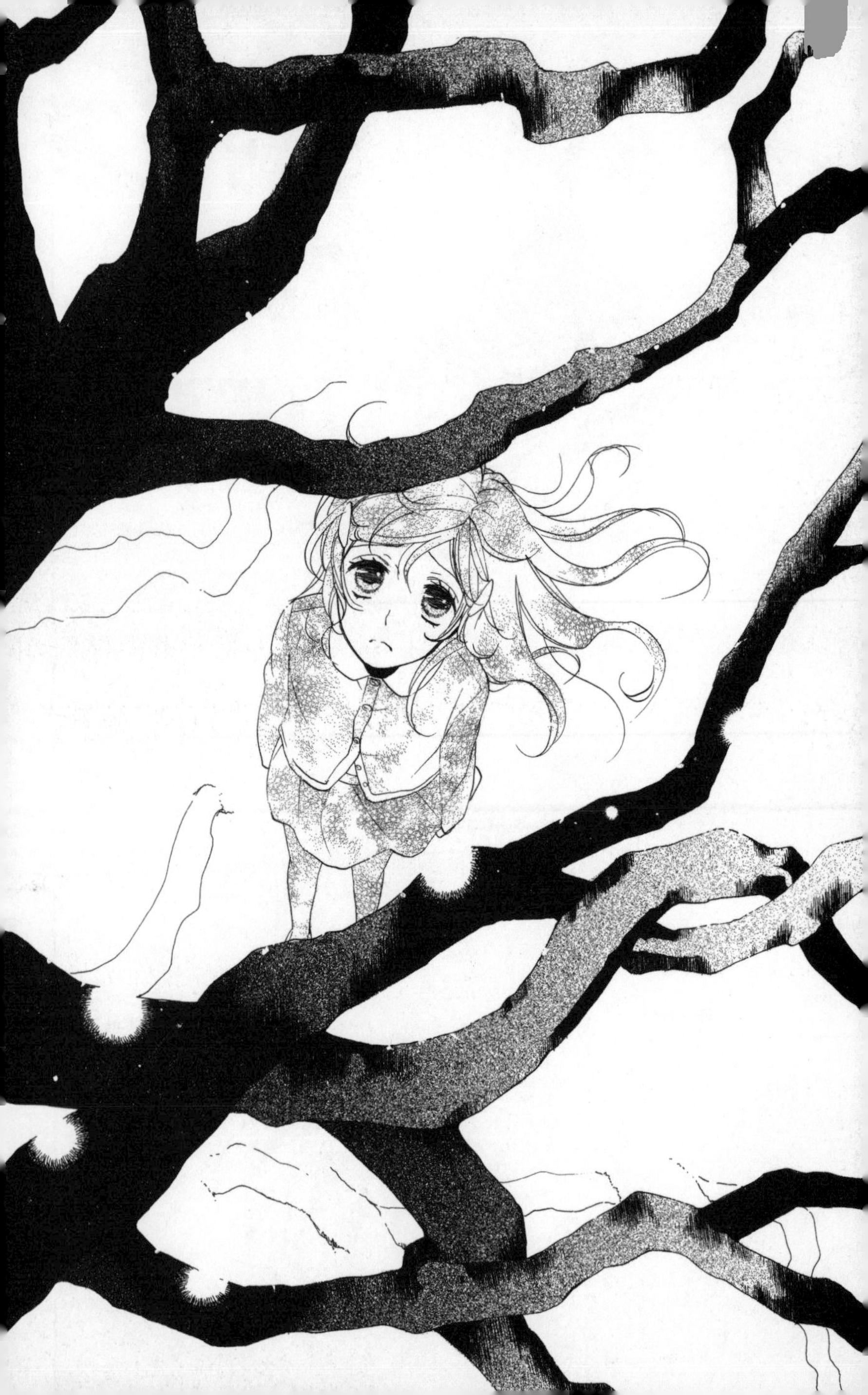

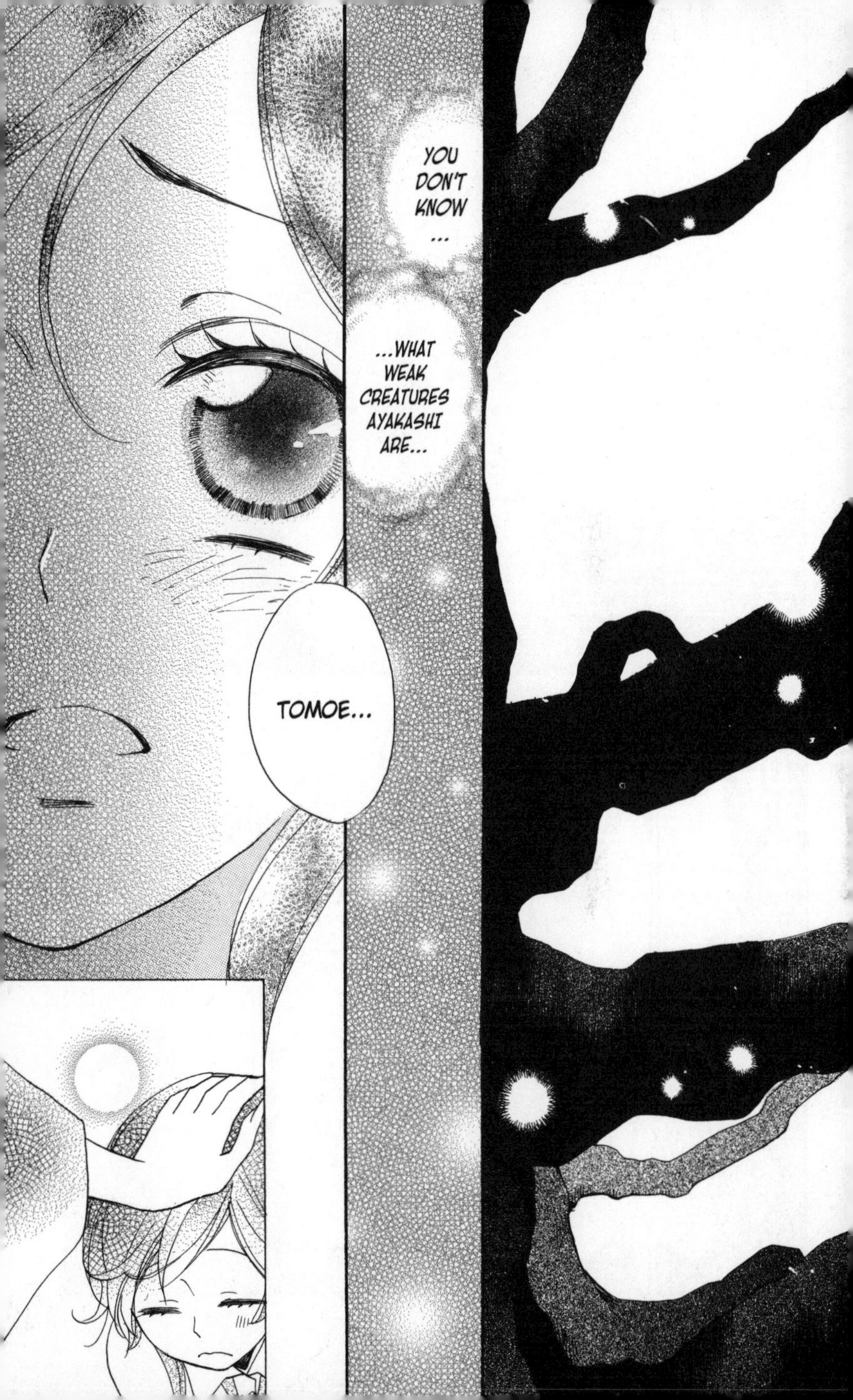
YOU DON'T KNOW ...
...WHAT WEAK CREATURES AYAKASHI ARE...
TOMOE...

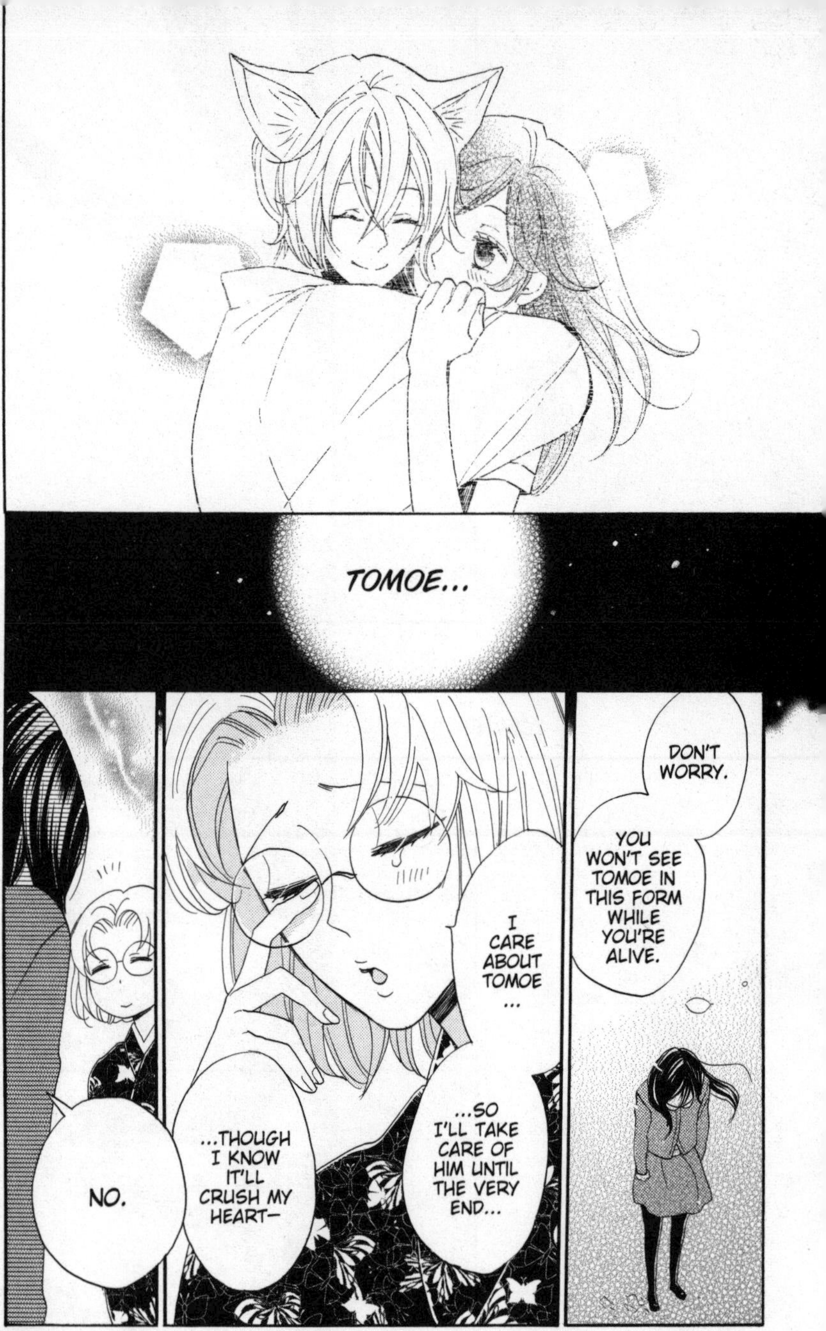
TOMOE...
DON'T WORRY.
YOU WON'T SEE TOMOE IN THIS FORM WHILE YOU'RE ALIVE.
I CARE ABOUT TOMOE ...
...SO I'LL TAKE CARE OF HIM UNTIL THE VERY END...
...THOUGH I KNOW IT'LL CRUSH MY HEART—
NO.

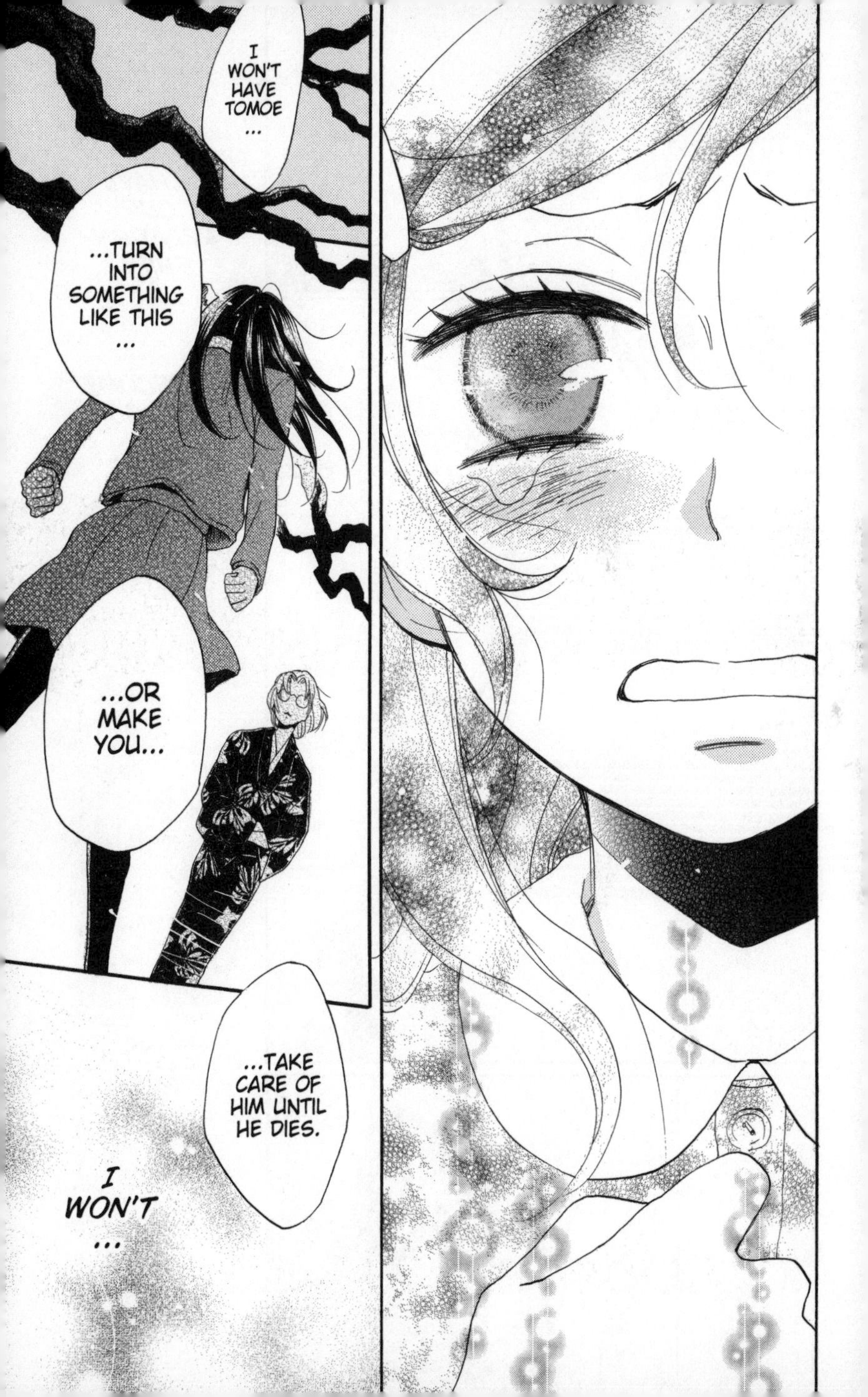
I WON'T HAVE TOMOE ...
...TURN INTO SOMETHING LIKE THIS ...
...OR MAKE YOU...
...TAKE CARE OF HIM UNTIL HE DIES.
I WON'T ...

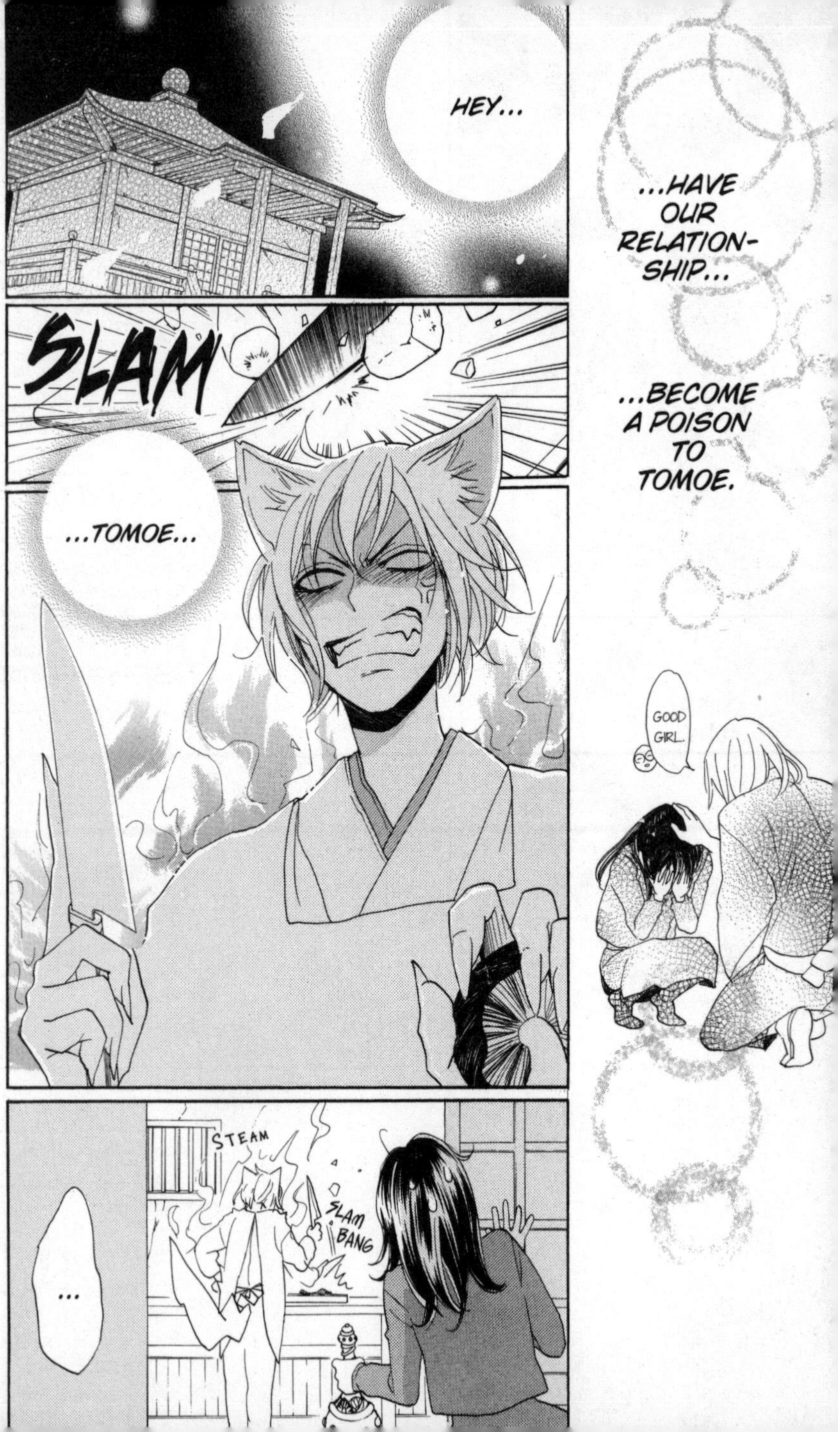
...HAVE OUR RELATIONSHIP...
...BECOME A POISON TO TOMOE.
GOOD GIRL.
HEY...
SLAM
...TOMOE...
STEAM
SLAM
BANG
...

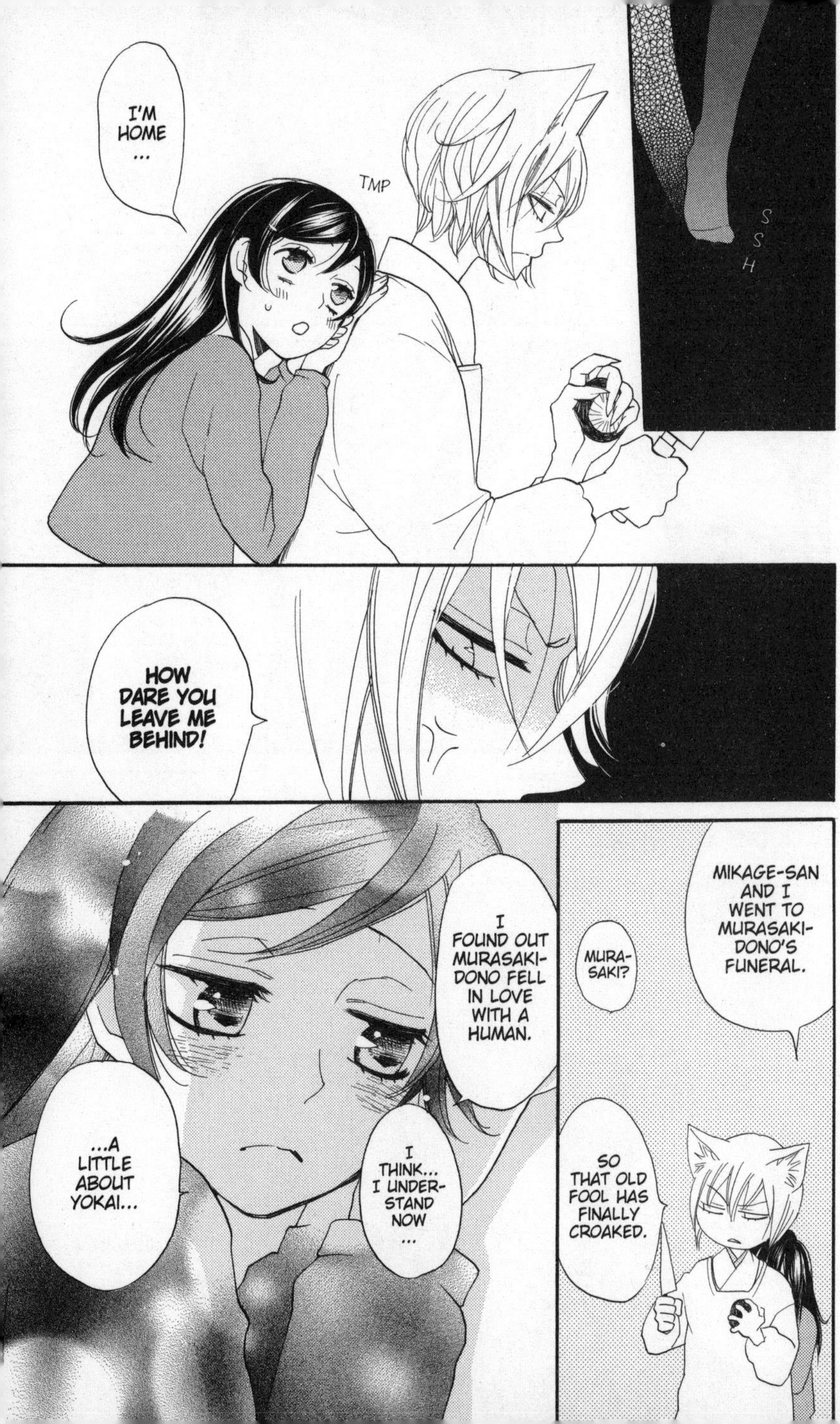
SSH
TMP
I'M HOME...
HOW DARE YOU LEAVE ME BEHIND!
MIKAGE-SAN AND I WENT TO MURASAKI-DONO'S FUNERAL.
MURA-SAKI?
SO THAT OLD FOOL HAS FINALLY CROAKED.
I FOUND OUT MURASAKI-DONO FELL IN LOVE WITH A HUMAN.
I THINK... I UNDER-STAND NOW...
...A LITTLE ABOUT YOKAI...

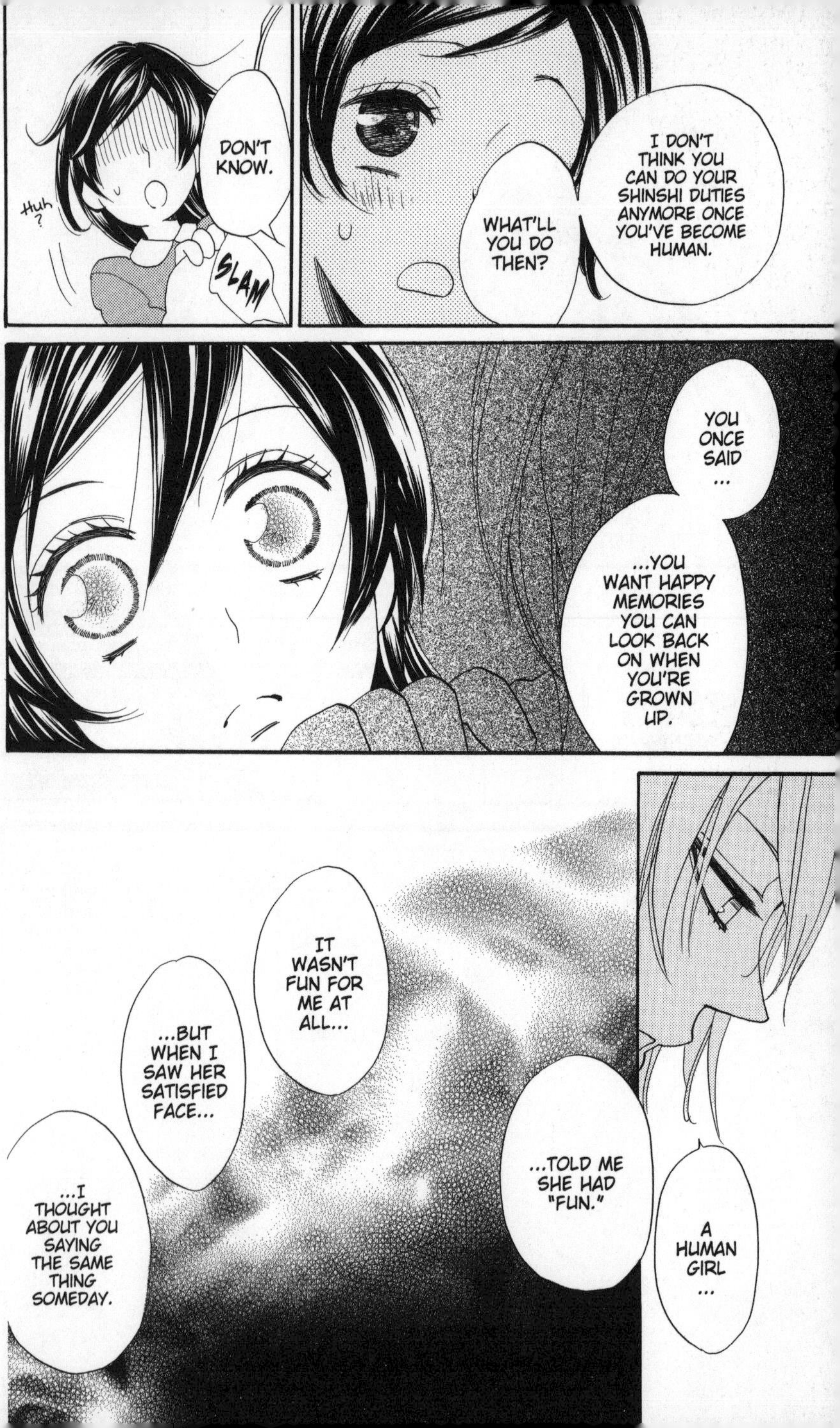
I DON'T THINK YOU CAN DO YOUR SHINSHI DUTIES ANYMORE ONCE YOU'VE BECOME HUMAN.
WHAT'LL YOU DO THEN?
DON'T KNOW.
Huh?
SLAM
YOU ONCE SAID ...
...YOU WANT HAPPY MEMORIES YOU CAN LOOK BACK ON WHEN YOU'RE GROWN UP.
A HUMAN GIRL ...
...TOLD ME SHE HAD "FUN."
IT WASN'T FUN FOR ME AT ALL...
...BUT WHEN I SAW HER SATISFIED FACE...
...I THOUGHT ABOUT YOU SAYING THE SAME THING SOMEDAY.

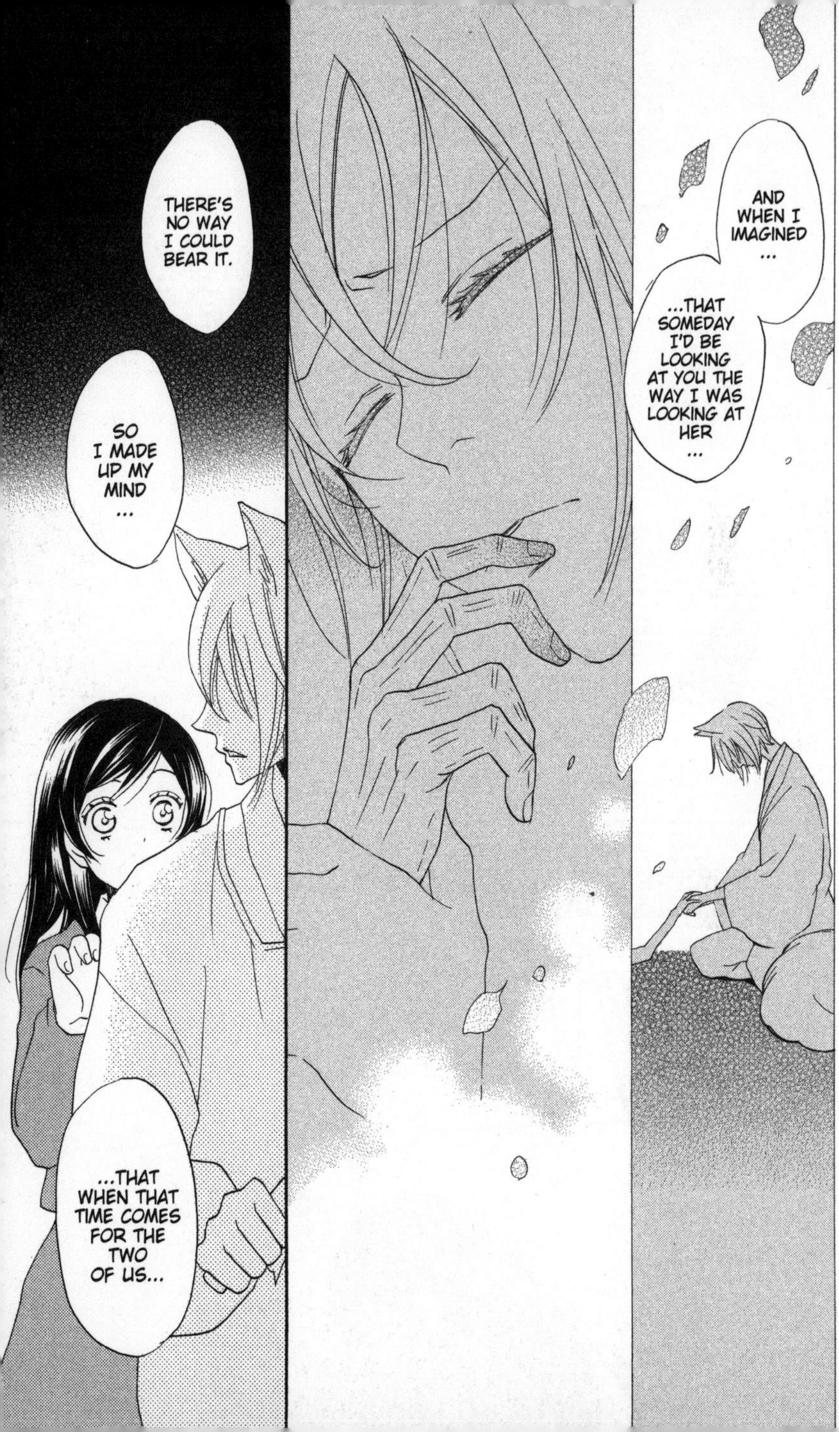
AND WHEN I IMAGINED ...
...THAT SOMEDAY I'D BE LOOKING AT YOU THE WAY I WAS LOOKING AT HER ...
THERE'S NO WAY I COULD BEAR IT.
SO I MADE UP MY MIND ...
...THAT WHEN THAT TIME COMES FOR THE TWO OF US...

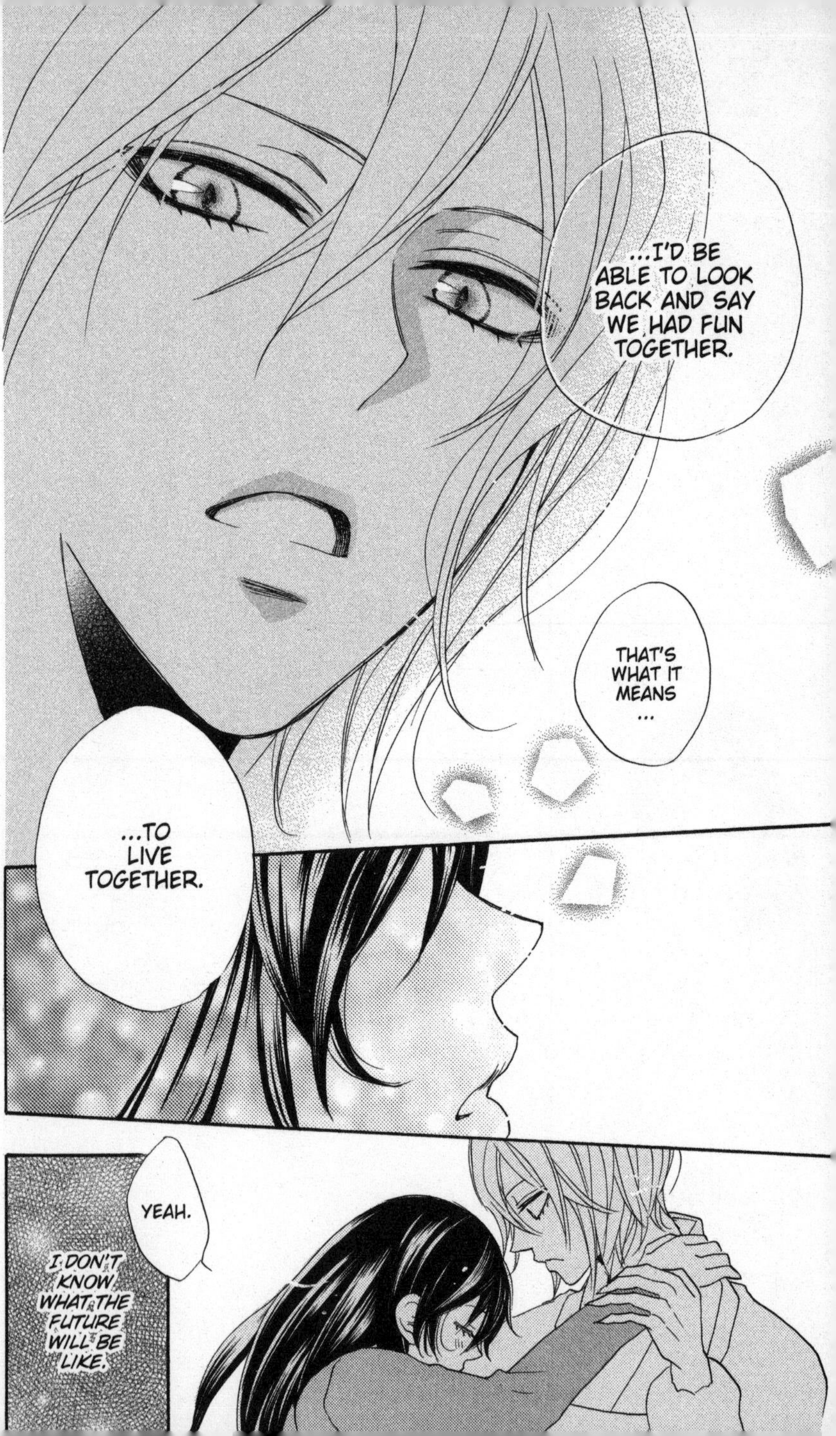
...I'D BE ABLE TO LOOK BACK AND SAY WE HAD FUN TOGETHER.
THAT'S WHAT IT MEANS...
...TO LIVE TOGETHER.
YEAH.
I DON'T KNOW WHAT THE FUTURE WILL BE LIKE.

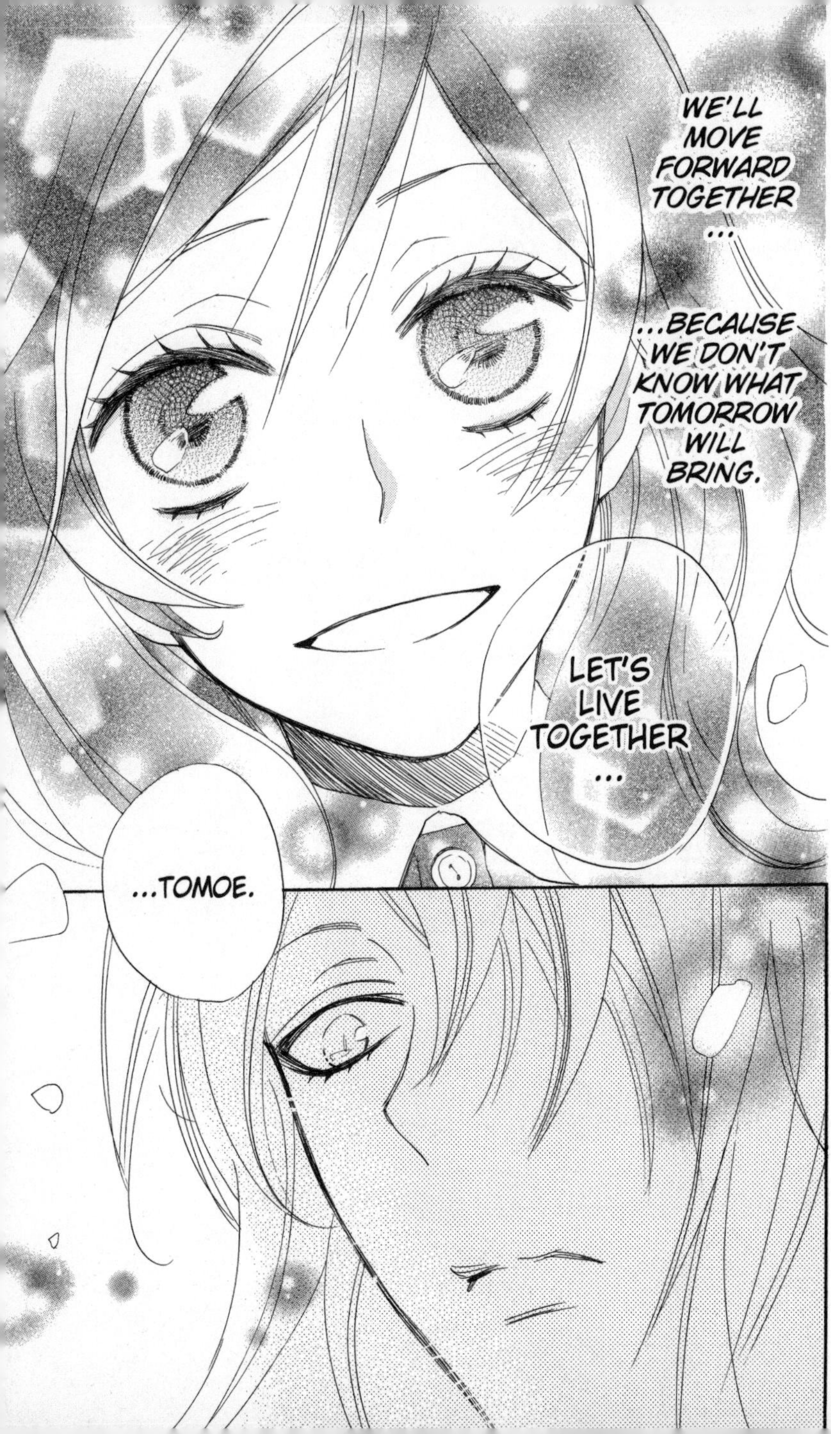
WE'LL MOVE FORWARD TOGETHER ...
...BECAUSE WE DON'T KNOW WHAT TOMORROW WILL BRING.
LET'S LIVE TOGETHER ...
...TOMOE.

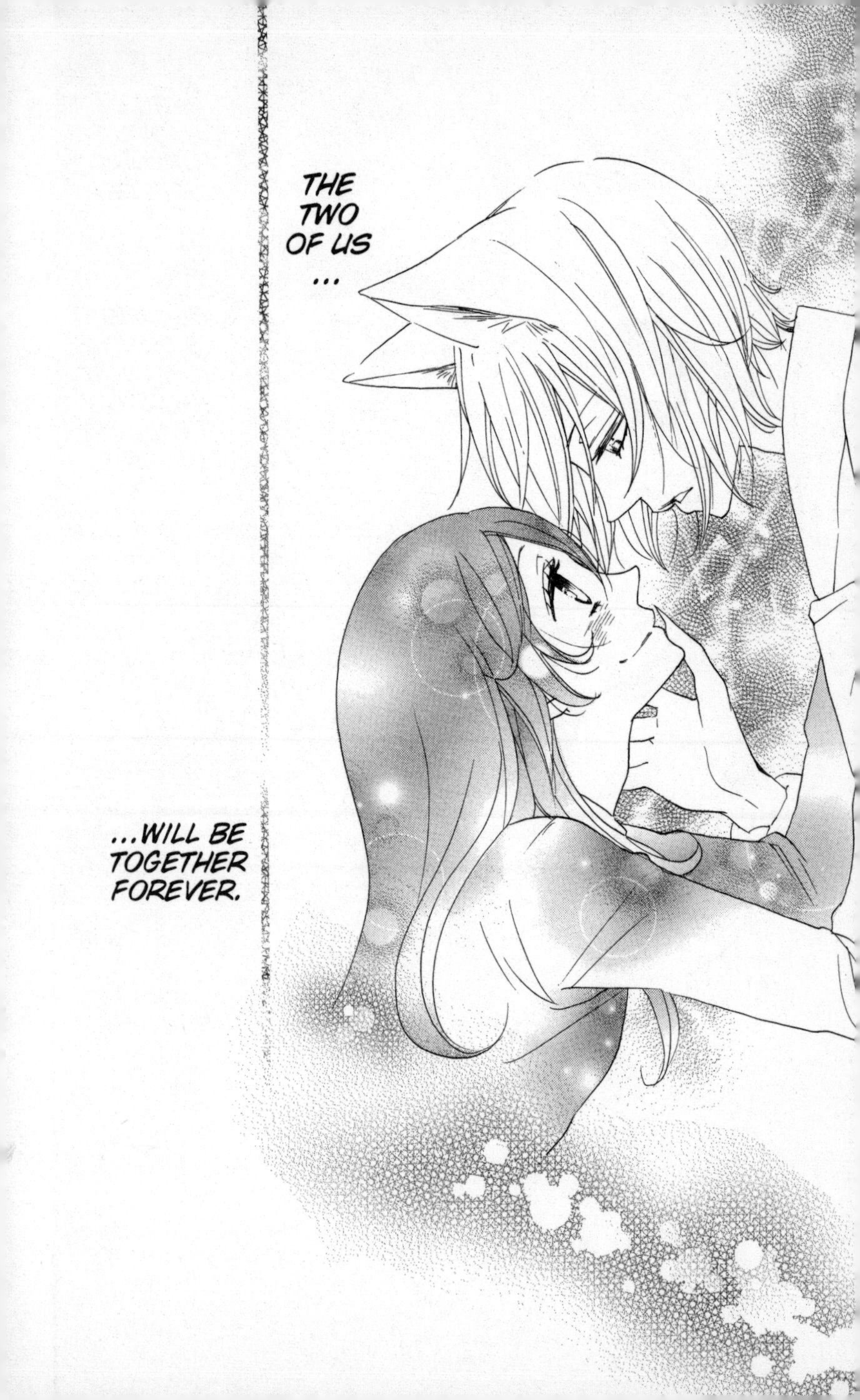
THE TWO OF US ...
...WILL BE TOGETHER FOREVER.

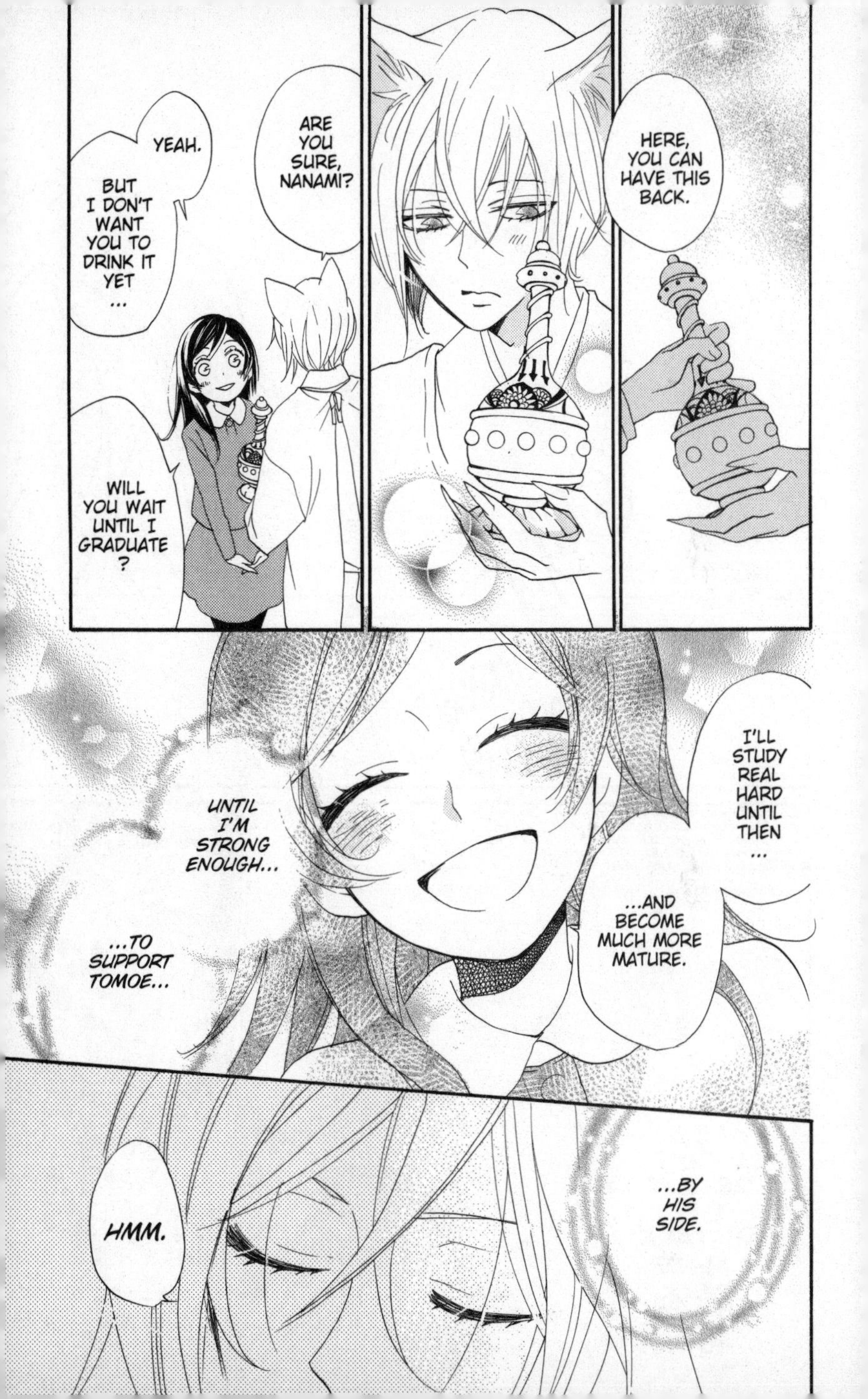
HERE, YOU CAN HAVE THIS BACK.
ARE YOU SURE, NANAMI?
YEAH.
BUT I DON'T WANT YOU TO DRINK IT YET...
WILL YOU WAIT UNTIL I GRADUATE?
I'LL STUDY REAL HARD UNTIL THEN...
...AND BECOME MUCH MORE MATURE.
UNTIL I'M STRONG ENOUGH...
...TO SUPPORT TOMOE...
...BY HIS SIDE.
HMM.

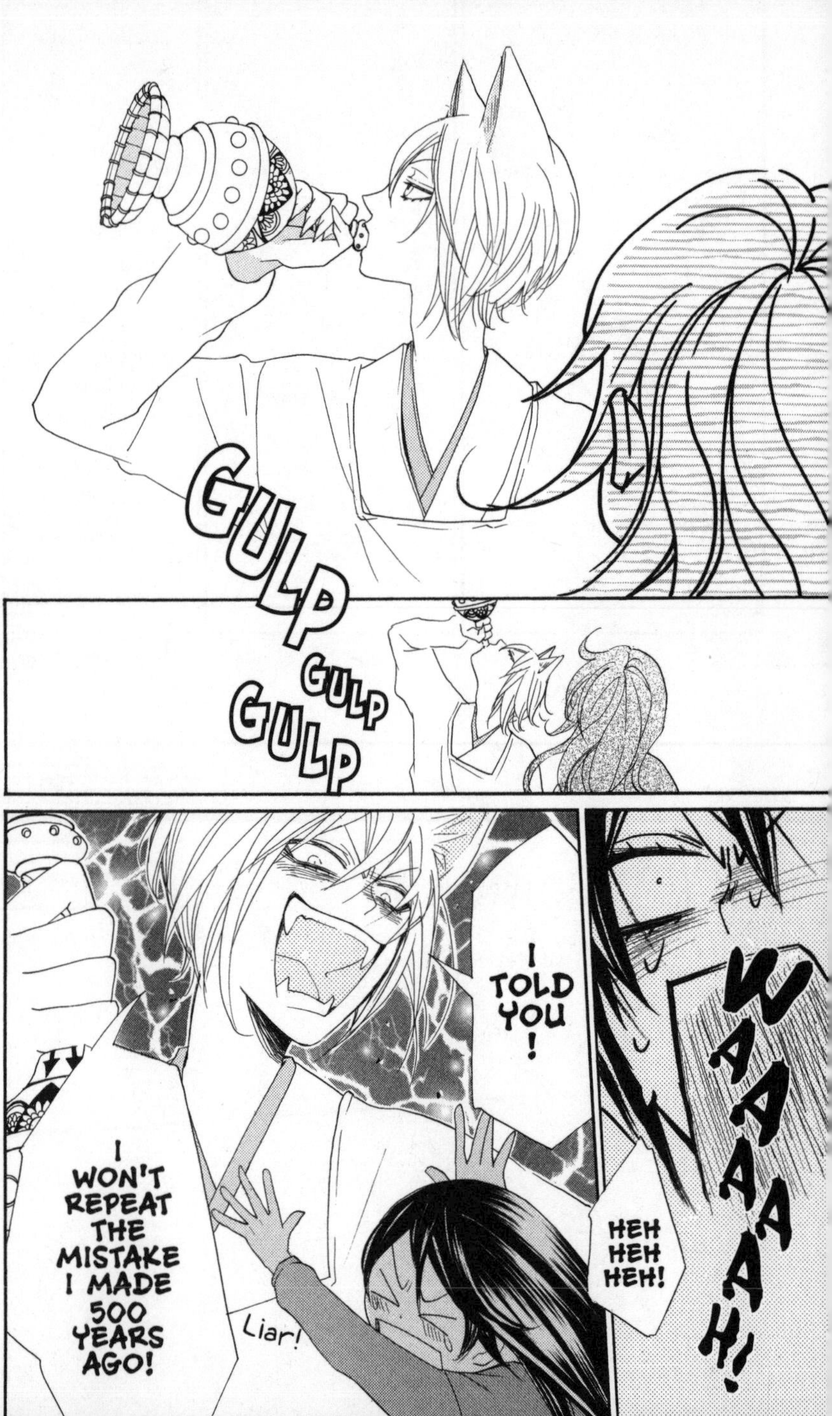
GULP
GULP
GULP
WAAAAAH!
HEH HEH HEH!
I TOLD YOU!
I WON'T REPEAT THE MISTAKE I MADE 500 YEARS AGO!
Liar!

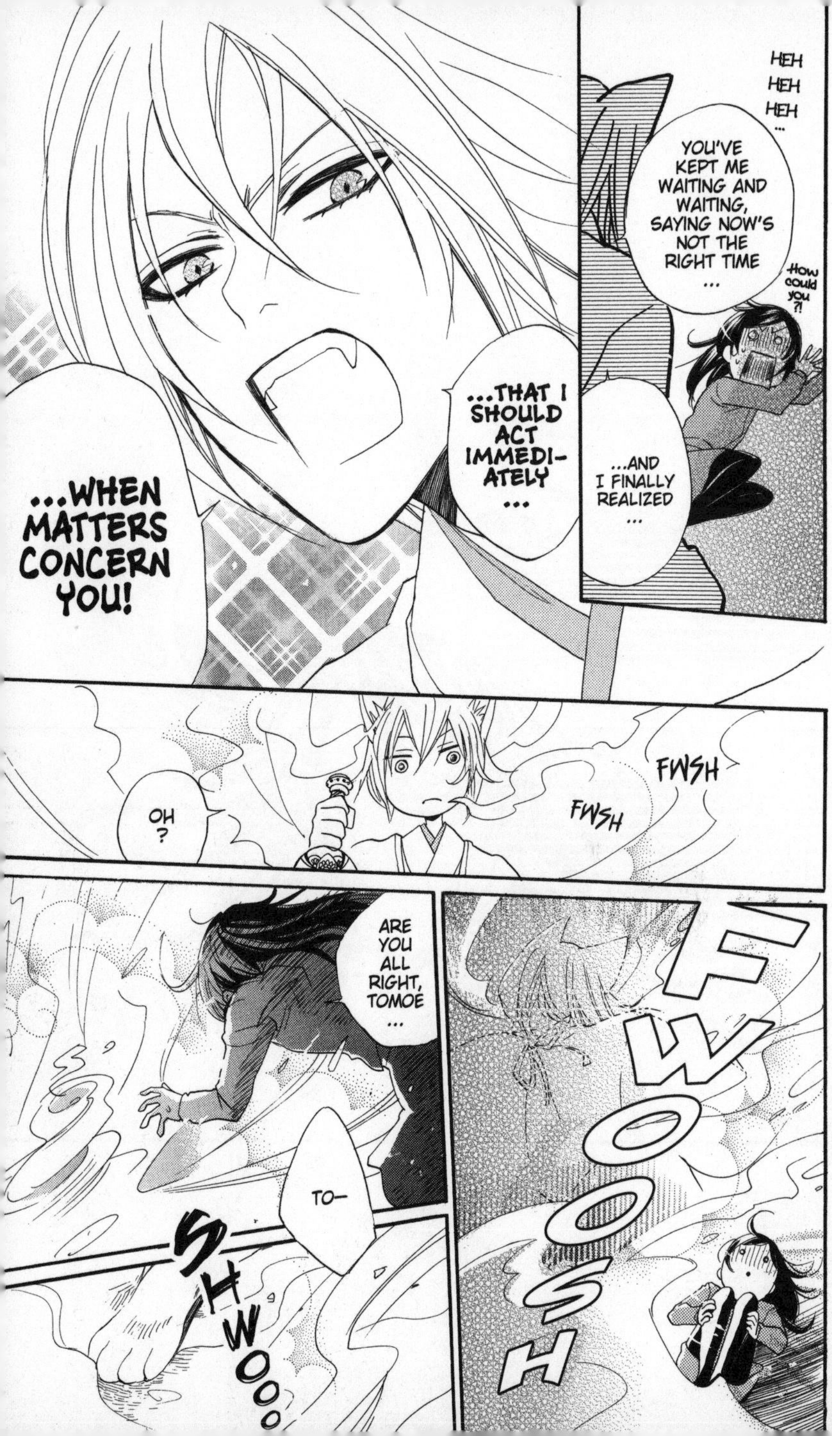
HEH HEH HEH ...
YOU'VE KEPT ME WAITING AND WAITING, SAYING NOW'S NOT THE RIGHT TIME ...
How could you?!
...AND I FINALLY REALIZED ...
...THAT I SHOULD ACT IMMEDIATELY ...
...WHEN MATTERS CONCERN YOU!
FWSH
FWSH
OH?
FWOOOSH
ARE YOU ALL RIGHT, TOMOE ...
TO-
SHWOOO

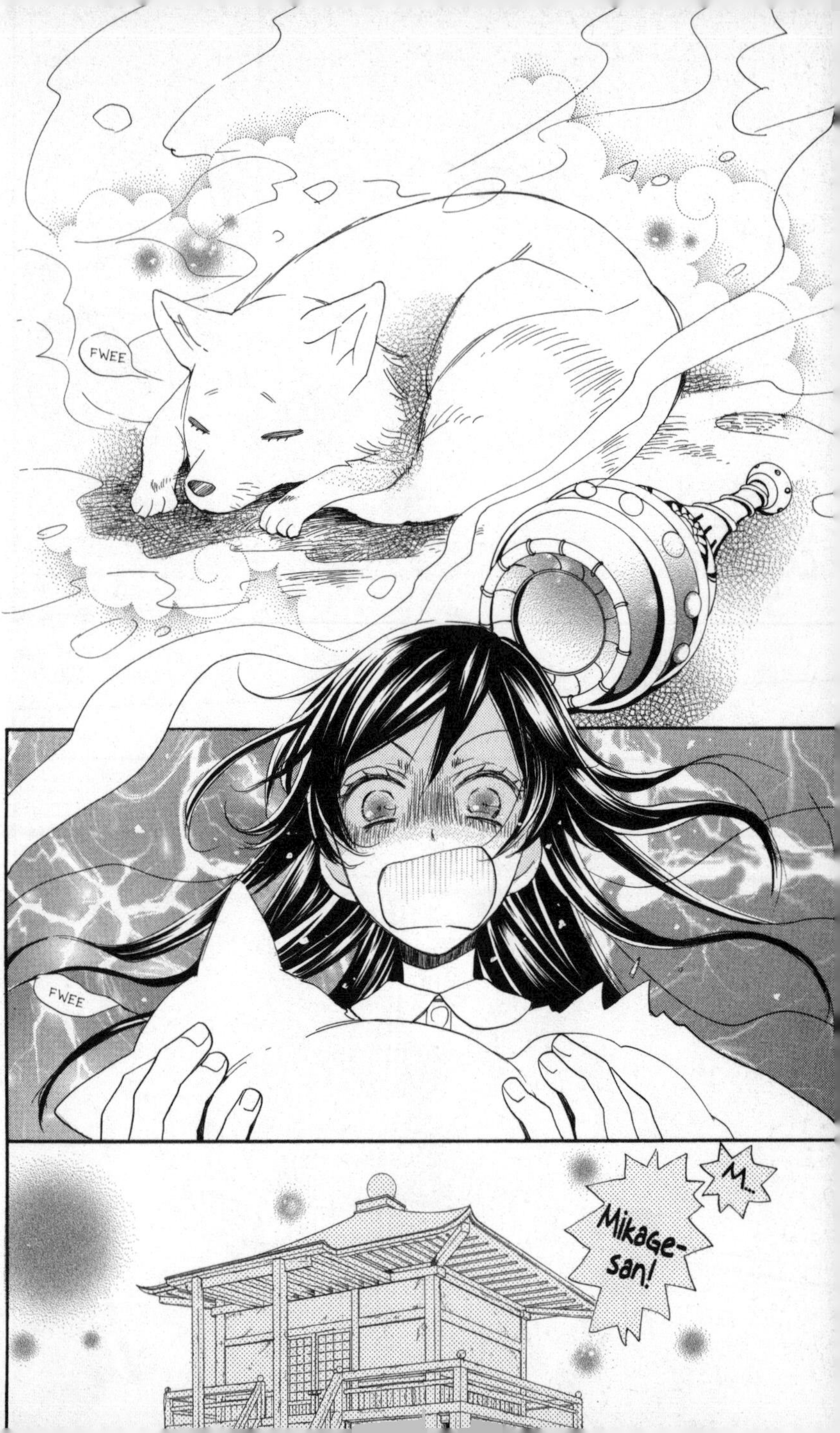
FWEE
FWEE
M...
Mikage-san!

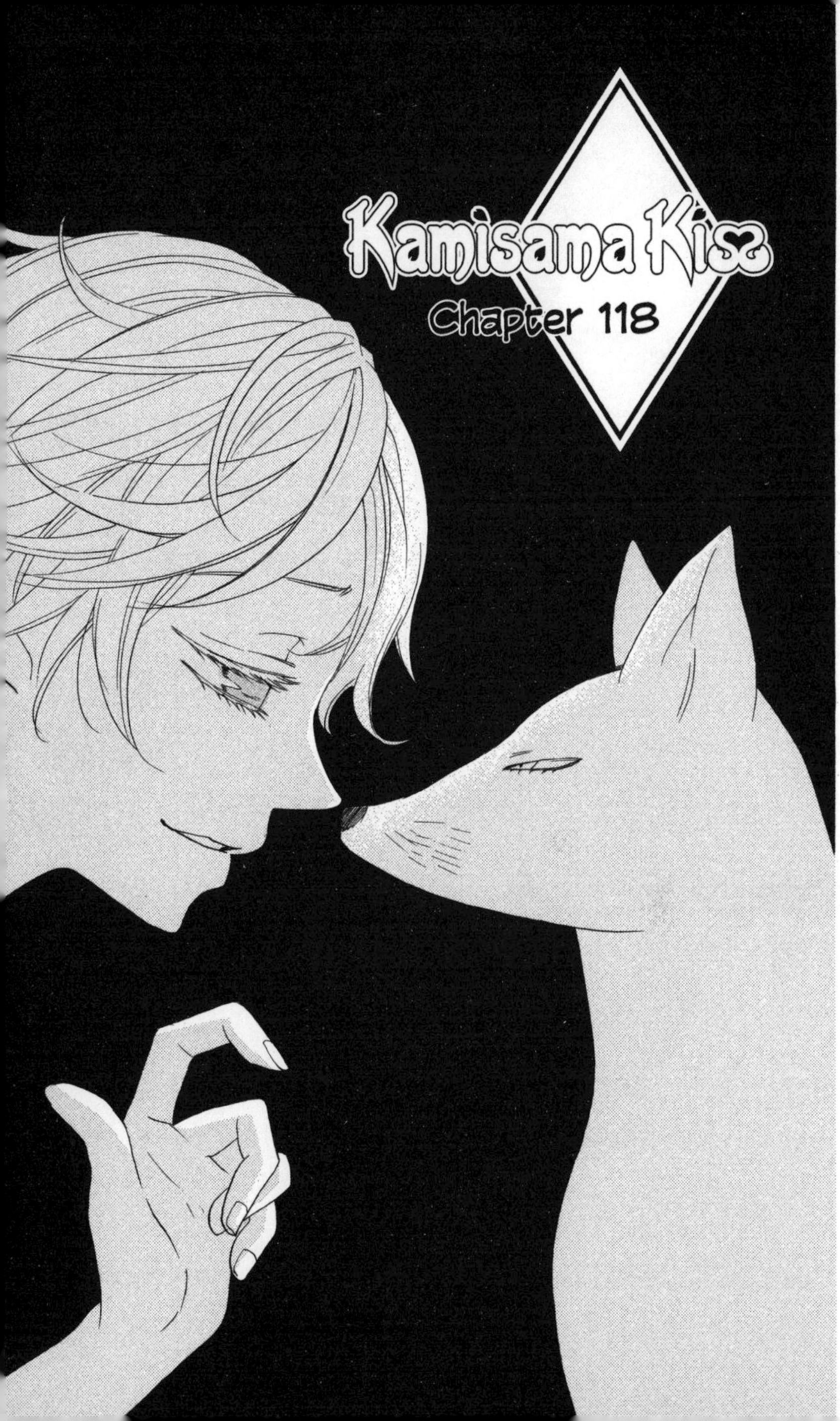
Kamisama Kiss
Chapter 118

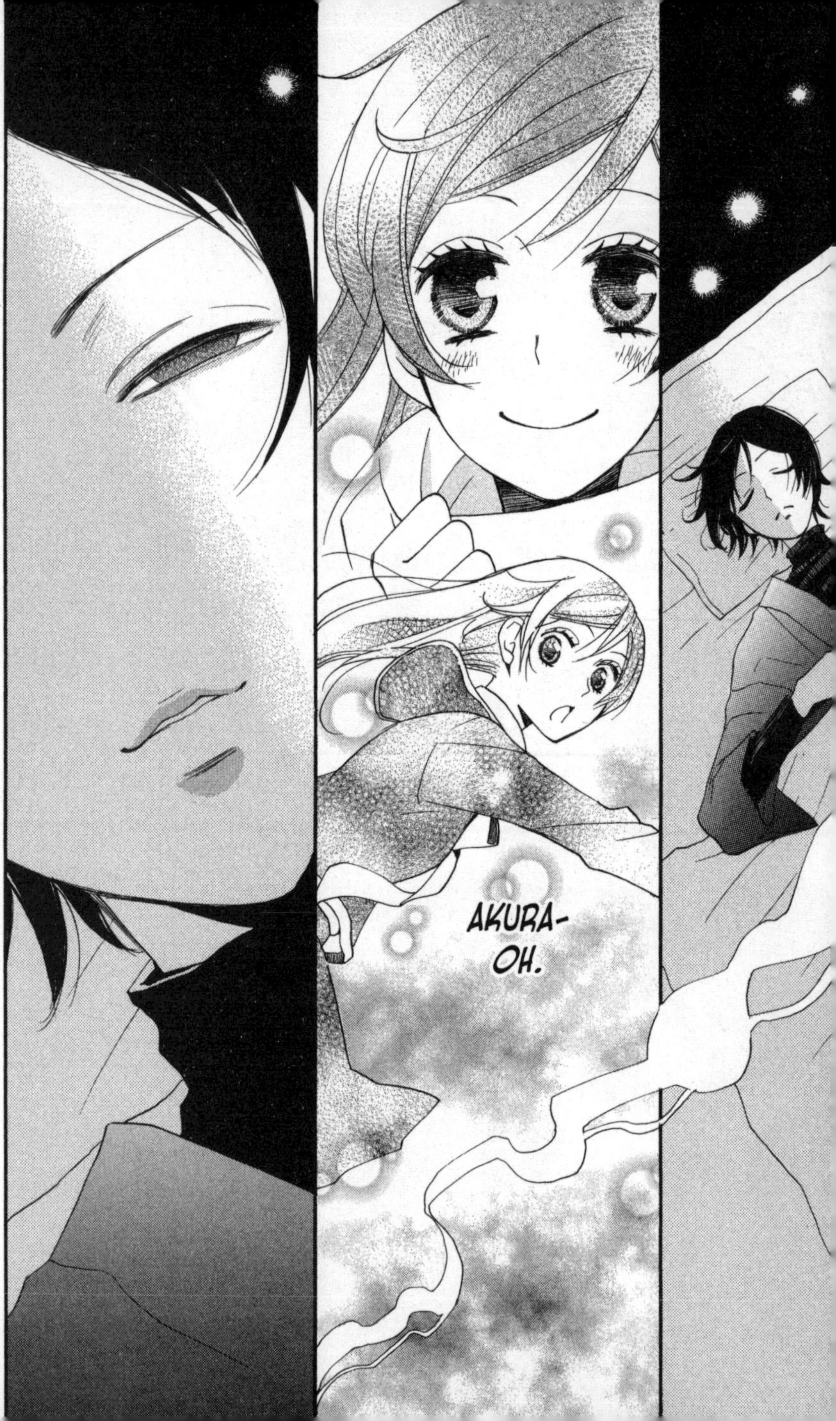
AKURA-OH.

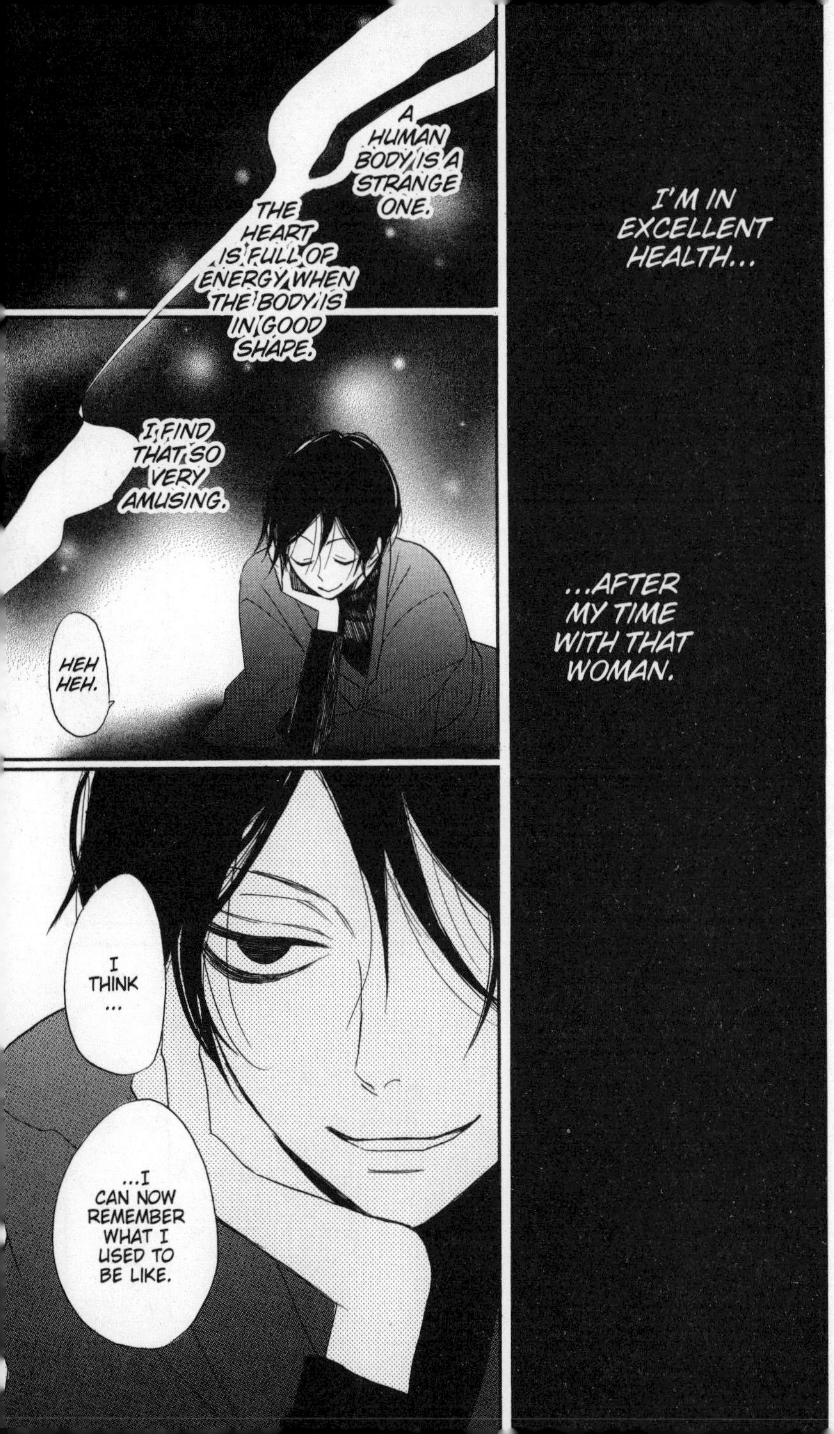
I'M IN EXCELLENT HEALTH...
...AFTER MY TIME WITH THAT WOMAN.
A HUMAN BODY IS A STRANGE ONE.
THE HEART IS FULL OF ENERGY WHEN THE BODY IS IN GOOD SHAPE.
I FIND THAT SO VERY AMUSING.
HEH HEH.
I THINK...
...I CAN NOW REMEMBER WHAT I USED TO BE LIKE.

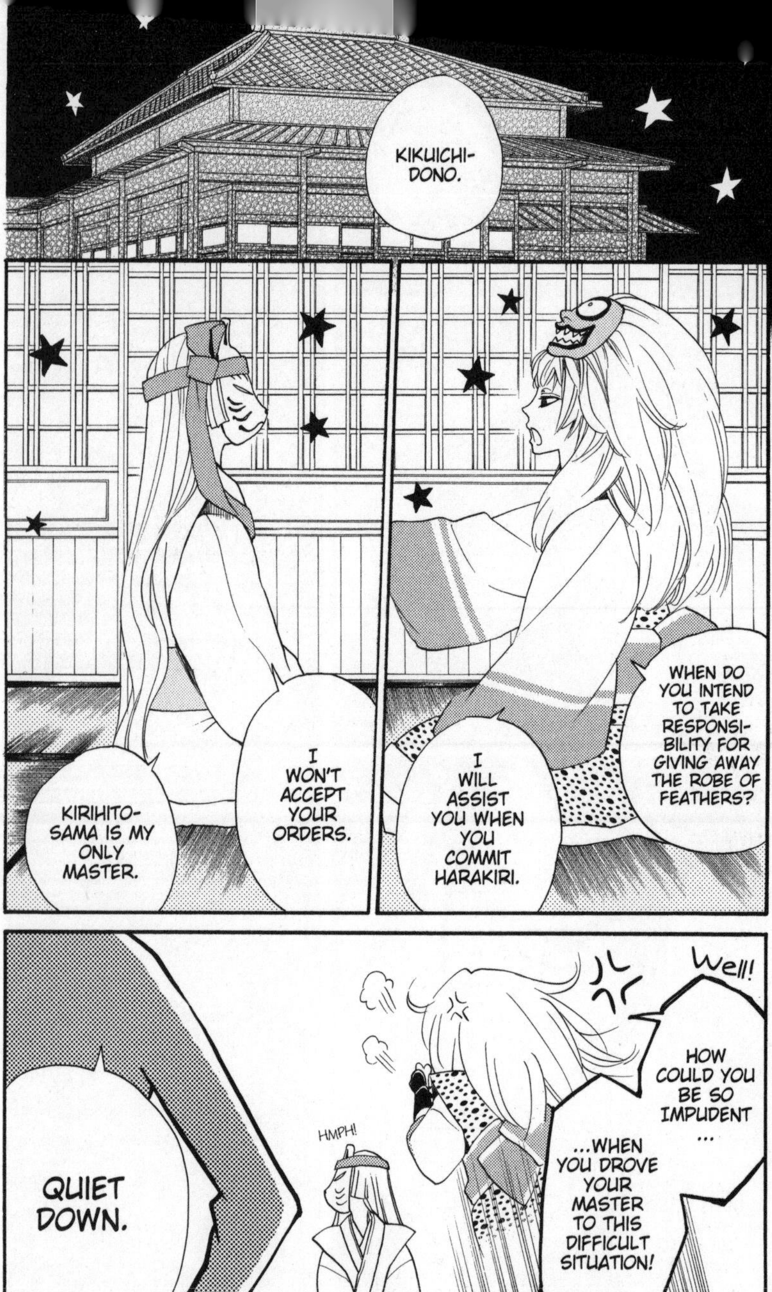
KIKUICHI-DONO.
WHEN DO YOU INTEND TO TAKE RESPONSIBILITY FOR GIVING AWAY THE ROBE OF FEATHERS?
I WILL ASSIST YOU WHEN YOU COMMIT HARAKIRI.
I WON'T ACCEPT YOUR ORDERS.
KIRIHITO-SAMA IS MY ONLY MASTER.
Well!
HOW COULD YOU BE SO IMPUDENT ...
...WHEN YOU DROVE YOUR MASTER TO THIS DIFFICULT SITUATION!
HMPH!
QUIET DOWN.

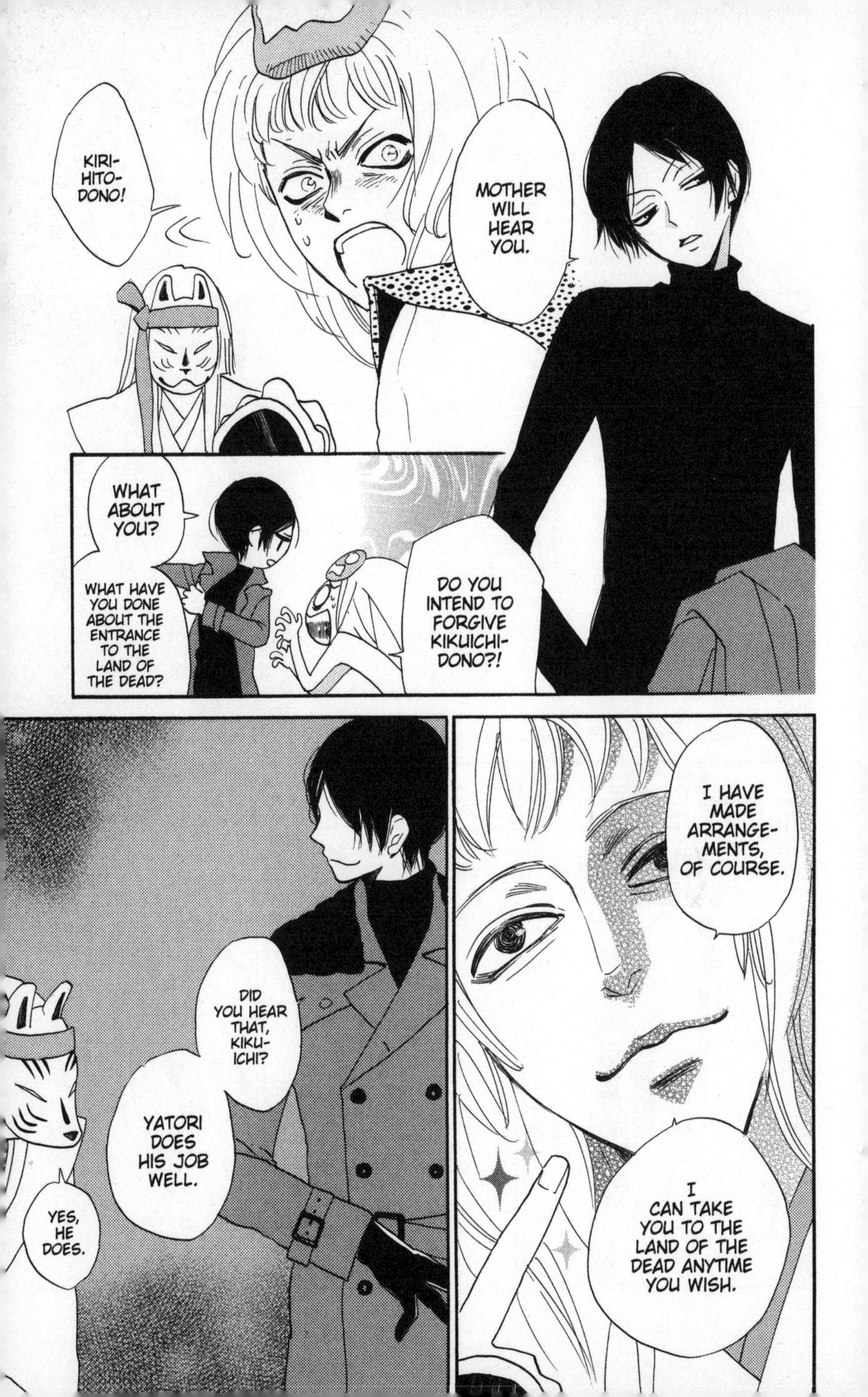
MOTHER WILL HEAR YOU.
KIRIHITO-DONO!
DO YOU INTEND TO FORGIVE KIKUICHI-DONO?!
WHAT ABOUT YOU?
WHAT HAVE YOU DONE ABOUT THE ENTRANCE TO THE LAND OF THE DEAD?
I HAVE MADE ARRANGEMENTS, OF COURSE.
I CAN TAKE YOU TO THE LAND OF THE DEAD ANYTIME YOU WISH.
DID YOU HEAR THAT, KIKUICHI?
YATORI DOES HIS JOB WELL.
YES, HE DOES.

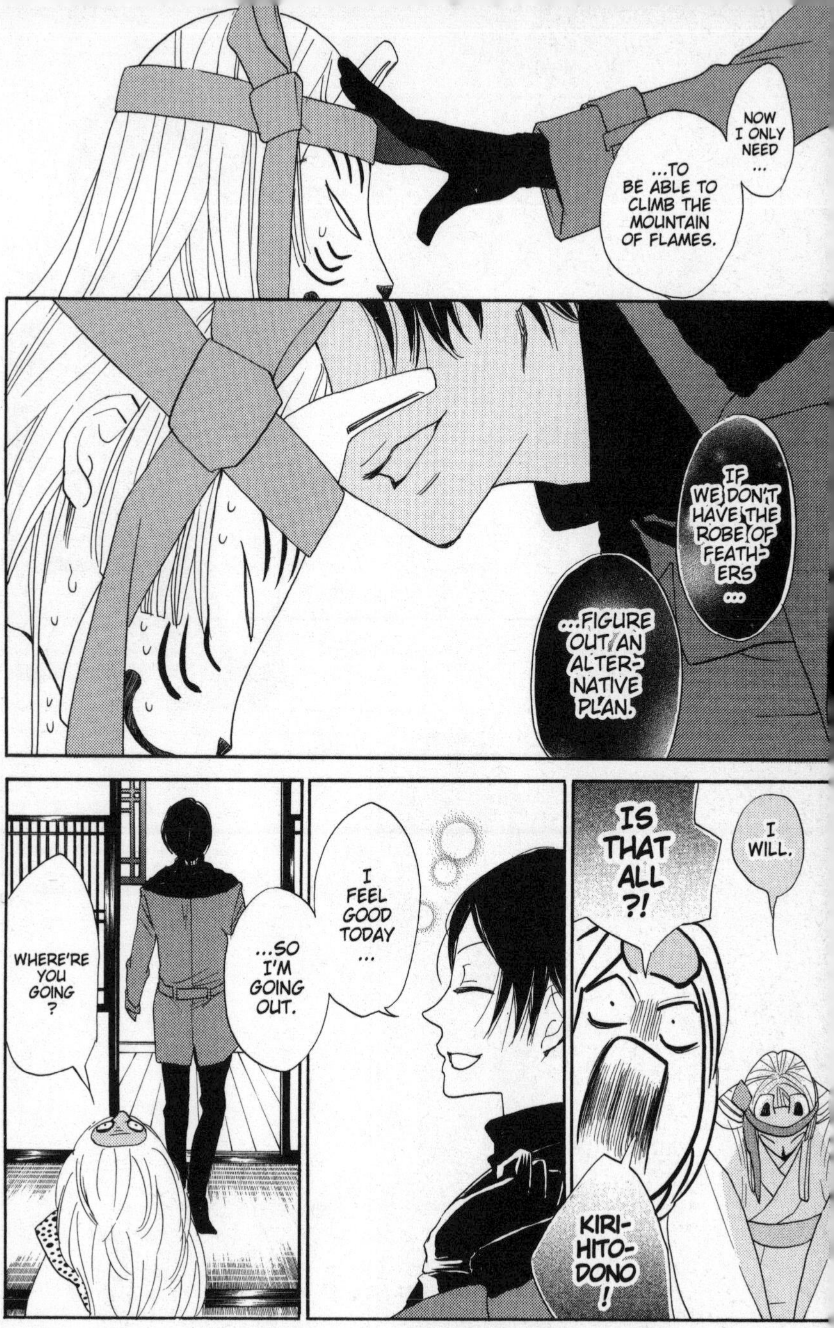
NOW I ONLY NEED...
...TO BE ABLE TO CLIMB THE MOUNTAIN OF FLAMES.
IF WE DON'T HAVE THE ROBE OF FEATHERS...
...FIGURE OUT AN ALTERNATIVE PLAN.
I WILL.
IS THAT ALL?!
KIRIHITO-DONO!
I FEEL GOOD TODAY...
...SO I'M GOING OUT.
WHERE'RE YOU GOING?

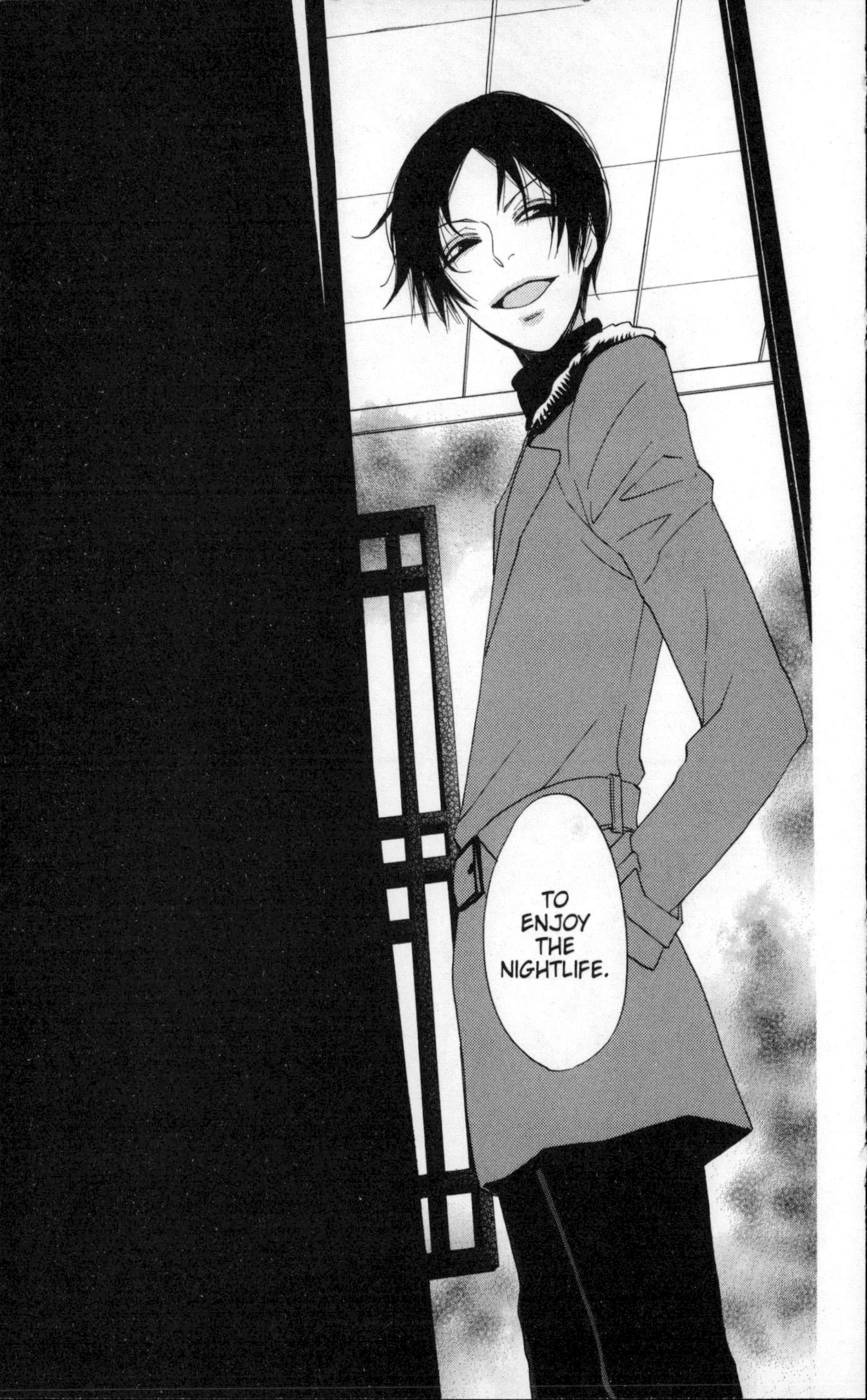
TO ENJOY THE NIGHTLIFE.

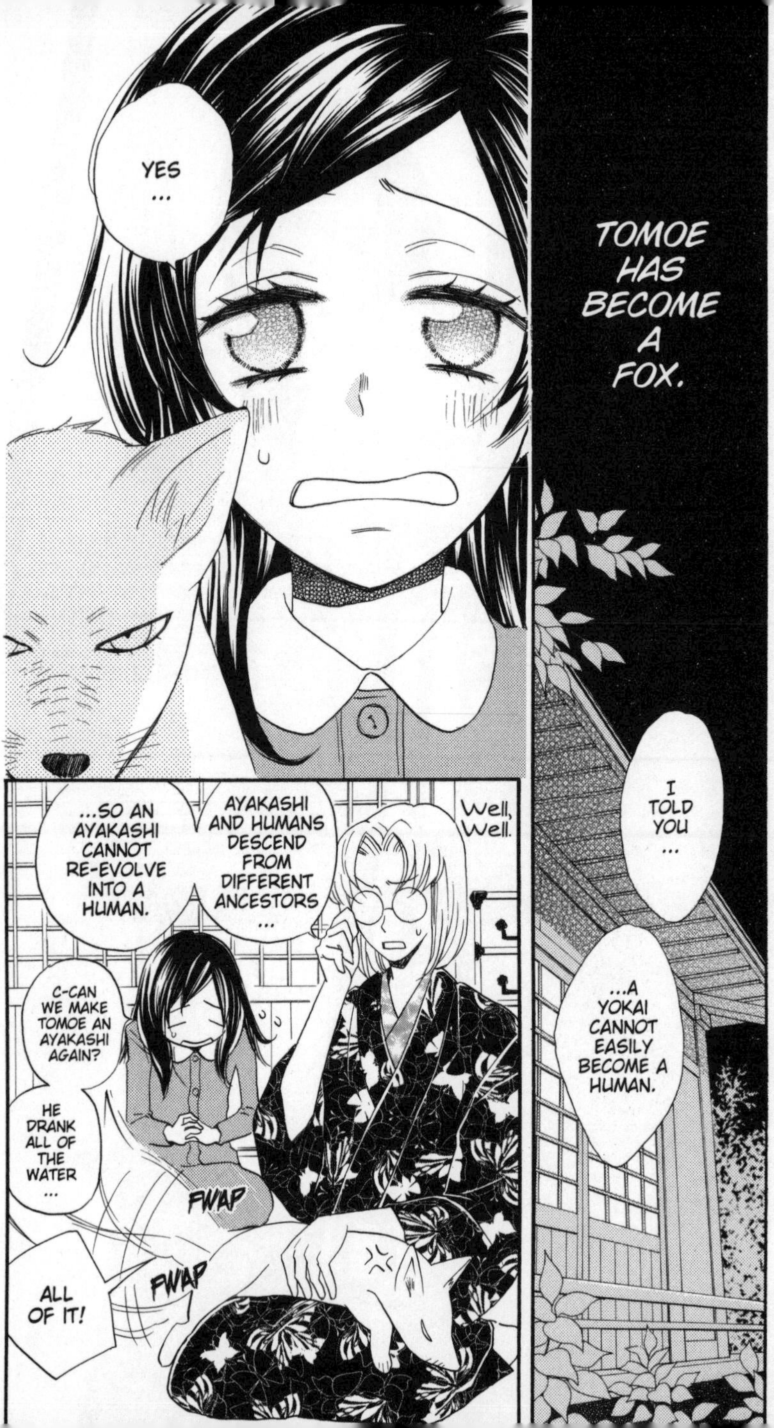
TOMOE HAS BECOME A FOX.
I TOLD YOU ...
...A YOKAI CANNOT EASILY BECOME A HUMAN.
YES ...
Well, Well.
AYAKASHI AND HUMANS DESCEND FROM DIFFERENT ANCESTORS ...
...SO AN AYAKASHI CANNOT RE-EVOLVE INTO A HUMAN.
C-CAN WE MAKE TOMOE AN AYAKASHI AGAIN?
HE DRANK ALL OF THE WATER ...
FWAP
FWAP
ALL OF IT!

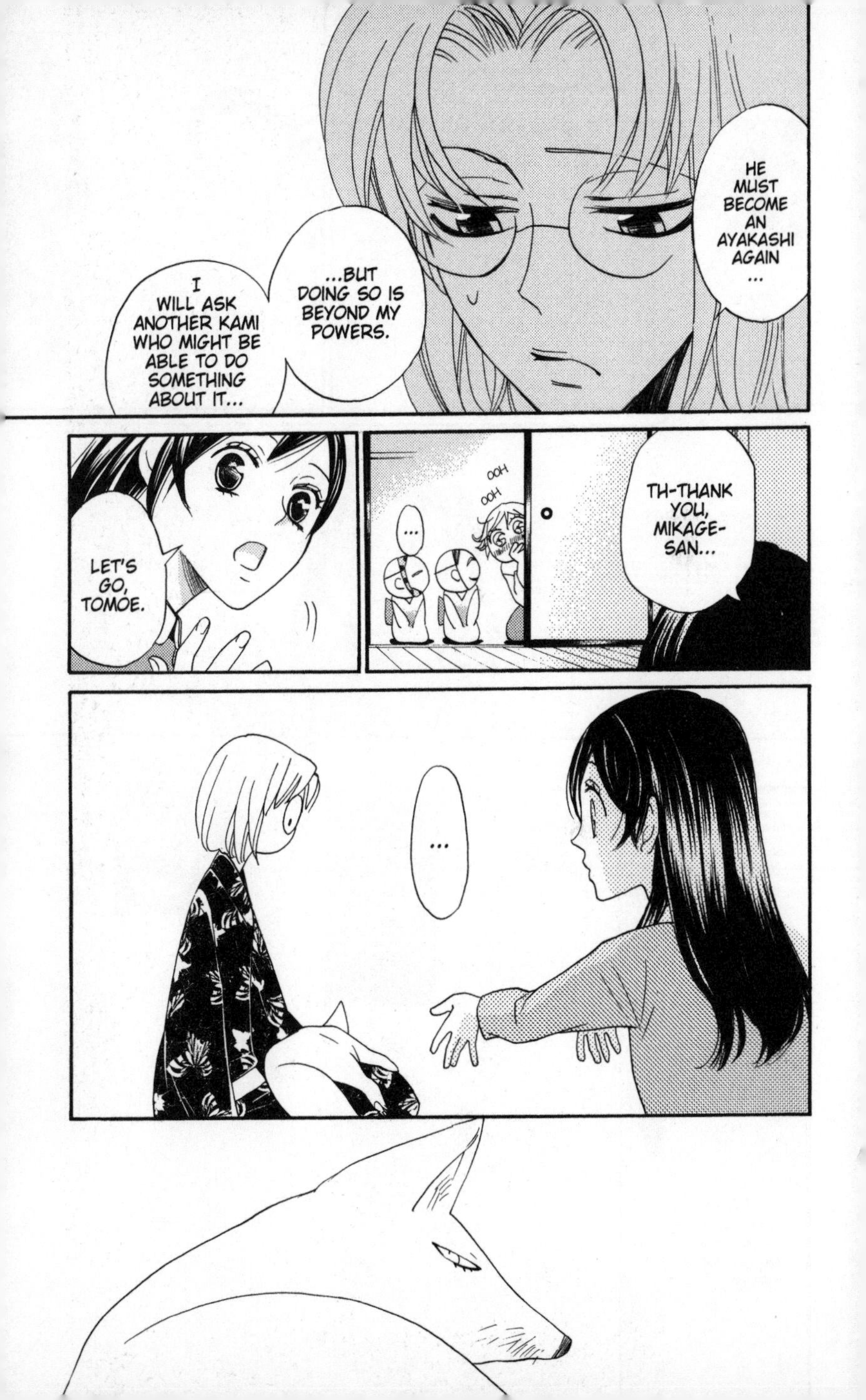
HE MUST BECOME AN AYAKASHI AGAIN...
...BUT DOING SO IS BEYOND MY POWERS.
I WILL ASK ANOTHER KAMI WHO MIGHT BE ABLE TO DO SOMETHING ABOUT IT...
TH-THANK YOU, MIKAGE-SAN...
OOH
OOH
...
LET'S GO, TOMOE.
...

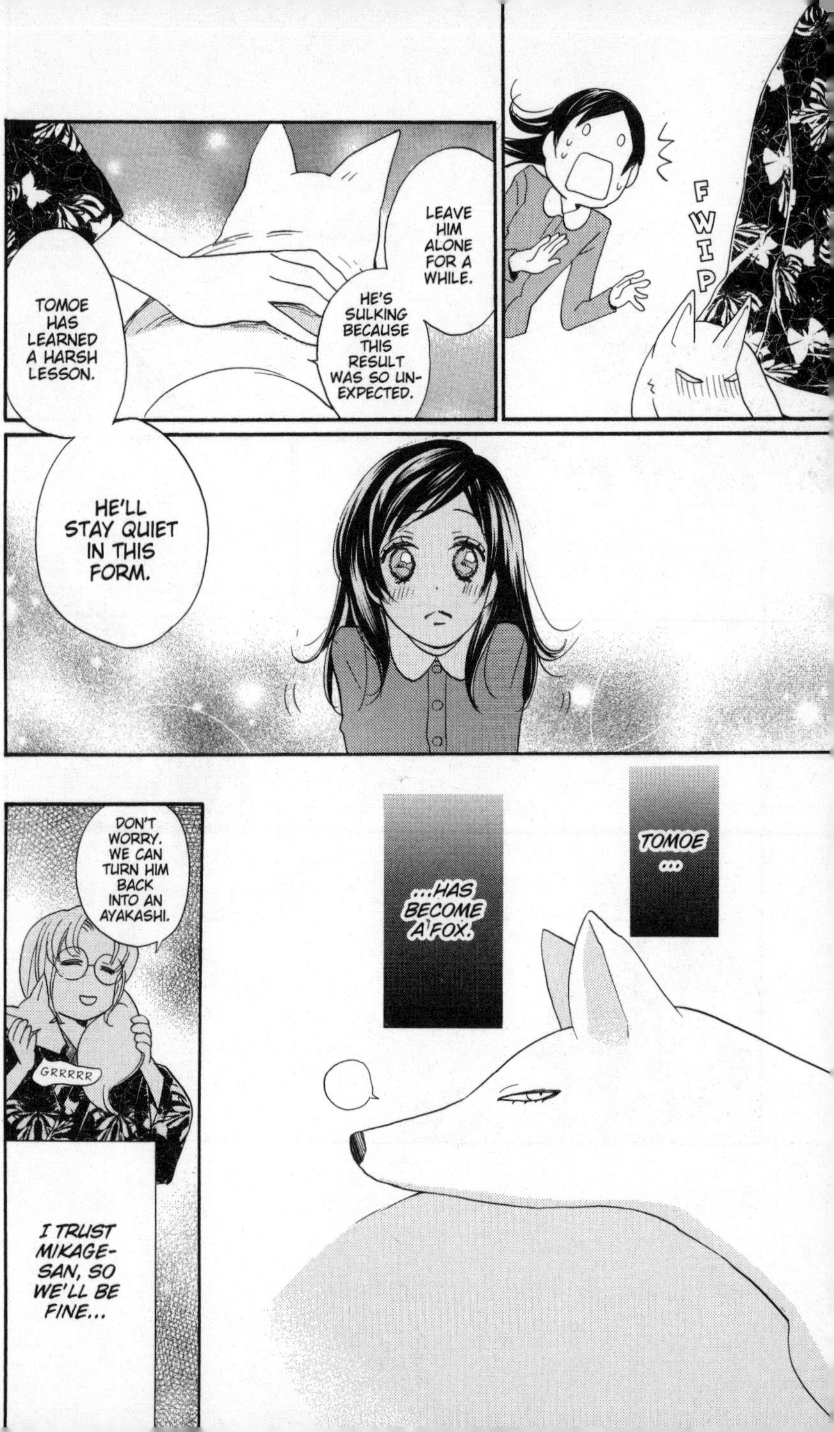
FWIP
LEAVE HIM ALONE FOR A WHILE.
HE'S SULKING BECAUSE THIS RESULT WAS SO UN-EXPECTED.
TOMOE HAS LEARNED A HARSH LESSON.
HE'LL STAY QUIET IN THIS FORM.
TOMOE...
...HAS BECOME A FOX.
DON'T WORRY. WE CAN TURN HIM BACK INTO AN AYAKASHI.
GRRRRR
I TRUST MIKAGE-SAN, SO WE'LL BE FINE...

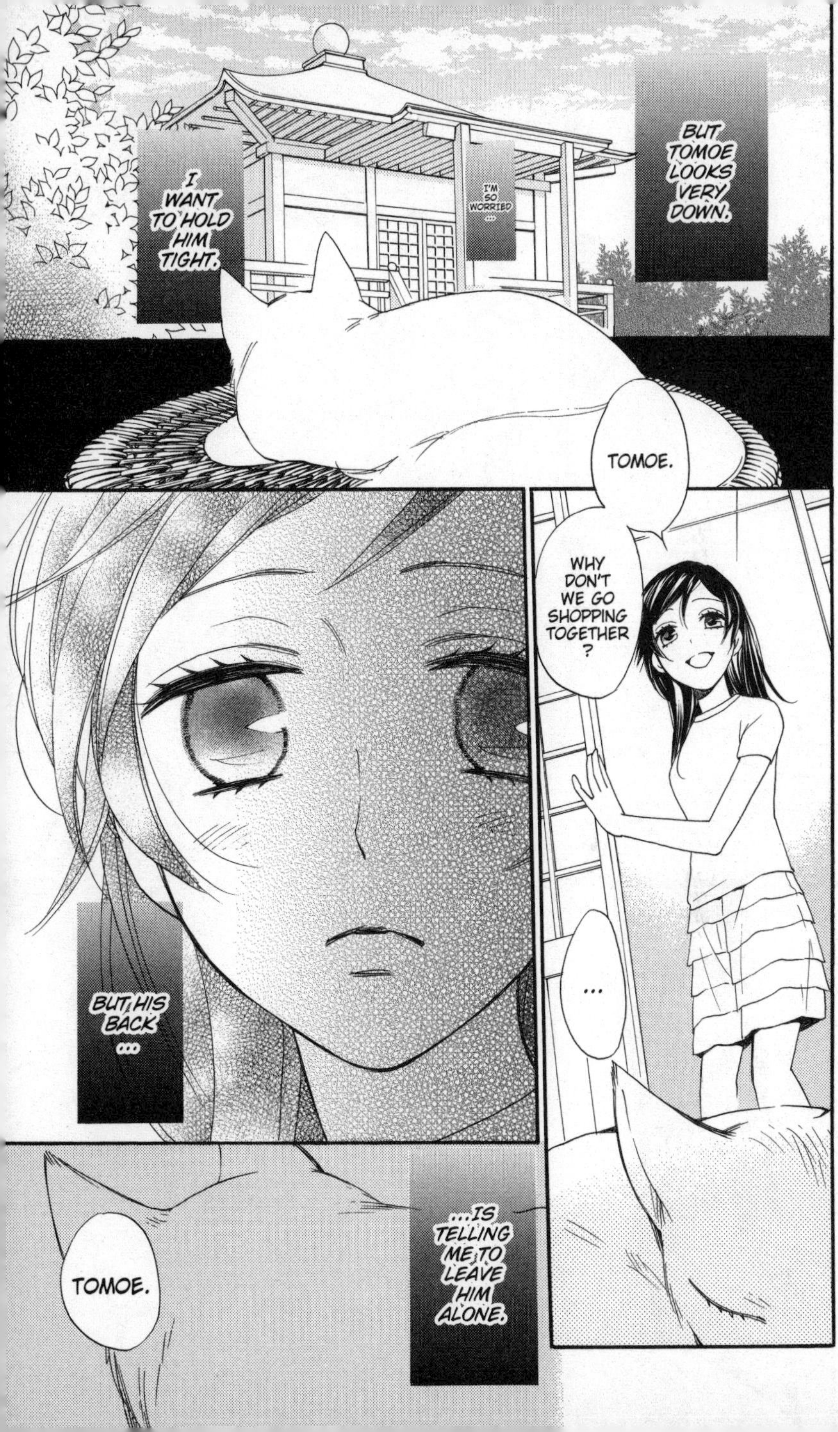
BUT TOMOE LOOKS VERY DOWN.
I'M SO WORRIED...
I WANT TO HOLD HIM TIGHT.
TOMOE.
WHY DON'T WE GO SHOPPING TOGETHER?
...
BUT HIS BACK...
...IS TELLING ME TO LEAVE HIM ALONE.
TOMOE.

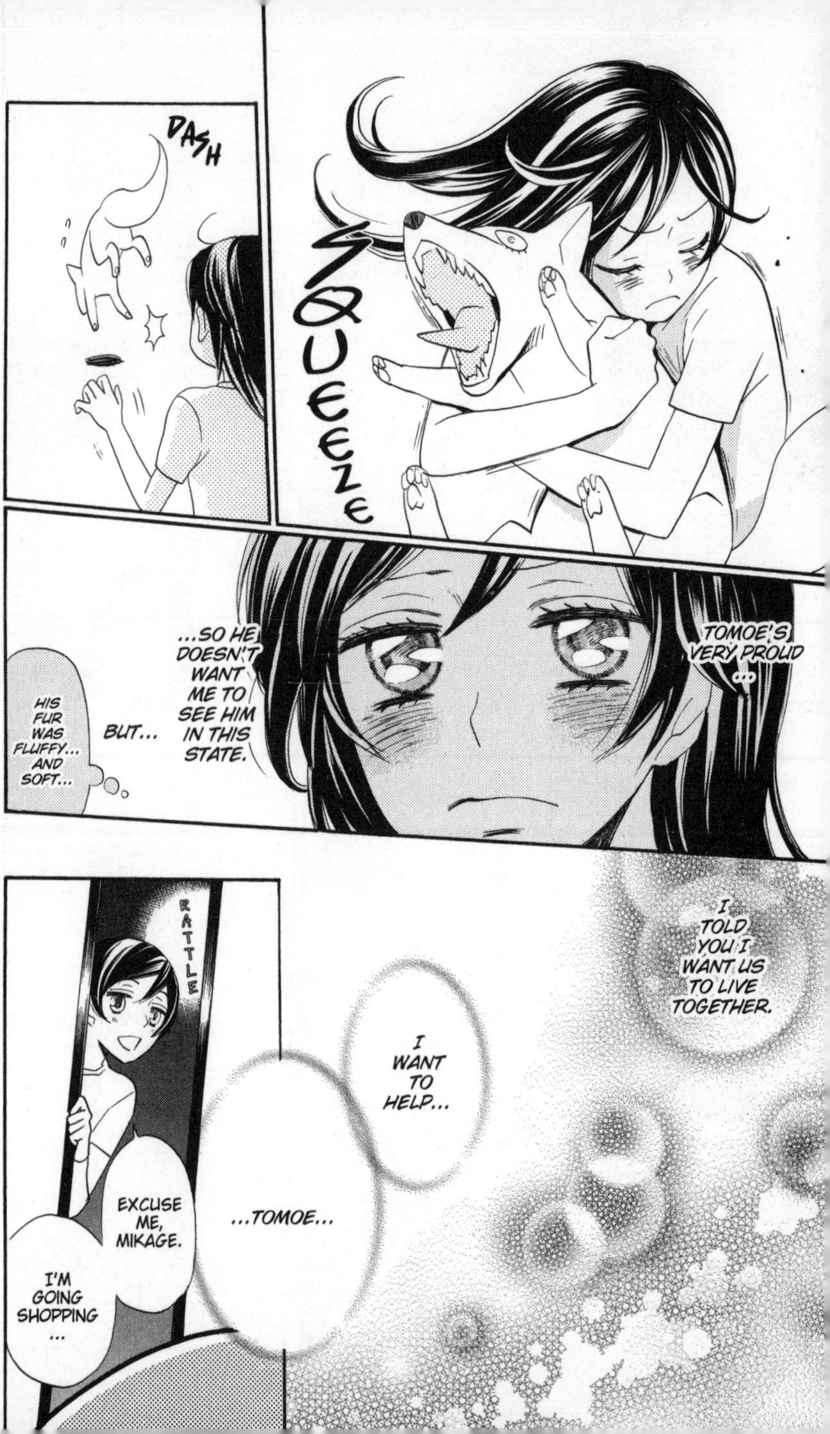
SQUEEZE
DASH
TOMOE'S VERY PROUD ...
...SO HE DOESN'T WANT ME TO SEE HIM IN THIS STATE.
BUT...
HIS FUR WAS FLUFFY... AND SOFT...
I TOLD YOU I WANT US TO LIVE TOGETHER.
I WANT TO HELP...
...TOMOE...
RATTLE
EXCUSE ME, MIKAGE.
I'M GOING SHOPPING ...

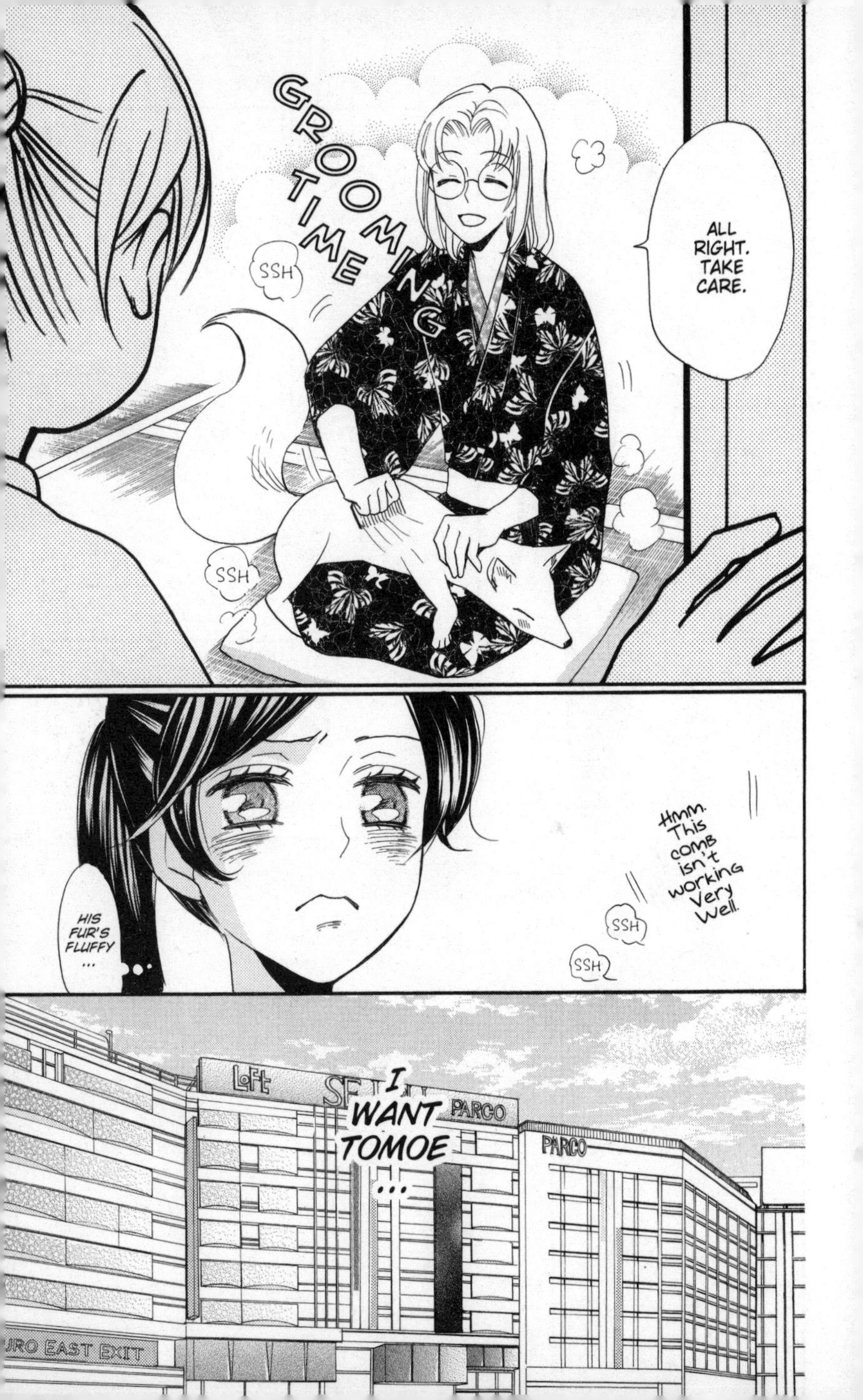
ALL RIGHT. TAKE CARE.
GROOMING TIME
SSH
SSH
Hmm. This comb isn't working very well.
SSH
SSH
HIS FUR'S FLUFFY ...
I WANT TOMOE ...
LoFt
PARCO
PARCO
URO EAST EXIT

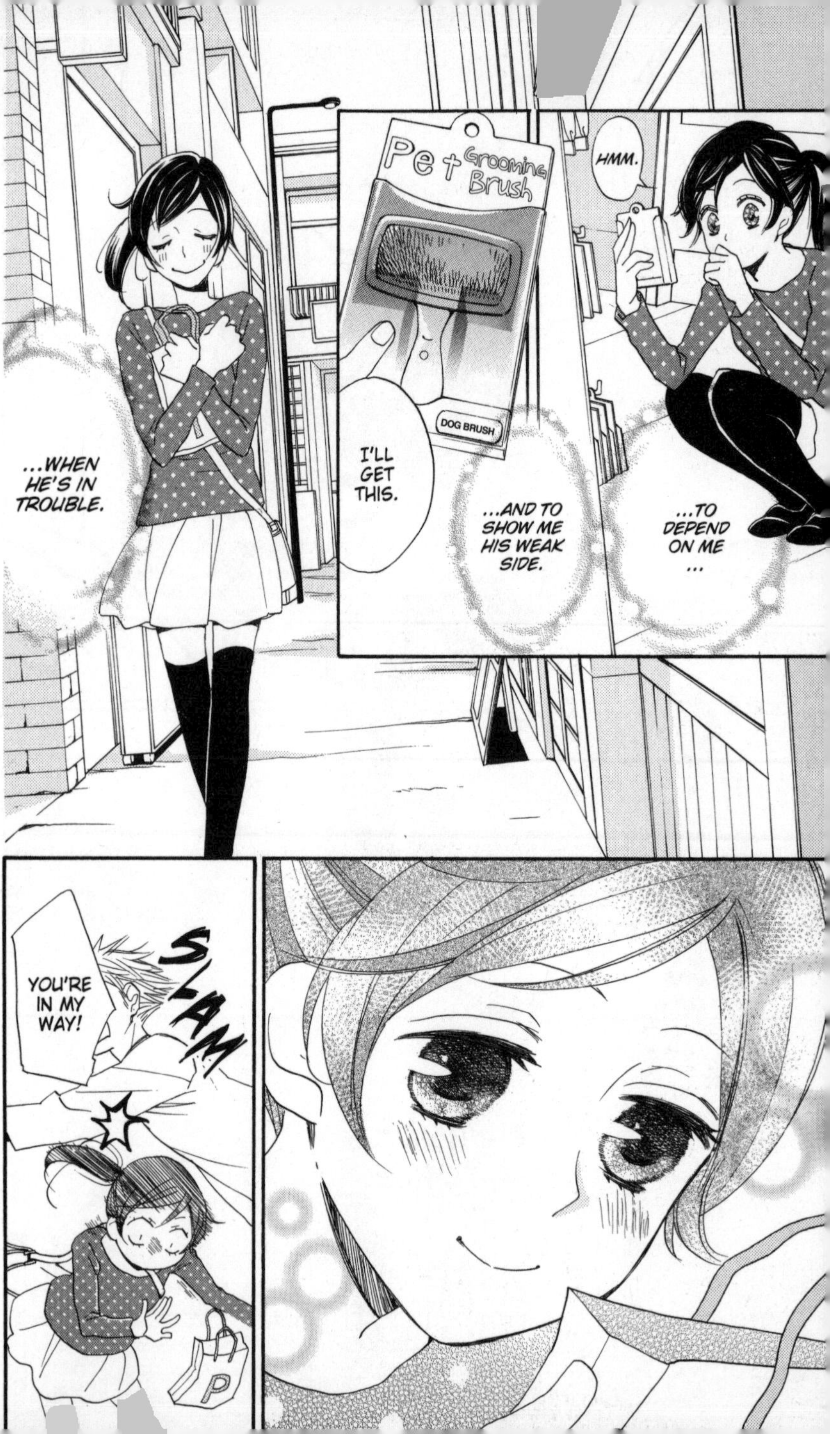
HMM.
...TO DEPEND ON ME ...
Pet Grooming Brush
DOG BRUSH
I'LL GET THIS.
...AND TO SHOW ME HIS WEAK SIDE.
...WHEN HE'S IN TROUBLE.
SLAM
YOU'RE IN MY WAY!

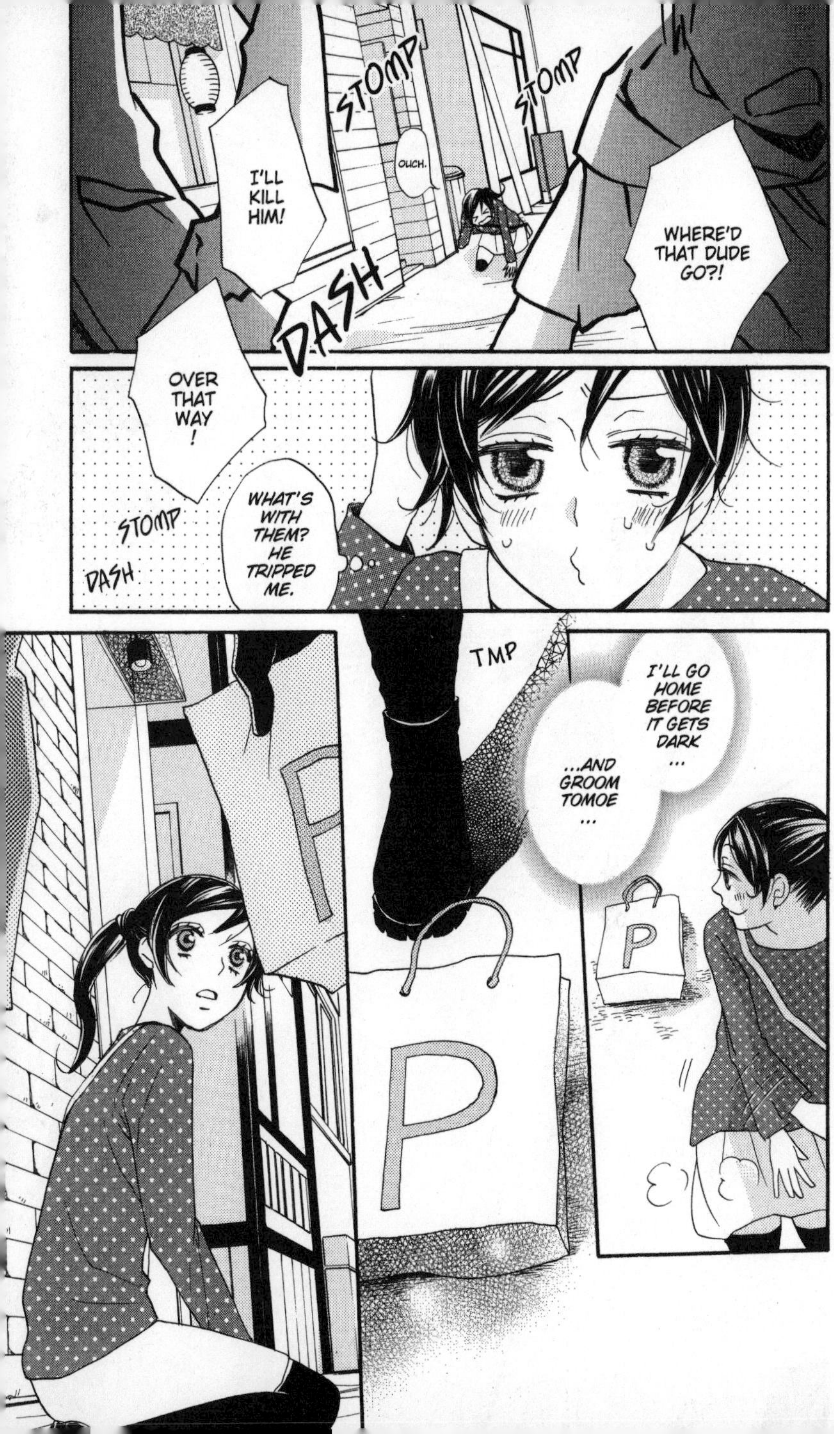
WHERE'D THAT DUDE GO?!
STOMP
STOMP
OUCH.
I'LL KILL HIM!
DASH
OVER THAT WAY!
WHAT'S WITH THEM? HE TRIPPED ME.
STOMP
DASH
I'LL GO HOME BEFORE IT GETS DARK...
...AND GROOM TOMOE...
TMP

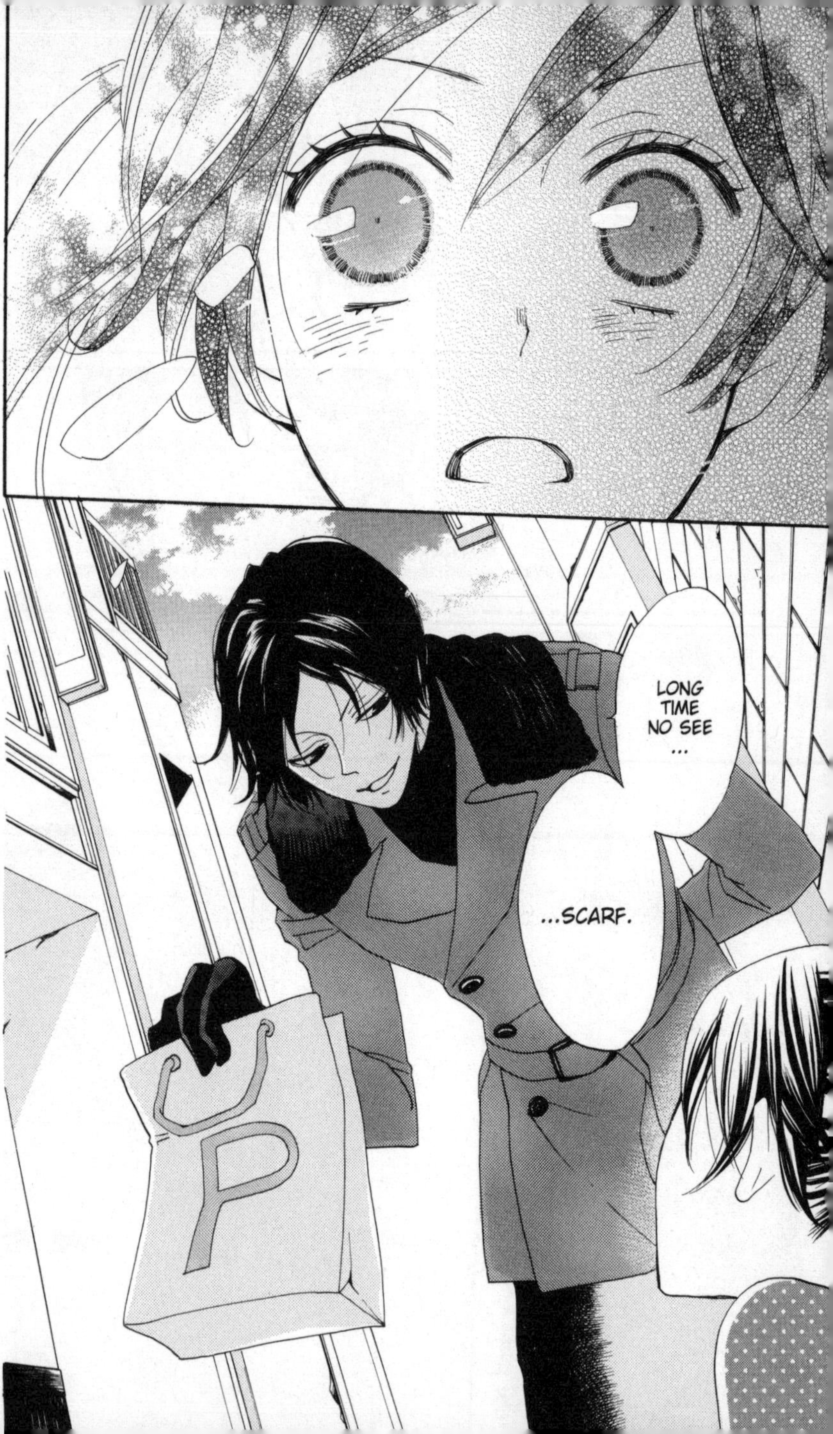
LONG TIME NO SEE ...
...SCARF.

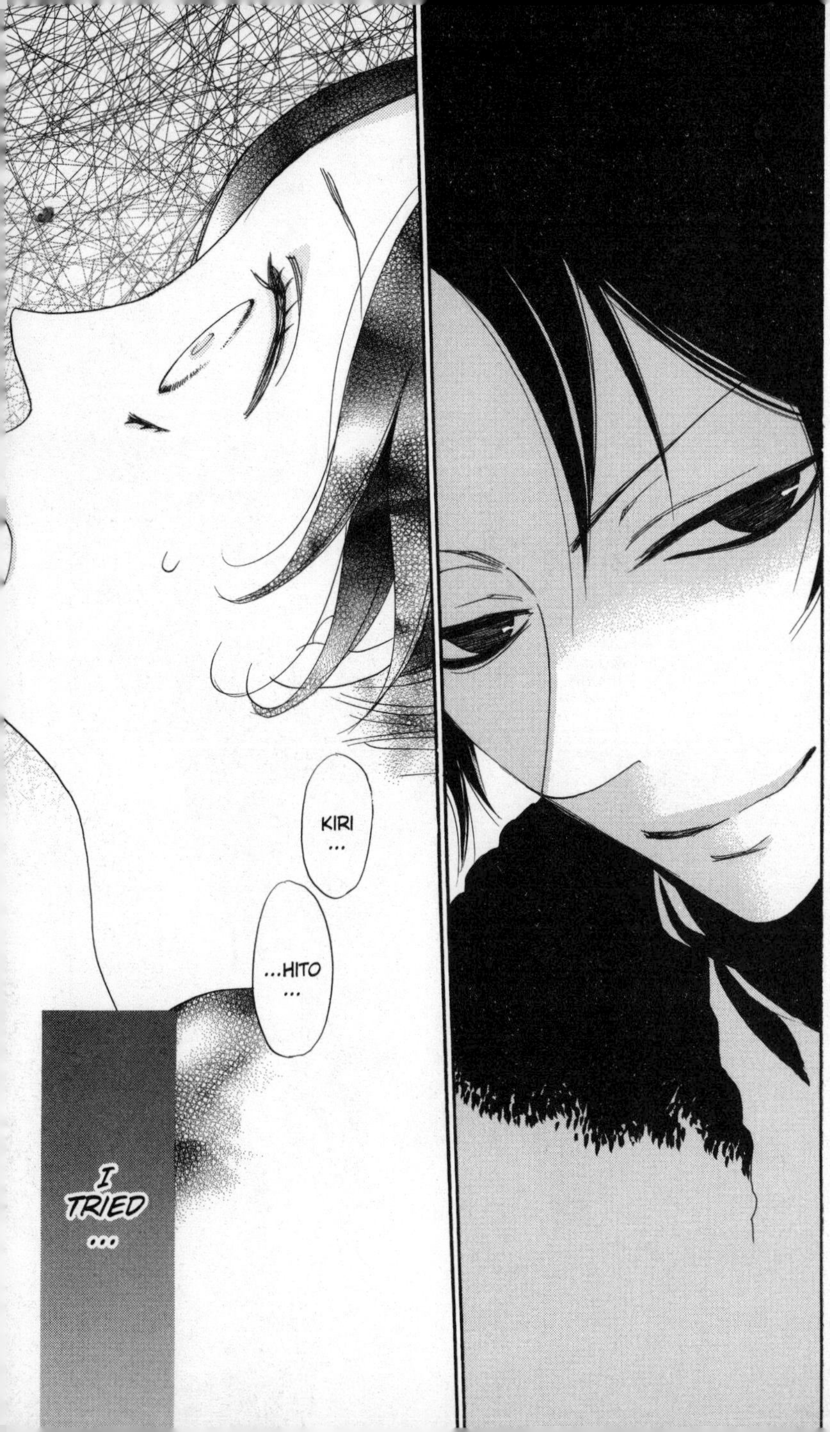
KIRI...
...HITO...
I TRIED...

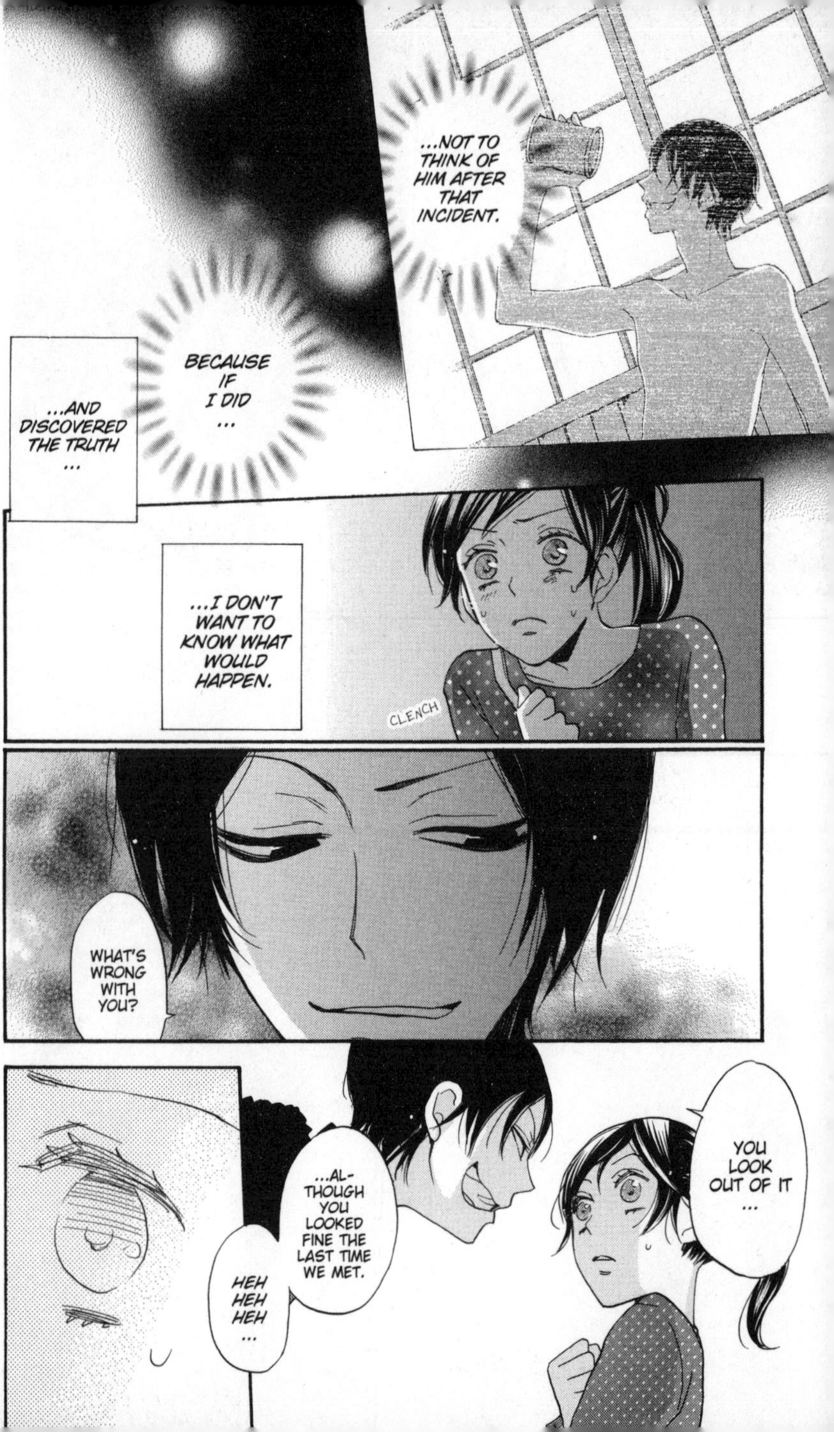
...NOT TO THINK OF HIM AFTER THAT INCIDENT.
BECAUSE IF I DID ...
...AND DISCOVERED THE TRUTH ...
...I DON'T WANT TO KNOW WHAT WOULD HAPPEN.
CLENCH
WHAT'S WRONG WITH YOU?
YOU LOOK OUT OF IT ...
...AL-THOUGH YOU LOOKED FINE THE LAST TIME WE MET.
HEH HEH HEH ...

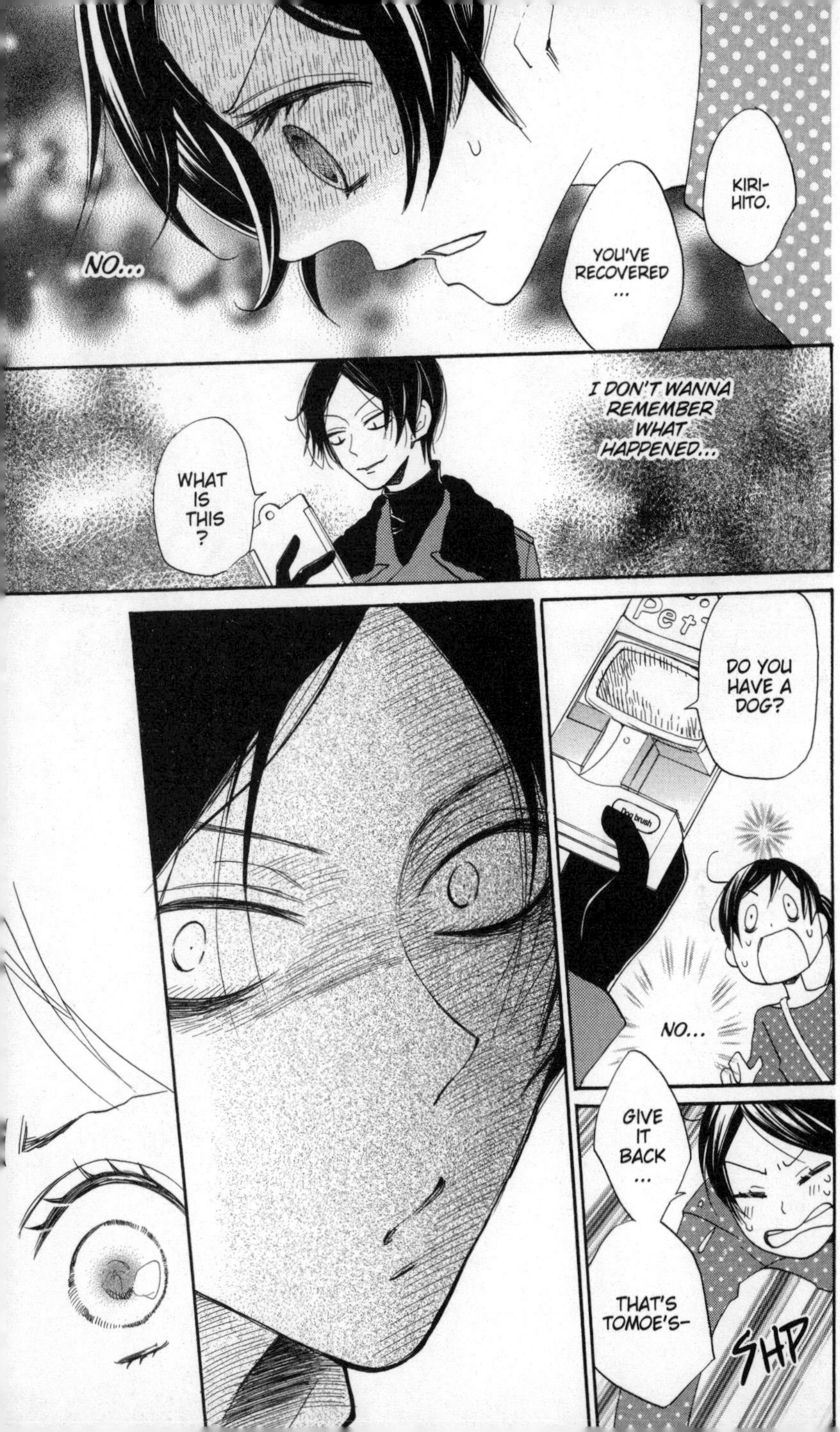
KIRI-HITO.
YOU'VE RECOVERED ...
NO...
I DON'T WANNA REMEMBER WHAT HAPPENED...
WHAT IS THIS ?
Pet
Dog brush
DO YOU HAVE A DOG?
NO...
GIVE IT BACK ...
THAT'S TOMOE'S-
SHP

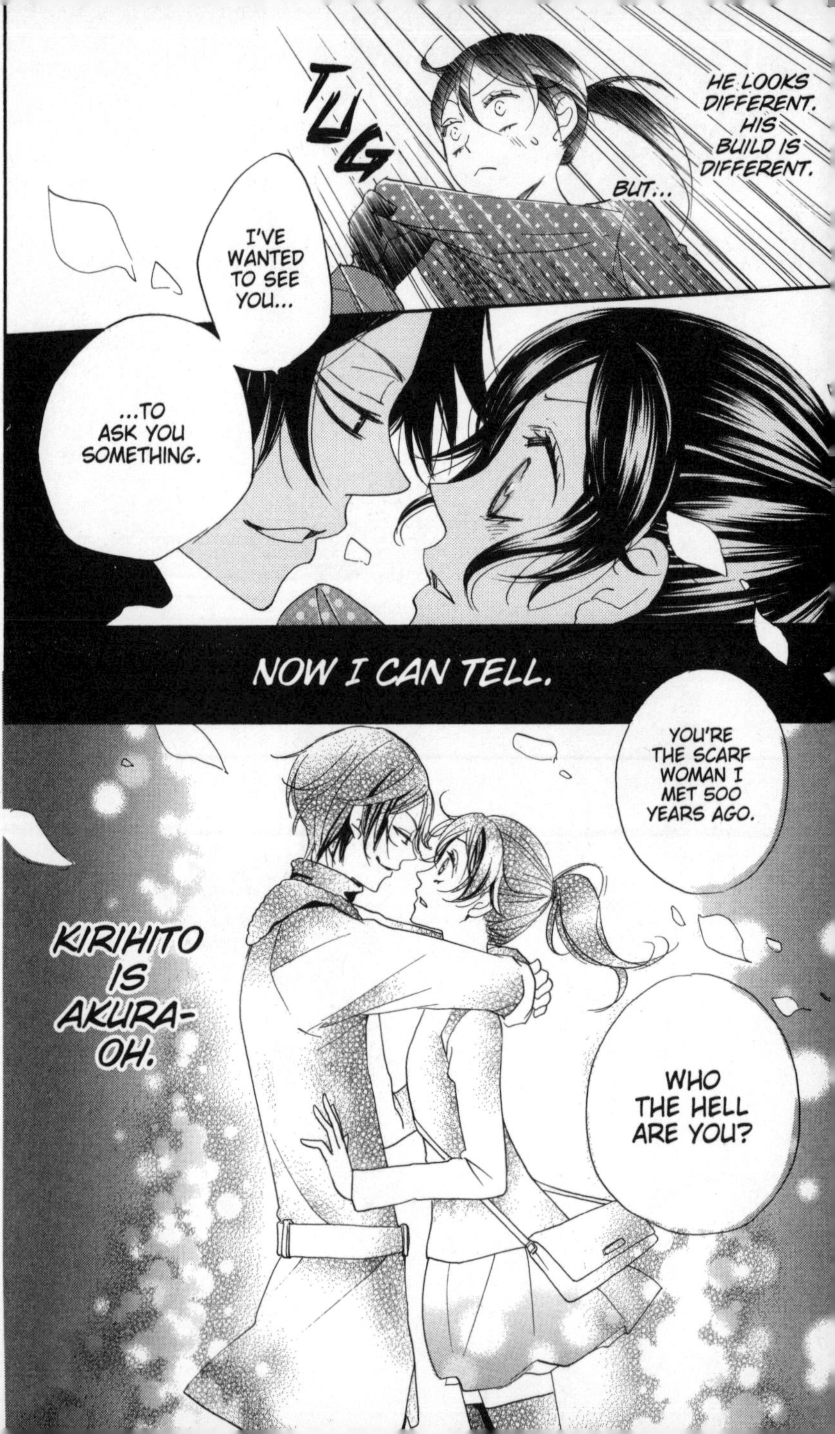
HE LOOKS DIFFERENT. HIS BUILD IS DIFFERENT.
BUT...
TUG
I'VE WANTED TO SEE YOU...
...TO ASK YOU SOMETHING.
NOW I CAN TELL.
YOU'RE THE SCARF WOMAN I MET 500 YEARS AGO.
KIRIHITO IS AKURA-OH.
WHO THE HELL ARE YOU?

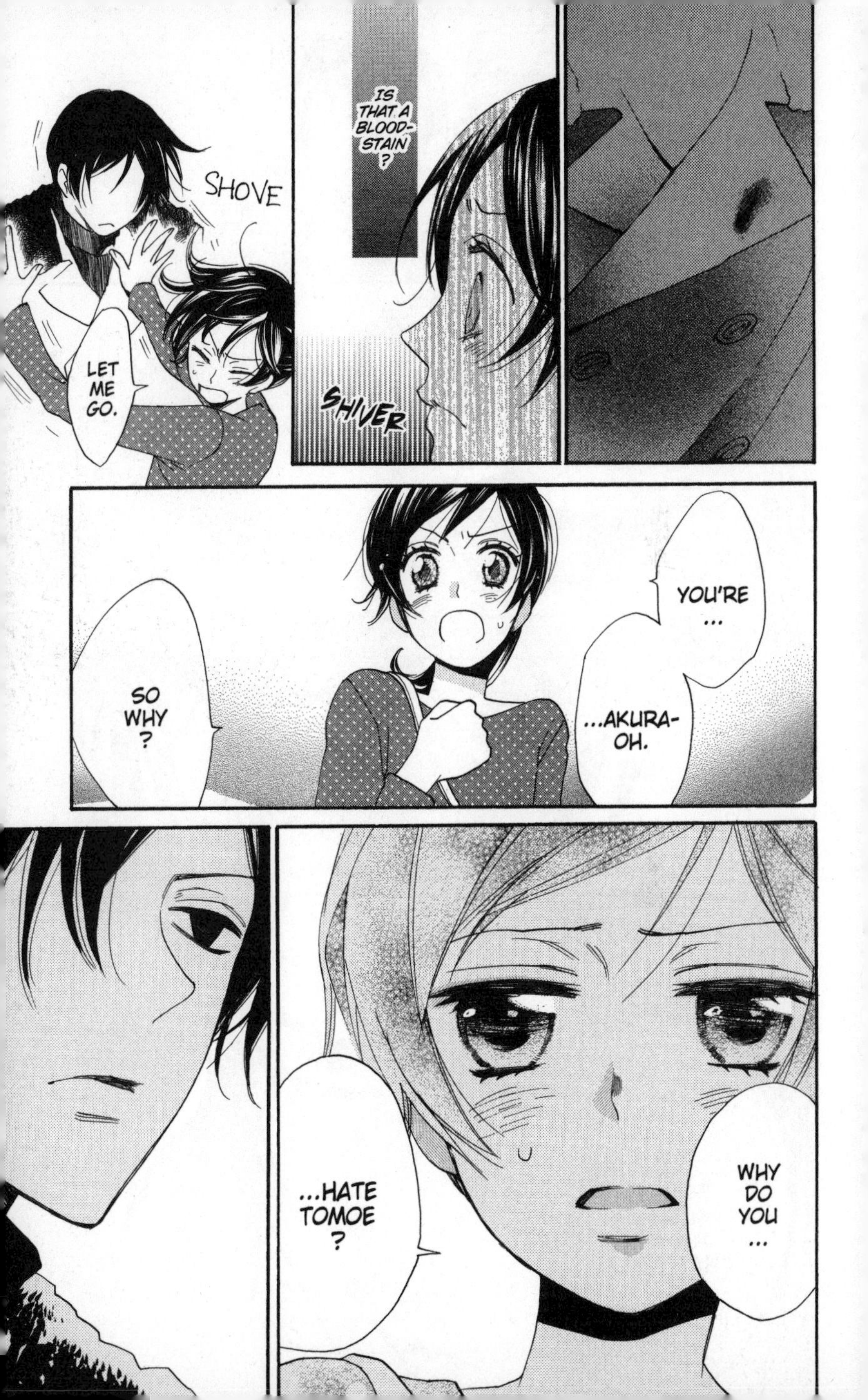
IS THAT A BLOOD-STAIN?
SHIVER
SHOVE
LET ME GO.
YOU'RE...
...AKURA-OH.
SO WHY?
WHY DO YOU...
...HATE TOMOE?

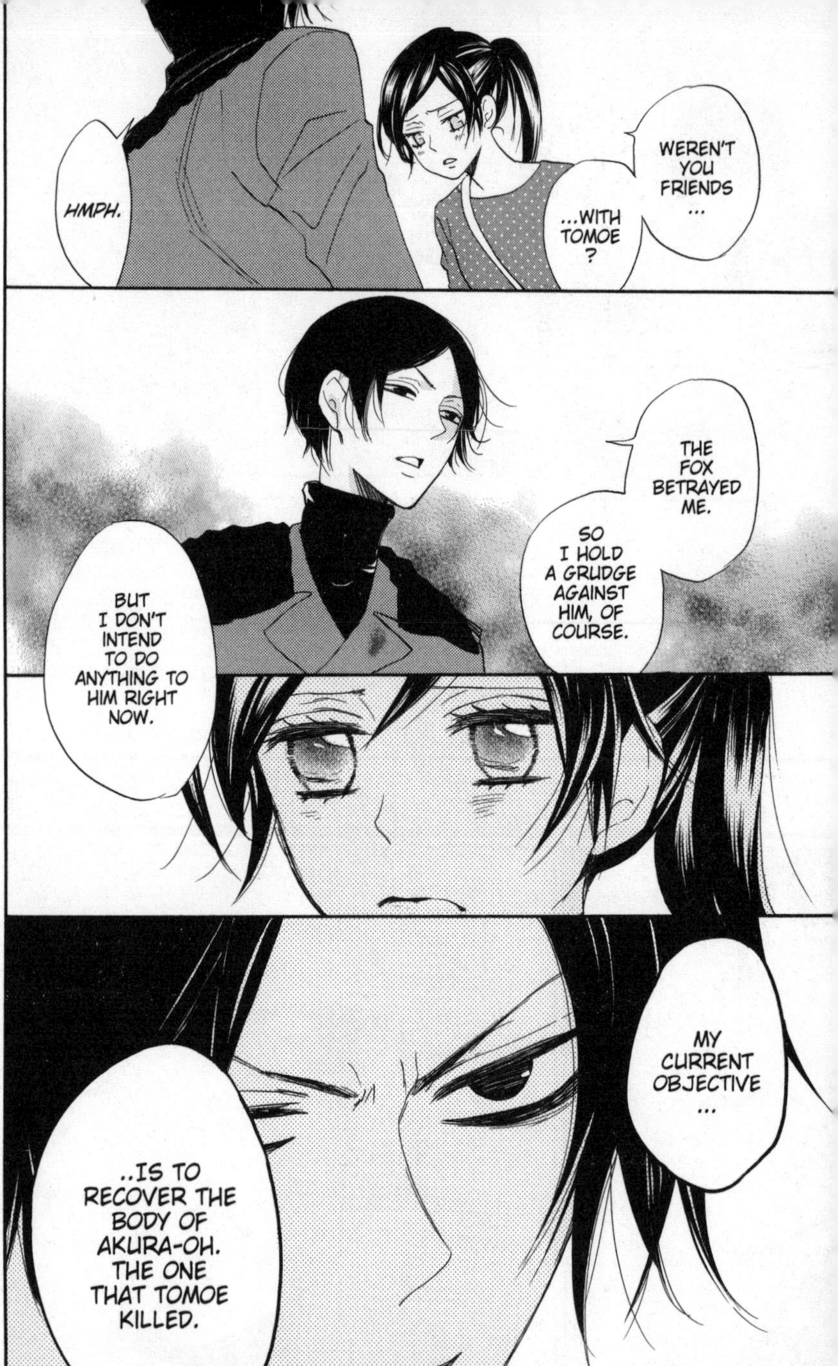
WEREN'T YOU FRIENDS ...
...WITH TOMOE ?
HMPH.
THE FOX BETRAYED ME.
SO I HOLD A GRUDGE AGAINST HIM, OF COURSE.
BUT I DON'T INTEND TO DO ANYTHING TO HIM RIGHT NOW.
MY CURRENT OBJECTIVE ...
..IS TO RECOVER THE BODY OF AKURA-OH. THE ONE THAT TOMOE KILLED.

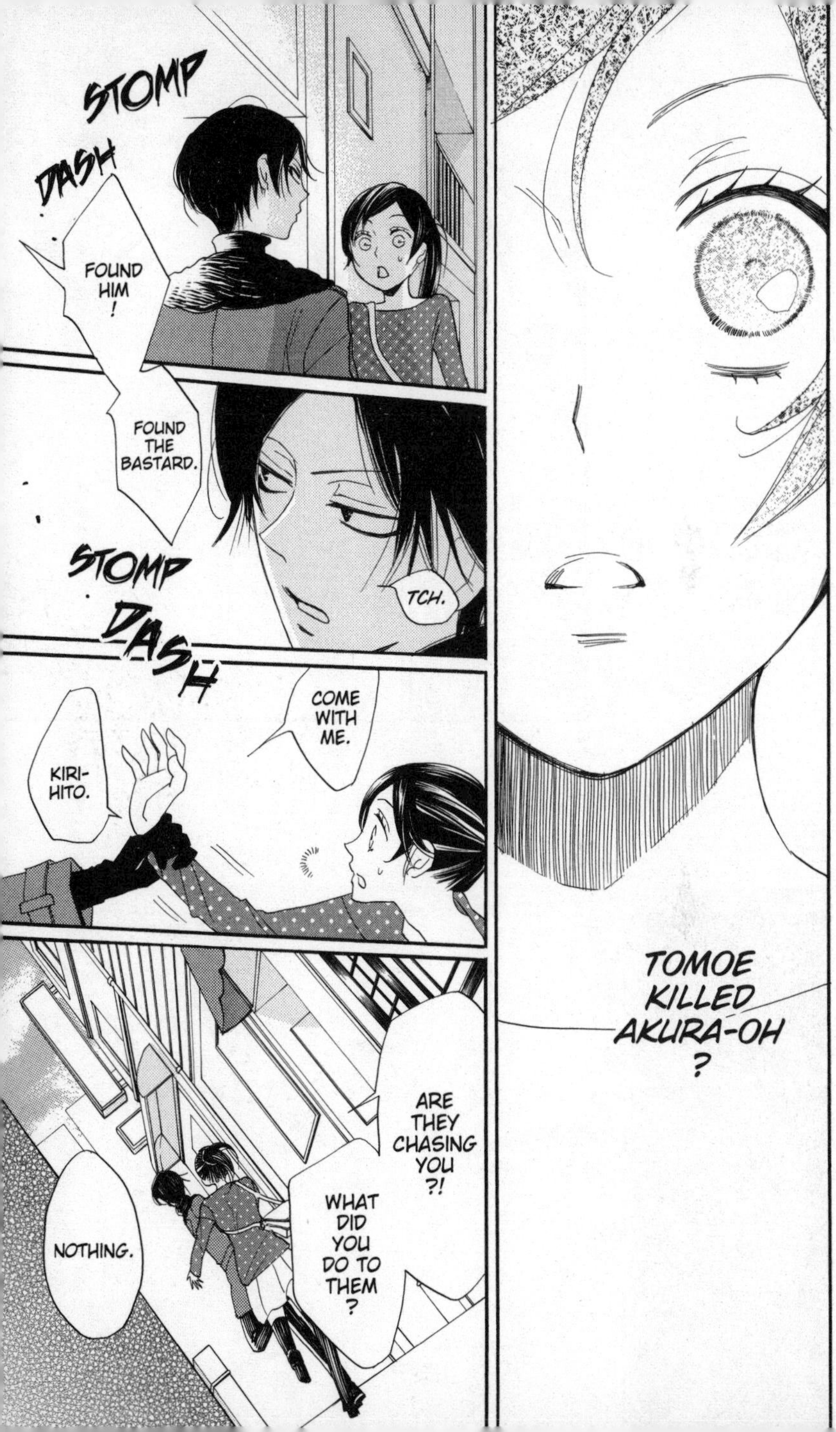
TOMOE KILLED AKURA-OH?
STOMP
DASH
FOUND HIM!
FOUND THE BASTARD.
STOMP
TCH.
DASH
COME WITH ME.
KIRI-HITO.
ARE THEY CHASING YOU?!
WHAT DID YOU DO TO THEM?
NOTHING.

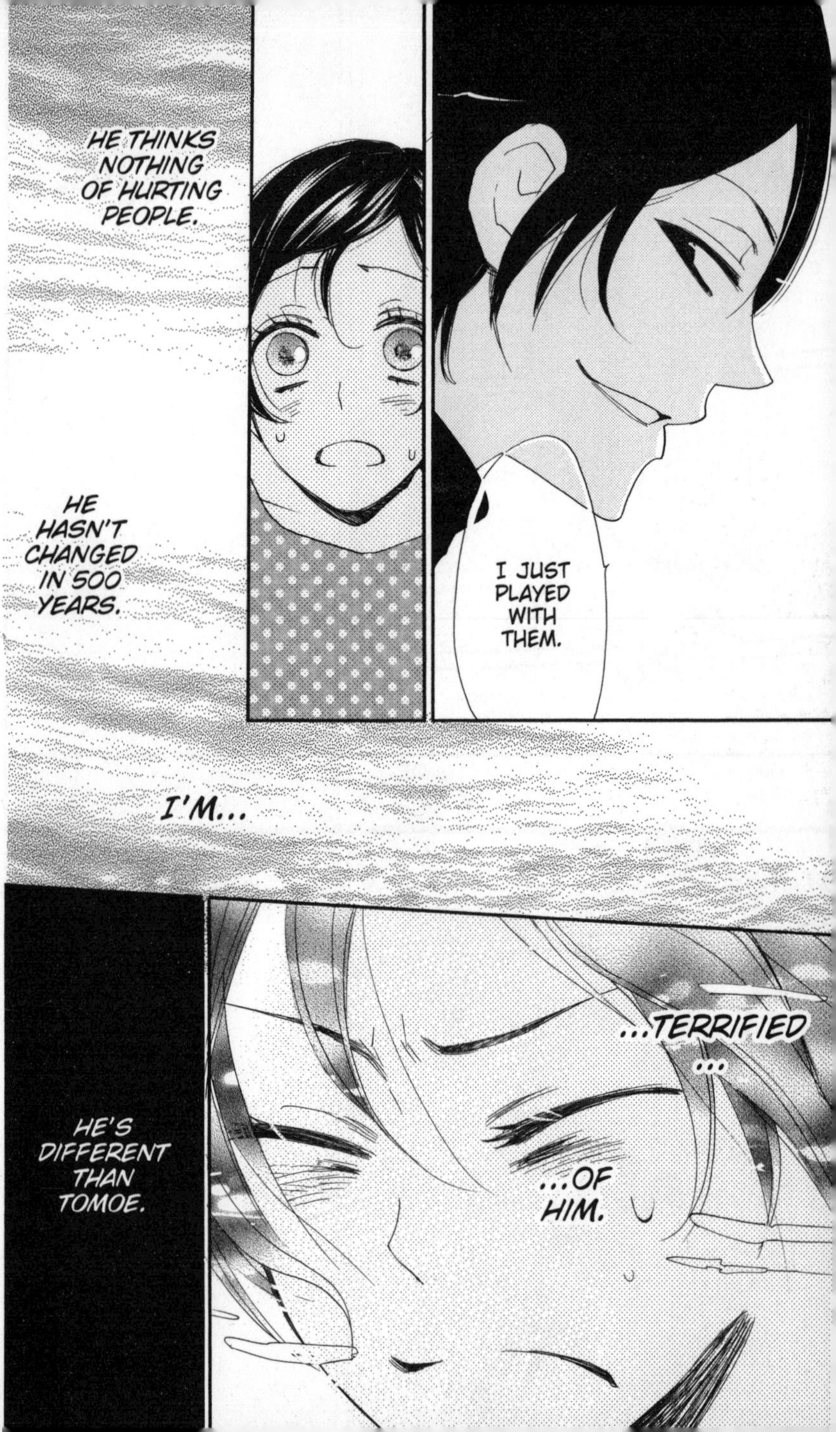
I JUST PLAYED WITH THEM.
HE THINKS NOTHING OF HURTING PEOPLE.
HE HASN'T CHANGED IN 500 YEARS.
I'M...
...TERRIFIED...
...OF HIM.
HE'S DIFFERENT THAN TOMOE.

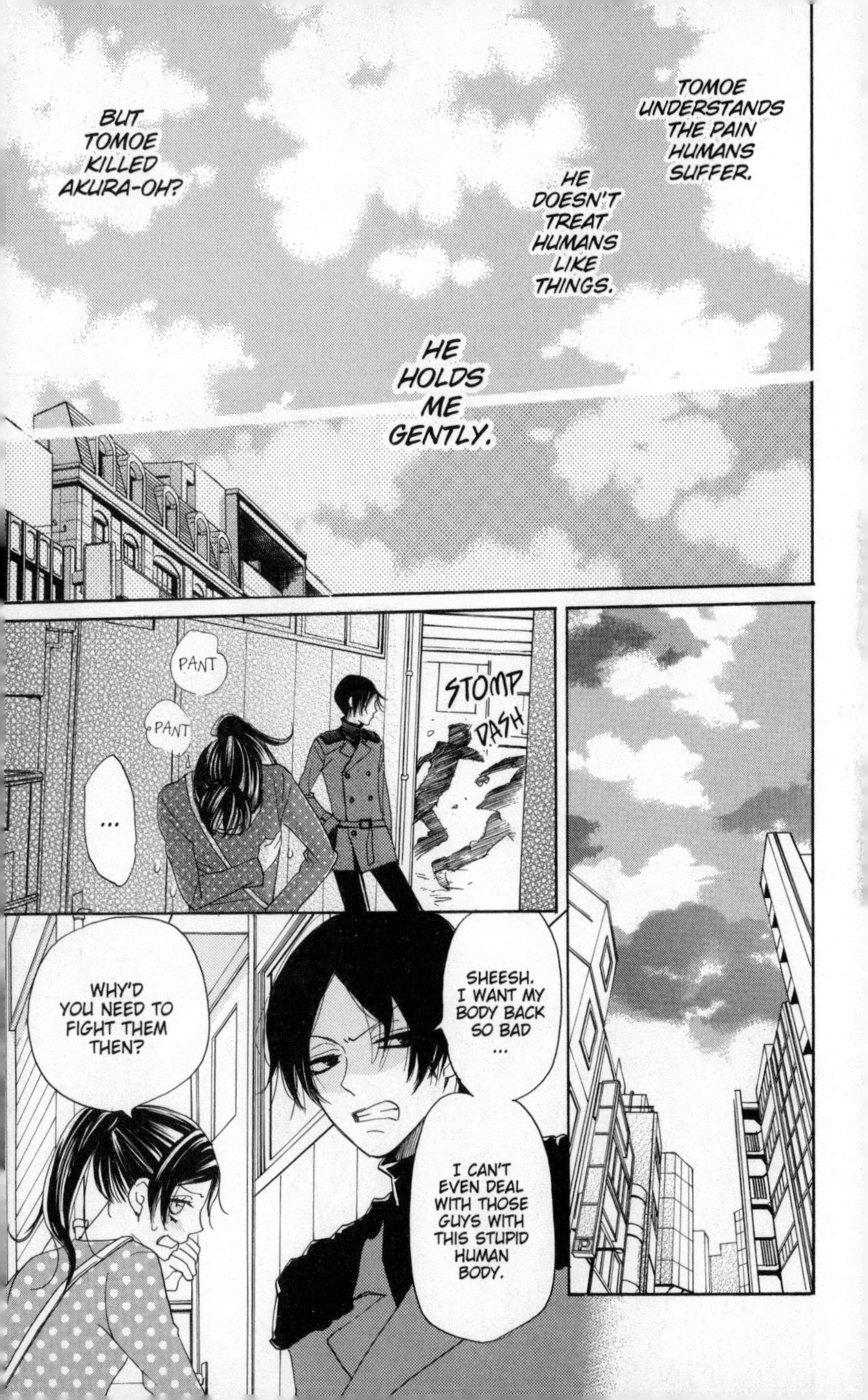
TOMOE UNDERSTANDS THE PAIN HUMANS SUFFER.
HE DOESN'T TREAT HUMANS LIKE THINGS.
HE HOLDS ME GENTLY.
BUT TOMOE KILLED AKURA-OH?
STOMP
DASH
PANT
PANT
...
SHEESH. I WANT MY BODY BACK SO BAD ...
I CAN'T EVEN DEAL WITH THOSE GUYS WITH THIS STUPID HUMAN BODY.
WHY'D YOU NEED TO FIGHT THEM THEN?

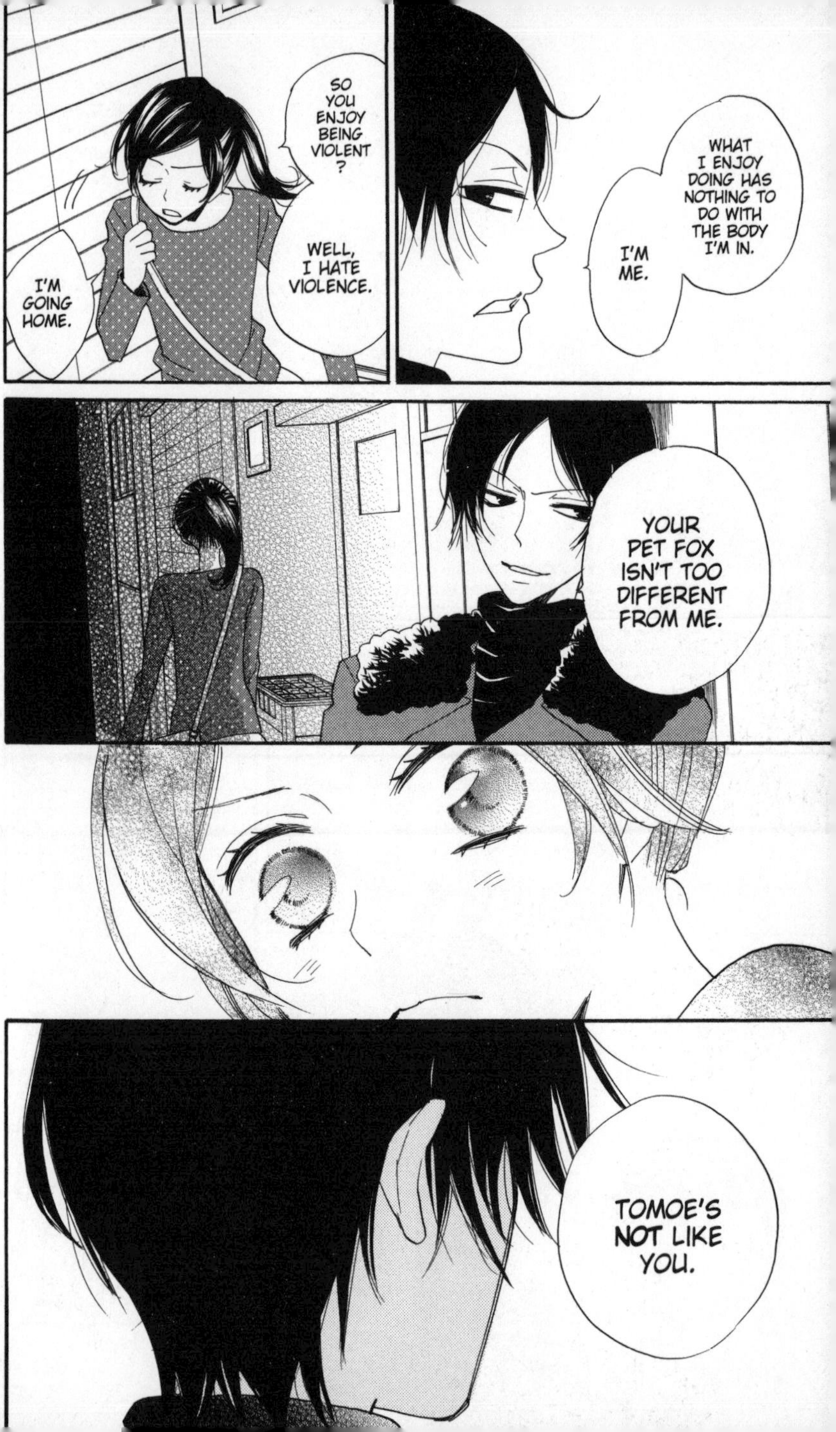
WHAT I ENJOY DOING HAS NOTHING TO DO WITH THE BODY I'M IN.
I'M ME.
SO YOU ENJOY BEING VIOLENT?
WELL, I HATE VIOLENCE.
I'M GOING HOME.
YOUR PET FOX ISN'T TOO DIFFERENT FROM ME.
TOMOE'S NOT LIKE YOU.

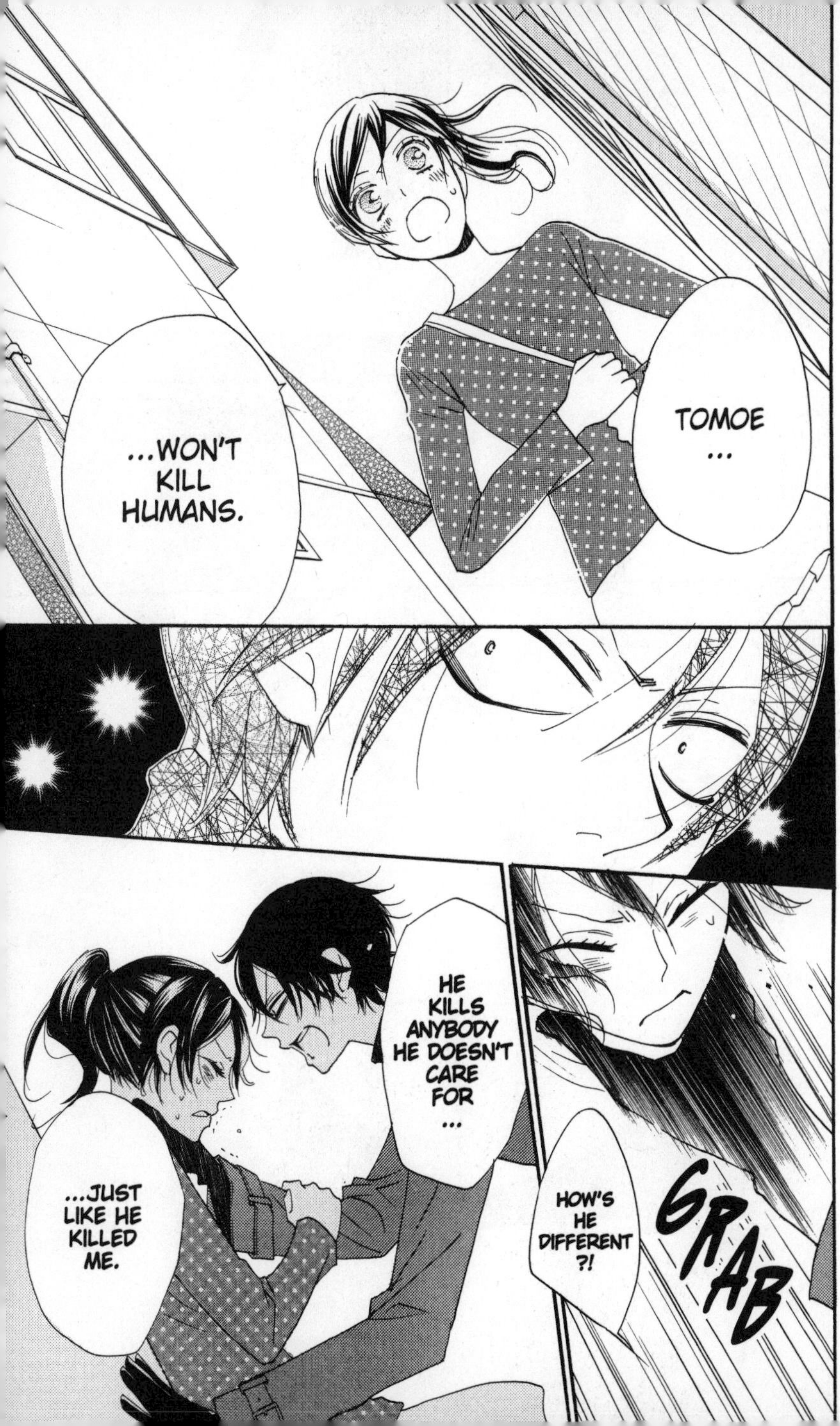
TOMOE ...
...WON'T KILL HUMANS.
GRAB
HOW'S HE DIFFERENT ?!
HE KILLS ANYBODY HE DOESN'T CARE FOR ...
...JUST LIKE HE KILLED ME.

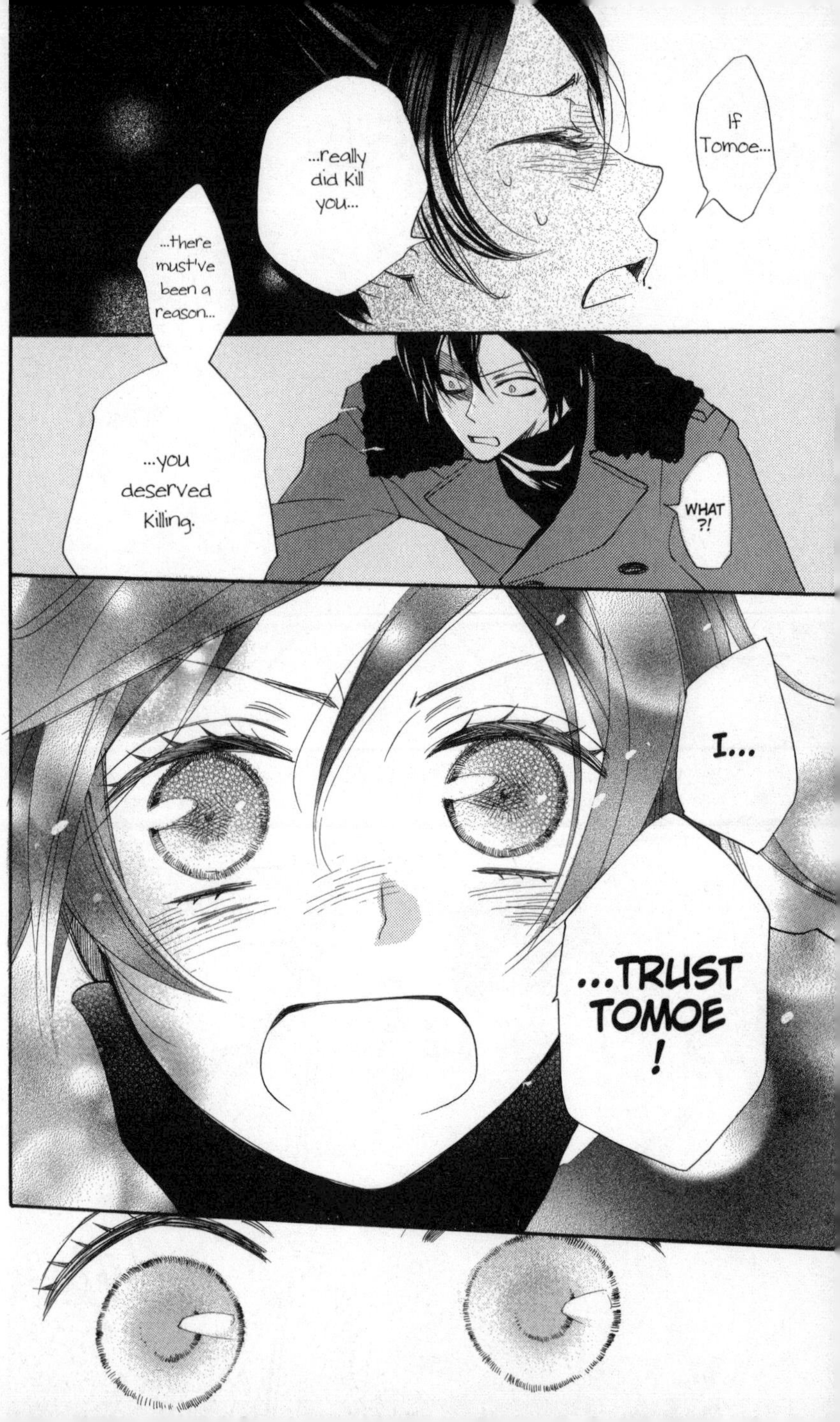
If Tomoe...
...really did kill you...
...there must've been a reason...
...you deserved killing.
WHAT ?!
I...
...TRUST TOMOE !

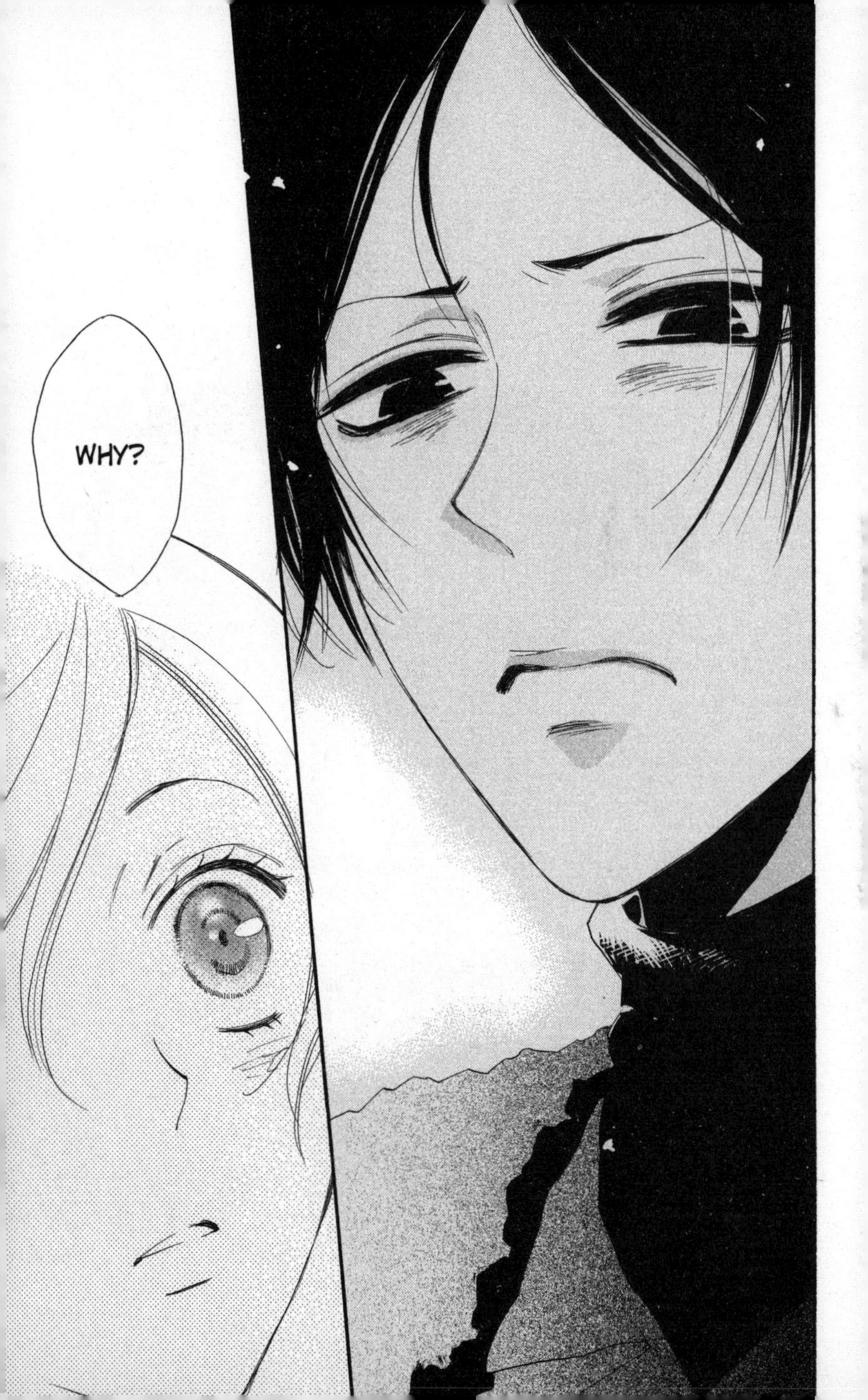
WHY?

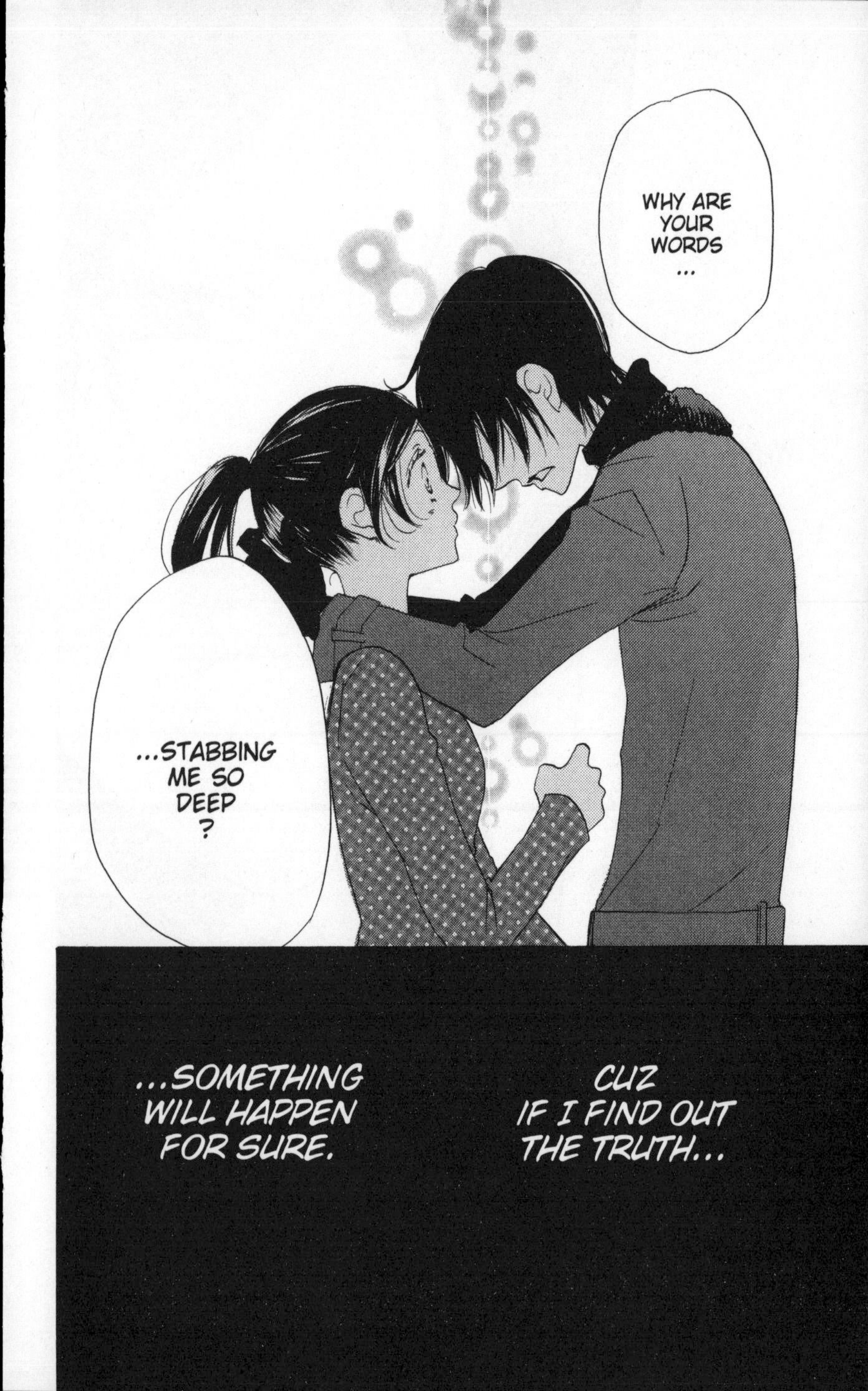
WHY ARE YOUR WORDS ...
...STABBING ME SO DEEP ?
CUZ IF I FIND OUT THE TRUTH...
...SOMETHING WILL HAPPEN FOR SURE.

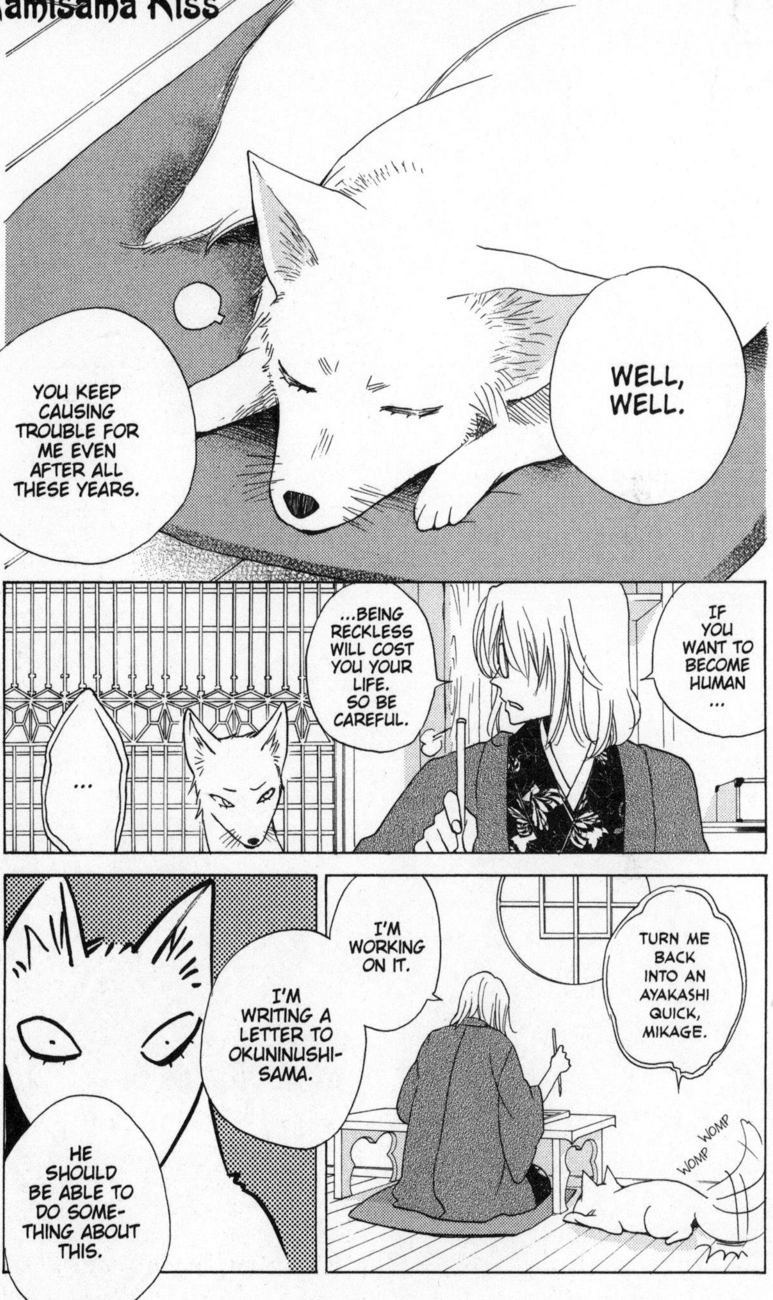
WELL, WELL.
YOU KEEP CAUSING TROUBLE FOR ME EVEN AFTER ALL THESE YEARS.
IF YOU WANT TO BECOME HUMAN...
...BEING RECKLESS WILL COST YOU YOUR LIFE. SO BE CAREFUL.
...
TURN ME BACK INTO AN AYAKASHI QUICK, MIKAGE.
I'M WORKING ON IT.
I'M WRITING A LETTER TO OKUNINUSHI-SAMA.
WOMP WOMP
HE SHOULD BE ABLE TO DO SOME-THING ABOUT THIS.

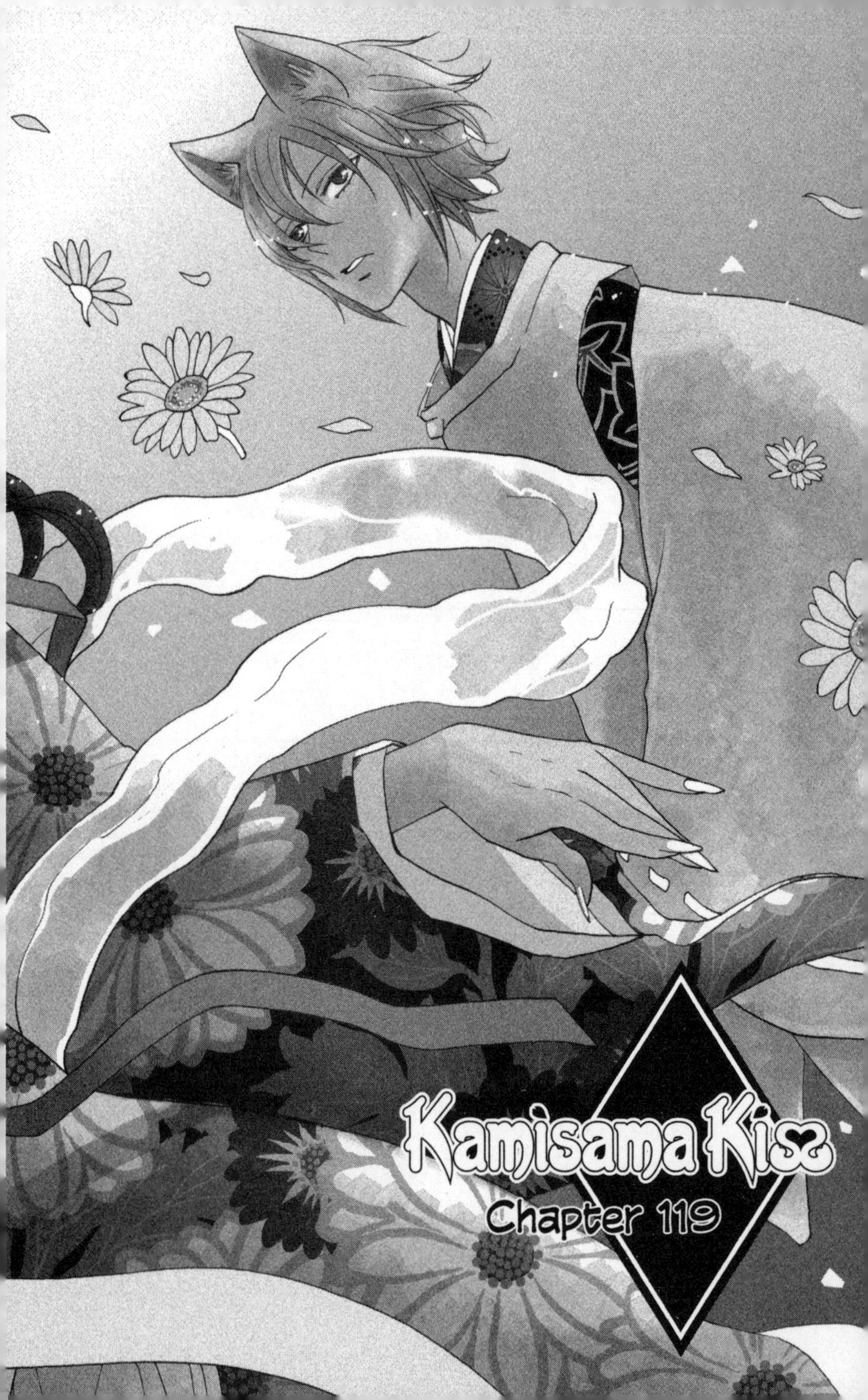
Kamisama Kiss
Chapter 119

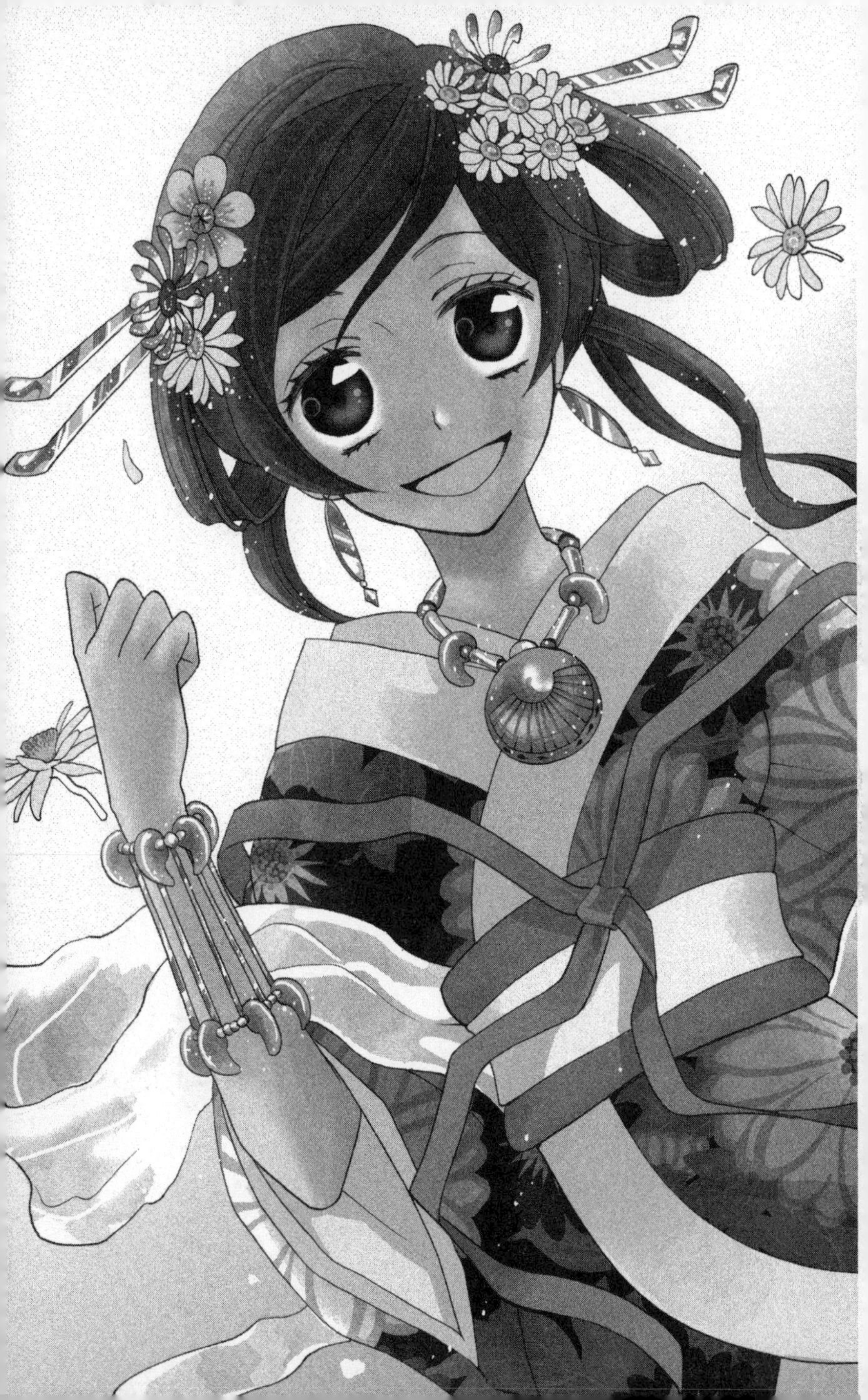

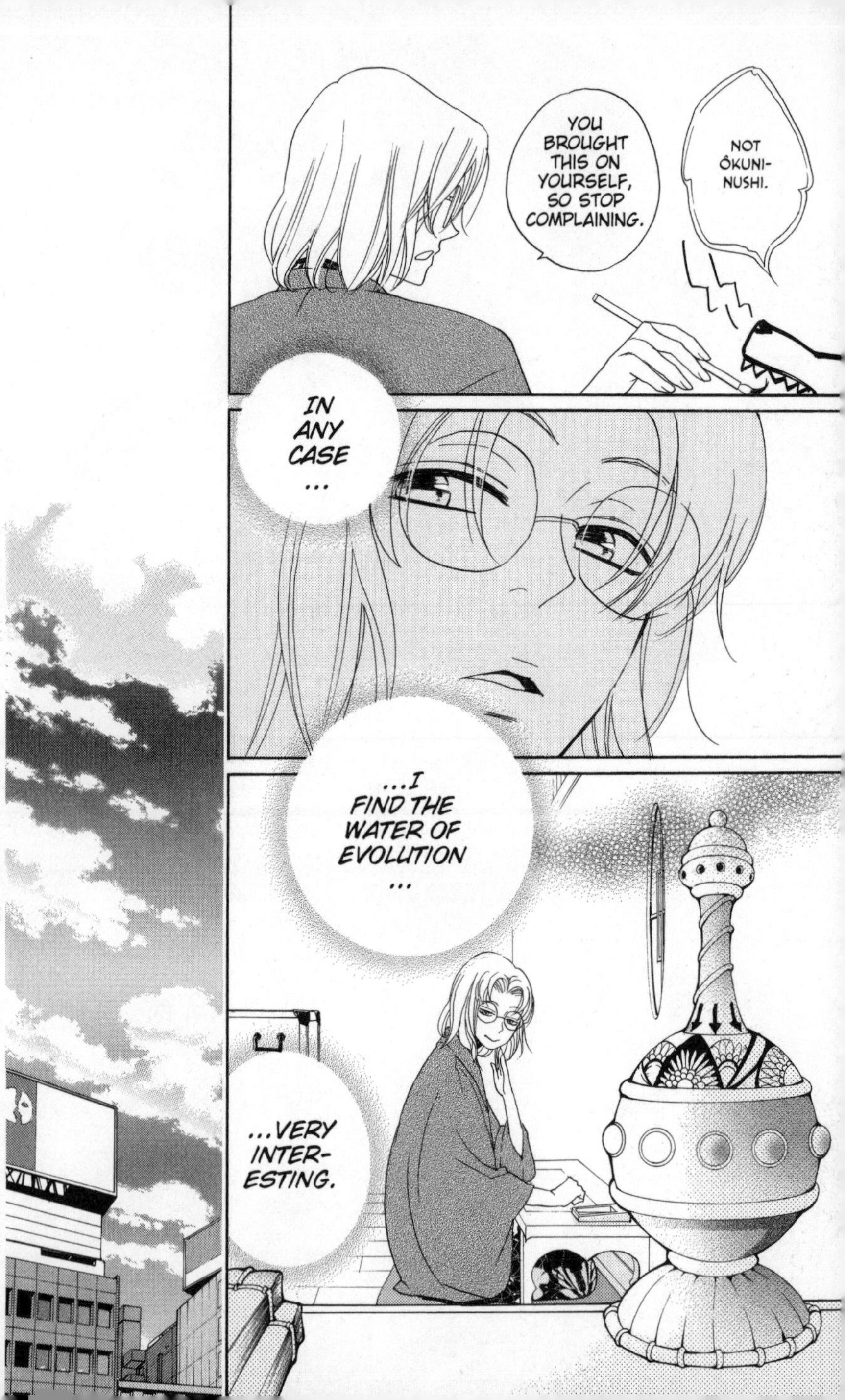
NOT ÔKUNI-NUSHI.
YOU BROUGHT THIS ON YOURSELF, SO STOP COMPLAINING.
IN ANY CASE ...
...I FIND THE WATER OF EVOLUTION ...
...VERY INTER-ESTING.

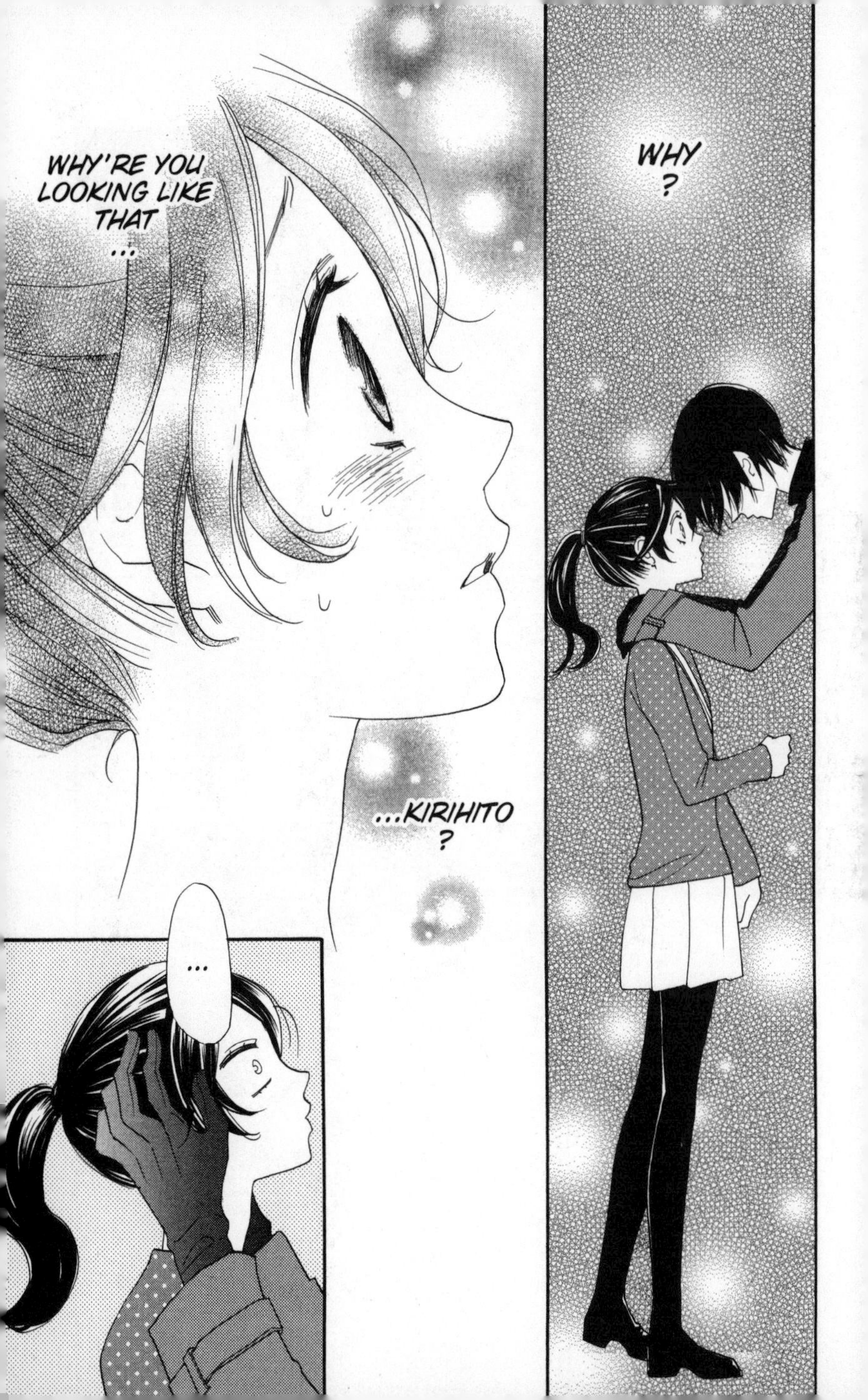
WHY ?
WHY'RE YOU LOOKING LIKE THAT ...
...KIRIHITO ?
...

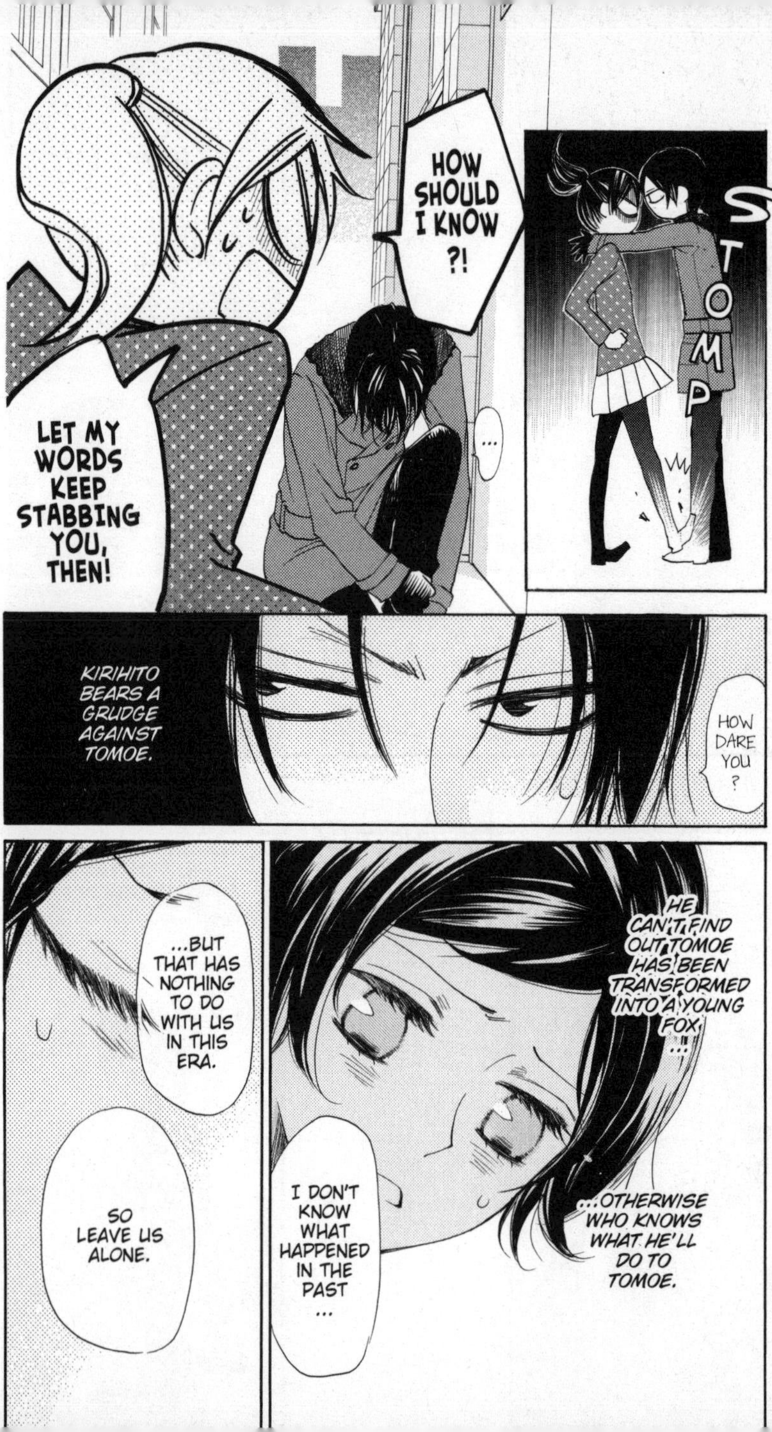
STOMP
HOW SHOULD I KNOW ?!
...
LET MY WORDS KEEP STABBING YOU, THEN!
HOW DARE YOU ?
KIRIHITO BEARS A GRUDGE AGAINST TOMOE.
HE CAN'T FIND OUT TOMOE HAS BEEN TRANSFORMED INTO A YOUNG FOX...
...OTHERWISE WHO KNOWS WHAT HE'LL DO TO TOMOE.
I DON'T KNOW WHAT HAPPENED IN THE PAST...
...BUT THAT HAS NOTHING TO DO WITH US IN THIS ERA.
SO LEAVE US ALONE.

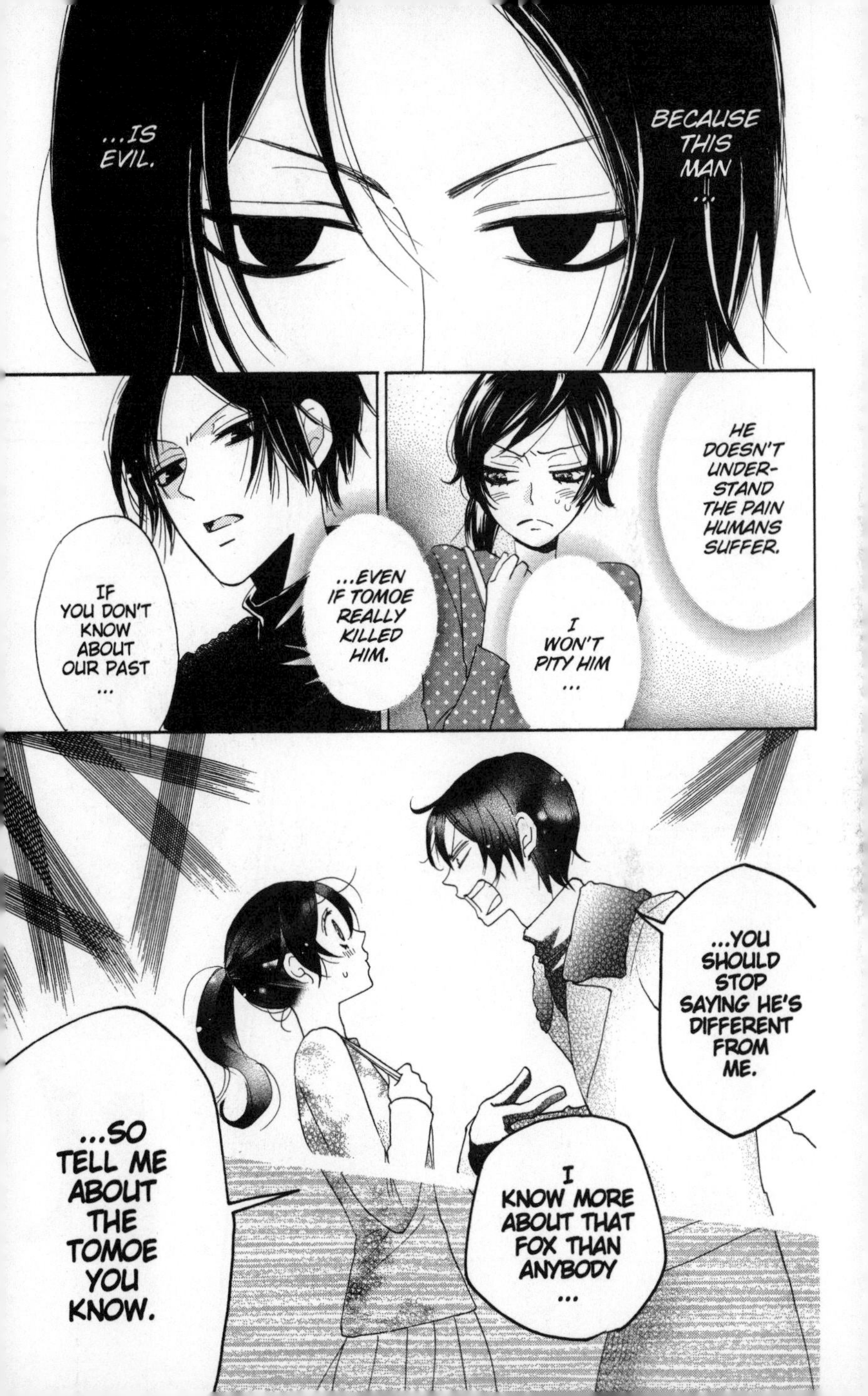
BECAUSE THIS MAN ...
...IS EVIL.
HE DOESN'T UNDER-STAND THE PAIN HUMANS SUFFER.
I WON'T PITY HIM ...
...EVEN IF TOMOE REALLY KILLED HIM.
IF YOU DON'T KNOW ABOUT OUR PAST ...
...YOU SHOULD STOP SAYING HE'S DIFFERENT FROM ME.
I KNOW MORE ABOUT THAT FOX THAN ANYBODY ...
...SO TELL ME ABOUT THE TOMOE YOU KNOW.

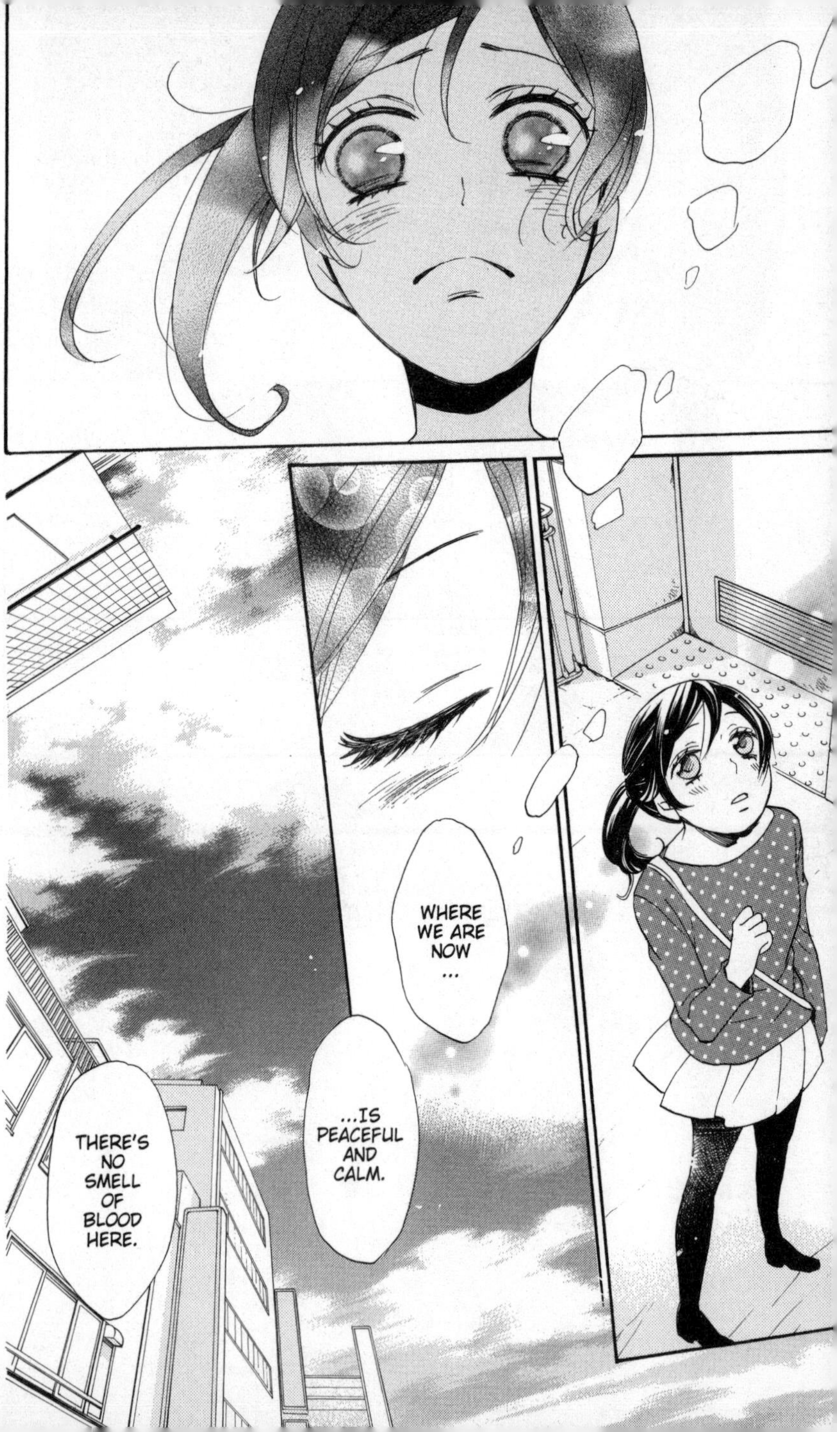
WHERE WE ARE NOW ...
...IS PEACEFUL AND CALM.
THERE'S NO SMELL OF BLOOD HERE.

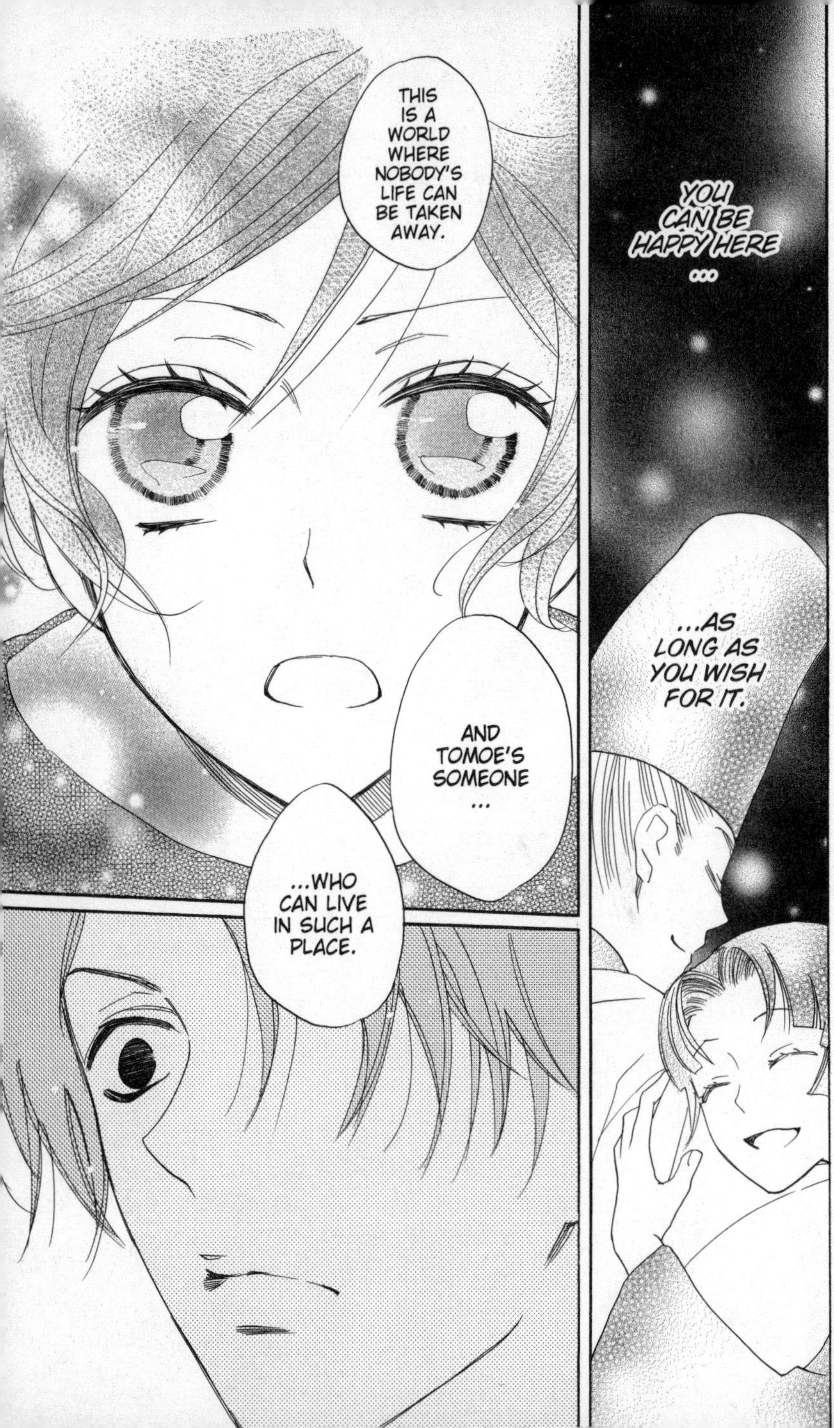
YOU CAN BE HAPPY HERE ...
...AS LONG AS YOU WISH FOR IT.
THIS IS A WORLD WHERE NOBODY'S LIFE CAN BE TAKEN AWAY.
AND TOMOE'S SOMEONE ...
...WHO CAN LIVE IN SUCH A PLACE.

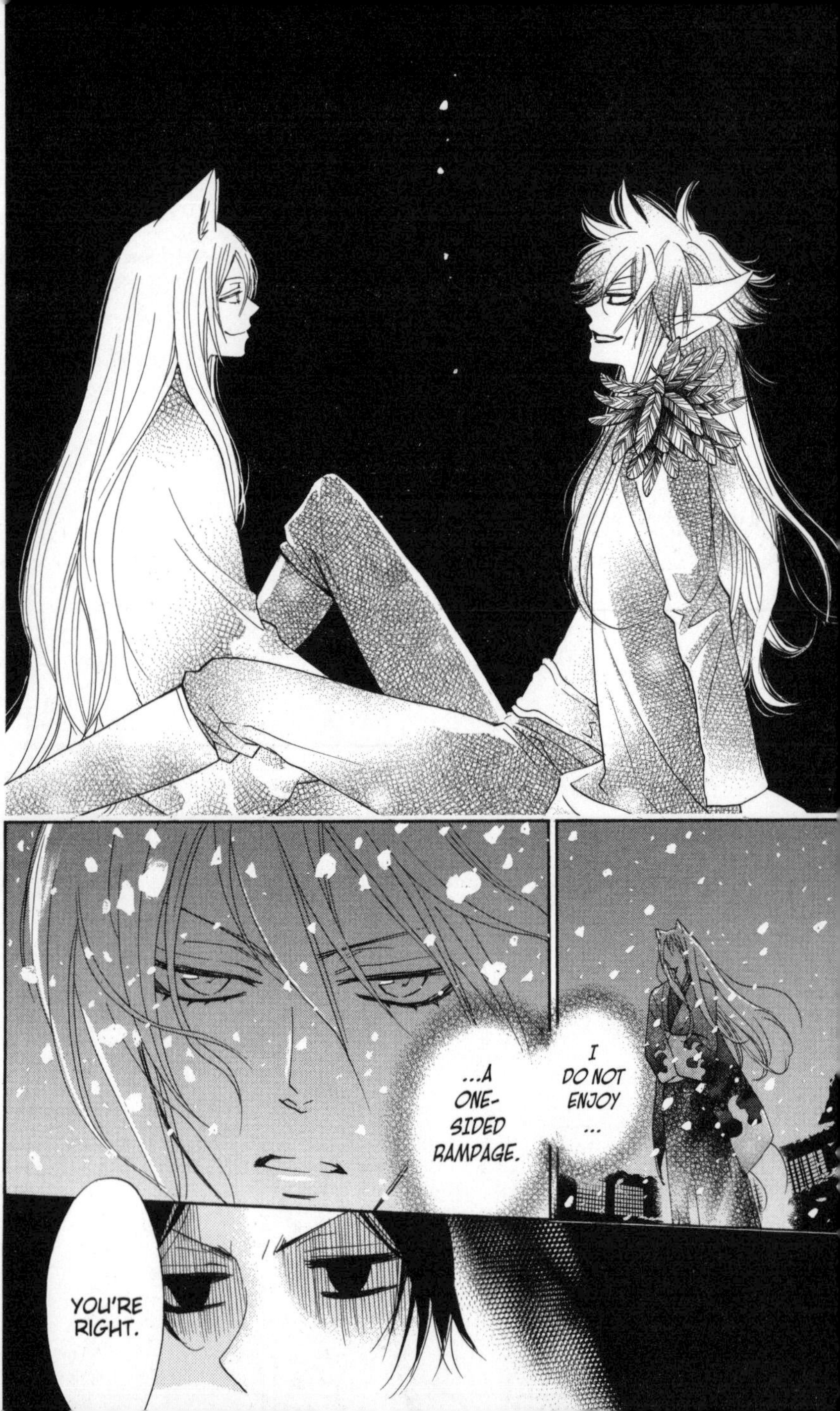
I DO NOT ENJOY ...
...A ONE-SIDED RAMPAGE.
YOU'RE RIGHT.

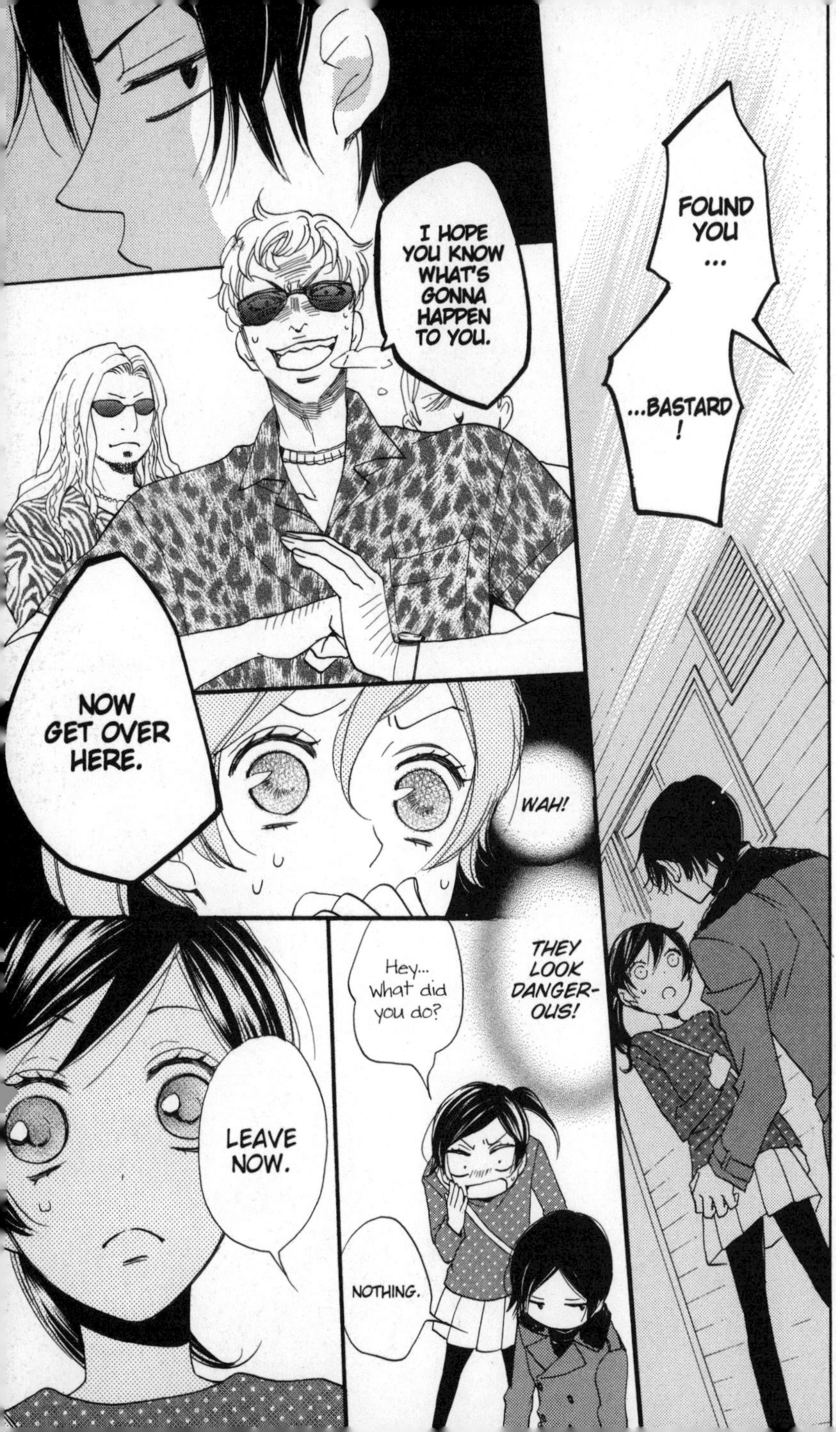
FOUND YOU ...
...BASTARD !
I HOPE YOU KNOW WHAT'S GONNA HAPPEN TO YOU.
NOW GET OVER HERE.
WAH!
THEY LOOK DANGER-OUS!
Hey... What did you do?
NOTHING.
LEAVE NOW.

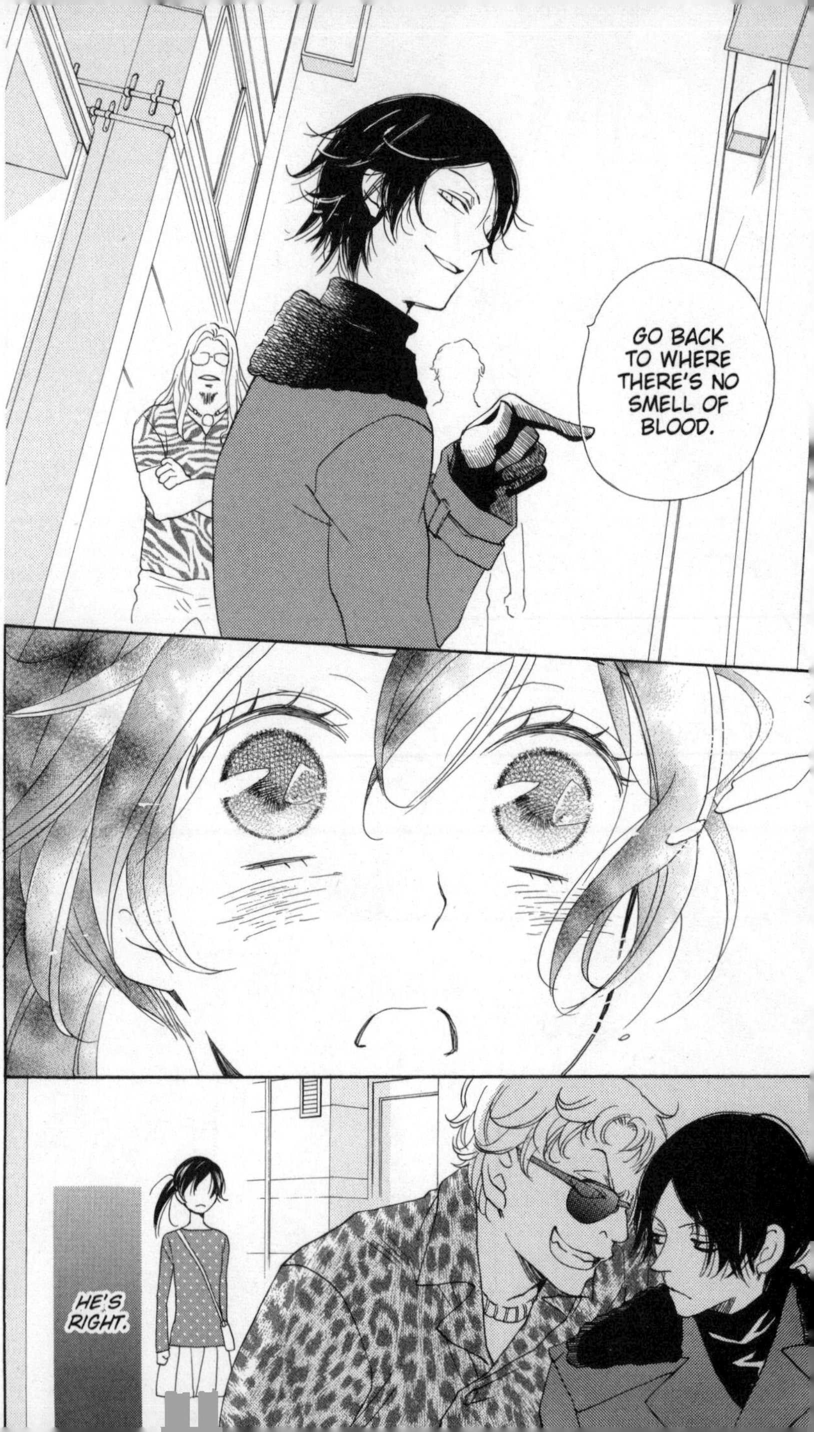
GO BACK TO WHERE THERE'S NO SMELL OF BLOOD.
HE'S RIGHT.

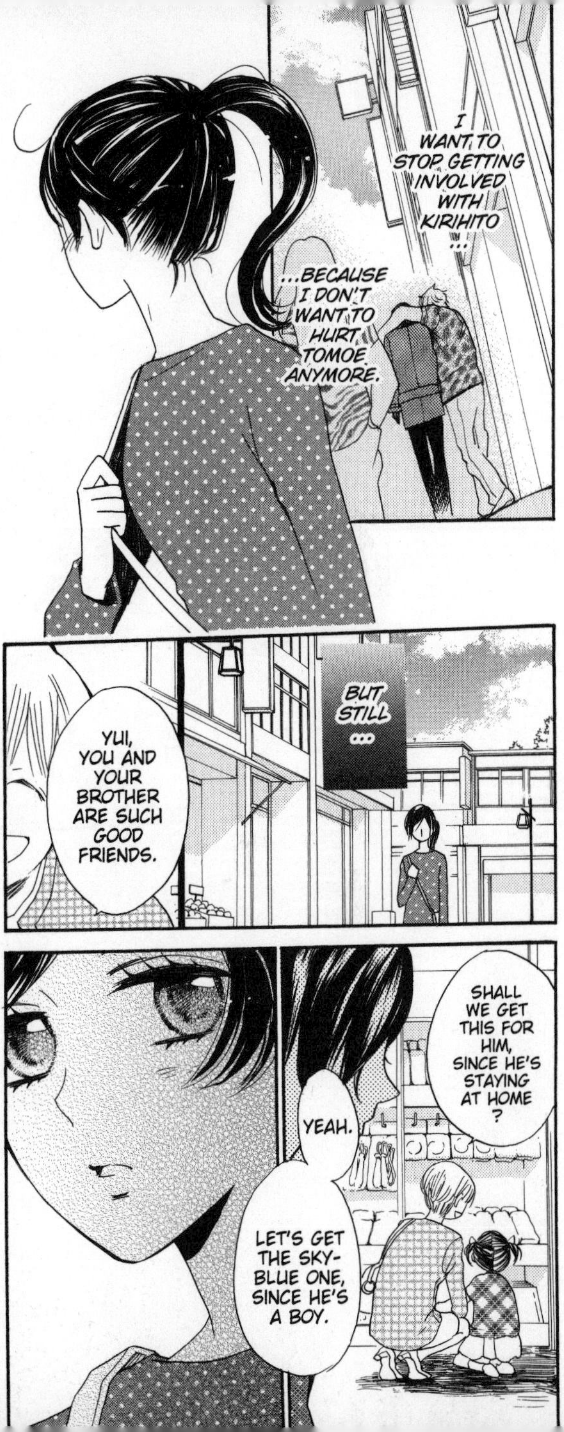
I WANT TO STOP GETTING INVOLVED WITH KIRIHITO...
...BECAUSE I DON'T WANT TO HURT TOMOE ANYMORE.
BUT STILL...
YUI, YOU AND YOUR BROTHER ARE SUCH GOOD FRIENDS.
SHALL WE GET THIS FOR HIM, SINCE HE'S STAYING AT HOME?
YEAH.
LET'S GET THE SKY-BLUE ONE, SINCE HE'S A BOY.

Thank you for reading this far!

If you have any comments and thoughts about volume 20, I'd love to hear from you!

The address is...

Julietta Suzuki
c/o Shojo Beat
VIZ Media, LLC
P.O. Box 77010
San Francisco
CA 94107

I have a blog and a twitter account, so please take a look at them too.

I hope we'll be able to meet again in the next volume...

-Juli

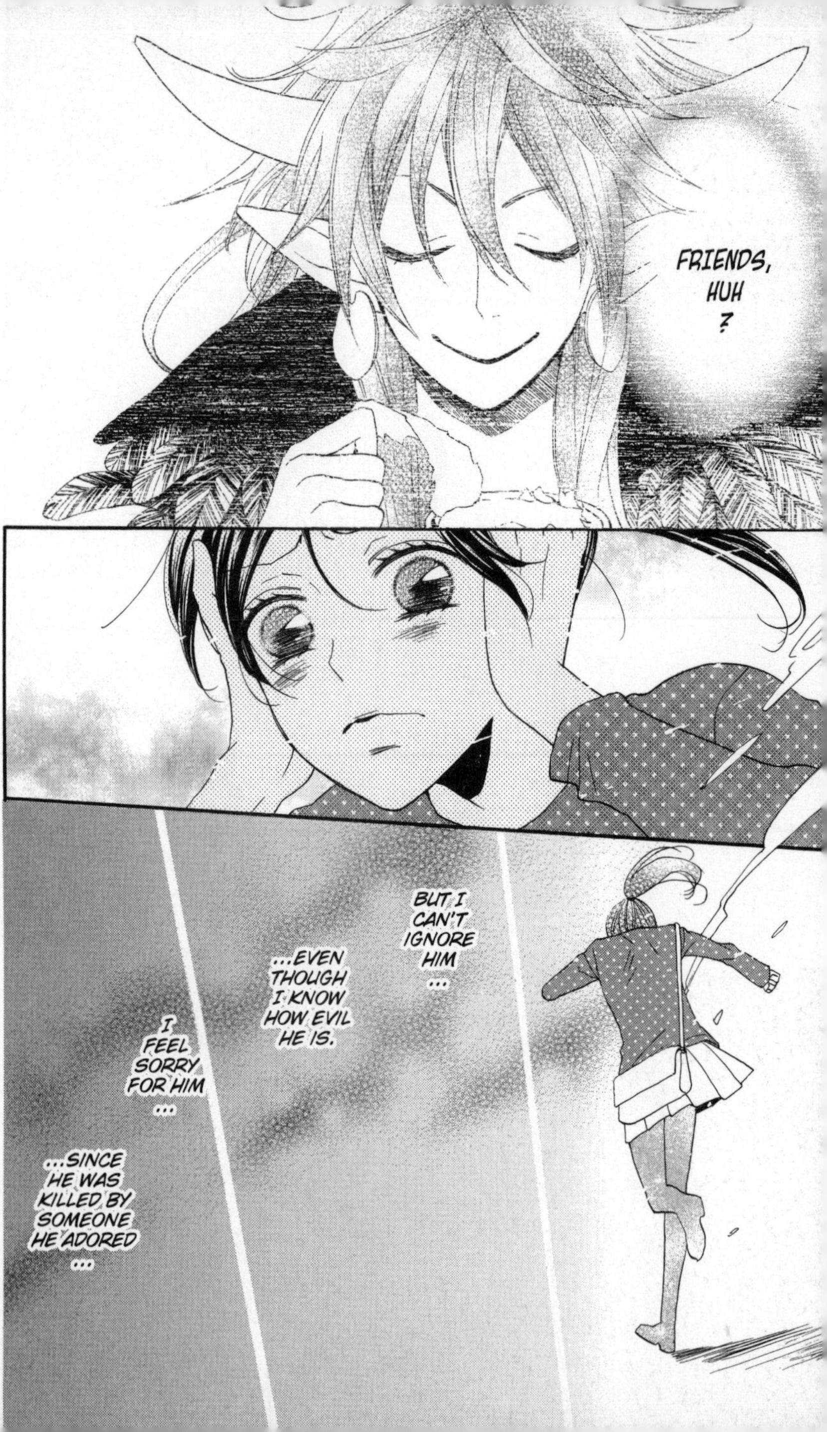
FRIENDS, HUH?
BUT I CAN'T IGNORE HIM...
...EVEN THOUGH I KNOW HOW EVIL HE IS.
I FEEL SORRY FOR HIM...
...SINCE HE WAS KILLED BY SOMEONE HE ADORED...

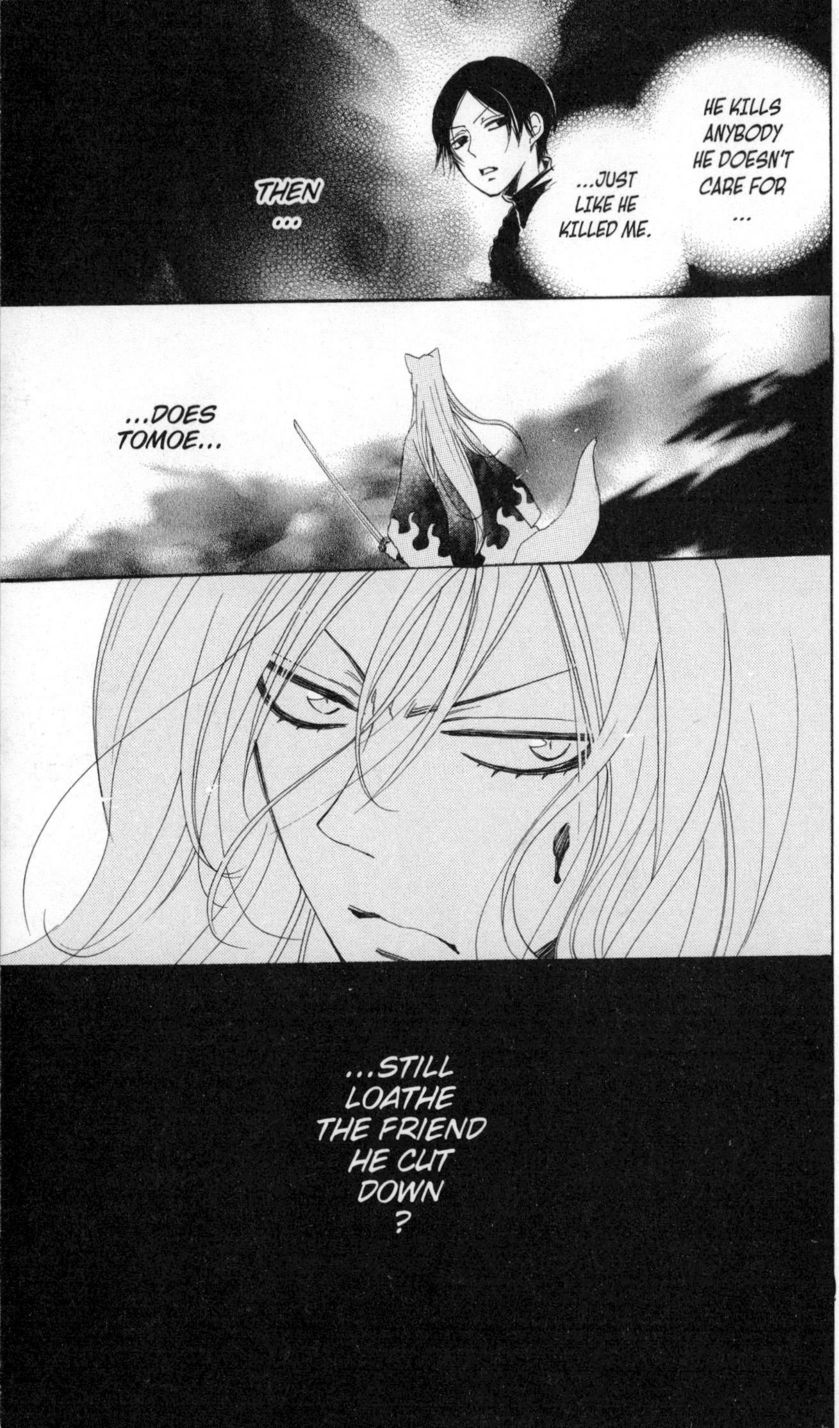
HE KILLS ANYBODY HE DOESN'T CARE FOR ...
...JUST LIKE HE KILLED ME.
THEN ...
...DOES TOMOE...
...STILL LOATHE THE FRIEND HE CUT DOWN ?

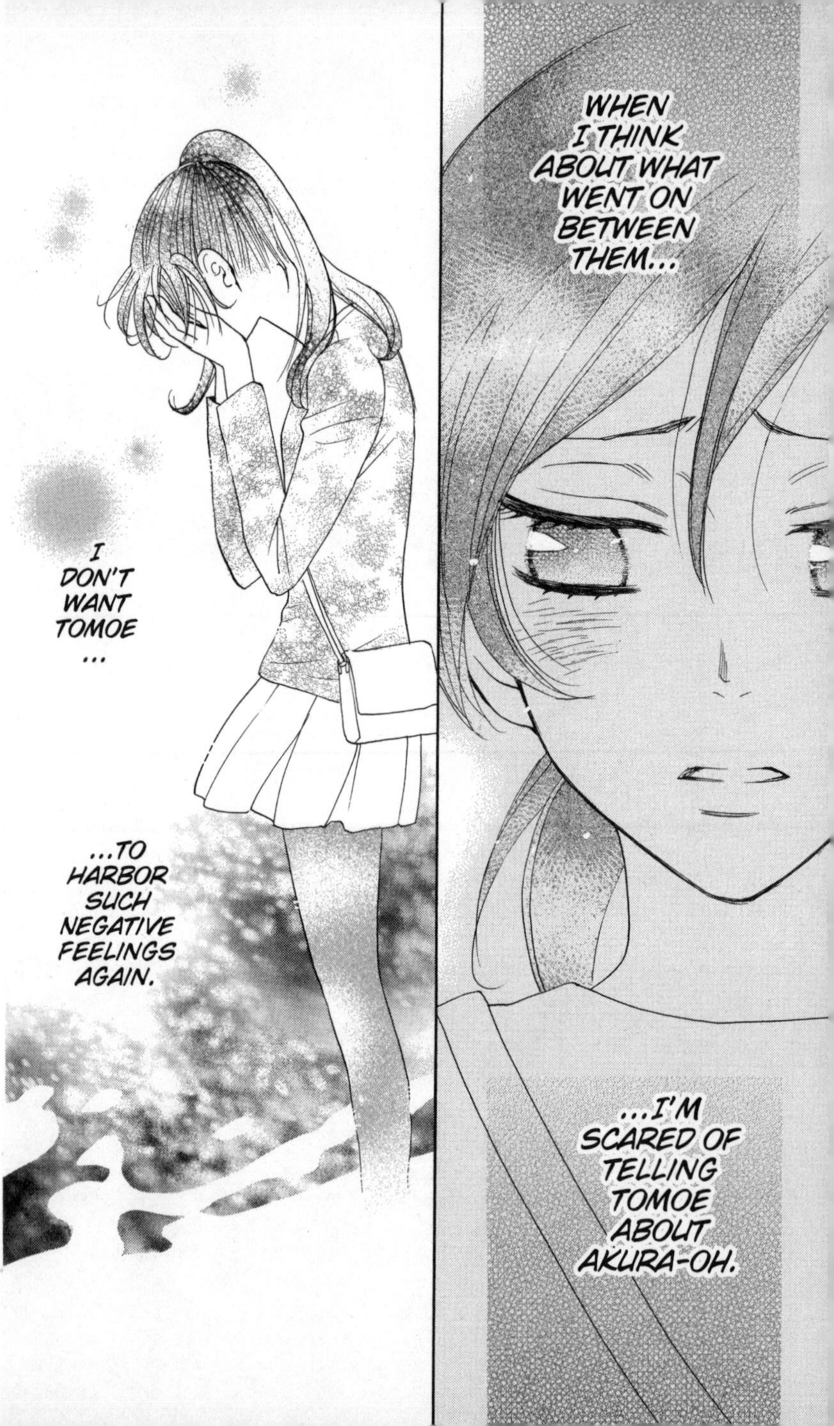
WHEN I THINK ABOUT WHAT WENT ON BETWEEN THEM...
...I'M SCARED OF TELLING TOMOE ABOUT AKURA-OH.
I DON'T WANT TOMOE...
...TO HARBOR SUCH NEGATIVE FEELINGS AGAIN.

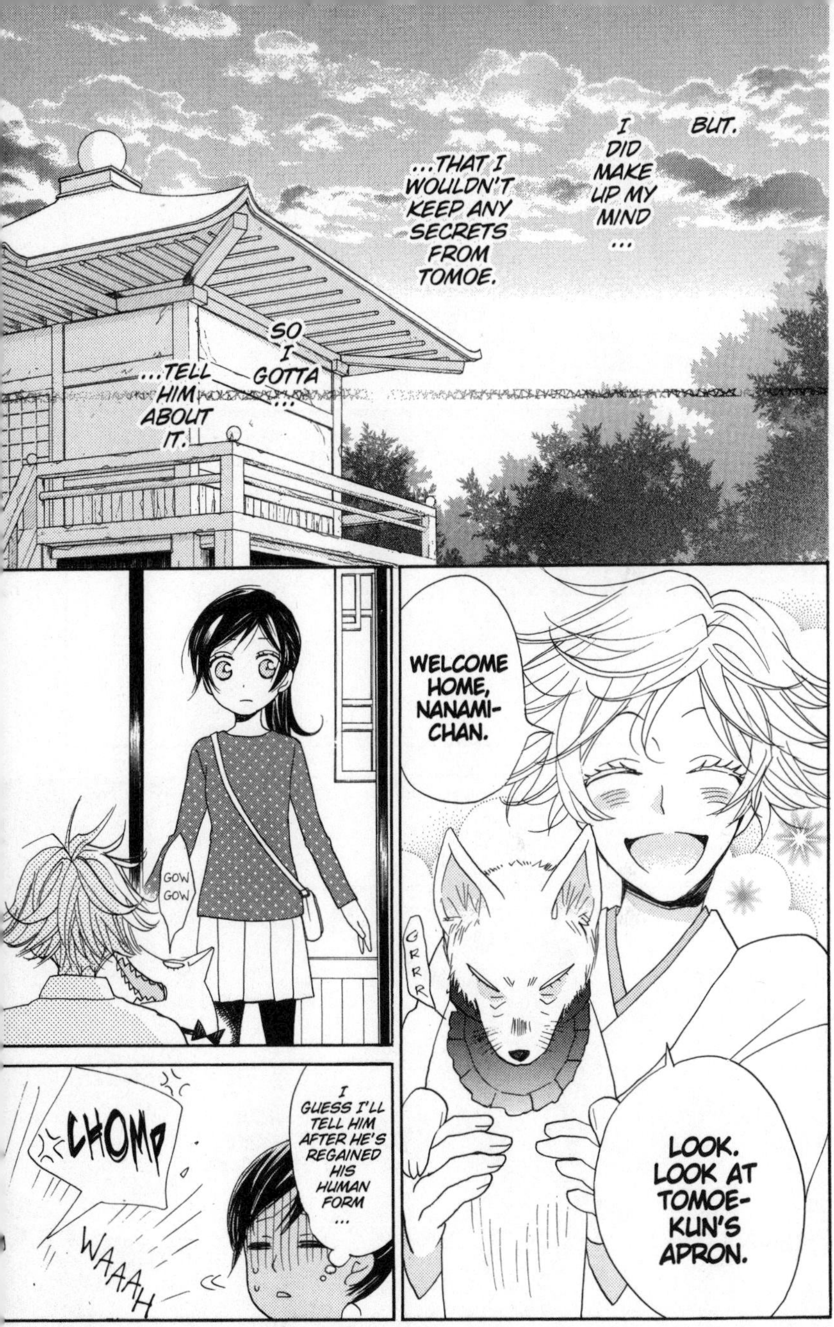
BUT.
I DID MAKE UP MY MIND ...
...THAT I WOULDN'T KEEP ANY SECRETS FROM TOMOE.
SO I GOTTA ...
...TELL HIM ABOUT IT.
WELCOME HOME, NANAMI-CHAN.
GRRR
LOOK. LOOK AT TOMOE-KUN'S APRON.
GOW GOW
I GUESS I'LL TELL HIM AFTER HE'S REGAINED HIS HUMAN FORM ...
CHOMP
WAAAH

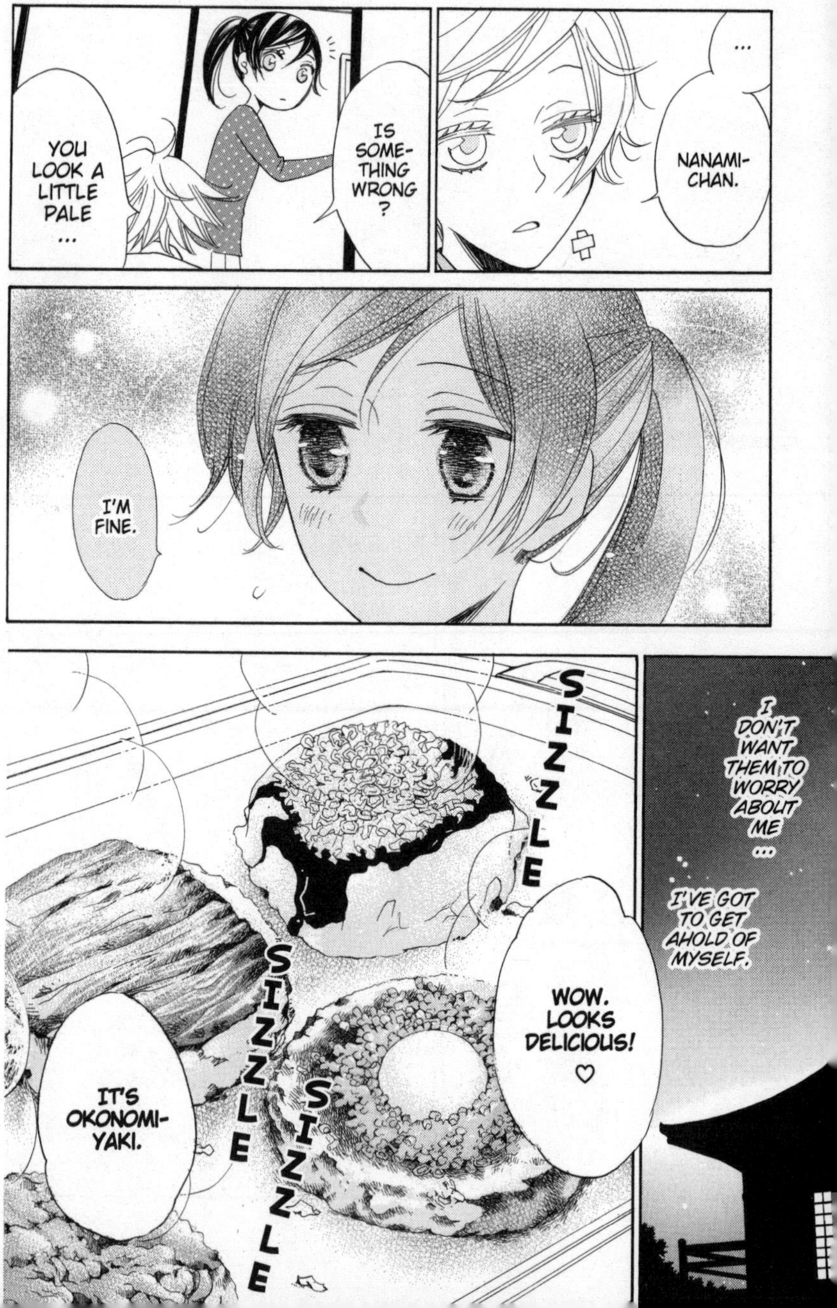
...
NANAMI-CHAN.
IS SOMETHING WRONG?
YOU LOOK A LITTLE PALE...
I'M FINE.
I DON'T WANT THEM TO WORRY ABOUT ME...
I'VE GOT TO GET AHOLD OF MYSELF.
SIZZLE
WOW. LOOKS DELICIOUS! ♡
SIZZLE
SIZZLE
IT'S OKONOMI-YAKI.

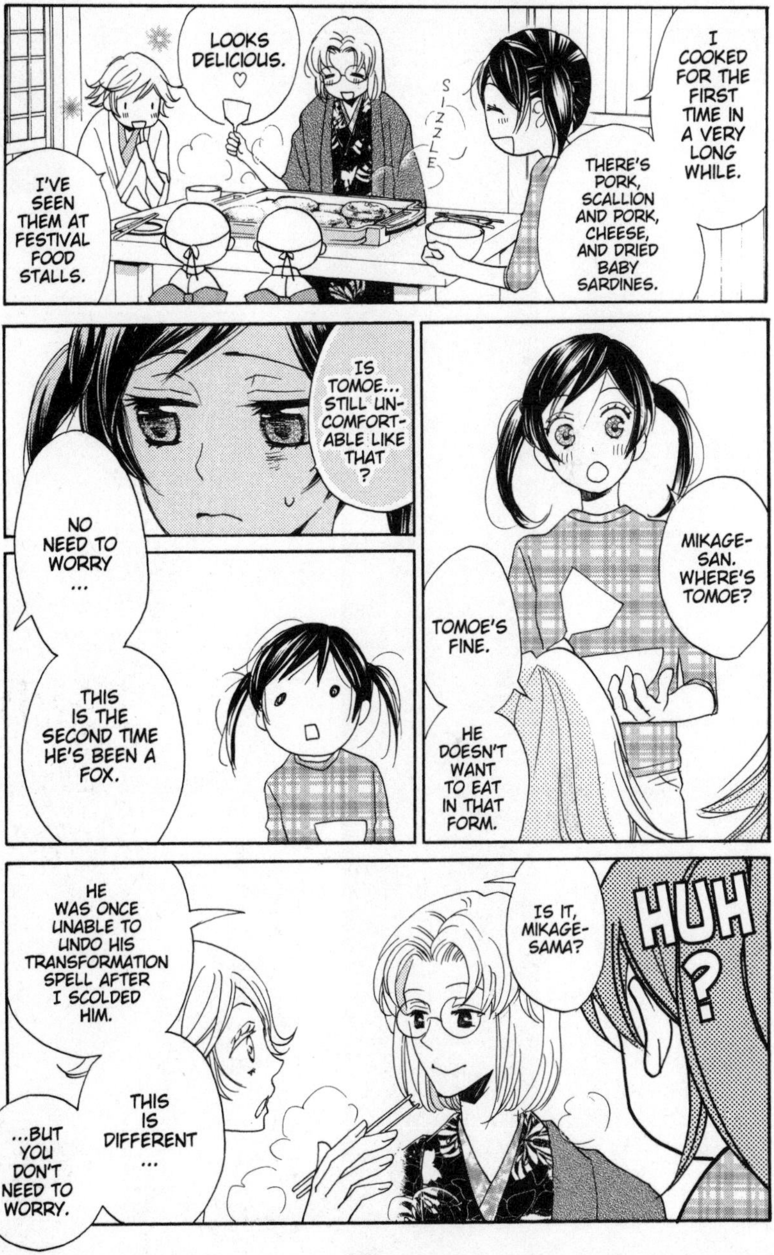
I COOKED FOR THE FIRST TIME IN A VERY LONG WHILE.
THERE'S PORK, SCALLION AND PORK, CHEESE, AND DRIED BABY SARDINES.
SIZZLE
LOOKS DELICIOUS. ♡
I'VE SEEN THEM AT FESTIVAL FOOD STALLS.
MIKAGE-SAN. WHERE'S TOMOE?
TOMOE'S FINE.
HE DOESN'T WANT TO EAT IN THAT FORM.
IS TOMOE... STILL UN-COMFORTABLE LIKE THAT?
NO NEED TO WORRY...
THIS IS THE SECOND TIME HE'S BEEN A FOX.
HUH?
IS IT, MIKAGE-SAMA?
HE WAS ONCE UNABLE TO UNDO HIS TRANSFORMATION SPELL AFTER I SCOLDED HIM.
THIS IS DIFFERENT...
...BUT YOU DON'T NEED TO WORRY.

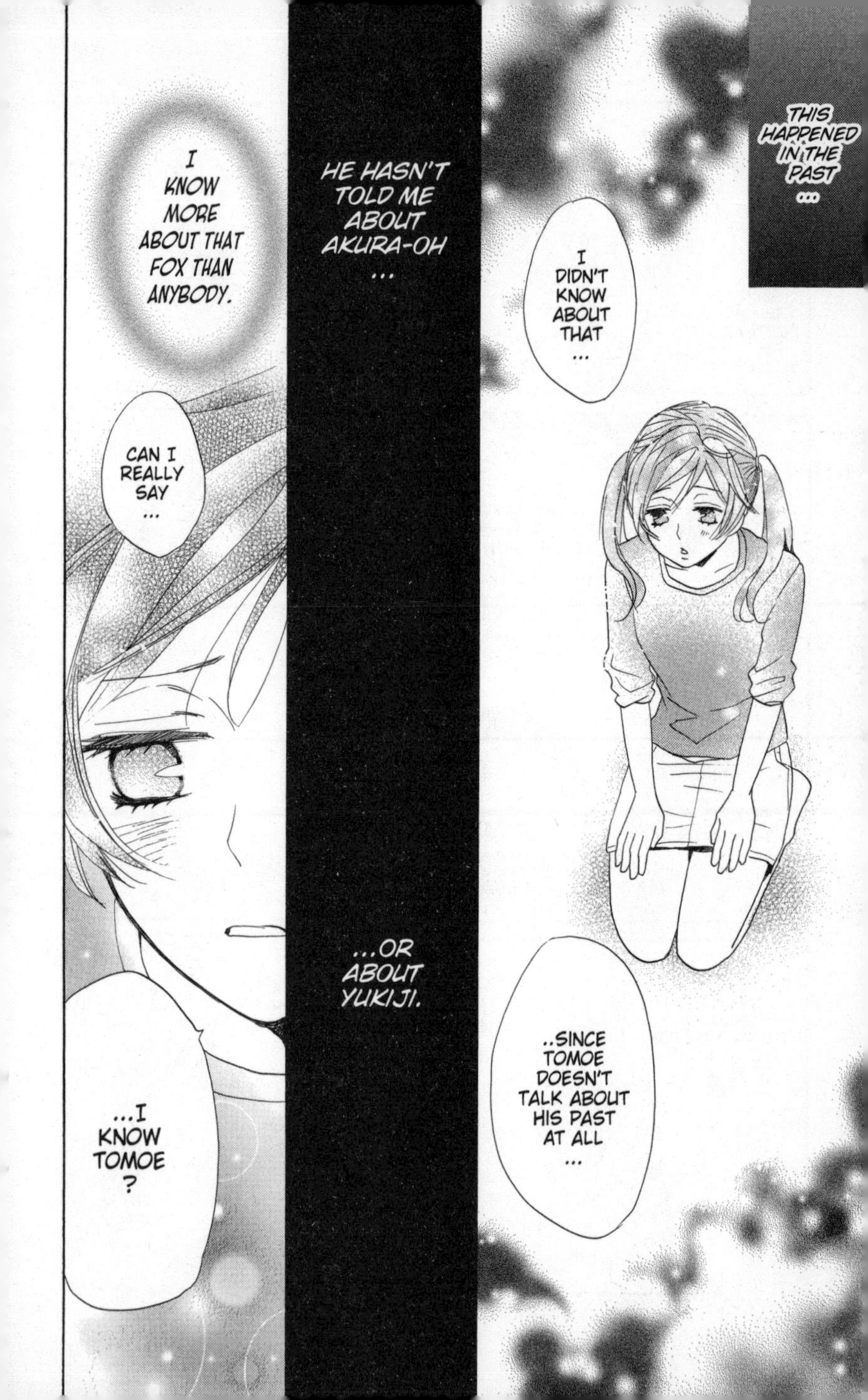
THIS HAPPENED IN THE PAST...
I DIDN'T KNOW ABOUT THAT...
..SINCE TOMOE DOESN'T TALK ABOUT HIS PAST AT ALL...
HE HASN'T TOLD ME ABOUT AKURA-OH...
...OR ABOUT YUKIJI.
I KNOW MORE ABOUT THAT FOX THAN ANYBODY.
CAN I REALLY SAY...
...I KNOW TOMOE?

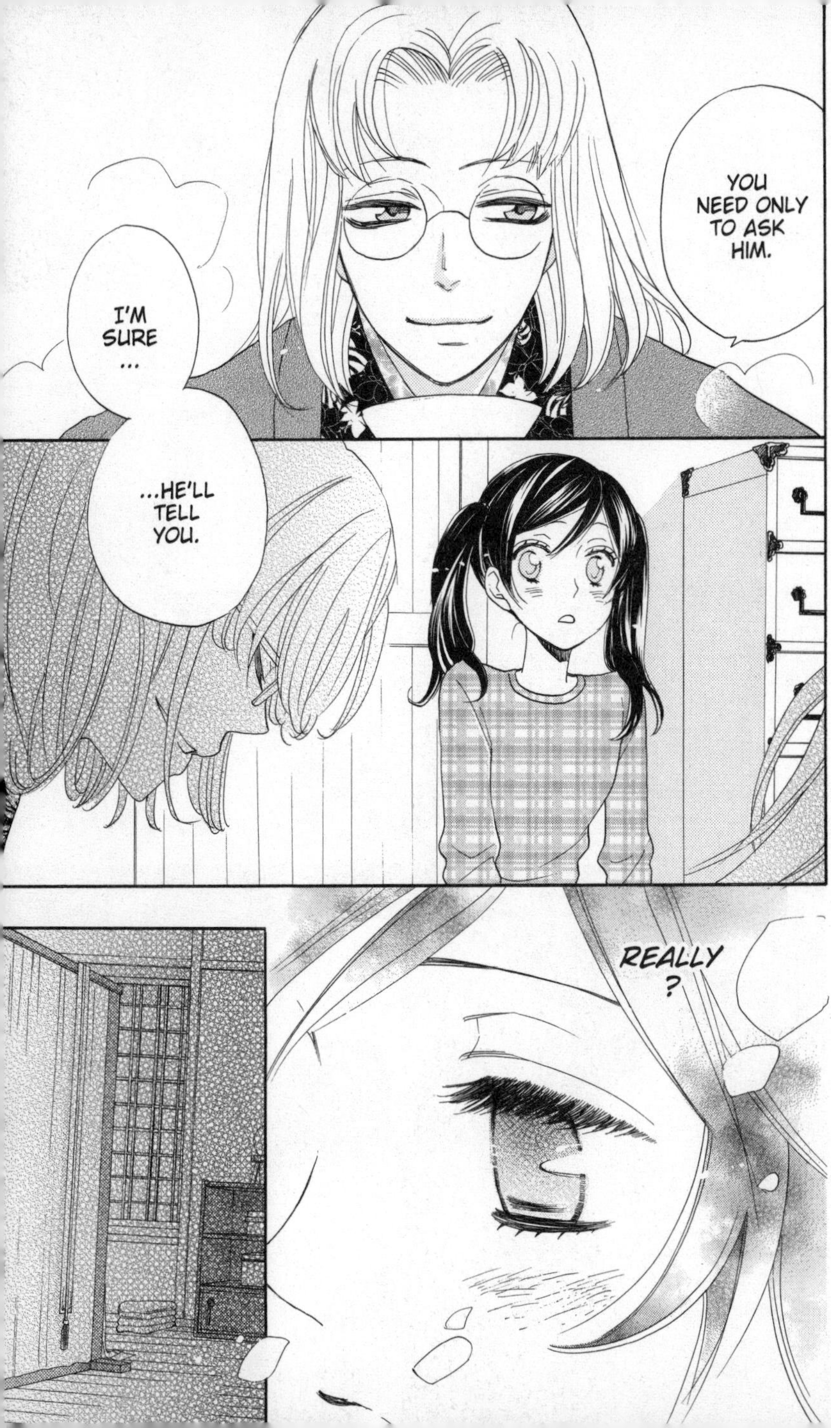
YOU NEED ONLY TO ASK HIM.
I'M SURE ...
...HE'LL TELL YOU.
REALLY ?

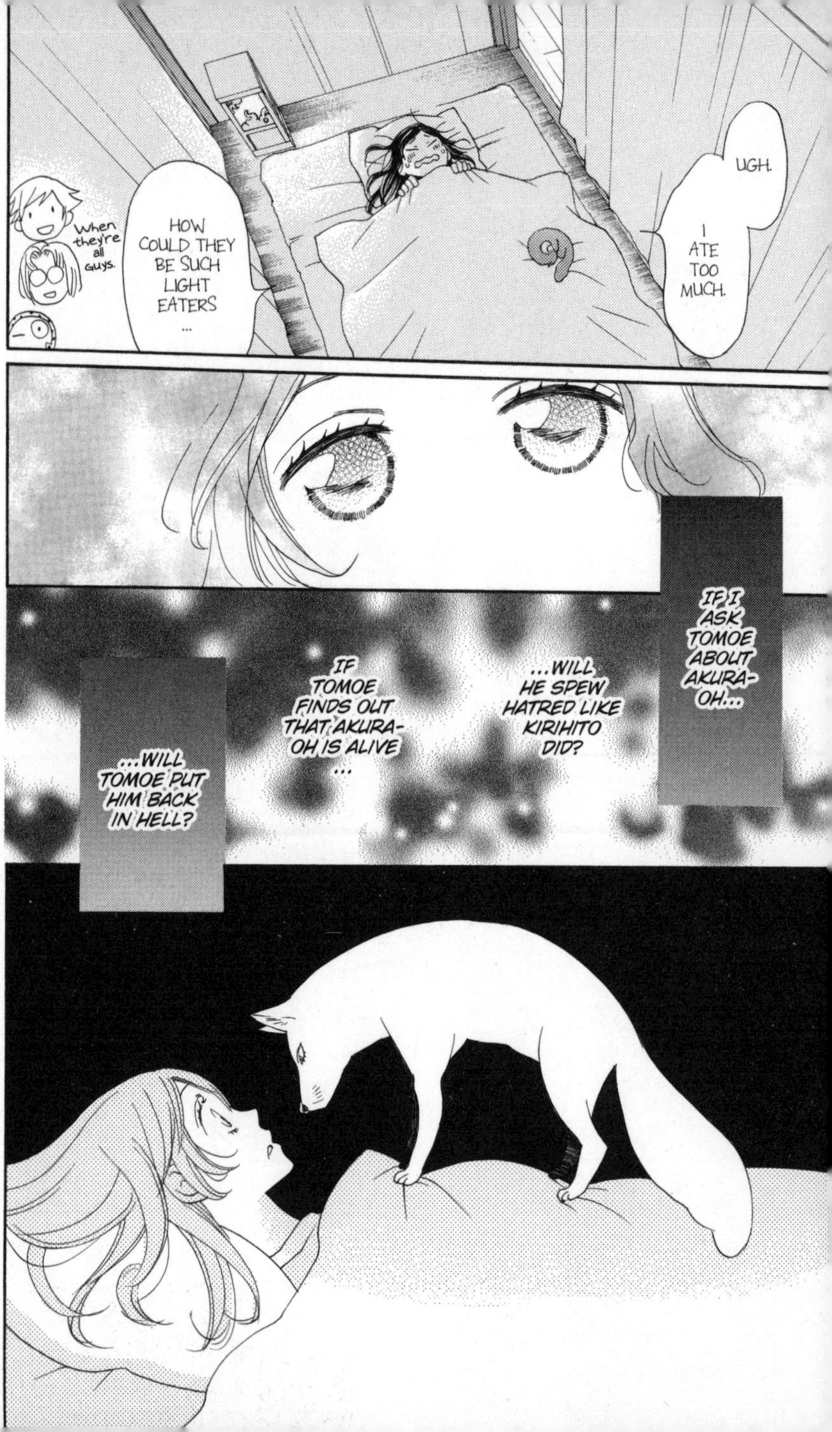
UGH. I ATE TOO MUCH.
HOW COULD THEY BE SUCH LIGHT EATERS ...
When they're all guys.
IF I ASK TOMOE ABOUT AKURA-OH...
...WILL HE SPEW HATRED LIKE KIRIHITO DID?
IF TOMOE FINDS OUT THAT AKURA-OH IS ALIVE ...
...WILL TOMOE PUT HIM BACK IN HELL?

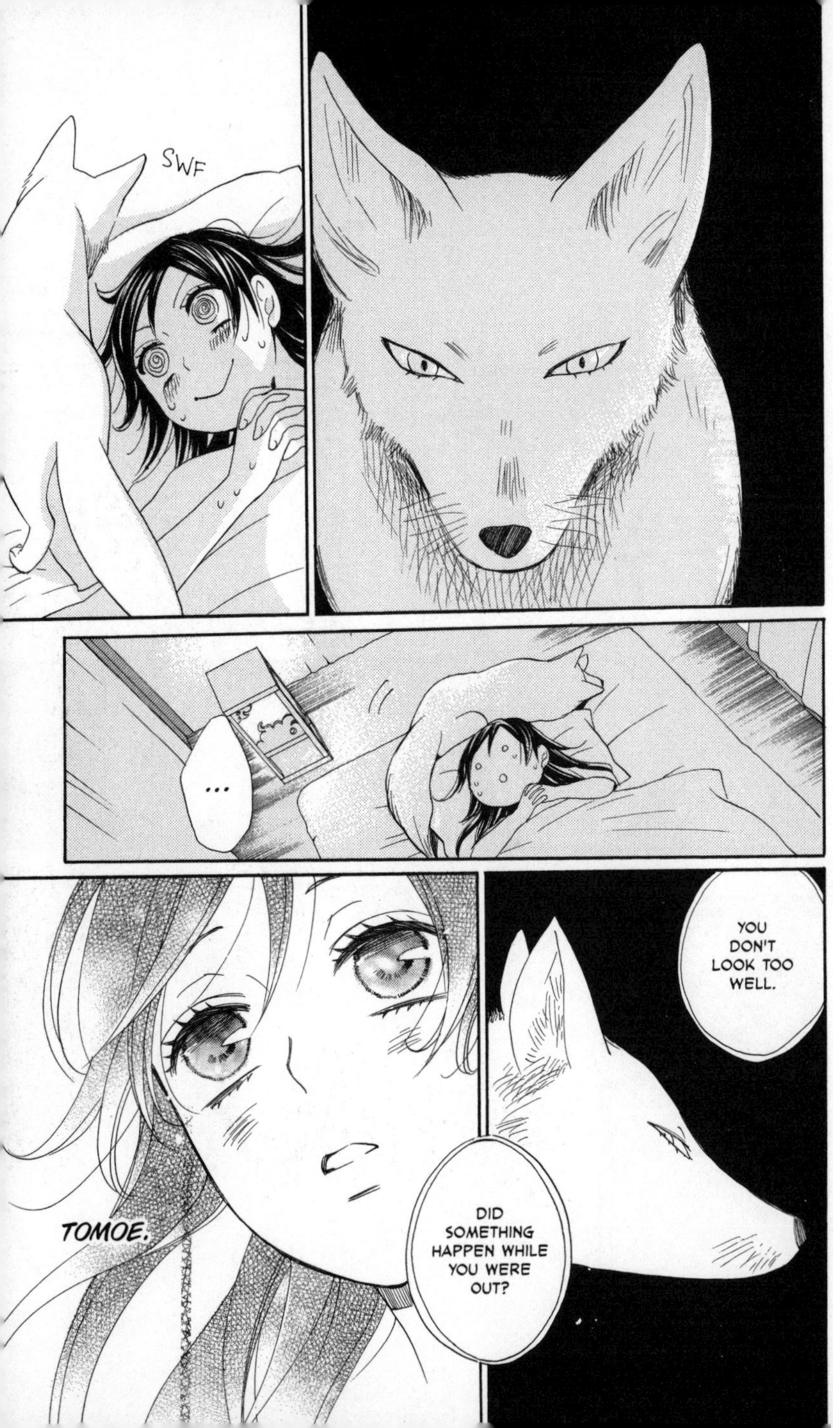
SWF
...
YOU DON'T LOOK TOO WELL.
DID SOMETHING HAPPEN WHILE YOU WERE OUT?
TOMOE.

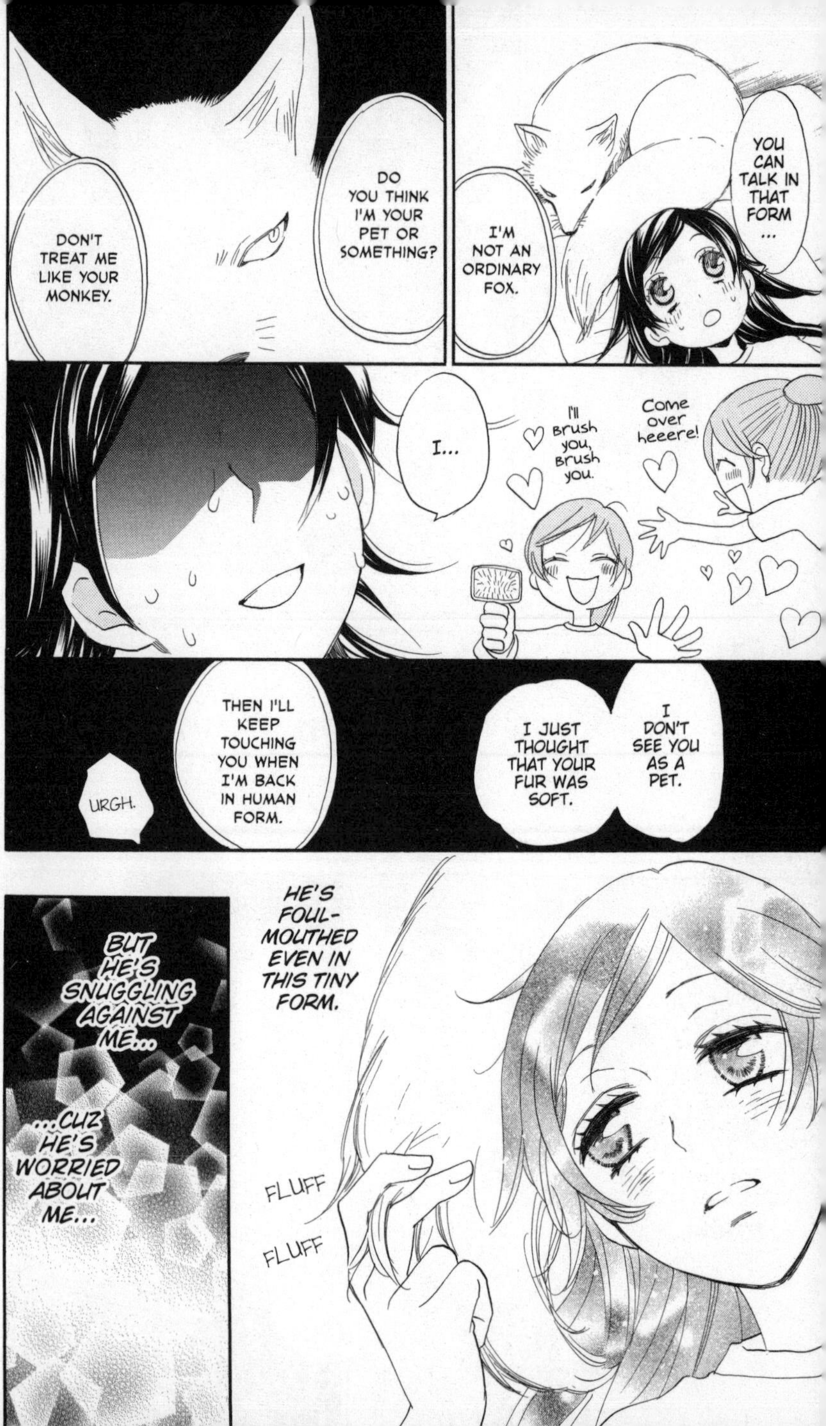
YOU CAN TALK IN THAT FORM ...
I'M NOT AN ORDINARY FOX.
DO YOU THINK I'M YOUR PET OR SOMETHING?
DON'T TREAT ME LIKE YOUR MONKEY.
Come over heeere!
I'll brush you, brush you.
I...
I DON'T SEE YOU AS A PET.
I JUST THOUGHT THAT YOUR FUR WAS SOFT.
THEN I'LL KEEP TOUCHING YOU WHEN I'M BACK IN HUMAN FORM.
URGH.
HE'S FOUL-MOUTHED EVEN IN THIS TINY FORM.
FLUFF
FLUFF
BUT HE'S SNUGGLING AGAINST ME...
...CUZ HE'S WORRIED ABOUT ME...

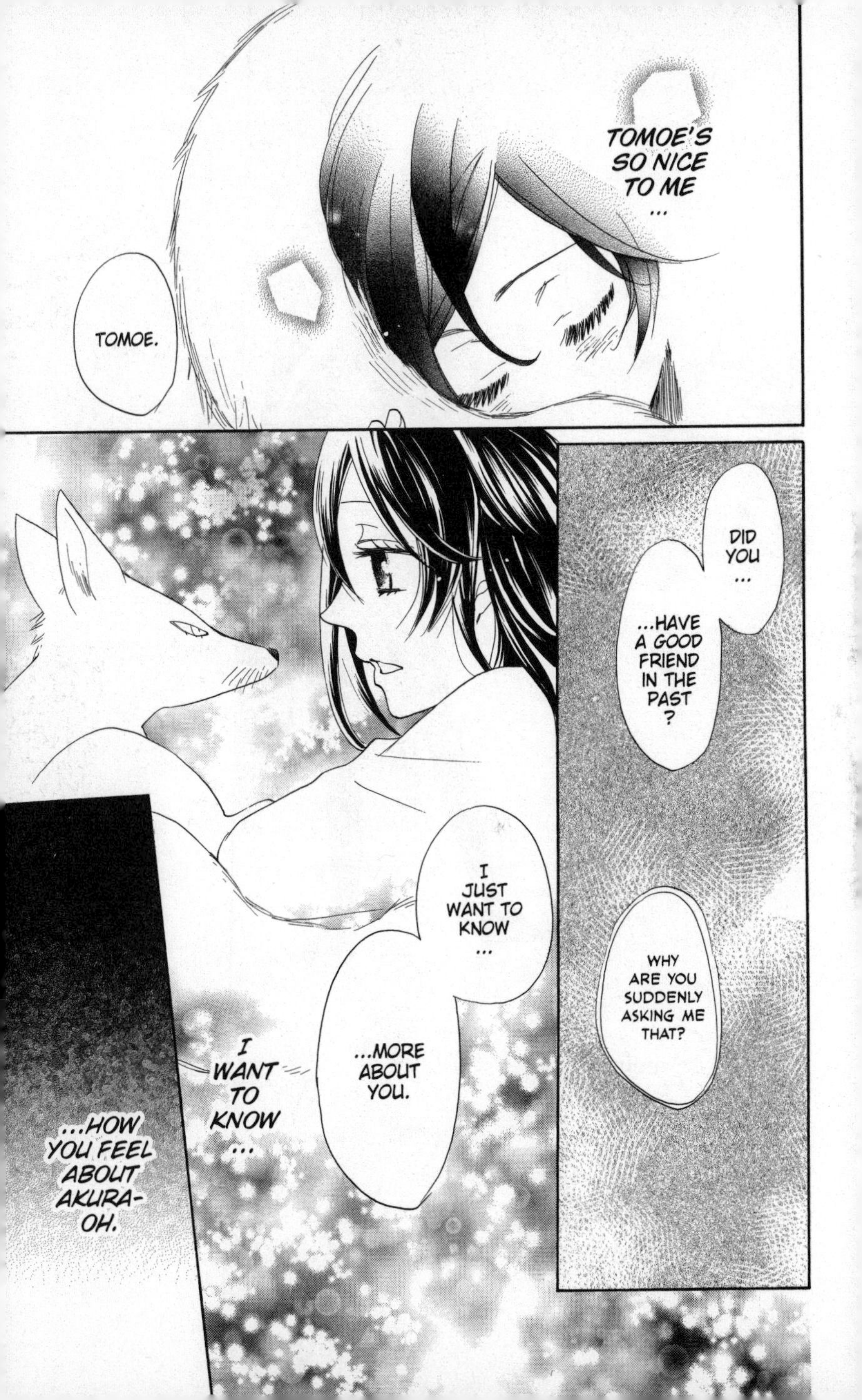
TOMOE'S SO NICE TO ME ...
TOMOE.
DID YOU ...
...HAVE A GOOD FRIEND IN THE PAST?
WHY ARE YOU SUDDENLY ASKING ME THAT?
I JUST WANT TO KNOW ...
...MORE ABOUT YOU.
I WANT TO KNOW ...
...HOW YOU FEEL ABOUT AKURA-OH.

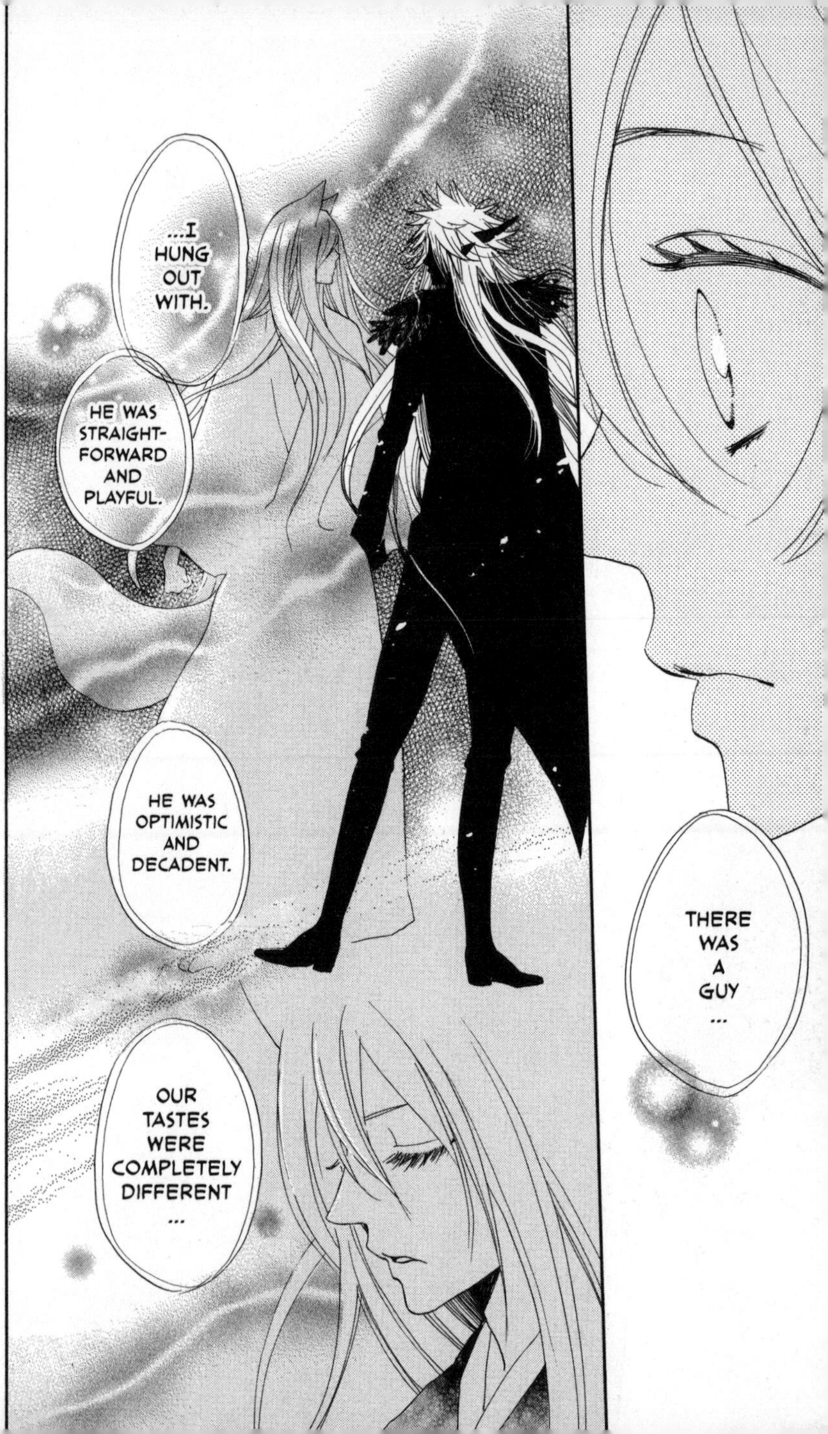
THERE WAS A GUY...
...I HUNG OUT WITH.
HE WAS STRAIGHT-FORWARD AND PLAYFUL.
HE WAS OPTIMISTIC AND DECADENT.
OUR TASTES WERE COMPLETELY DIFFERENT...

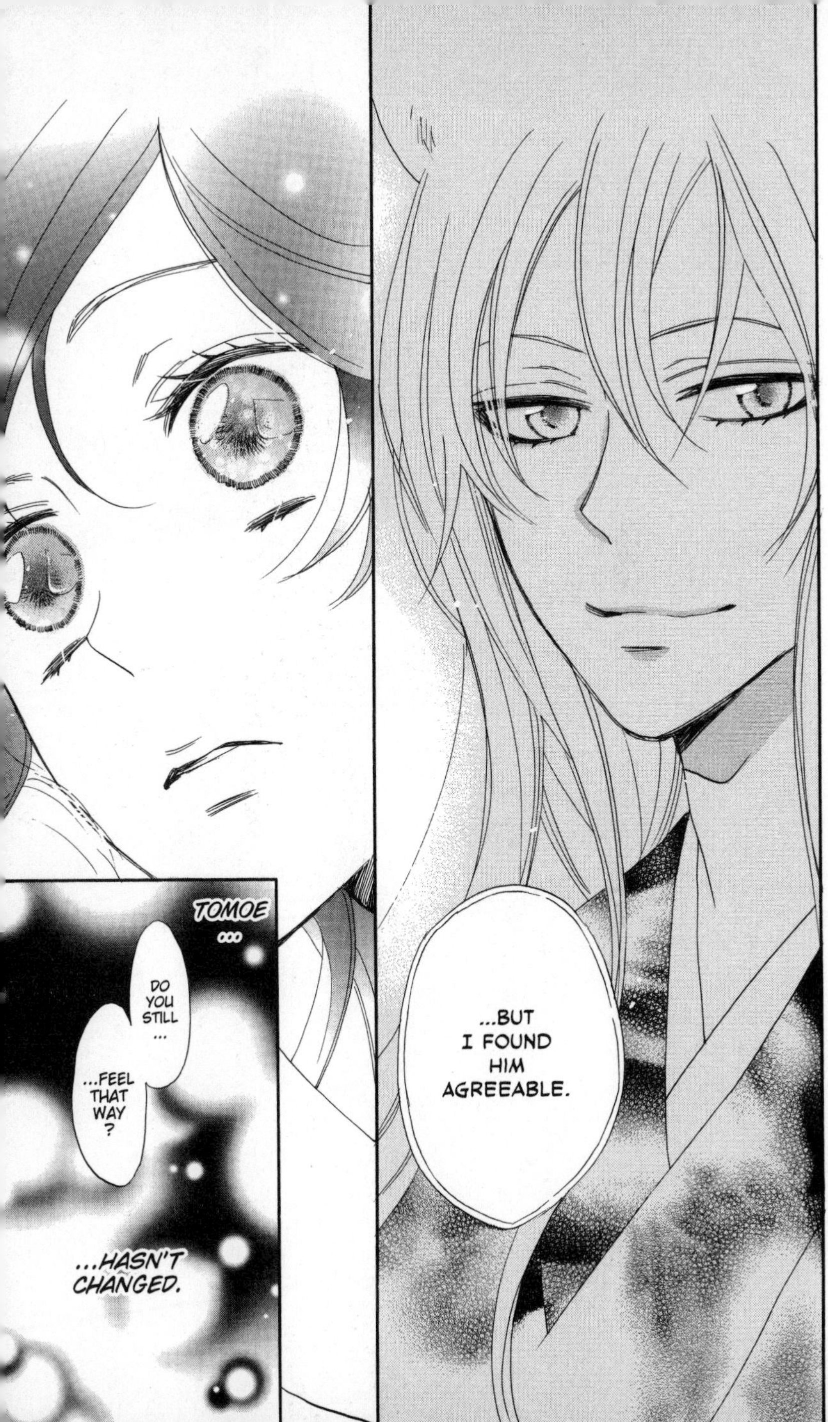
...BUT I FOUND HIM AGREEABLE.
TOMOE ...
DO YOU STILL ...
...FEEL THAT WAY ?
...HASN'T CHANGED.

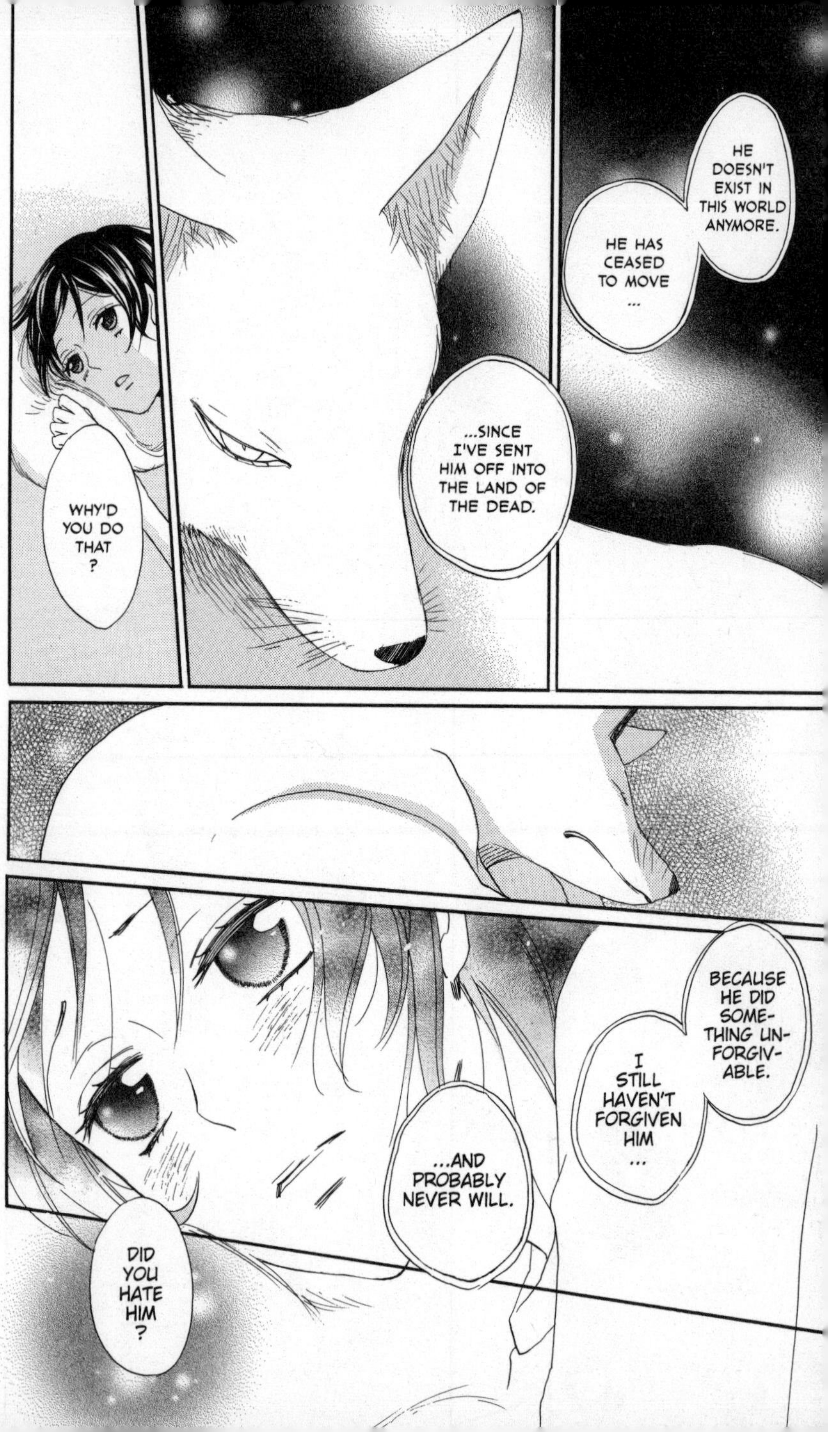
HE DOESN'T EXIST IN THIS WORLD ANYMORE.
HE HAS CEASED TO MOVE ...
...SINCE I'VE SENT HIM OFF INTO THE LAND OF THE DEAD.
WHY'D YOU DO THAT ?
BECAUSE HE DID SOME-THING UN-FORGIV-ABLE.
I STILL HAVEN'T FORGIVEN HIM ...
...AND PROBABLY NEVER WILL.
DID YOU HATE HIM ?

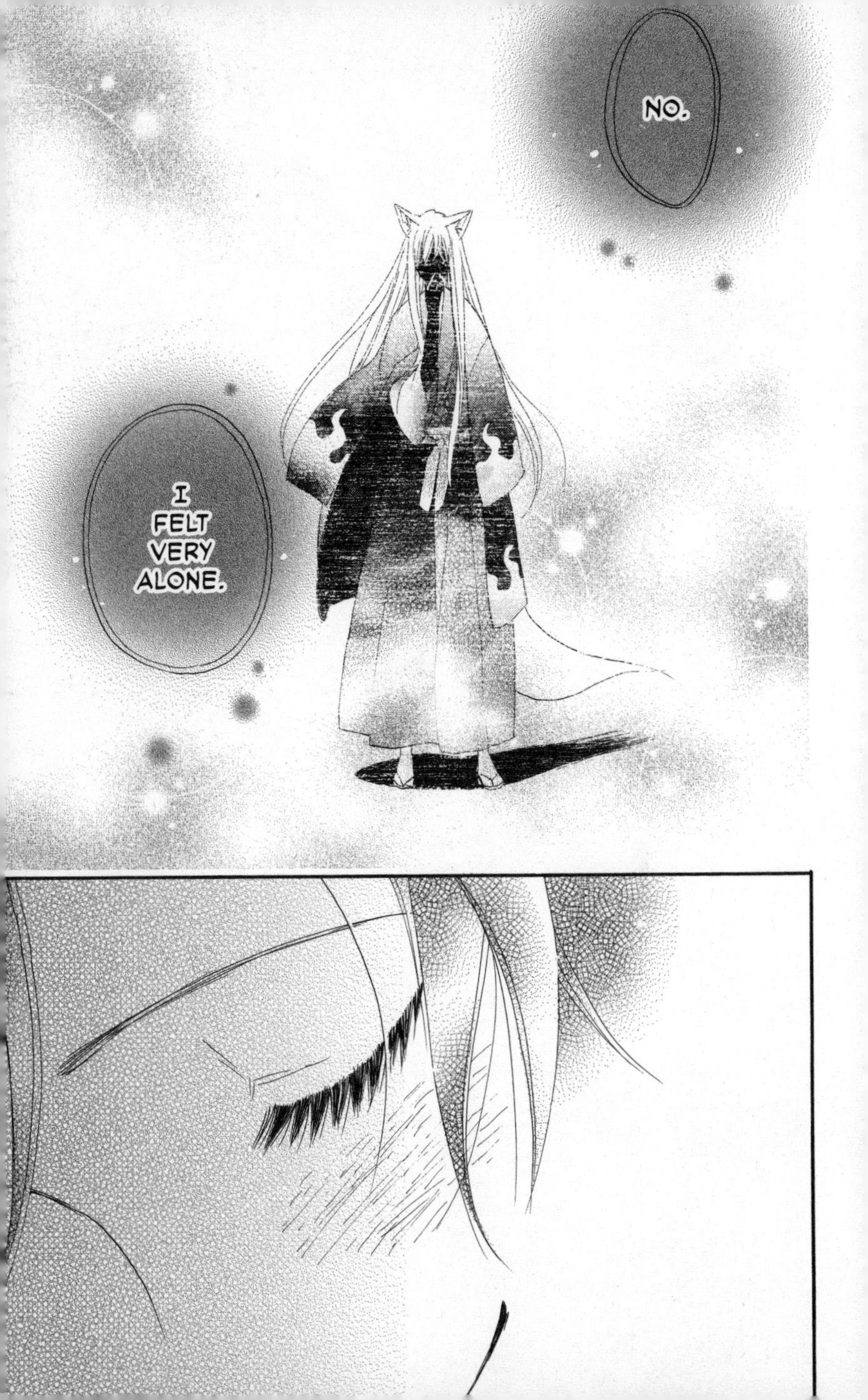
NO.
I FELT VERY ALONE.

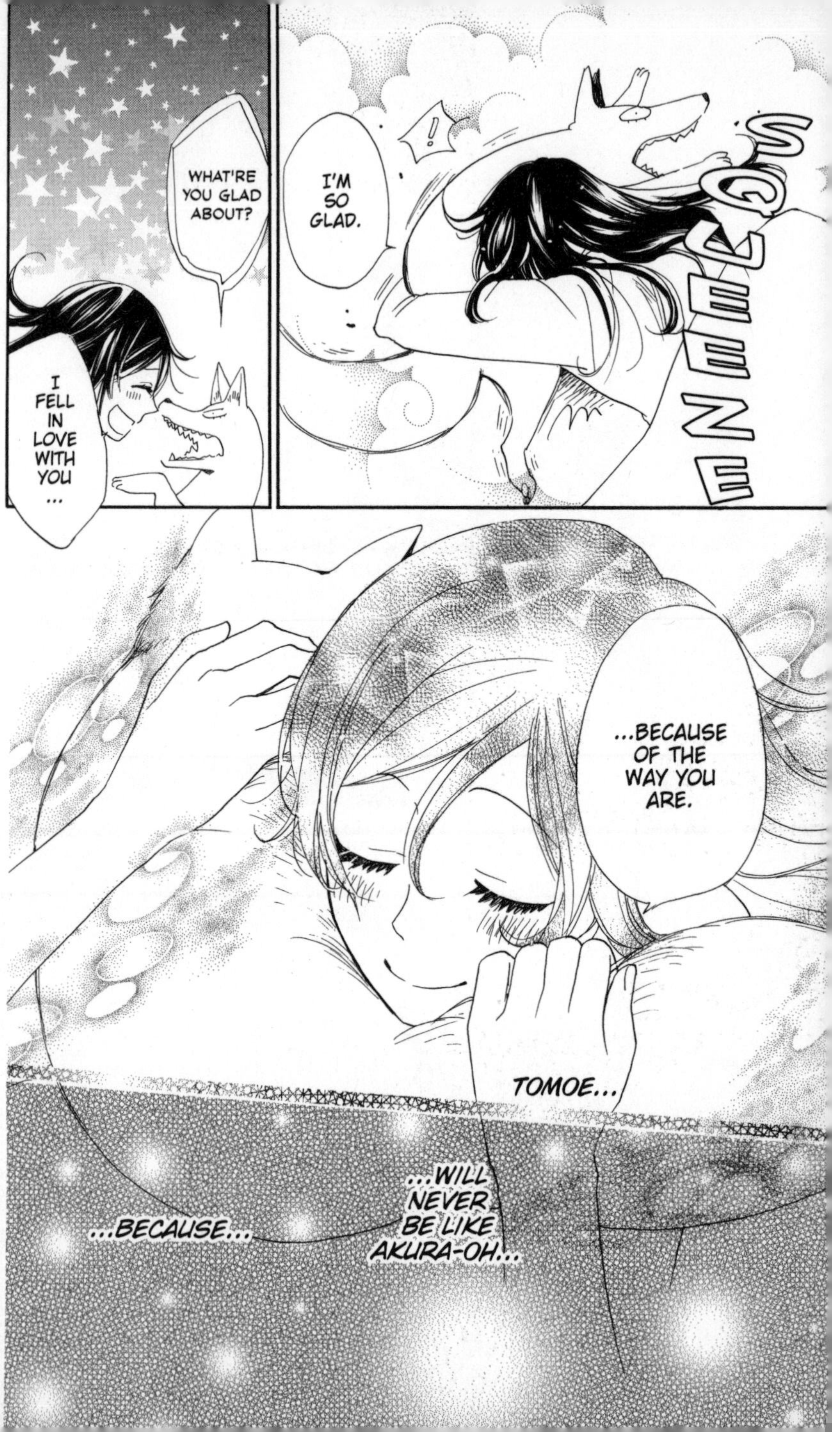
SQUEEZE
!
I'M SO GLAD.
WHAT'RE YOU GLAD ABOUT?
I FELL IN LOVE WITH YOU ...
...BECAUSE OF THE WAY YOU ARE.
TOMOE...
...WILL NEVER BE LIKE AKURA-OH...
...BECAUSE...

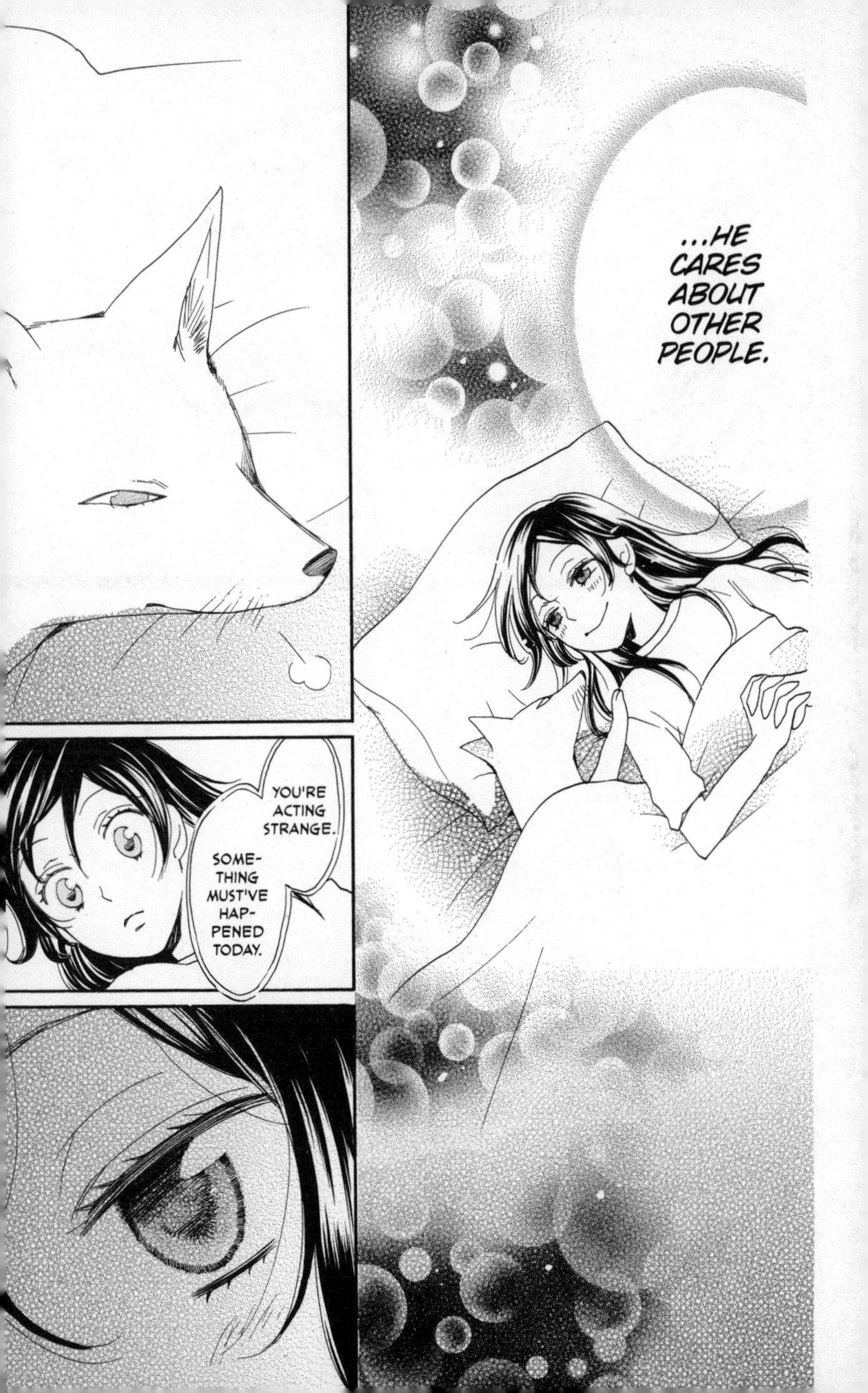
...HE CARES ABOUT OTHER PEOPLE.
YOU'RE ACTING STRANGE.
SOME-THING MUST'VE HAP-PENED TODAY.

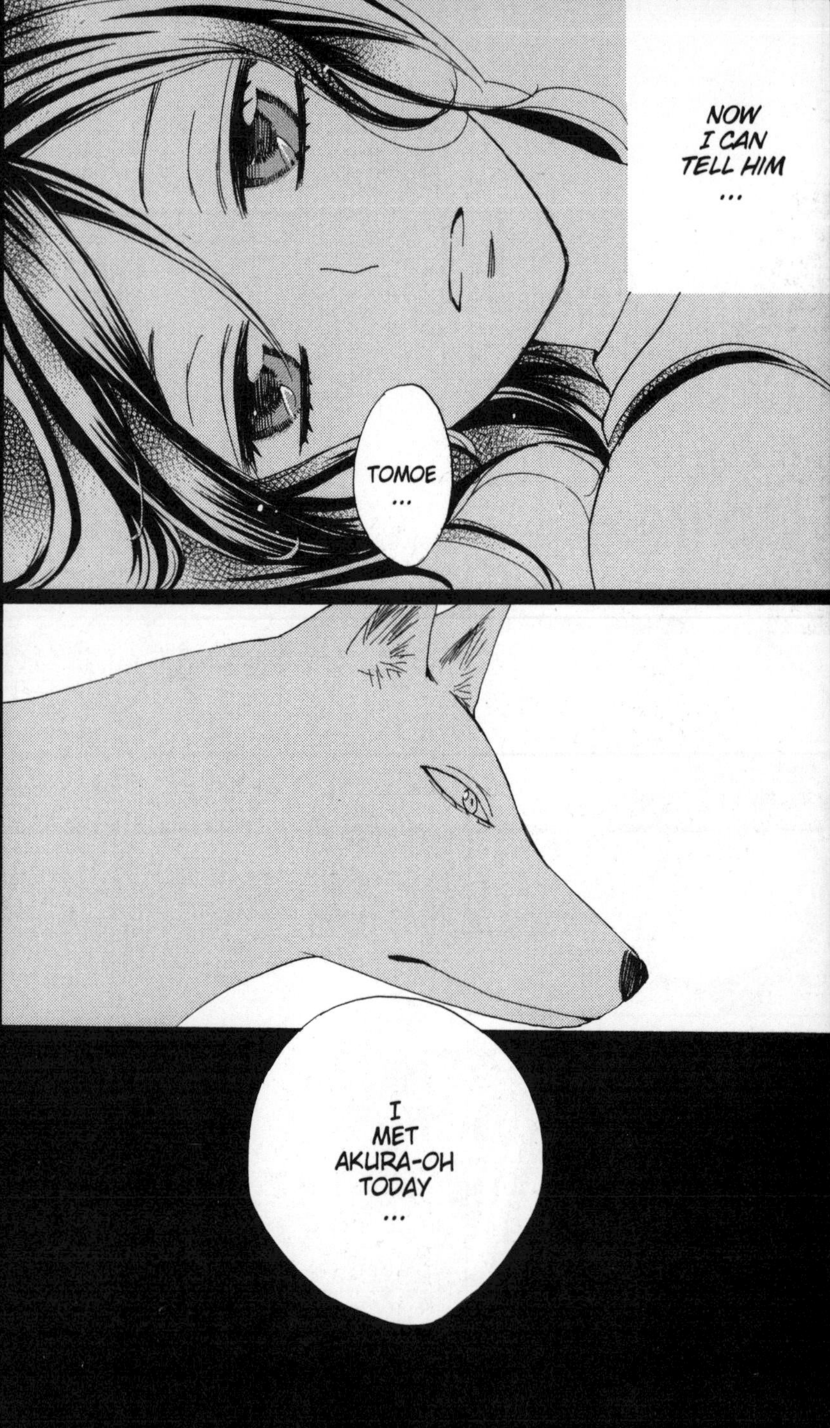
NOW I CAN TELL HIM ...
TOMOE ...
I MET AKURA-OH TODAY ...

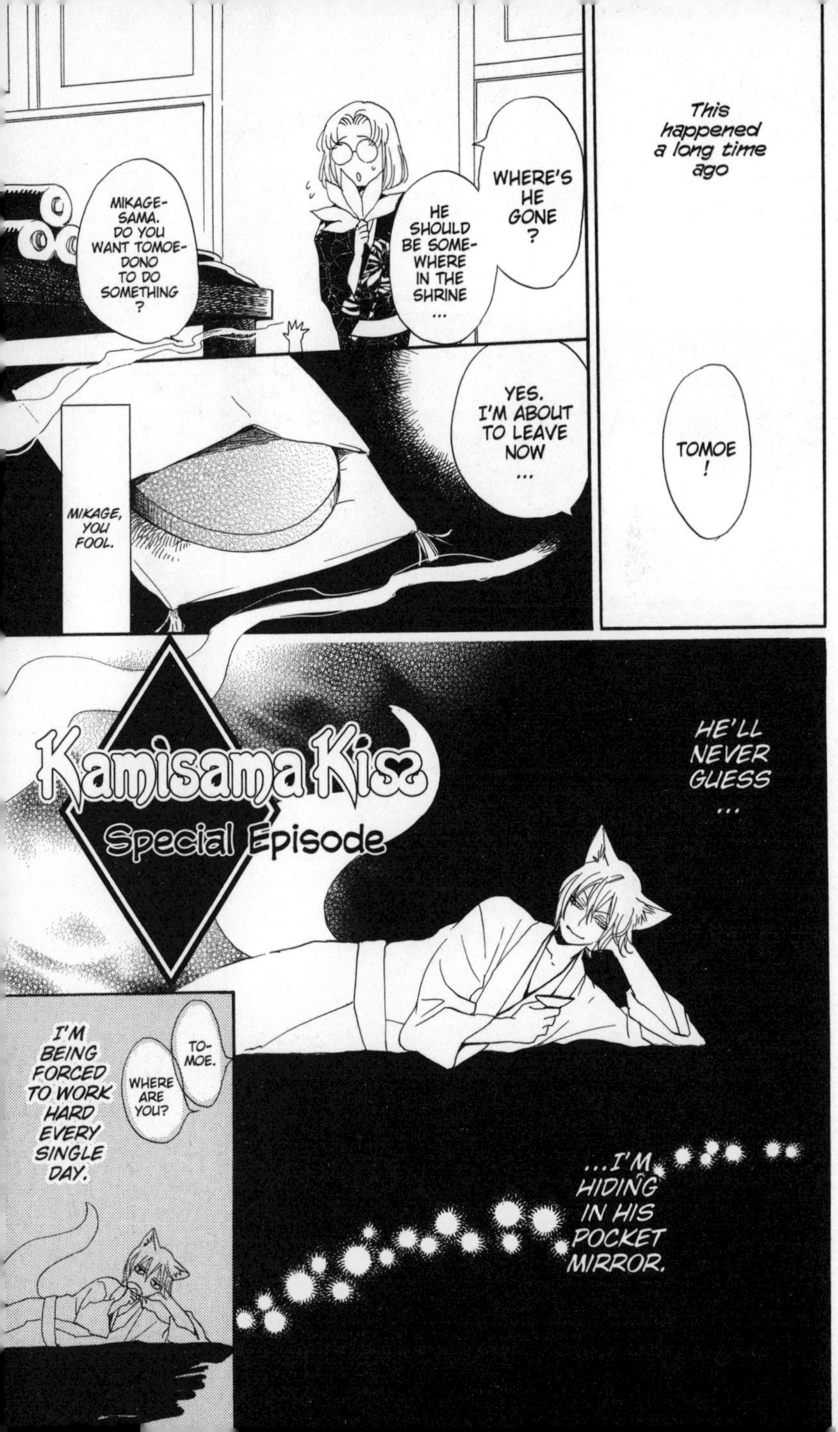
This happened a long time ago
TOMOE!
WHERE'S HE GONE?
HE SHOULD BE SOMEWHERE IN THE SHRINE...
MIKAGE-SAMA. DO YOU WANT TOMOE-DONO TO DO SOMETHING?
YES. I'M ABOUT TO LEAVE NOW...
MIKAGE, YOU FOOL.
Kamisama Kiss
Special Episode
HE'LL NEVER GUESS...
...I'M HIDING IN HIS POCKET MIRROR.
TO-MOE.
WHERE ARE YOU?
I'M BEING FORCED TO WORK HARD EVERY SINGLE DAY.

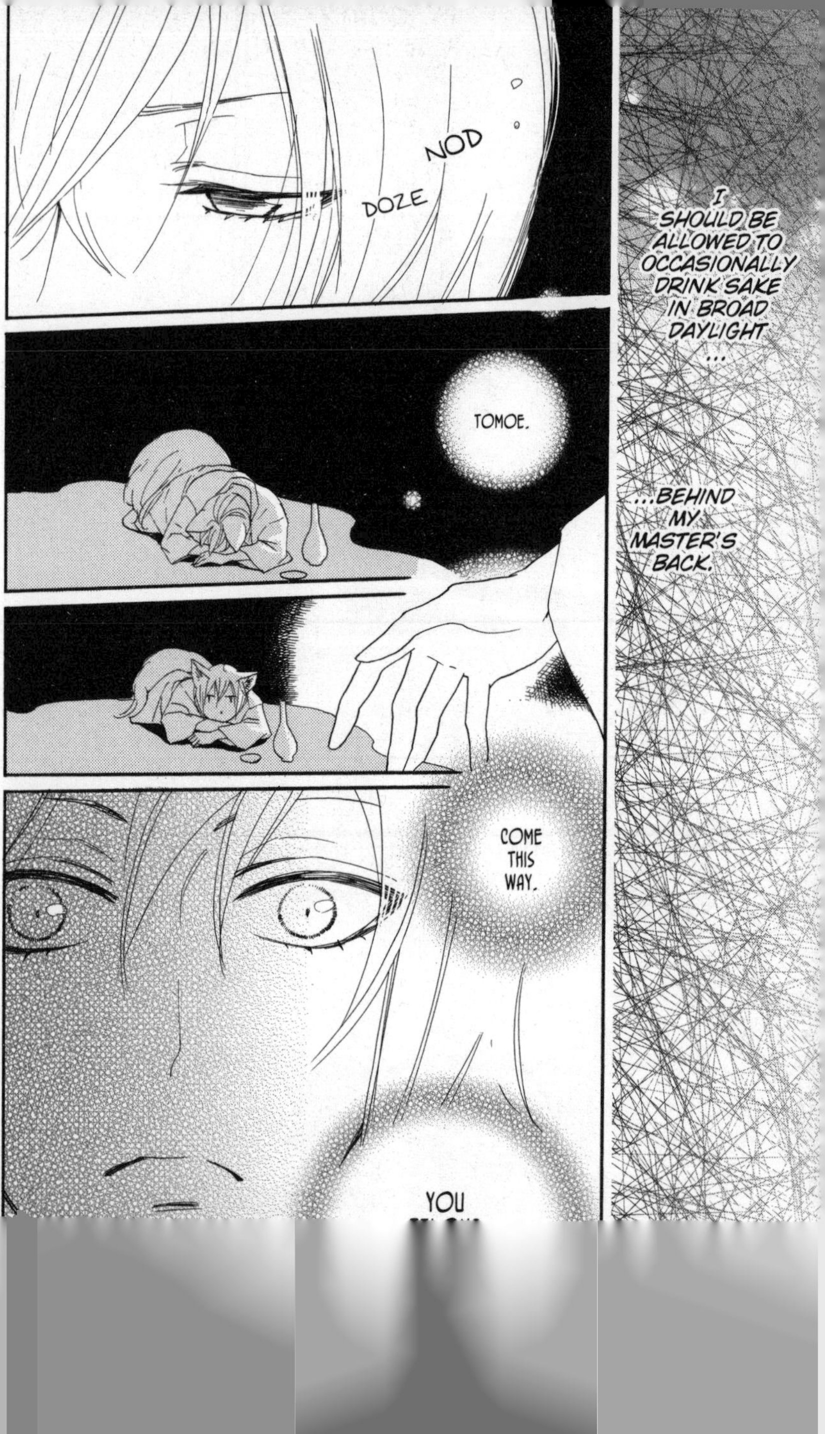
I SHOULD BE ALLOWED TO OCCASIONALLY DRINK SAKE IN BROAD DAYLIGHT...
...BEHIND MY MASTER'S BACK.
NOD
DOZE
TOMOE.
COME THIS WAY.
YOU

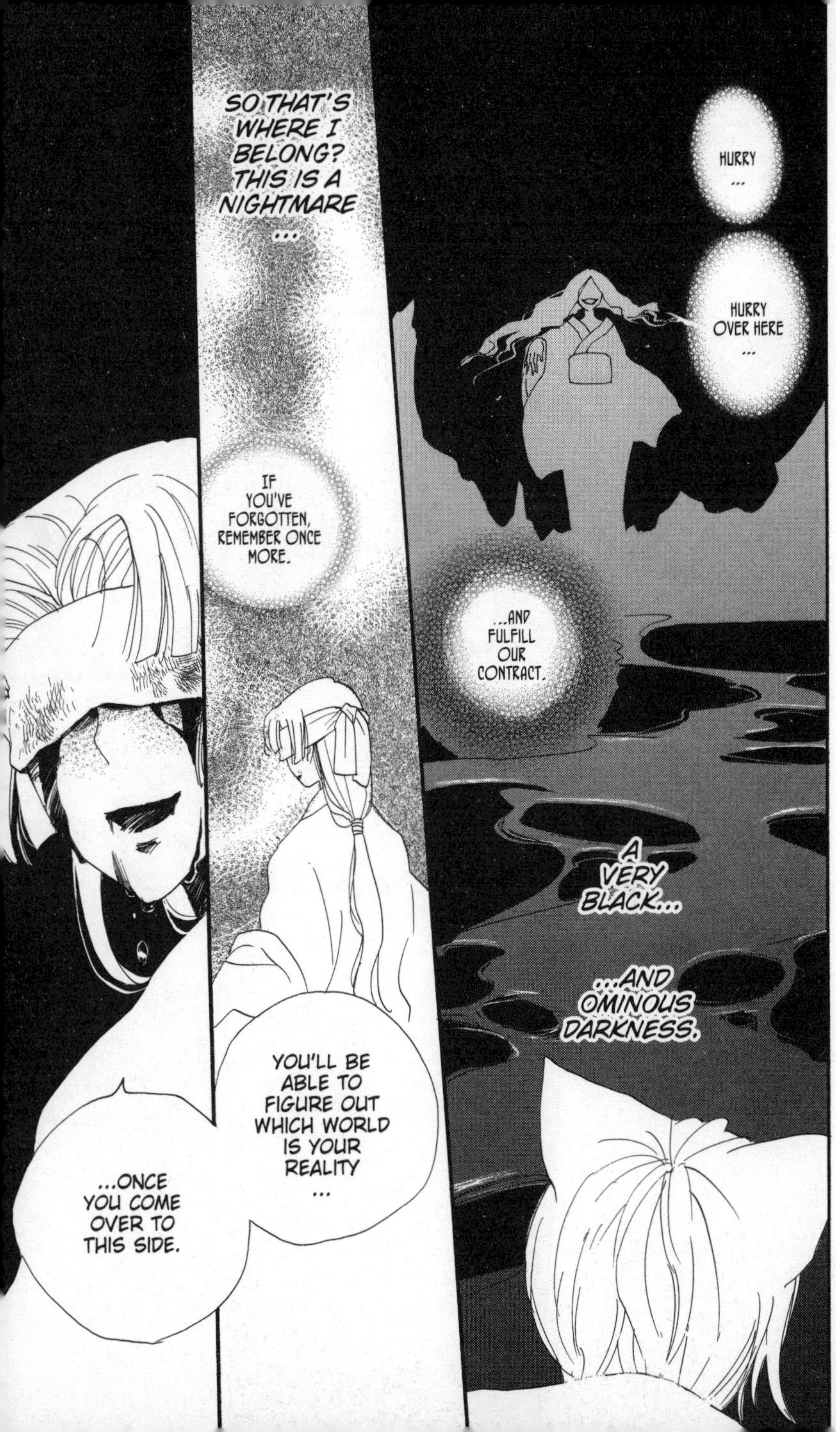
HURRY ...
HURRY OVER HERE ...
...AND FULFILL OUR CONTRACT.
A VERY BLACK...
...AND OMINOUS DARKNESS.
SO THAT'S WHERE I BELONG? THIS IS A NIGHTMARE ...
IF YOU'VE FORGOTTEN, REMEMBER ONCE MORE.
YOU'LL BE ABLE TO FIGURE OUT WHICH WORLD IS YOUR REALITY ...
...ONCE YOU COME OVER TO THIS SIDE.

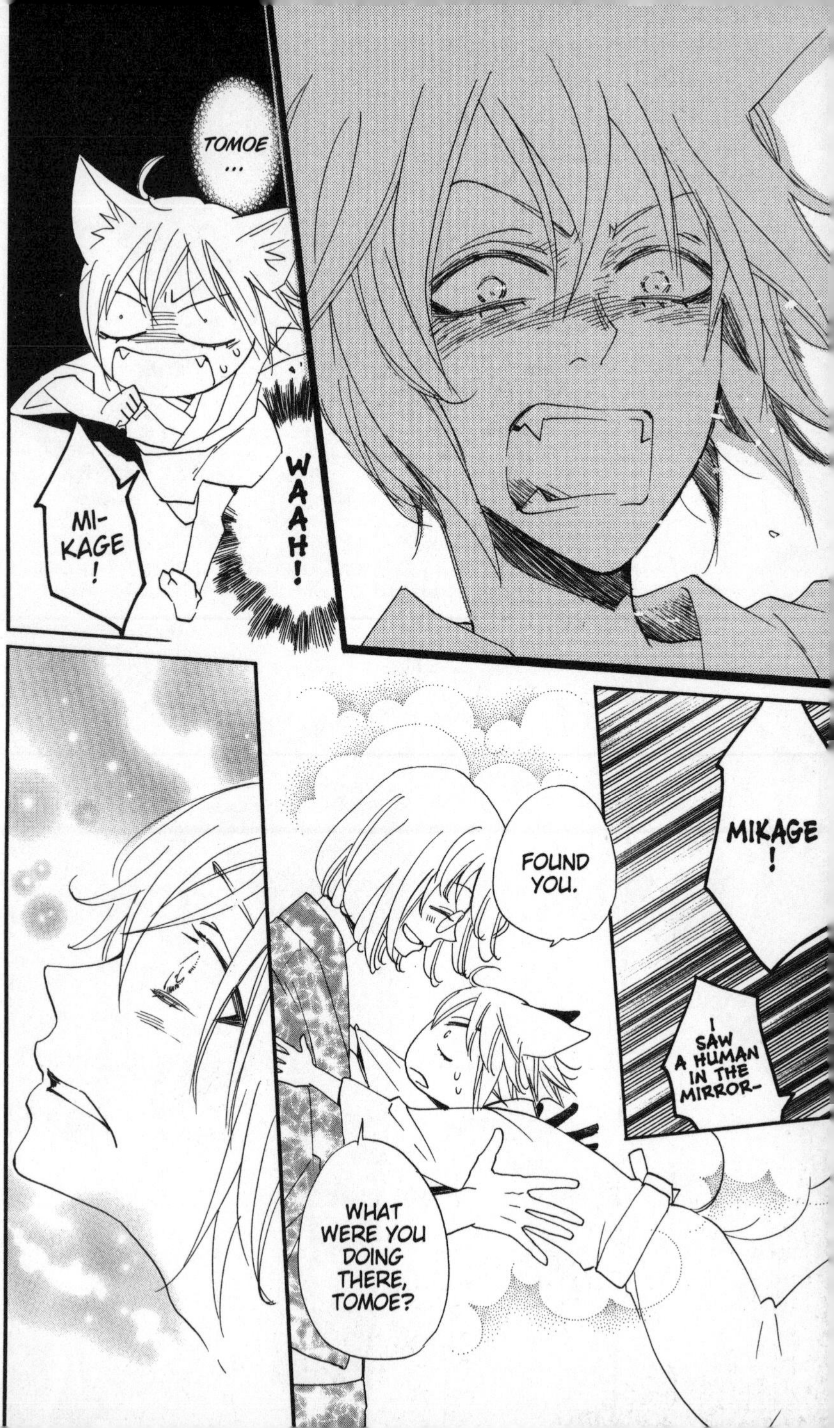
TOMOE ...
WAAAH!
MI-KAGE!
MIKAGE!
I SAW A HUMAN IN THE MIRROR-
FOUND YOU.
WHAT WERE YOU DOING THERE, TOMOE?

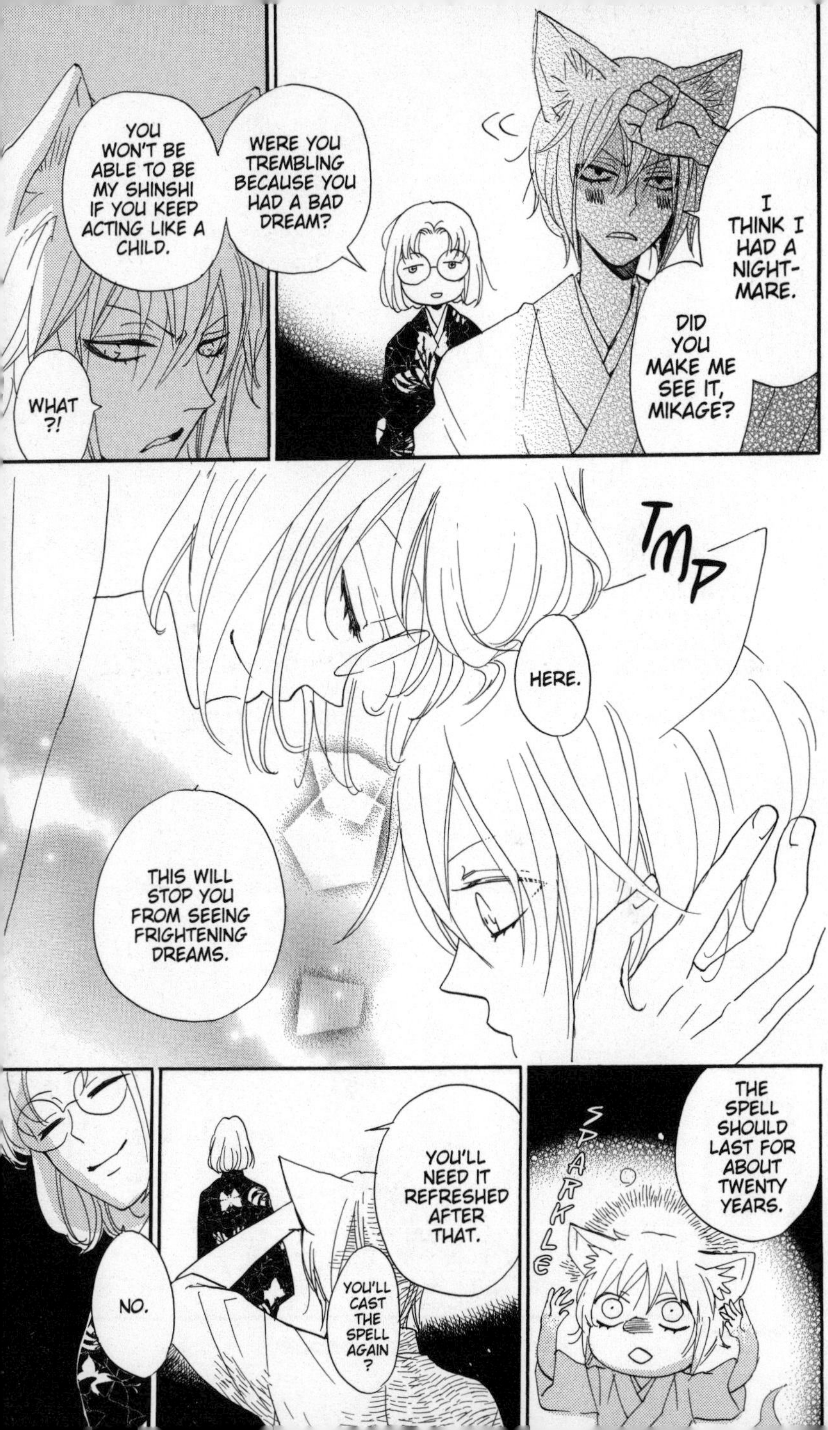
I THINK I HAD A NIGHTMARE.
DID YOU MAKE ME SEE IT, MIKAGE?
WERE YOU TREMBLING BECAUSE YOU HAD A BAD DREAM?
YOU WON'T BE ABLE TO BE MY SHINSHI IF YOU KEEP ACTING LIKE A CHILD.
WHAT ?!
TMP
HERE.
THIS WILL STOP YOU FROM SEEING FRIGHTENING DREAMS.
SPARKLE
THE SPELL SHOULD LAST FOR ABOUT TWENTY YEARS.
YOU'LL NEED IT REFRESHED AFTER THAT.
YOU'LL CAST THE SPELL AGAIN?
NO.

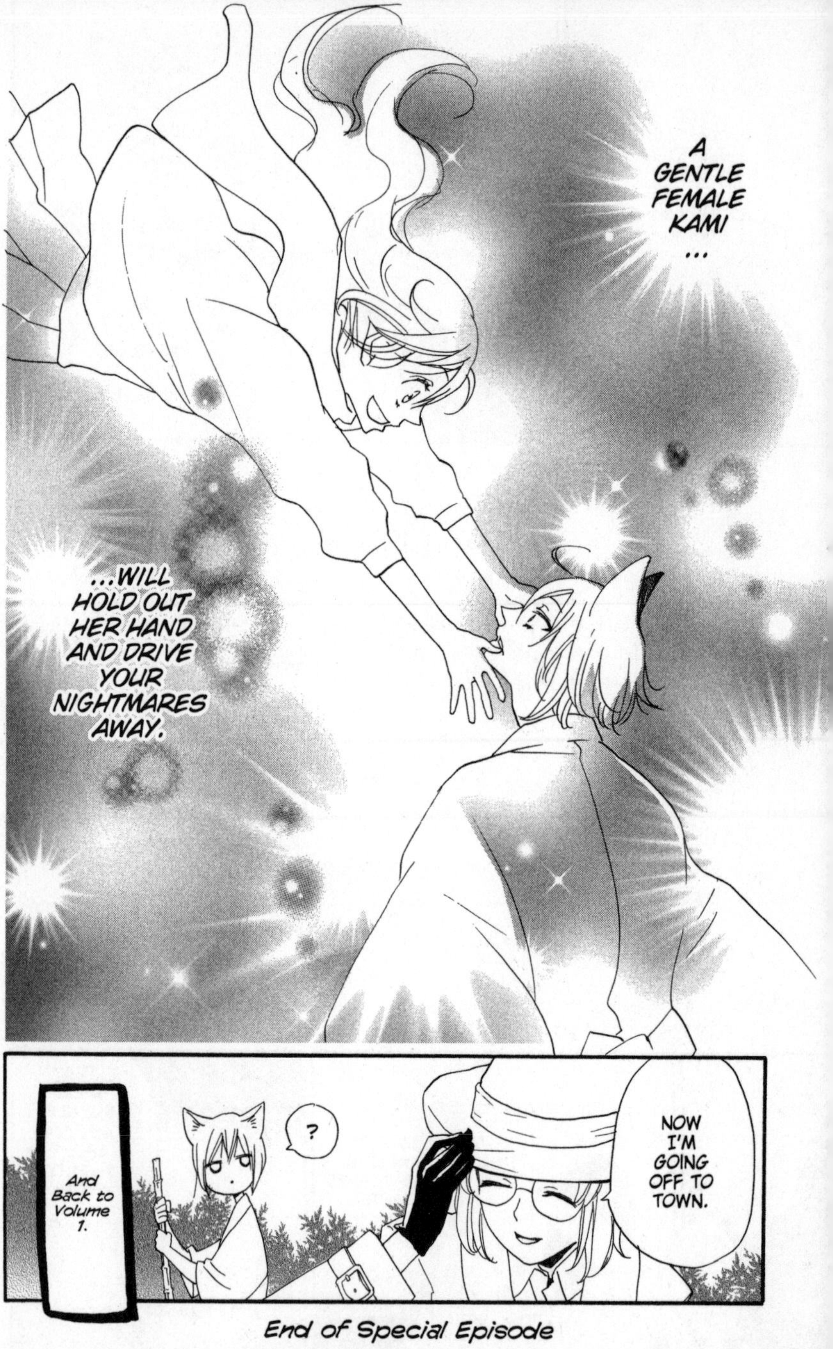
A GENTLE FEMALE KAMI...
...WILL HOLD OUT HER HAND AND DRIVE YOUR NIGHTMARES AWAY.
NOW I'M GOING OFF TO TOWN.
?
And Back to Volume 1.

End of Special Episode

The Otherworld

Ayakashi is an archaic term for yokai.

Kami are Shinto deities or spirits. The word can be used for a range of creatures, from nature spirits to strong and dangerous gods.

Komainu are a pair of guardian statues placed at the gate of a shrine, usually carved of stone. Depending on the shrine, they can be lions, foxes or cows.

Onibi-warashi are like will-o'-the-wisps.

Shinshi are birds, beasts, insects or fish that have a special relationship with a kami.

Tengu are a type of yokai. They are sometimes associated with excess pride.

Tochigami (or *jinushigami*) are deities of a specific area of land.

Yokai are demons, monsters or goblins.

Honorifics

-chan is a diminutive most often used with babies, children or teenage girls.

-dono roughly means "my lord," although not in the aristocratic sense.

-kun is used by persons of superior rank to their juniors. It can sometimes have a familiar connotation.

-san is a standard honorific similar to Mr., Mrs., Miss or Ms.

-sama is used with people of much higher rank.

Notes

Page 13, panel 5: Kokusai Dori
Kokusai Dori ("International Street") is a popular tourist spot in Naha. The street is lined with souvenir shops, restaurants and bars.

Page 35, panel 1: Bukubuku tea
Okinawan tea served with a huge mountain of foam on top.

Page 45, panel 4: Muscovado lumps
Sugar cane is grown in Okinawa, so muscovado (partially refined brown sugar) is a specialty of the area.

Page 70, panel 1: Chinsuko, Manta chin, Sata andagi
Chinsuko are biscuit-like Okinawan sweets that have been made since the times of the Ryukyu Kingdom. *Manta chin* are chinsuko that are shaped like manta rays. *Sata andagi* are Okinawan donuts.

Page 177, panel 2: Tomoe-kun's apron
Fox statues at inari shrines usually wear red aprons.

Page 178, panel 5: Okonomiyaki
Okonomiyaki is a Japanese dish resembling a thick pancake that has any variety of vegetables, meat, seafood or noodles mixed in.

Julietta Suzuki's debut manga *Hoshi ni Naru Hi* (The Day One Becomes a Star) appeared in the 2004 *Hana to Yume Plus*. Her other books include *Akuma to Dolce* (The Devil and Sweets) and *Karakuri Odette*. Born in December in Fukuoka Prefecture, she enjoys having movies play in the background while she works on her manga.

KAMISAMA KISS
VOL. 20
Shojo Beat Edition

STORY AND ART BY
Julietta Suzuki

English Translation & Adaptation/Tomo Kimura
Touch-up Art & Lettering/Joanna Estep
Design/Yukiko Whitley
Editor/Pancha Diaz

KAMISAMA HAJIMEMASHITA by Julietta Suzuki
© Julietta Suzuki 2014
All rights reserved.
First published in Japan in 2014 by HAKUSENSHA, Inc., Tokyo.
English language translation rights arranged with
HAKUSENSHA, Inc., Tokyo.

Printed in the U.S.A.

Published by VIZ Media, LLC
P.O. Box 77010
San Francisco, CA 94107

10 9 8 7 6 5 4 3 2 1
First printing, February 2016

www.viz.com   www.shojobeat.com

Kyoko Mogami followed her true love Sho to Tokyo to support him while he made it big as an idol. But he's casting her out now that he's famous enough! Kyoko won't suffer in silence—she's going to get her sweet revenge by beating Sho in show biz!

Vol. 1 ISBN: 978-1-4215-4226-3

Vol. 2 ISBN: 978-1-4215-4227-0

Vol. 3 ISBN: 978-1-4215-4228-7

Show biz is sweet...but revenge is sweeter!

Only **$14.99** for each volume! ($16.99 in Canada)

Skip·Beat!

Story and Art by YOSHIKI NAKAMURA

In Stores Now!

www.viz.com

Escape to the World of the

Young, Rich & Sexy

Ouran High School

Host Club

By Bisco Hatori

This is the last page.

In keeping with the original Japanese comic format, this
book reads from right to left—so action, sound effects, and
word balloons are completely reversed. This preserves the
orientation of the original artwork—plus, it's fun! Check out
the diagram shown here to get the hang of things, and then turn
to the other side of the book to get started!